John Lydgate

Troy Book: Selections

Middle English Texts

General Editor

Russell A. Peck
University of Rochester

Associate Editor

Alan Lupack
University of Rochester

Advisory Board

Rita Copeland
University of Minnesota

Thomas G. Hahn
University of Rochester

Lisa Kiser
Ohio State University

Thomas Seiler
Western Michigan University

R. A. Shoaf
University of Florida

Bonnie Wheeler
Southern Methodist University

The Middle English Texts Series is designed for classroom use. Its goal is to make available to teachers and students texts which occupy an important place in the literary and cultural canon but which have not been readily available in student editions. The series does not include those authors such as Chaucer, Langland, the Pearl-poet, or Malory, whose English works are normally in print in good student editions. The focus is, instead, upon Middle English literature adjacent to those authors that teachers need in compiling the syllabuses they wish to teach. The editions maintain the linguistic integrity of the original work but within the parameters of modern reading conventions. The texts are printed in the modern alphabet and follow the practices of modern capitalization and punctuation. Manuscript abbreviations are expanded, and u/v and j/i spellings are regularized according to modern orthography. Hard words, difficult phrases, and unusual idioms are glossed on the page, either in the right margin or at the foot of the page. Textual and explanatory notes appear at the end of the text. The editions include short introductions on the history of the work, its merits and points of topical interest, and also include briefly annotated bibliographies.

John Lydgate

Troy Book: Selections

Edited by
Robert R. Edwards

Published for TEAMS
(The Consortium for the Teaching of the Middle Ages)
in Association with the University of Rochester

by

Medieval Institute Publications

WESTERN MICHIGAN UNIVERSITY

Kalamazoo, Michigan –1998

Library of Congress Cataloging-in-Publication Data

Lydgate, John, 1370?-1451?
  [Troy book. Selections]
  Troy book : selections / John Lydgate ; edited by Robert R.
Edwards.
        p.   cm. -- (Middle English texts)
  Text in English and Middle English.
  Based on Guido's Historia destructionis Trojae.
  Includes bibliographical references.
  ISBN 1-879288-99-0 (alk. paper)
  1. Trojan War--Romances. 2. Troy (Extinct city)--Romances.
3. Epic poetry, Latin (Medieval and modern)--Adaptations. 4. Epic
poetry, English (Middle)   I. Colonne, Guido delle, 13th cent.
Historia destructionis Trojae.   II. Title. III. Series: Middle
English texts (Kalamazoo, Mich.)
  PR2034. T7L93   1998   97-47781
  821'.2--dc21   CIP

ISBN 1-879288-99-0

Printed in the United States of America

Cover design by Elizabeth King

For Pat and Colin

Contents

Preface

The aim of this book is to make John Lydgate's *Troy Book* accessible to non-specialist readers and to students of Middle English and Renaissance literature. The selections made for the present edition were chosen for their place in Lydgate's overall narrative, for their importance to literary history, and for their intrinsic interest and merit. Though some material has been omitted for lack of space, I believe the text and bridging summaries convey the rich mythographic frame within which medieval readers viewed the Troy story. The selections also demonstrate the complex relation of Lydgate to Chaucer in particular and to literary culture generally. The text, reedited for this edition, is not, however, a document to be consulted primarily for the external links to its historical age and poetic milieu. Lydgate composed a poem that simultaneously celebrated chivalric ideals and displayed their internal tensions and contradictions. In the Introduction and Notes, I have tried to incorporate the best contemporary scholarship on Lydgate and to give some orientation toward productive ways of reading *Troy Book*.

In the course of preparing this book, I have had the benefit of substantial research support from the Department of English and the Institute for the Arts and Humanistic Studies at Penn State. As a scholar, I have had the advantage of advice from colleagues who know Lydgate's poetry well and who indeed have given contemporary discussion of *Troy Book* its direction and defining qualities — Derek Pearsall, A. S. G. Edwards, A. C. Spearing, C. David Benson, Carol M. Meale, and Stephen Reimer. Professor Reimer made available materials from his own research on the Lydgate canon, and I wish to record my indebtedness to his remarkable generosity. In drafting the Introduction and grappling with textual and interpretive problems, I have had the fortune of good advice from Stephen Spector and Patrick Cheney. What errors and infelicities that remain are my creations and not those of the scholars who have made this a better book than it would have been otherwise. Russell Peck has been a patient and supportive editor. What I have learned from studying Lydgate's poem owes directly to his kind invitation to undertake this project. To Alan Lupack, Russell Peck, Jennifer Church, and the TEAMS staff I am indebted for their suggestions and preparation of the camera-ready copy. The Glossorial Database for Chaucer, Gower, and the Chaucer Apocrypha, under development by Larry D. Benson and Joseph Wittig, has facilitated consultation. Thomas Seiler and Juleen Eichinger at Western Michigan University saw the volume through press. I gratefully acknowledge permission from the British Library to quote from MS Cotton Augustus A.iv, the base text for the present edition, and from the Bodleian Library to quote from manuscripts in its collections.

Troy Book

I am grateful to the National Endowmment for the Humanities for its generous support in producing the volume. My thanks, as always, go to my wife, Emily Rolfe Grosholz, and to our children, Benjamin, Robert, William, and Mary-Frances. They have been gracious hosts to the monk of Bury whose sojourn has been slightly longer than could have been anticipated. Finally, I want to thank my graduate research assistants for this project, Patricia Nickinson and Colin Fewer, to whom this book is dedicated in recognition and thanks for all their splendid work.

Troy Book

Introduction

Troy Book is one of the most ambitious attempts in medieval vernacular poetry to recount the story of the Trojan war. John Lydgate, monk of the great Benedictine abbey of Bury St. Edmunds in Suffolk, began composing the poem in October 1412 on commission from Henry, Prince of Wales, later King Henry V, and he completed it in 1420. Lydgate's poem is a translation and expansion of Guido delle Colonne's *Historia destructionis Troiae*, a Latin prose account written in 1287 but based, without acknowledgement, on Benoît de Sainte-Maure's Old French *Roman de Troie* (c. 1160). *Troy Book* presents the full narrative and mythographic sweep that the Middle Ages expected for the story of Troy's tragic downfall. Though Lydgate wrote the poem some three decades after Chaucer's *Troilus and Criseyde*, it furnishes the essential background that educated medieval readers would have brought to Chaucer's poem and to Chaucer's source, Boccaccio's *Filostrato*. It is background as well for the myths of origins adopted by medieval nations and regions, which claimed descent from the heroes driven to new lands by Troy's fall.

Lydgate's poem is one of several translations of Guido's *Historia* into Middle English. The *Laud Troy Book* and the alliterative *Destruction of Troy* are near contemporaries. All three poems follow the arc of Guido's narrative as it moves from the remote origins of the war in Jason's quest for the Golden Fleece to the heroic battles and downfall of Priam's Troy and finally to the catastrophes awaiting the Greek victors on their homecoming. Lydgate gives, however, a defining shape to Guido's account where the other translations are content to reproduce its sequence of action. In a gesture of acknowledgement and homage to Chaucer's "litel tragedye," Lydgate brings a five-book structure to Guido's thirty-five shorter books. He thereby balances the opening and closing movements and makes Hector's death in Book 3 the narrative center and turning point of the story. *Troy Book* also differs from its contemporaries by making significant additions to the outlines of Guido's story. Lydgate adds materials from Ovid, Christine de Pisan (for Hector's death), and authorities like Fulgentius (for mythology), Isidore of Seville (for mythography), Jacobus de Cessolis (for the invention of chess), and John Trevisa (for the labors of Hercules). The result is a poem longer, more diffuse in focus, and more consciously learned than its predecessors or contemporaries. As Derek Pearsall remarks, "The *Troy Book* is a homily first, an encyclopedia second, and an epic nowhere" (1970, p. 129).

In the late Middle Ages and Renaissance, *Troy Book* enjoyed considerable reputation and influence. Not long after it was composed, it served as the source for a prose *Sege of Troy*, which retold the story through the fall of the city at the end of Lydgate's Book 4. In *The Recuyell of the Historyes of Troye* (STC 15375), the first book printed in English (c. 1475), William Caxton professes that there is no need for him to translate the portion of his French source, Raoul Lefèvre's *Recueil des Histoires de Troie*, dealing with the fall of Troy: "And as for the thirde book whiche treteth of the generall and last destruccioun of Troye Hit nedeth not to translate hit into englissh ffor as moche as that worshifull and religyous man dan John lidgate monke of Burye did translate hit but late // after whos werke I fere to take upon me that am not worthy to bere his penner and ynke horne after hym, to medle me in that werke" (Epilogue to Book 2). *Troy Book*'s classical topic, narrative scope, and moral purpose probably had something to do with William Dunbar's inclusion of Lydgate with Chaucer and John Gower as a triad of originary English poets in his early-sixteenth-century "Lament for the Makaris": "The noble Chaucer, of makaris flour, / The Monk of Bery, and Gower, all thre" (lines 50–51). Richard Pynson printed the first edition of *Troy Book* in 1513, under the title *The hystorye / sege and dystruccyon of Troye* (STC 5579). As A. S. G. Edwards and Carol M. Meale note, Pynson's edition was printed at the command of Henry VIII to manipulate public opinion in his first French compaign (p. 99). Thomas Marshe printed a second edition in 1555, with a prefatory epistle by Robert Braham (STC 5580). The continuing influence of *Troy Book* can be detected in Thomas Heywood's modernization, printed in 1614 as *The Life and Death of Hector* (STC 13346a), and in the works of Robert Henryson, Thomas Kyd, Christopher Marlowe, and William Shakespeare. The sense of Trojan history and particularly of Cressida's character in Shakespeare's *Troilus and Cressida* bear the imprint of Lydgate's poem.

Troy Book incorporates a distinctly medieval approach to its subject matter. As Chaucer shows in the *House of Fame* and *Troilus and Criseyde*, medieval writers knew Homer only as a name. Moreover, they discounted the poetic tradition associated with him, even as they recognized its cultural authority and struggled ambivalently to appropriate it to their own ends. For them, the claims of the Troy story lie not in the fables of the poets but in the truth of what they took to be historical witness. Such witness was provided by Dares and Dictys, who were supposedly contemporary observers of the war. A fragment of a Greek text of Dictys survives, but the chief sources are Dares's *De excidio Troiae historia* and Dictys's *Ephemeridos belli Troiani*, two late Latin texts purporting to translate Greek originals. However spare their accounts of heroes and battles may be, these accounts established the idea for the Middle Ages that the Trojan War could be approached as history with the same factual basis as found in chronicles. Joseph of Exeter's *Frigii Daretis*

Introduction

Ylias (dated 1188–90) is one example of the continuing claim to historicity that surrounded such chronicle writing. Benoît drew on Dares and Dictys to compose his *Roman de Troie*. He goes beyond the accounts in his sources, however, to introduce an exotic and chivalric locale that figures prominently in subsequent medieval versions of the story. Geoffrey of Monmouth's *Historia Regum Britanniae* (dated 1135) claimed a Trojan origin for the British monarchy and people. The poet of *Sir Gawain and the Green Knight* deliberately frames his Arthurian romance with references to the fall of Troy. In addition to its narrative, the Troy story offered an example to be studied for its lessons in statecraft and moral conduct. Greeks and Trojans participate in the same chivalric culture, and their actions serve as examples of how to govern both a kingdom and its aristocratic subjects.

The medieval approach to the Troy story also implies a particular sense of authorship. Lois Ebin argues that Lydgate regards his literary role as that of "an orderer and civilizer of men" (1985, p. 39) who transmits the lessons of the past. Lydgate makes it clear that he sees his poetic task as "making" (the technical composition of verse) rather than original creation. Like Chaucer, he does not call himself a poet. His translation follows medieval literary conventions by rendering the sense of Guido's text rather than striving for word-for-word equivalences (2.180). Just as Guido supposedly follows Dares and Dictys so that "in effecte the substaunce is the same" (Pro. 359) in both source and translation, so Lydgate hopes that, despite any flaws in meter, his readers will find "[t]he story pleyn, chefly in substaunce" (5.3543). Lydgate ascribes to Guido a rhetorical skill (Pro. 360–69) that other readers might well dispute, but he understood Guido's intentions accurately. As Guido explains at the end of the *Historia* (Book 35), his work presents a truthful historical account ("ueram noticiam") embellished by rhetorical colors and figures. Lydgate regards his source and, by extension, himself as part of a tradition of chroniclers for whom language is superficial and external to actual meaning. "Ye may beholde in her wrytyng wel," he says confidently, "The stryfe, the werre, the sege and everydel, / Ryghte as it was, so many yeres passyd" (Pro. 247–49).

The truth of such historical writing ostensibly sets it apart from poetry. Lydgate's way of expressing this difference is to contrast the transparency of history and the opacity of poetry. The chronicle story of Troy is open and plain; we can grasp its "substaunce" apart from any rhetorical effects. The poets use "veyn fables" in order to "hyde trouthe falsely under cloude, / And the sothe of malys for to schroude" (Pro. 265–66). Homer's honey-sweet words only disguise the gall inside. Ovid and Vergil fall under the same suspicion:

Ovide also poetycally hath closyd — *clothed*
Falshede with trouthe, that maketh men ennosed — *confused*
To whiche parte that thei schal hem holde;
His mysty speche so hard is to unfolde

That it entriketh rederis that it se.	*ensnares*
Virgile also for love of Enee	*Aeneas*
In *Eneydos* rehersyth moche thyng	*Aeneid*
And was in party trewe of his writyng,	
Exsepte only that hym lyst som whyle	
The tracys folwe of Omeris stile.	*traces (ideas)*
(Pro. 299–308)	

Here and elsewhere, Lydgate uses the same images for poets that he applies in the narrative to characters who employ deceitful language to mislead others and subvert just deliberation.

Besides historical truth, the Troy story carries exemplary meaning for medieval and Renaissance culture. Walter Schirmer observes that the tales connected with Troy were regarded "as a historical work containing all the moral and political lessons which history was expected to teach" (p. 44). An important feature of Lydgate's moralizing is its rather precise focus. The lessons of *Troy Book* apply on one level to kingship and statecraft and on another to the individual within an aristocratic, chivalric world. The capacity to foresee consequences or control anger, for example, serves a king in his political role as a governor and a hero in his public office as an adviser, advocate, or warrior. Conspicuous by its absence is a larger social vision. *Troy Book* concedes the need in several places to account for popular opinion. Priam's rebuilding of Troy in Book 2, for example, incorporates the gesture of vesting its builders with citizenship so that the founding of a new city is simultaneously the creation of a new state. But Lydgate offers nothing really comparable to John Gower's appeal in his *Confessio Amantis* to the commons as a source for political legitimacy or to the estates as a basis of stable government and institutions. Lydgate's moralization of Troy's history offers an aristocratic perspective rather than a social vision. It is a mirror for kings and nobles.

The principal lesson that Lydgate's Troy story offers its royal, aristocratic, and noble readers is the virtue of prudence. In Book 6 of the *Nicomachean Ethics*, Aristotle defines prudence as an intellectual virtue by which one can deliberate about particular goods and the practical steps toward attaining them. Prudence considers means rather than ends, and it addresses things that are variable rather than true and unchanging. Thomas Aquinas's phrase "recta ratio agibilium" — right reason directed toward what can be done — captures the spirit of Aristotle's idea and shows its application to politics and statecraft. Prudence is commonly described as an "imperative" virtue, governing all the others. The importance of prudence for rulers is a standard precept from medieval political theorists like John of Salisbury and Marsilius of Padua to Lydgate's English contemporaries, Thomas Hoccleve and Thomas Usk. Chaucer signals its importance in The Tale of Melibee and makes it the virtue Criseyde lacks (*Troilus and Criseyde* 5.744). In the imitation of the pseudo-Aristotelian *Secreta secretorum* that he undertook at the

4

very end of his life, Lydgate has prudence rule over the other virtues needed by a king.

At the end of *Troy Book* (Env. 36–42), Lydgate presents Solomon as the Biblical model of prudence. But the character who best embodies prudence in Lydgate's poem is Hector, the figurative root of all chivalry (2.244). Hector's prudence extends from practical wisdom in infantry tactics to political governance, moral example, skill in debate and deliberation, self-containment, and foresight. As Lydgate describes him, he is an ideal because of his traits of character and judgment: "He had in hym sovereine excellence, / And governaunce medlid with prudence, / That nought asterte him, he was so wis and war" (3.489–91). Significantly, it is Hector who urges restraint when Priam seeks support from the Trojan council to avenge Hesione's abduction by Telamon after the fall of Lamedon's Troy:

But first I rede, wysely in your mynde	*advise*
To cast aforn and leve nat behynde,	
Or ye begynne, discretly to adverte	*reflect*
And prudently consyderen in your herte	
Al, only nat the gynnyng but the ende	*not only*
And the myddes, what weie thei wil wende,	
And to what fyn Fortune wil hem lede:	*end*
Yif ye thus don, amys ye may nat spede.	
(2.2229–36)	

His death "thorugh necligence only of his shelde" (3.5399) is surely the most interesting contradiction of Lydgate's poem. Hector's fatal lapse, which Lydgate adds to Guido's narrative, does not compromise Hector's heroic stature so much as challenge the primacy of prudence as a virtue that can be applied to so many facets of human experience.

Lydgate's depiction of prudence also reveals the way in which he expects his moralizations and the exemplarity of the Troy story to be understood. C. David Benson points out that Lydgate's moralizing is practical rather than spiritual (1980, pp. 116–24). In particular, prudence seems to offer a remedy to Fortune and the transitory world. Lydgate's panorama of pagan history from Jason's quest outward through Ulysses's return home sketches a world of unknown and hidden consequences. Remote, even trivial causes set tragic events in motion: "of sparkys that ben of syghte smale / Is fire engendered that devoureth al" (1.785–86). Thus Lamedon's discourtesy in denying Jason temporary respite in his land initiates a cycle of vengeance that destroys Troy twice. The governing mechanism of history is Boethian Fortune, a compound of sheer accident and of consequences proceeding from hidden and only partially understood choices. Boethius's remedy is to see past the mutability of the world and finally reject the secular for the transcendent. But for pagans trapped in their history and for Christian chivalry and rulers who cannot abandon the duties of worldly governance, prudence offers the only means for navigating the reversals of Fortune. Still, if prudence is the chief virtue of *Troy Book*, it also generates the profound moral contradiction that inhabits the center of Lydgate's poem. In the Troy story, prudence means right reason, foresight, cleverness, eloquence, and practical wisdom, but it also comes to mean cunning, deceit, and false language. While Lydgate extols the value of prudence throughout the story, he ends Book 5 of *Troy Book* by asserting the fragility of human institutions before Fortune and giving a final definition to prudence. "For oure lyf here is but a pilgrymage," he says, citing a medieval commonplace. If men would "toforn prudently adverte" (5.3573), they would put little trust in worldly things. Through the example of Troy, princes, lords, and kings can see that in this life none of them "may have ful sureté" (5.3578).

To judge from the reception of *Troy Book* and the marginal commentary recorded in the manuscripts, medieval and early Renaissance readers understood Lydgate's moralizations on the level he intended them and not necessarily in their fuller, tragic implications. On the fly leaf at the end of one *Troy Book* manuscript (Rawlinson poet. 144), an anonymous sixteenth-century reader takes to heart Lydgate's protest that he writes true meaning but with little craft. Ancient English books, says this reader, show little art; ignorance darkened understanding in those earlier times, "but mark the substance of this book / In wiche this mownk such paynes hath vndertook" (Bergen 4:52). He then goes on, without any sense of contradiction, to connect Lydgate with precisely the poetic fabrication from which he strives to distinguish *Troy Book* in his Prologue:

> A, story tys sone writt, thats nothing true,
> And poets haue it decte, with vading hewe.
> So lydgat hath a poets lycence tooke
> By vayne discowrce, with lyes to farce this book,
> Yet dothe his paynes, Joynd with Obedience,
> Deserve dew prayse, & worthy recompence.

Various manuscripts preserve marginal responses to Lydgate's sententious passages in *Troy Book*. In Pierpont Morgan Library, MS M.876, Agamemnon's speech to Menelaus, counseling him to disguise his grief at Helen's loss (2.4337–4429), carries the marginal reminder, "note thes | and follow." In Rawlinson C.446, a sixteenth-century reader has added verses on the dishonorable deaths of Hector and Troilus at the hands of Achilles. In the Pierpont Morgan manuscript and in slightly later manuscripts (dating from the mid-fifteenth century onwards), pointing hands mark various passages in the text, especially those dealing with the supposed perfidy of women.

Manuscript illustrations provide another means of grasping how Lydgate's contemporaries might have read his poem. Eight manuscripts, including the four oldest witnesses, have miniatures, and at least six others have decorated borders or initials. The textual and visual layout of the manuscripts show that *Troy Book* was a prestige item, appearing as the sole text in the earliest witnesses and with the *Siege of Thebes* and the romance *Generydes* in several later manuscripts. One manuscript, which cannot be identified from among extant witnesses and may not have survived, was, of course, a presentation copy for Lydgate's patron, Henry V. Coats of arms indicate that *Troy Book* manuscripts were owned by fifteenth-century gentry and, in at least one instance, by aristocracy. In the later case (Royal 18.D.ii), the conventional portrait of Lydgate presenting the poem to the king is displaced by a scene that shows the owner, Sir William Herbert, First Earl of Pembroke and his second wife, Anne Devereux, in postures of homage to the king.

Kathleen L. Scott proposes that the manuscript was intended as a presentation gift to Henry VI or Edward IV and that it may register Herbert's shift of allegiance from the Lancastrian to the Yorkist cause (1996, 2:282–84). Lesley Lawton observes that there is a uniform sequence of miniatures in the manuscripts which reflects Lydgate's structural reordering of Guido's narrative into five books. Miniatures introduce the Prologue and the first major incident of each of the five books; they are visual markers of the formal divisions of the text. The opening of Book 2, where Lydgate complains about Fortune, occasions some divergence among the illustrations. Four manuscripts have a miniature of the goddess Fortuna, while the other four represent Priam's siege (2.203), the first event in the narrative. For Books 3 and 4, Royal 18.D.ii adds illustrations to highlight Troilus. Even when the number of miniatures is increased in manuscripts from the later fifteenth century, the basic program remains intact. In addition, a "decorative hierarchy" governs the use of initials in the text, emphasizing such features as seasonal descriptions and other examples of Lydgate's amplification. Royal 18.D.ii contains extensive rubrics to guide the reader. The overall effect of the miniatures, initials, and rubrics in *Troy Book* manuscripts is to delineate the formal order of Lydgate's poem rather than provide a visual representation parallel to the written text. Pynson's edition retains these manuscript features, while dividing the text into both Lydgate's five books and a reminiscence of Guido's original thirty-five books plus Lydgate's Prologue and final materials. Marshe's 1555 edition eliminates the woodcuts but uses rubrics and blank spaces to mark structural divisions.

For a full understanding of *Troy Book*, Lydgate's historical and literary contexts prove as important as the narrative scope and thematic complexity of the poem. Ebin describes *Troy Book* and the *Siege of Thebes*, the poem composed directly after it and finished in 1422, as "public poems" (p. 39). Pearsall calls *Troy Book* "an instrument of national prestige" as well as a chivalric and moral exemplar (1970, p. 69). Schirmer proposes that Henry's commission involved a poetic rivalry with Benoît's *Roman de Troie* and Guido's *Historia* (pp. 42–43). Certainly, Lydgate's description of Henry's motives bears out some of this claim. Henry seeks to preserve the worthiness of true knighthood and "the prowesse of olde chivalrie" so that his contemporaries can find examples for pursuing virtue and rejecting sloth and idleness. He commissions Lydgate to make the exemplary force of the story available to all by creating an English equivalent to the French and Latin histories:

> By cause he wolde that to hyghe and lowe   *wished*
> The noble story openly wer knowe   *were known*
> In oure tonge, aboute in every age,
> And ywriten as wel in oure langage
> As in Latyn and in Frensche it is,
> That of the story the trouthe we nat mys
> No more than doth eche other nacioun:
> This was the fyn of his entencioun.   *goal*
>   (Pro. 111–18)

That Henry should choose Lydgate, a monk of Bury St. Edmunds, to carry out such a weighty task reflects political allegiances and an intricate network of personal connections. Bury St. Edmonds had a long association with the English crown, and it actively supported royal interests during the late fourteenth and early fifteenth centuries. Far from retreating from the world, the great monasteries of the day cultivated economic and political ties with secular institutions. Lydgate's profession as a monk makes him in some measure an agent of ecclesiastical public policy. Though he entered the monastery at about age fifteen, he spent much of his life outside and even overseas, until his retirement to St. Edmunds in the early 1440s. From the commission to write *Troy Book* in 1412, he served in effect as a court poet, and the record of later commissions, such as the *Fall of Princes* for Duke Humphrey, shows his popularity and adaptability to occasions. Some recent scholars have proposed that one of the underlying objectives of Lydgate's work is to affirm Lancastrian legitimacy. Lydgate's address to Henry in the Envoy of *Troy Book* subtly raises these issues. The poet addresses his sovereign not only as the source of knighthood but as one "born also by discent of lyne / As rightful eyr by title to atteyne, / To bere a crowne of worthi rewmys tweyne" (Env. 5–7). Though the immediate reference is to English claims to the French crown, the effect is tacitly to affirm Henry IV's usurpation of the English throne and Henry V's legitimate succession of his father.

The link with Henry also has some enticing biographical dimensions. Lydgate spent time at Oxford in Gloucester College, which the Benedictines maintained for monks engaged in university study. Henry had studied at Queen's College in 1394, and sometime between 1406 and 1408 wrote Lydgate's abbot asking for permission for Lydgate to continue his studies, either in divinity or canon law. Henry's letter mentions that he has heard good reports about Lydgate; it does not indicate necessarily that the Prince of Wales and the monk had a personal acquaintance. John Norton-Smith proposes, however, that Lydgate resided in Oxford from approximately 1397 to 1408 and that he met Henry

8

(p. 195n). The rubrics of Lydgate manuscripts owned by the fifteenth-century antiquarian John Shirley suggest that Lydgate and Henry shared interests in the liturgy, but these are textual sources that postdate *Troy Book*. Henry's religious fervor matched his enthusiasm for tales of chivalry. Schirmer argues that Lydgate's attitude differs from his patron's endorsement of military adventure. He contends, for example, that Lydgate initially invokes Mars (Pro. 1–37) but reproves him (4.4440–4536) after Henry becomes king. In his view, the line "[a]lmost for nought was this strif begonne" (2.7855) refers not just to the Trojan War but also to the pointlessness of the French war. Lydgate's peace sentiments seem, however, more the expression of commonplace counsel than a rejection of Henry's policies. To be sure, there are profound tensions and contradictions in *Troy Book*, but they grow out of the narrative that Lydgate recounts and embellishes and not from a kind of authorial resistance. In its immediate historical context, the poem aims to affirm chivalric virtues, offer examples and moral precepts, and celebrate the national myth of Trojan origins.

The literary rather than the historical context of *Troy Book* is a more likely source of ambivalence. Lydgate situates himself conspicuously within literary tradition, even if he knows many of the authors who comprise that tradition only at second hand. Guido is the author whose achievement he serves, Chaucer is his acknowledged master, and the treasures of encyclopedic learning and anthology literature lie about as sources for embellishing the Troy narrative with scientific, mythographic, and historical commentary. E. B. Atwood proposes that, for Lydgate, Guido has completely superseded Benoît, the poet who initially gave the medieval Troy story its admixture of classical and chivalric elements. All the details on which Lydgate and Benoît agree, says Atwood, are also contained in Guido, and so there is no direct influence on Lydgate from the original French source of his story. Of the classical *auctores*, Lydgate knew only Ovid well. He goes to the Ovidian sources to add more when Guido cites them and uses Ovid elsewhere as a supplement to Guido. Lydgate's acquaintance with Vergil is by all accounts scant or indirect. His references to the *Aeneid* show, for instance, that he depended on the story of Dido contained in Chaucer's *The Legend of Good Women*. Other classical authors he knew largely through anthologies and grammars. The library at Bury St. Edmunds gives some sense of the practical form literary culture might have taken for Lydgate. It contained over 2,000 volumes in Lydgate's day, and it was notable for its holdings among Patristic writers, later commentators on the Bible, classical authors, theologians, and encyclopedic writers. It contained two manuscripts of Guido and possibly a copy of Gower's *Confessio Amantis*. All the materials for embellishing an authoritative historical text with the apparatus of learned comments, excursus, and interpolations lay readily to hand. The one manuscript positively associated with Lydgate (Bodleian Library MS Laud 233) has two works by Isidore, sermons by Hilbert of Le Mons, and brief quotations from Vergil and Horace.

Troy Book

The bookishness of this literary context shows itself perhaps most apparently in Lydgate's rhetorical amplifications. Pearsall observes, "Lydgate's expansiveness clearly forms part of a deliberate poetic style" (1970, p. 7), but for *Troy Book* it may be still nearer the case to speak of a poetics of amplification. The conceptual and thematic counterpart to the poet's task of "making" is the addition of new materials suitable to the passage that Lydgate is translating at any given point. Lydgate finds the warrant for such practice in Guido himself. Guido adds rhetorical colors to "[t]his noble story" and "many riche flour / Of eloquence to make it sownde bet / He in the story hath ymped in and set" (Pro. 363–66). Lydgate's amplifications take the form of learned digressions on mythography and science, additional speeches, set-piece descriptions, formal laments, and seasonal descriptions. The aim of such amplification is not, however, merely dilation. Ebin contends that the additions are part of a program directed toward securing a place within literary culture: "Lydgate's changes in the *Troy Book* reveal his concern with elevating the narrative and creating a monumental version of the story in English, loftier and more impressive than any before him" (1985, p. 51). Moreover, the additions afford Lydgate the opportunity to develop his own thematic interests. His reproval of Guido's antifeminism, though by no means unproblematic (see note to 3.4343–4448), is one example. Benson argues that Lydgate uses Christine de Pisan's *Epistre Othea* to introduce a new view of Hector and the value of prudence (1980, pp. 124–29). Schirmer finds three major themes in Lydgate's formal digressions: transitoriness, war and discord, and encyclopedic learning (p. 47).

The other defining feature of Lydgate's literary context is the influence of Chaucer as both inspiration and rival. *Troy Book* contains laudatory passages that not only offer praise for Chaucer but also shape literary history by establishing him as the father of English poetry. Robert O. Payne observes that Chaucer offered Lydgate a double model of poetic originator and craftsman (p. 255). Chaucer is "Noble Galfride, poete of Breteyne" (2.4697). His great achievement is to have exploited the rhetorical possibilities of English and thereby to have established it as a literary idiom comparable to classical languages and other European vernaculars. He was the firste "to reyne / The gold dewedropis of rethorik so fyne, / Oure rude langage only t'enlwmyne" (2.4698–4700). He is the "chefe poete" (3.4256), the English counterpart of Petrarch as poet laureate.

> For he owre Englishe gilte with his sawes,   *gilded; tales*
> Rude and boistous firste be olde dawes,   *Unpolished; rough; days*
> That was ful fer from al perfeccioun
> And but of litel reputacioun,
> Til that he cam and thorugh his poetrie
> Gan oure tonge firste to magnifie   *make greater in importance*
> And adourne it with his elloquence . . .
>   (3.4237–41)

10

Introduction

Elsewhere Lydgate says that the death of "[t]he noble rhetor" (3.553) leaves him without counsel or correction, and so he goes "[c]olourles" — without rhetorical figures — to his composition. When he later submits the finished work for correction to his readers, he invokes the image of Chaucer as a gentle and beneficent master who genially overlooks defects in the works offered to him: "Hym liste nat pinche nor gruche at every blot" (5.3522).

It is unlikely that Lydgate actually knew or ever met Chaucer. He did have connections with Thomas Chaucer and Thomas's daughter, Alice, the Duchess of Suffolk. Some recent criticism wants to see in these connections a link between establishing the Chaucer canon and furthering Lancastrian politics. The important point, however, is that Lydgate constructs the paternal figure of Chaucer and, through that figure, his own literary pose of discipleship and "dullness" — the persona of a belated, deferential, and supposedly inadequate latter-day follower. Chaucer had, of course, already perfected the role of the humble literary artisan, its commonplaces of modesty and inability, and its characteristic phrasing. Lydgate's innovation is to position himself with respect to Chaucer just as Chaucer had positioned himself with respect to the classical *auctores*. Later writers show that the process can go a step further. Lydgate's discipleship can be transmitted to his successors. Caxton says that Lydgate's version of Troy's fall is too strong to emulate. In his *Pastime of Pleasure* (1509), Stephen Hawes claims to write without rhetoric or "colour crafty": "Nothynge I am/ experte in poetry / As the monke of Bury/ floure of eloquence / Whiche was in tyme/ of grete excellence" (lines 26–28).

Lydgate's echoes and allusions make it clear that he had access to Chaucer's work, though monastic libraries possessed few vernacular manuscripts, still fewer in English. Lydgate obviously knew *The Book of the Duchess*, *The House of Fame*, *The Legend of Good Women*, and a number of the pieces comprising the *Canterbury Tales*. In his description of the Greeks' landing to destroy Lamedon's Troy (1.3907–43), Lydgate goes so far as to hazard an imitation of the opening of the General Prologue to the *Canterbury Tales*, with disastrous results. The Notes to the present edition give examples of the wide range of allusion to Chaucer that runs throughout *Troy Book*. Atwood divides the borrowings into classical material for which Chaucer served as an intermediary and "miscellaneous fine phrases and descriptive passages" (pp. 35–36). At those points where he strives most to represent himself within the poem, Lydgate recalls Chaucer's narrative persona, even if the occasional efforts at comic deflation fail, as in the uneven, shifting tone of his reproval of Guido's misogyny.

Troilus and Criseyde is, of course, the poem that bears most immediately on *Troy Book* and Lydgate's relation to Chaucer. Chaucer's poem is Lydgate's subtext, even though Lydgate's subject matter furnishes the background for Chaucer's poem. More important, *Troilus and Criseyde* is the literary work that fully embodies Chaucer for Lydgate, as it did for readers in the Renaissance. Lydgate concedes there is no need for him to retell the lovers' story after Chaucer, but he goes on to summarize it and echo the style and content of its conclusion (3.4196–4230). He even works mention of Chaucer's description of Criseyde (*Troilus and Criseyde* 5.803–26) into his own adaptation of Chaucer's inability topos (2.4676–93). Benson would find in *Troy Book* the beginnings of a distinct historical sense, derived from *Troilus and Criseyde*, that views pagan antiquity as a remote and radically different cultural world to be investigated almost ethnographically for its rites and beliefs, false though they be. At the same time that it proclaims discipleship, however, *Troy Book* competes with Chaucer's poem in the scope of its ambition. Chaucer's genius, following from Boccaccio's *Filostrato*, is to portray the intimate, private sphere of antiquity and the epic. Lydgate gives the larger, encompassing story. As Anna Torti rightly points out, the love story of Troilus and Criseyde is one of many love stories counterpointing the war in Guido and Lydgate (p. 180). Following perhaps the narrator's suggestion in *Troilus and Criseyde* (1.144–45) that "the Troian gestes" can be found "[i]n Omer, or in Dares, or in Dite" for whoever can read them, Lydgate seeks to go beyond his master.

Chaucer's influence shows in the style of *Troy Book* as well as in the narrative and thematic elements. The pentameter couplets are modeled on Chaucer's later work in the *Canterbury Tales*, while the rhyme royal stanzas of the Envoy recall the *Parliament of Fowls, Troilus*, and works probably composed earlier and then added to the *Canterbury Tales*. Lydgate's ambition is to write in an elevated style appropriate to his subject matter. This leads to an English verse approximation of what he claims to recognize as the high style of Guido's prose. The most common effect is to distort the natural order of syntax, abandoning the "conversational tone" that characterizes Chaucer's most mature writing. Lydgate seeks instead to emulate Latin models by using devices of accretion, parallelism, and subordination. Constructions such as the ablative absolute, syntactic inversion, and anacoluthon (lack of sequence in a sentence) are common. Pearsall remarks that one of Lydgate's major traits is the use of "unrelated participles instead of finite verbs" (1970, p. 58). Few run-on lines disrupt the patterning of phrases and clauses within Lydgate's couplets. At times, when he reaches for his most complex effects, the syntax can fail altogether; at others, as in the laments and passages expressing his authorial response, he achieves a fluid, more direct elegiac verse.

The designation often given to Lydgate's verse is aureate style or diction. "Aureate," meaning both "golden" and "eloquent," refers generally to the effort to reproduce the elevated effects of Latin in English. Lydgate originated the term and the concept, and it exerted a strong influence on both the Scottish Chaucerians and English Renaissance poets. The style depends essentially on the importation of Latin vocabulary, though the number of words Lydgate introduced into Middle English is now reckoned fewer than once thought. Norton-Smith contends that Lydgate always uses the term with strong metaphoric associations, and he notes that these associations are with rhetorical skill, eloquent language, and inspiration (pp. 192–95). The style produces a poetry based on exuberant elaboration rather than master images or controlling symbols. Scholars would limit most applications of "aureate" to Lydgate's religious poetry and would distinguish his borrowing of Latin vocabulary for purely artistic effect from borrowings of Latin technical and scientific terms. In a broad sense, however, what matters most to Lydgate's style is the combination of Latinate vocabulary with intricate syntactic structures.

Lydgate's meter, like his style, has been the topic of much aesthetic debate. Alain Renoir traces most dismissals of Lydgate's metrical skill to the early nineteenth century, which reversed centuries of opinion that ranked Lydgate with or above Chaucer in prosodic skill as well as rhetorical eloquence. Lydgate's assertion that "moche thing is wrong, / Falsly metrid, bothe of short and long" (5.3483–84) is, as Schirmer observed (p. 71), a modesty formula rather than a description of his actual composition or poetic ambitions. The basic model of prosody in *Troy Book* is Chaucer's iambic pentameter line, which regularly placed a caesura after the fourth or sixth syllable and permitted the addition of an unaccented syllable at the end of the line. Lydgate also follows Chaucerian practice in sounding final *-e* as needed for meter, even though the spoken language dropped this feature of the grammatical case system in the second half of the fourteenth century. Josef Schick distinguished five kinds of lines in Lydgate's poetry. Iambic pentameter (Type A) is the most common line. Trochaic feet sometimes appear before the caesura (Type B) and in the first foot (Type E) of a line. More characteristic are a headless line (Type D), with the first syllable missing, and the so-called "Lydgate line" or "broken-backed line," in which the unaccented syllable is missing after the caesura so that two accented syllables stand next to each other (Type C). In the following example, the manuscripts preserve a Lydgate line with stressed syllables on both sides of the caesura: "That his entent | | can no man bewreye" (1.224). In Chaucer manuscripts, which are also fifteenth-century witnesses, the Lydgate line is commonly treated as a scribal error rather than an intentional form; most editors emend the line, frequently without notice. The pattern is intentional with Lydgate, however. In general, the metrical features that Chaucer used occasionally and even then with a rhythmic purpose in mind become frequent and systematic. Chaucer's metrical variants are the recurring elements of Lydgate's metrical program.

The present edition of *Troy Book* offers a selection of Lydgate's text from the vast and encyclopedic narrative that Lydgate composed. Its aim is to present key episodes, while preserving the overall shape of a narrative running to 30,117 lines. Prose summaries recount the material left out between the passages. The Prologue and Epilogue as well as the openings of each book are printed as markers of the poem's formal divisions and stylistic examples that differ significantly from Lydgate's narration. The selections for Book 1 seek to balance the Jason and Medea story with the events that precipitate the war. The passages from Book 2 alternate between narrative elements and set pieces, such as Priam's rebuilding of Troy, Lydgate's apostrophe to Priam on kingship, and the speeches made by Hector and Agamemnon. The episodes chosen from Book 3 sketch the evolving catastrophe of the war: the death of Patroclus, Hector's blunder in not pursuing his tactical advantage in battle, Achilles's plot to murder Hector, the exchange of Thoas for Antenor that prepares for the betrayal of Troy, and the sequence that begins with Andromache's prophetic dream and moves through Hector's death and enshrinement. The last of these is a fascinating reminiscence of the exotic element that Benoît introduced to the medieval Troy story. The episodes taken from Book 4 reflect the final stages of Troy's downfall. Achilles succeeds in killing Troilus, the second Hector, but falls in love with Polyxena and subsequently dies in a murder plot. Though the Amazons give Troy some respite by entering the war, the conspiracy to betray the city succeeds, and after Troy's destruction, Achilles's son Pyrrhus exacts a brutal and unjust vengeance on Polyxena. The selections from Book 5, which recounts the return of the Greek heroes, focus on the story of Ulysses. The resolution reached by his sons, Telemachus and Telegonus, mirrors a larger pattern of peacemaking between Trojans and Greeks that Lydgate sees as an example for the current strife between England and France. Throughout these selections, passages and episodes of particular literary interest have been included, such as Lydgate's remarks on translation (2.134–202) and the many references to Chaucer and to *Troilus and Criseyde* (2.4677–4762, 2.4861–95, 3.550– 57, 3.4077–4448, 3.4820–4869, and 4.2029–2177). From the text and intervening summaries, the reader can follow the main line of Lydgate's story and examine its major rhetorical and narrative elements.

The text of *Troy Book* survives in twenty-three manuscripts and fragments. Pynson's first edition seems to have relied on another early manuscript with a good text. Despite the claims to sober editorial judgment made in Braham's prefatory epistle, the 1555 edition printed by Marshe reproduces Pynson's text and emends it freely with no manuscript authority. An extract from Lydgate's reproval of Priam (2.1849–56) appears in one manuscript of the *Canterbury Tales* (Royal 18.C.ii). In two late manuscripts (Douce 148 and Cambridge Kk.V.30), fragments of a fifteenth-century Scots translation of Guido are inserted. Douce 148 was "mendit" by John Asloan, and both manuscripts descend from the same exemplar that was the ancestor of Arundel 99. A portrait of Lydgate presenting *Troy Book* to Henry appears in Cotton Augustus A.iv, Digby 232, Rawlinson C.446, Rylands English 1, and Trinity College, MS 0.5.2. The same themes and details of the portrait reappear in a woodcut from Pynson's edition; Pynson also introduces Lydgate's complaint on Hector's death with a portrait of the poet writing at a desk. The earliest manuscripts, it has been suggested, might have been written and illustrated at Bury St. Edmunds for the monastery's great poet, but the London booktrade now seems a more likely source.

As A. S. G. Edwards points out, manuscript study over the past two decades has added much important detail about the material production of *Troy Book* (1981, pp. 16–19). The illuminations of Rawlinson C.446 have been connected to the atelier of a follower of John Siferwas, a master miniaturist (Spriggs, p. 200 n. 2). Rylands English 1 was illuminated by an artist close stylistically to William Abell, the mid-fifteenth English illuminator who reacted against developments in Netherlandish and Italian Renaissance painting (Alexander, pp. 169–70). Decorations in a fragment of *Troy Book* attached to the front of a manuscript of the *Canterbury Tales* (Rawlinson poet. 223) are linked to the "owl" atelier, so called for the trademark used by one artist who decorated the borders of books in a London illuminating shop around 1465; the text was written elsewhere (Scott, 1968, pp. 189–91). Rawlinson C. 446 and Digby 230 were written by the same scribe in the 1420s; the space left for coats of arms to be inserted in illuminated initials indicates they were destined for noble owners (Doyle and Parkes, pp. 201 n. 100, 210 n. 128). There also seems to have been a "Lydgate scribe" active in the mid-fifteenth century who was responsible for the text of *Troy Book* in Arundel 99 and for other Lydgate poems (Edwards, 1981, pp. 17–19). His presence suggests that a complex publishing organization existed to produce and disseminate Lydgate's work. A. I. Doyle speaks of a "long-standing Lydgate workshop" in East Anglia possibly composed of monks and laymen (p. 7).

The most important textual sources for *Troy Book* are the four earliest manuscripts: Cotton Augustus A.iv, Bristol MS 8, Digby 232, and Rawlinson C.446. None of them is Lydgate's original, and each was copied independently from the others. Cotton Augustus A.iv is usually thought to be the earliest witness; Bergen dated it 1420–30, the other three 1420–35. Scott suggests revised dates of 1430–40 for Cotton Augustus A.iv, c. 1420–35 for Digby 232, and c. 1420–25 for Rawlinson C.446 (1996, 2:261). The Cotton MS is virtually complete, lacking only six lines of the full text; the other three are missing portions of text that run between two thousand and five thousand lines. Bristol 8, which suffered the greatest loss of text, was mutilated for the miniatures. The large folio layout of the early manuscripts and the extent of decoration indicate that all of them could have been presentation copies, but no one manuscript can be identified as the *Troy Book* that Lydgate presented to Henry. The evidence of later manuscripts indicates that the poem retained its value as a prestige possession and found an audience among provincial gentry. Rylands English 1, for example, shows up in an inventory of Markeaton Hall, Derbyshire, compiled in 1545.

Cotton Augustus A.iv is the base text chosen for this edition of selections from *Troy Book*, as it was for Henry Bergen's complete edition of the poem prepared for the Early English Text Society early in this century. Cotton Augustus offers the most complete early text. Written on vellum leaves measuring 26 x 15 inches, the manuscript is composed of 155 folios, gathered in eight-leaf quires. The script is an Anglicana formata, with the characteristic double-lobed *a*, *e*, and *g*. The letter *d* is looped. Both *s* and long *s* are used. The two-shaped *r* replaces the regular *r* after the letter *o*, but the forked *r* does not appear. Cotton Augustus contains only *Troy Book*. The text is arranged in double columns of 49 lines, except for the rhyme royal stanzas of the Envoy and the two eight-line stanzas of the final Envoy and *Verba translatoris*. The first miniature (fol. 1ra) contains the arms of Sir Thomas Chaworth (d. 1458) and his second wife, Isabella de Ailesbury below the portrait of Lydgate and Henry V. A short description of the manuscript appears in the British Museum catalogue compiled by H. L. D. Ward and J. A. Herbert. A more extensive description is contained in Bergen's edition (4:1–4).

The text presented here follows the readings of Cotton Augustus A.iv, except for the emendations recorded in the accompanying Notes. Emendations have been made where sense requires and where metrical changes are needed to avoid clearly defective lines. Final -e has been added as needed for meter, most notably in forms like *myght*, *hert*, and *gret*, which are spelled inconsistently. A MS form like *ageyns* is emended to *ageynes*, particularly at the beginning of a line. Obvious spelling errors have been corrected. In accordance with the conventions of the TEAMS series, the letters *i/j* and *u/v* have been normalized. Thorn has been transcribed as *th*, yogh as *y* or *g* or *gh*, and the scribal ampersand as *and*. Unless spelled *ee* (e.g., *secree* 1.2001), the accented final -e is printed *é*, as in *pité*. Double consonants at the beginning of a line have been treated as capitals, so, for example, MS *fful* appears as *Ful*. Suspension marks and common abbreviations have been silently expanded. Capitalization and word division are editorial. The noun *nothing*, for example, is distinguished from the adverbial form *no thing* (not at all, in no way). Punctuation follows modern practice, but there are points where the complications of Lydgate's syntax make any effort to show the structure of subordination among clauses, phrases, and parenthetical expressions only approximate.

Every reader of *Troy Book* owes a debt to Henry Bergen, and any later editor's debt must be greater still. As the Notes make clear, I have relied frequently on his suggestions for final -e and for additions needed for sense and meter. My editorial practice is somewhat more conservative, however, in retaining substantive readings from the base manuscript. I preserve some wording that Bergen would change and phrasings that he would transpose. MS forms of the past participles *avenget* (1.4255), *conselit* (4.6739), *defoulit* (2.545), *flickerit* (3.4179), *forget* (1.3218, 2.2508, 4.6938), and *plounget* (5.3551) are allowed to stand, as are a number of idiomatic constructions attested in Chaucer and the *Middle English Dictionary*. In some places I read the MS differently from Bergen and in others follow the MS order where Bergen transposes lines. Bergen proposes a number of metrical emendations at points where I have chosen to let the Lydgate lines stand. My punctuation of the text is somewhat lighter than Bergen's Victorian punctuation; on occasion, the structure of Lydgate's long parallel clauses is broken into shorter sentences as an aid to reading and comprehension.

Select Bibliography

Manuscripts

Bristol, City Reference Library, MS 8.

Cambridge, Trinity College, MS O.5.2.

Cambridge, University Library, MS Kk.5.30.

Cambridge, Massachusetts, Houghton Library, Harvard University, MS Eng 752 (formerly Harvard-Ashburnham MS).

Geneva, Fondation Martin Bodmer, MS Bodmer 110 (formerly Phillipps 3113).

Gloucester, Cathedral Library, MS 5.

London, British Library, MS Arundel 99.

London, British Library, MS Cotton Augustus A.iv.

London, British Library, MS Royal 18.D.ii.

London, British Library, MS Royal 18.D.vi.

London, Inner Temple Library, MS Petyt 524 (fragment).

Manchester, John Rylands Library, MS English 1.

New York, Pierpont Morgan Library, MS M.876 (formerly Helmingham Hall and Tollemache MS).

Oxford, Bodleian Library, MS Digby 230.

Oxford, Bodleian Library, MS Digby 232.

Oxford, Bodleian Library, MS Douce 148.

Oxford, Bodleian Library, MS Rawlinson C.446.

Troy Book

Oxford, Bodleian Library, MS Digby 232.

Oxford, Bodleian Library, MS Douce 148.

Oxford, Bodleian Library, MS Rawlinson C.446.

Oxford, Bodleian Library, MS Rawlinson D.913 (fragment).

Oxford, Bodleian Library, MS Rawlinson poet. 144.

Oxford, Bodleian Library, MS Rawlinson poet. 223 (fragment).

Oxford, Christ Church Library, MS 153 (fragment).

Oxford, Exeter College, MS 129.

Oxford, St. John's College, MS 6.

Editions

Bergen, Henry, ed. *Lydgate's Troy Book*. 4 vols. Early English Text Society, e.s. 97, 103, 106, 126. London: Kegan Paul, Trench, Trübner & Co. and Oxford University Press for the Early English Text Society, 1906–35.

Neilson, W. A., and K. G. T. Webster, eds. *The Chief British Poets of the Fourteenth and Fifteenth Centuries: Selected Poems*. Boston: The Riverside Press / Houghton Mifflin Co., 1916. [*Troy Book* 2.479–768.]

Norton-Smith, John, ed. *John Lydgate: Poems*. Clarendon Medieval and Tudor Series. Oxford: Clarendon Press, 1966. [*Troy Book* 2.479–551, 565–72, 578–631, 638–41, 651–67, 681–92, 695–710.]

Steiner, George, ed. *Homer in English*. New York: Penguin, 1996. [*Troy Book* Pro. 145–75, 2.7852–75, 3.5423–74, 4.7058–7108.]

Introduction

Other Sources

Benoît de Sainte-Maure. *Roman de Troie*. Ed. Leopold Constans. Société des anciens textes français. 6 vols. Paris: Firmin-Didot, 1904–12.

——. *Chaucer's Boccaccio: Sources of "Troilus" and the "Knight's" and "Franklin's Tales."* Trans. N. R. Havely. Chaucer Studies 3. Cambridge: D. S. Brewer, 1980. Pp. 167–80, 213–14. [Excerpts from *Le Roman de Troie*.]

Brie, Friedrich. "Zwei mittelenglische Prosaromane: The Sege of Thebes und The Sege of Troy." *Archiv für das Studium der neueren Sprachen und Literaturen* 130 (1913), 40–52, 269–85.

Chaucer, Geoffrey. *The Riverside Chaucer*. Gen. ed. Larry D. Benson. Third ed. Boston: Houghton Mifflin, 1987.

Colonne, Guido delle. *Historia destructionis Troiae*. Ed. Nathaniel Griffin. Medieval Academy of America Publications 26. Cambridge, Mass.: Medieval Academy of America, 1936.

——. *The History of the Destruction of Troy*. Trans. Mary Elizabeth Meek. Bloomington: Indiana University Press, 1974.

Dares Phyrygius. *De excidio Troiae historia*. Ed. Ferdinand Meister. Leipzig: Teubner, 1873, 1991.

Dictys Cretensis. *Ephemeridos belli Troiani*. Ed. Werner Eisenhut. Leipzig: Teubner, 1973.

Frazer, Richard M., Jr., trans. *The Trojan War: The Chronicles of Dictys of Crete and Dares the Phyrigian*. Bloomington: Indiana University Press, 1966.

The "Gest Hystoriale" of the Destruction of Troy. Ed. G. A. Panton and D. Donaldson. Early English Text Society, o.s. 39 and 56. London: John Childs and Son, 1869 and 1874; rpt. in one vol. Oxford: Oxford University Press, 1968.

Joseph of Exeter. *The Iliad of Dares Phrygius*. Trans. Gildas O. Roberts. Ph.D. Diss. The Ohio State University, 1966. Cape Town: A. A. Balkema, 1970.

——. *Frigii Daretis Ylias: De bello Troiano*. In *Werke und Briefe von Joseph Iscanus*. Ed. Ludwig Gompf. Leiden: Brill, 1970.

The Laud Troy Book. Ed. J. E. Wülfing. Early English Text Society, o.s. 121 and 122. London: Kegan Paul, Trench, Trübner & Co., 1902–03.

Bibliographical Sources

Edwards, A. S. G. "Additions and Corrections to the Bibliography of John Lydgate." *Notes and Queries* ns 32 [230] (1985), 450–52.

——. "A Lydgate Bibliography, 1926–68." *Bulletin of Bibliography and Magazine Notes* 27.4 (1970), 95–98.

——. "Lydgate Scholarship: Progress and Prospects." In *Fifteenth-Century Studies: Recent Essays*. Ed. Robert F. Yeager. Hamden, Conn.: Archon Books, 1984. Pp. 29–47.

Lee, Sidney. "Lydgate." In *Dictionary of National Biography*. Ed. Sir Leslie Stephen and Sir Sidney Lee. London: Oxford University Press, 1921–22. Pp. 306–16.

Reimer, Stephen R. "The Lydgate Canon: A Project Description." *Literary and Linguistic Computing* 5 (1990), 248–49.

Renoir, Alain, and C. David Benson. "John Lydgate." In *A Manual of the Writings in Middle English, 1050–1500*. Ed. J. Burke Severs and rev. Albert E. Hartung. 9 vols. New Haven: Connecticut Academy of Arts and Sciences, 1967–. 6: 1809–1920, 2071–2175.

Rice, Joanne A. *Middle English Romance: An Annotated Bibliography, 1955–1985*. New York: Garland, 1987. Pp. 153–60, 533–36.

Ward, H. L. D., and J. A. Herbert. *Catalogue of Romances in the Department of Manuscripts in the British Museum*. 3 vols. London: British Museum, 1883–1910.

Selected Criticism and Scholarship

Alexander, Jonathan. "William Abell 'lymnour' and 15th Century English Illumination." In *Kunsthistorische Forschungen Otto Pächt zu seinem 70. Geburtstag*. Ed. Artur Rosenauer and Gerold Weber. Salzburg: Residenz Verlag, 1972. Pp. 166–72.

Introduction

Ambrisco, Alan S., and Paul Strohm. "Succession and Sovereignty in Lydgate's Prologue to *Troy Book*." *Chaucer Review* 30 (1995–96), 40–57.

Atwood, E. Bagby. "Some Minor Sources of Lydgate's *Troy Book*." *Studies in Philology* 35 (1938), 25–42.

Ayers, Robert W. "Medieval History, Moral Purpose and the Structure of Lydgate's *Siege of Thebes*." *PMLA* 73 (1958), 463–74.

Benson, C. David. "The Ancient World in John Lydgate's *Troy Book*." *American Benedictine Review* 24 (1973), 299–312.

———. "Chaucer's Influence on the Prose *Sege of Troy*." *Notes and Queries* ns 18 [216] (1971), 127–30.

———. "Critic and Poet: What Lydgate and Henryson Did to Chaucer's *Troilus and Criseyde*." *Modern Language Quarterly* 53 (1992), 23–40.

———. *The History of Troy in Middle English Literature: Guido delle Colonne's "Historia Destructionis Troiae" in Medieval England*. Woodbridge, Suffolk: D. S. Brewer; Totowa, N. J.: Rowman and Littlefield, 1980.

———. "Prudence, Othea, and Lydgate's Death of Hector." *American Benedictine Review* 26 (1975), 115–23.

Boffey, Julia. "The Reputation and Circulation of Chaucer's Lyrics in the Fifteenth Century." *Chaucer Review* 28 (1993), 23–40.

Bornstein, Dean. "Chivalric Idealism in Lydgate's *Troy Book*." *The Lydgate Newsletter* 1 (1972), 8–13.

Buuren-Veenenbos, Catherine C. van. "Notes and News: John Asloan, an Edinburgh Scribe." *English Studies* 47 (1966), 365–72.

Doyle, A. I. "Book Production by the Monastic Orders in England (*c.* 1375–1530): Assessing the Evidence." In *Medieval Book Production: Assessing the Evidence*. Ed. Linda L. Brownrigg. Los Altos Hills, Calif.: Anderson-Lovelace / The Red Gull Press, 1990. Pp. 1–19.

—— and M. B. Parkes. "The Production of Copies of the *Canterbury Tales* and the *Confessio Amantis* in the Early Fifteenth Century." In *Medieval Scribes, Manuscripts and Libraries: Essays Presented to N. R. Ker.* Ed. M. B. Parkes and Andrew G. Watson. London: Scolar Press, 1978. Pp. 163–210.

Dwyer, R. A. "Some Readers of John Trevisa." *Notes and Queries* ns 14 [212] (1965), 291–92.

Ebin, Lois. "Chaucer, Lydgate, and the 'Myrie Tale.' " *Chaucer Review* 13 (1978–79), 316–36.

——. *John Lydgate.* Twayne English Authors Series 407. Boston: Twayne, 1985.

Edwards, A. S. G. "Lydgate Manuscripts: Some Directions for Future Research." In *Manuscripts and Readers in Fifteenth-Century England: The Literary Implications of Manuscript Study.* Ed. Derek Pearsall. Cambridge: D. S. Brewer, 1981. Pp. 15–26.

——. "Lydgate's Attitudes to Women." *English Studies* 51 (1970), 436.

——. "An Unidentified Extract from Lydgate's *Troy Book*." *Notes and Queries* ns 36 [234] (1989), 307–08.

—— and Carol M. Meale. "The Marketing of Printed Books in Late Medieval England." *The Library*, sixth series, 15 (1993), 95–124.

Finlayson, John. "Guido de Columnis' *Historia destructionis Troiae*, the *'Gest Hystorial'* *of the Destruction of Troy*, and Lydgate's *Troy Book*: Translation and the Design of History." *Anglia* 113 (1995), 141–62.

Fisher, John H. *The Importance of Chaucer.* Carbondale: Southern Illinois University Press, 1992.

——. "A Language Policy for Lancastrian England." *PMLA* 107 (1992), 1168–80.

Griffin, Nathaniel. See Colonne, Guido delle, above.

Horstmann, Carl, ed. *Barbour's des schotttischen Nationaldichters Legendensammlung nebst den Fragmenten seines Trojanerkrieges zum ersten Mal herausgegeben und kritisch Bearbeitet.* 2 vols. Heilbronn: Gebr. Henninger, 1881–82.

Introduction

Kempe, Dorothy. "A Middle English Tale of Troy." *Englische Studien* 29 (1901), 1–26.

Krochalis, Jeanne E. "The Books and Reading of Henry V and His Circle." *Chaucer Review* 23 (1988–89), 50–77.

Lawton, Lesley. "The Illustration of Late Medieval Secular Texts, with Special Reference to Lydgate's 'Troy Book.' " In *Manuscripts and Readers in Fifteenth-Century England: The Literary Implications of Manuscript Study*. Ed. Derek Pearsall. Cambridge: D. S. Brewer, 1981. Pp. 41–69.

Marquardt, W. F. "A Source for the Passage on the Origin of Chess in Lydgate's *Troy Book*." *Modern Language Notes* 64 (1949), 87–88.

McIntosh, Angus. "Some Notes on the Language and Textual Transmission of the *Scottish Troy Book*." *Archivum Linguisticum* 10 (1979), 1–19.

Meek, Mary Elizabeth. See Colonne, Guido delle, above.

Mieszkowski, Gretchen. "The Reputation of Criseyde, 1155–1500." *Transactions of the Connecticut Academy of Arts and Sciences* 43 (1971), 71–153.

Patterson, Lee. "Making Identities in Fifteenth-Century England: Henry V and John Lydgate." In *New Historical Literary Study: Essays on Reproducing Texts, Representing History*. Ed. Jeffrey N. Cox and Larry J. Reynolds. Princeton: Princeton University Press, 1993. Pp. 69–107.

Payne, Robert O. "Late Medieval Images and Self-Images of the Poet: Chaucer, Gower, Lydgate, Henryson, Dunbar." In *Vernacular Poetics in the Middle Ages*. Ed. Lois Ebin. Kalamazoo, Mich.: Medieval Institute Publications, 1984. Pp. 249–61.

Pearsall, Derek. "Chaucer and Lydgate." In *Chaucer Traditions: Studies in Honour of Derek Brewer*. Ed. Ruth Morse and Barry Windeatt. Cambridge: Cambridge University Press, 1990. Pp. 39–53.

———. "Hoccleve's *Regement of Princes*: The Poetics of Royal Self-Representation." *Speculum* 69 (1994), 386–410.

———. *John Lydgate*. Medieval Authors: Poets of the Later Middle Ages. London: Routledge and Kegan Paul; Charlottesville: University Press of Virginia, 1970.

23

————. "Notes on the Manuscript of *Generydes*." *The Library*, fifth series, 16 (1961), 205–10.

Renoir, Alain. "Attitudes Toward Women in Lydgate's Poetry." *English Studies* 42 (1961), 1–14.

————. *The Poetry of John Lydgate*. Cambridge, Mass.: Harvard University Press, 1967.

Schick, Josef. *Lydgate's Temple of Glas*. Early English Text Society, e.s. 60. London: Kegan Paul, Trench, Trübner & Co., 1891.

Schirmer, Walter F. *John Lydgate: A Study in the Culture of the XVth Century*. Trans. Ann E. Keep. London: Methuen; Berkeley: University of California Press, 1961. English trans. of *John Lydgate: Ein Kulturbild aus dem 15. Jahrhundert*. Tübingen: Max Niemeyer, 1952.

Scott, Kathleen L. *Later Gothic Manuscripts: 1390–1490*. 2 vols. Vol. 6 of A Survey of Manuscripts Illuminated in the British Isles. London: Harvey Miller, 1996.

————. "A Mid-Fifteenth-Century English Illuminating Shop and Its Customers." *Journal of the Warburg and Courtauld Institutes* 31 (1968), 170–96.

Skeat, Walter W. "Flaskisable." *Notes and Queries*, seventh series, 12 (1891), 146.

Spearing, A. C. *Medieval to Renaissance in English Poetry*. Cambridge: Cambridge University Press, 1985.

Spriggs, Gereth M. "Unnoticed Bodleian Manuscripts, Illuminated by Herman Scheerre and His School." *Bodleian Library Record* 7 (1964), 193–203.

Strohm, Paul. "*Storie, Spelle, Geste, Romaunce, Tragedie*: Generic Distinctions in the Middle English Troy Narratives." *Speculum* 46 (1971), 348–59.

Studer, John. "History as Moral Instruction: John Lydgate's Record of *Troie Toun*." *Emporia State Research Studies* 19.1 (1970), 5–13, 22.

Sundwall, McKay. "The *Destruction of Troy*, Chaucer's *Troilus and Criseyde*, and Lydgate's *Troy Book*." *Review of English Studies* ns 26 (1975), 313–17.

Swithin, St. "Flaskisable." *Notes and Queries*, seventh series, 12 (1891), 215–16.

Introduction

Torti, Anna. "From 'History' to 'Tragedy': The Story of Troilus and Criseyde in Lydgate's *Troy Book* and Henryson's *Testament of Cresseid*." In *The European Tragedy of Troilus*. Ed. Piero Boitani. Oxford: Clarendon Press, 1989. Pp. 171–97.

Walsh, Elizabeth R. S. C. J. "John Lydgate and the Proverbial Tiger." In *The Learned and the Lewed: Studies in Chaucer and Medieval Literature*. Ed. Larry D. Benson. Harvard English Studies 5. Cambridge, Mass.: Harvard University Press, 1974. Pp. 291–303.

Watson, Nicholas. "Outdoing Chaucer: Lydgate's *Troy Book* and Henryson's *Testament of Cresseid* as Comparative Imitations of *Troilus and Criseyde*." In *Shifts and Transpositions in Medieval Narrative: A Festschrift for Dr. Elspeth Kennedy*. Ed. Karen Pratt. Woodbridge, Suffolk: D. S. Brewer, 1994. Pp. 89–108.

Prologue

  O Myghty Mars, that wyth thy sterne lyght   *who*
  In armys hast the power and the myght
  And named art from est til occident
  The myghty lorde, the god armypotent,   *omnipotent*
5 That wyth schynyng of thy stremes rede   *rays of red light*
  By influence dost the brydel lede
  Of chevalry as sovereyn and patrown,
  Ful hoot and drye of complexioun,
  Irows and wood and malencolyk   *Angry and mad*
10 And of nature brent and coleryk,   *hot (burnt)*
  Of colour schewyng lyche the fyré glede, *like the burning coal*
  Whos feerce lokes ben as ful of drede
  As the levene that alyghteth lowe   *lightning that strikes*
  Down by the skye from Jubiteris bowe   *Jupiter's*
15 (Thy stremes ben so passyng despitous,   *spiteful*
  To loke upon, inly furious,   *inwardly angry*
  And causer art wyth thy fery bemys   *cause; fiery*
  Of werre and stryf in many sondry rewmys),   *war; realms*
  Whos lordschype is most in Caprycorn
20 But in the Bole is thy power lorn   *Taurus (the bull); lost*
  And causer art of contek and of strif;   *anger*
  Now for the love of Vulcanus wyf   *Venus*
  Wyth whom whylom thou wer at meschef take,   *once*
  So helpe me now, only for hyr sake,
25 And for the love of thy Bellona *Mars's sister (goddess of war)*
  That wyth the dwellyth byyownd Cirrea *you; beyond Cirra (near Delphi)*
  In Lebyelonde upon the sondes rede; *land of Lybia; red sands*
  So be myn helpe in this grete nede   *need*
  To do socour my stile to directe *stylus (writing instrument)*
30 And of my penne the tracys to correcte   *written words*
  Whyche bareyn is of aureat lycour   *empty; golden fluid*
  But in thi grace I fynde som favour   *Unless*
  For to conveye it wyth thyn influence,

	That stumbleth ay for faute of eloquence	*always for lack*
35	For to reherse or writen any word;	*write*
	Now help, O Mars, that art of knyghthod lord	
	And hast of manhod the magnificence.	
	And Othea, goddesse of prudence,	*(see note)*
	This wirke t'exsplyte that ye nat refuse	*advance*
40	But maketh Clyo for to ben my muse	*Clio (the muse of history)*
	Wyth hir sustren that on Pernaso dwelle	
	In Cirrea by Elicon the welle,	*Syria; Helicon*
	Rennyng ful clere wyth stremys cristallyn	
	And callyd is the welle Caballyn	
45	That sprang by touche of the Pegasee.	*Pegasus*
	And helpe also, O thou Calliope,	*Calliope (muse of epic poetry)*
	That were moder unto Orpheus	
	Whos dites wern so mellodyus	*songs were*
	That the werbles of his resownyng harpe	*melodies*
50	Appese dyde the bitter Wyrdys scharpe	*Fates*
	Bothe of Parchas and Furies infernal	
	And Cerberus so cruel founde at al;	
	He coyede also beste, foule, and tree.	*He (Orpheus) calmed; beast*
	Now of thy grace be helpyng unto me	
55	And of thy golde dewe lat the lycour wete	
	My dulled brest that wyth thyn hony swete	
	Sugrest tongis of rethoricyens	*[You] sugar tongues*
	And maistresse art to musicyens;	
	Now be myn help t'enlumyne with this wirk	*illuminate*
60	Whyche am beset with cloudis dym and dirk	
	Of ygnoraunce, in makyng to procede,	*how to proceed in composition*
	To be lusty to hem that schal it rede.	*lively to them who*
	Also in hert I am so ful of drede	
	Whan prudent lysters herto schal take hede,	*listeners*
65	That in makyng more skylle can than I,	*Who know more art in composition*
	To whom I preie ful benignely	*meekly*
	Of her goodnesse to have compassioun	*their*
	Wher as I erre in my translacioun.	
	For God I take hyghly to wyttenesse	
70	That I this wirk of hertly lowe humblesse	
	Toke upon me of entencioun,	
	Devoyde of pride and presumpcioun,	

For to obeie withoute variaunce
My lordes byddyng fully and plesaunce,
75 Whiche hath desire, sothly for to seyn,   *truly*
Of verray knyghthod to remembre ageyn   *true*
The worthynes, yif I schal nat lye,
And the prowesse of olde chivalrie
By cause he hath joye and gret deynté   *refinement*
80 To rede in bokys of antiquité,
To fyn only vertu for to swe   *For the purpose; pursue*
Be example of hem and also for to eschewe   *them*
The cursyd vice of slouthe and ydelnesse.
So he enjoyeth in vertuous besynesse
85 In al that longeth to manhood, dar I seyn;   *pertains to*
He besyeth evere, and therto is so fayn   *He is active; eager*
To hawnte his body in pleies marcyal   *use; in warlike deeds*
Thorugh excersice t'exclude slouthe at al,
After the doctrine of Vygecius: *Vegetius*
90 Thus is he bothe manful and vertuous,
More passyngly than I can of hym write.
I wante connyng his highe renoun t'endite,   *lack the skill; to commend*
So moche of manhood men may in hym sen.   *see*
And for to witen whom I wolde mene —   *know whom I mean*
95 The eldest sone of the noble Kyng
Henri the Firthe, of knyghthood welle and spryng,   *Fourth*
In whom is schewed of what stok he grewe;
The rotys vertu thus can the frute renewe;   *power of the stock*
In every part the tarage is the same,   *quality*
100 Lyche his fader of maneris and of name,   *Like*
In sothefastnesse, this no tale is,   *truthfulness; falsehood*
Callid Henry ek, the worthy prynce of Walys,   *also; Wales*
To whom schal longe by successioun
For to governe Brutys Albyoun,
105 Whyche me comaunded the drery pitus fate
Of hem of Troye in Englysche to translate,
The sege also, and the destruccioun,
Lyche as the Latyn maketh mencioun,
For to compyle and after Guydo make,   *gather; versify*
110 So as I coude, and write it for his sake,
By cause he wolde that to hyghe and lowe   *wished*

29

The noble story openly wer knowe — *were known*
In oure tonge, aboute in every age,
And ywriten as wel in oure langage
115 As in Latyn and in Frensche it is,
That of the story the trouthe we nat mys
No more than doth eche other nacioun:
This was the fyn of his entencioun. — *goal*
The whyche emprise anoon I gynne schal — *undertaking at once; begin*
120 In his worschip for a memorial. — *historical record*
And of the tyme to make mencioun
Whan I began of this translacioun,
It was the yere, sothely for to seyne, — *truly*
Fourtene complete of his fadris regne,
125 The tyme of yere, schortly to conclude,
Whan twenty grees was Phebus altitude, — *degrees*
The hour whan he made his stedis drawe
His rosen chariet lowe under the wawe — *waves*
To bathe his bemys in the wawy see, — *beams; wavy sea*
130 Tressed lyche gold, as men myghte see,
Passyng the bordure of oure occian; — *ocean*
And Lucyna, of colour pale and wan — *the moon*
Hir cold arysyng in Octobre gan to dyght — *prepare*
T'enchace the dirknesse of the frosty nyght
135 In the myddes of the Scorpion;
And Esperus gan to wester doun — *Hesperus; to set in the west*
To haste hir cours ageyn the morwe graye;
And Lucifer, the nyght to voyde awaye, — *the morning star*
Is callyd than, messanger of day, — *then*
140 Our emysperye to put out of affraye — *hemisphere; alarm*
Wyth bright kalendis of Phebus upryst schene — *harbingers; rising brightly*
Out of the boundis Proserpina the Quene — *territory of*
Wher Pluto dwelleth, the dirke regioun,
And the Furies have her mansioun; — *their*
145 Til after sone Appollo lyst nat tarie — *soon; it pleases*
To take sojour in the Sagittarie.
Whyche tyme I gan the prolog to beholde
Of *Troye Boke*, imade be dayes olde,
Wher was remembrid of auctours us beforn
150 Of the dede the verreie trewe corn — *true grain*

So as it fil severid from the chaf,	*fell cut*
For in her honde they hilde for a staf	*their hands; held*
The trouthe only, whyche thei han compyled	
Unto this fyn — that we wer nat begyled	*end; deceived*
155 Of necligence thorugh foryetilnesse.	*forgetfulness*
The whiche serpent of age by processe	
Engendred is fersly us t'assaille,	
Of the trouth to make us for to faille;	
For nere writers, al wer out of mynde,	*if there were no*
160 Nat story only but of nature and kynde	*nature*
The trewe knowyng schulde have gon to wrak	*destruction*
And from science oure wittes put abak,	
Ne hadde oure elderis cerched out and sought	*searched*
The sothefast pyth, to ympe it in oure thought	*the substance of truth; implant*
165 Of thinges passed, fordirked of her hewe	*darkened*
But thorugh wrytyng thei be refresched newe,	*Unless*
Of oure auncetrys left to us byhynde	
To make a merour only to oure mynde	
To seen eche thing trewly as it was,	
170 More bryght and clere than in any glas.	
For ner her wrytyng nowe memorial,	*were not their*
Dethe with his swerde schulde have slayen al	
And ydymmed with his sodeyn schoures	*darkened; showers*
The grete prowes of thise conquerouris	
175 And dirked eke the brightnesse of her fame	*also; reputation*
That schyneth yet by report of her name;	
For unto us her bokes represent	
Withoute feynynge the weie that thei went	
In her daies, whan thei wer alyve.	
180 Ageyn the trouthe whoso evere stryve	
Or counterplete or make any debate,	*argue against; dissension*
The sothe is rad of highe or lowe estate	*truth*
Withoute favour, whoso list take hede.	*wishes*
For after deth clerkis lityl drede	
185 After desert for to bere witnesse	*worth*
Nor of a tyraunt the trouthe to expresse,	
As men disserve withoute excepcioun;	*have a rightful claim*
With lak or prys thei graunt hem her guerdoun.	*value; them their reward*
Wherfore me semeth every maner man	

190	Schulde be his live in al that ever he can	
	For vertu only eschewe to don amys,	
	For after dethe, pleynly as it is,	
	Clerkis wil write, and excepte noon,	*leave out*
	The pleyne trouthe whan a man is goon.	
195	And by olde tyme for her writing trewe	
	Thei cherisched werne of lordes that hem knewe	*were valued by*
	And honoured gretly in tho dawes;	*those days*
	For they enacted and gilte with her sawes	*gilded; their proverbs*
	Her hyghe renoun, her manhood and prowes,	*Their*
200	Her knyghthood eke and her worthynes,	*also*
	Her tryumphes also and victories,	
	Her famous conquest and her songe glories;	
	From poynt to poynt rehersyng al the trouthe	
	Withoute fraude, necligence, or slowthe	*sloth*
205	Thei dide her labour and her besynesse.	
	For elles certeyn the grete worthynesse	*otherwise*
	Of her dedis hadde ben in veyn;	*would have been*
	Fordirked age elles wolde have slayn	*Darkened; otherwise*
	By lenthe of yeris the noble worthi fame	*length*
210	Of conquerours and pleynly of her name	
	Fordymmed eke the lettris aureat,	*Obscured also; golden*
	And diffaced the palme laureat	
	Whiche that thei wan by knyghthod in her dayes,	
	Whos fretyng rust newe and newe assayes	*ornamentation rust again; attacks*
215	For to eclipse the honour and the glorie	
	Of highe prowes whiche clerkis in memorie	
	Han trewly set thorugh diligent labour	
	And enlumyned with many corious flour	*elaborate*
	Of rethorik, to make us comprehende	
220	The trouth of al, as it was in kende;	*nature*
	Besied hem, and feythfully travaylled	*Busied themselves; worked*
	Agayn al that that age wolde assaylled,	*diminish*
	In her bokes everythyng iset,	
	And with the keye of remembraunce it schet,	
225	Whiche lasteth yet and dureth ever in oon.	*endures*
	Recorde of Thebes that was so long agoon,	*Remember*
	Of whiche the rueyne and distruccioun	*ruin*
	Ye may beholde by gode inspeccioun,	

	Crop and rote, right as it was indede;	*Branch and root (i.e., the whole thing)*
230	On Stace loketh, and ther ye may it rede:	*Statius*
	How Polynece and Ethiocles,	*Oedipus's sons Polynices and Etiocles*
	The brether two, ne kowde nat lyve in pees	*peace*
	Til Thebes was brought unto ruyne,	
	And al the maner how thei dide fyne,	*died*
235	The deth also of worthi Tydeus;	
	And how Edippus with teris ful pytous	*Oedipus*
	Wepte oute his eyne and al his drery peyen;	*eyes; pain*
	And how the smokys departid wer in tweyen	*two*
	At the fest of fires funeral.	
240	In grete Stace ye may reden al:	
	The fyre engendered by brotherly hatrede,	
	Wherthorugh that deth was the cruel mede	*Through which; reward*
	In verray sothe of many worthi man	*full truth*
	Lyche as myn auctor wel reherse can;	
245	Of Troye also that was of latter yeres,	
	By dillygence of cronycleris	*chroniclers*
	Ye may beholde in her wrytyng wel	
	The stryfe, the werre, the sege, and everydel,	
	Ryghte as it was, so many yeres passyd.	*so long ago*
250	Whos story yit age hath nought diffaced,	*marred*
	Nor cruel deth with his mortal strokys;	
	For maugre deth, ye may beholde in bokys	*despite*
	The story fully rehersed new and newe	*again and again*
	And freschely floure of colour and of hewe	
255	From day to day, quyk and no thyng feynt.	*alive; not at all invented*
	For clerkys han this story so depeynt	*portrayed*
	That deth nor age by no maner weye	
	The trouthe may not maken for to deye,	*die*
	Albe that somme han the trouthe spared	*Although*
260	In her writyng and pleynly not declared	
	So as it was nor tolde out feithfully	
	But it transformed in her poysy	*poetry*
	Thorugh veyn fables, whiche of entencioun	*empty*
	They han contreved by false transumpcioun	*transferring materials*
265	To hyde trouthe falsely under cloude,	
	And the sothe of malys for to schroude,	*desire to injure; cloak*
	As Omer dide, the whiche in his writyng	*Homer*

	Ifeyned hathe ful many divers thyng	*Fabricated*
	That never was, as Guydo lyst devise,	*chose to explain*
270	And thingys done in another wyse	
	He hathe transformed than the trouthe was	
	And feyned falsly that goddis in this caas	
	The worthi Grekis holpen to werreye	*wage war*
	Ageyn Troyens, and howe that thei wer seye	*seen*
275	Lyche lyfly men amonge hem day by day.	*living; them*
	And in his dites that wer so fresche and gay	*writings*
	With sugred wordes under hony soote	*sweet*
	His galle is hidde lowe by the rote,	*bitterness; deeply hidden*
	That it may nought outewarde ben espied.	
280	And al for he with Grekis was allied,	*since*
	Therfor he was to hem favourable	
	In myche thing, whiche is nought commendable	
	Of hem that lyst to demen after ryght;	*them who wish to judge*
	For in makyng, love hath lost his syght,	*composing; blinded him*
285	To yeve a pris wher noon is disserved.	*ascribe worth*
	Cupide is blynde, whos domys ben observyd	*whose judgments follow*
	More after lust than after equité	
	Or after resoun, how the trouthe be.	*what the truth is*
	For singulerté and false affeccioun	
290	Reyseth ful ofte by veyne lausioun	*praise*
	A man to worschip that disserveth noon,	*honor who*
	By false reporte; and thus ful many oon	
	Withoute merit hath his fame blowe,	*trumpeted*
	Wher of another the renoun is unknowe,	*unknown*
295	That in armys hath mervelles wrought	
	Of whom paraunter speketh no man nought;	*perhaps*
	For favour only is fostered more than ryght,	
	That hyndered hath many worthi knyght.	
	Ovide also poetycally hath closyd	*clothed*
300	Falshede with trouthe, that maketh men ennosed	*confused*
	To whiche parte that thei schal hem holde;	
	His mysty speche so hard is to unfolde	
	That it entriketh rederis that it se.	*ensnares*
	Virgile also for love of Enee	*Aeneas*
305	In *Eneydos* rehersyth moche thyng	*Aeneid*
	And was in party trewe of his writyng,	

Exsepte only that hym lyst som whyle
The tracys folwe of Omeris stile.   *traces (ideas)*
And of this sege wrot eke Lollius,
310   But toforn alle Dares Frigius   *before*
Wrot moste trewly after that he fonde,   *according to what*
And Dytes eke of the Grekys lond.   *Dictys also*
They were present and seyen everydel,   *saw everything*
And as it fel they write trewe and wel,   *as it happened*
315   Eche in his tonge by swyche consonaunce   *with such agreement*
That in her bokys was no variaunce,   *their*
Whiche after wern unto Athenes brought
And by processe serched oute and sought
By dillygence of oon Cornelius   *Cornelius Nepos*
320   Whyche was nevewe unto Salustius,   *nephew*
Of Rome yborn, whiche dide his dever dewe   *proper obligation*
Hem to translate and the tracys sewe   *follow the written words*
Of thise auctours by good avisement.   *consideration*
But bycause he sette al his entent
325   For to be brefe, he lefte moche behynde
Of the story, as men in bokys fynde —
The firste mevyng and cause original
What was the gynnyng and rote in special;   *Which was the beginning; source*
Ne how thei come by lond or by navie;   *ship*
330   How firste the sparke was kyndeled of envie
Atwyxe Grekis and hem of Troye town,   *Between*
Of whiche Cornelye maketh no mencioun,
Or her schippes nor of her vitaille;   *food*
Nor how that Grece is called Gret Ytaille
335   And the lasse, as bokys verrefye,   *confirm*
Is named now the londe of Romanye;   *land of Italy*
What noumbre of kynges and of dukes went
Towarde the sege, al of oon assent,
To wynne worschip and for excersise
340   Of armys only in ful knyghtly wyse,
Abydyng there to sen the versioun   *overthrow*
Of the cité and noble Yllyoun;   *the citadel of noble Ilium (Troy)*
Nor what the maner was of her armure;
Nor at the sege who lengest dide endure;
345   In what wyse eche other dide assaile;

35

Nor how often thei metten in bataille;
How mony worthi loste ther his lyf   *many a worthy man*
Thorough olde hatrede wrought up with newe strif;
Nor of her dethe he dateth nat the yere,   *deaths*
350   For his writyng was particuler;   *incomplete*
Withoute frute he was compendious,
This forseyde Romeyne, this Cornelius.
Wherfore but late in comparisoun
Ther was an auctour of ful highe renoun
355   That besied hym the tracys for to swe   *follow the written words*
Of Dite and Dares, and cast hym nat transmwe   *Dictys; determine not to alter*
In al the story a worde as in sentence   *substance*
But folweth hem by swyche convenience
That in effecte the substaunce is the same;
360   And of Columpna Guydo was his name,
Whiche had in writyng passyng excellence.
For he enlumyneth by crafte and cadence   *rhythm*
This noble story with many fresche colour
Of rethorik, and many riche flour
365   Of eloquence to make it sownde bet   *better*
He in the story hathe ymped in and set,   *insert*
That in good feythe I trowe he hath no pere,   *believe; equal*
To rekne alle that write of this matere,   *subject matter*
As in his boke ye may byholde and se.
370   To whom I seie, knelyng on my knee:
Laude and honour and excellence of fame,   *Praise*
O Guydo maister, be unto thi name
That excellest by sovereinté of stile
Alle that writen this mater to compile.
375   Whom I schal folwe as nyghe as ever I may   *closely*
That God me graunt it be unto the pay   *liking*
Of hym for whom I have undertake
So as I can this story for to make,   *compose in verse*
Preynge to alle that schal it rede or se
380   Wher as I erre for to amenden me,
Of humble herte and lowe entencioun   *meek*
Commyttyng al to her correccioun,
And therof thanke; my wille is that thei wynne   *prosper*
For thorugh her support thus I wil begynne.

Book 1

In the regne and lond of Thesalye,	*Thessaly*
The whiche is now ynamed Salonye,	*Salonica*
Ther was a kyng callyd Pelleus,	*Peleus*
Wys and discrete and also vertuous.	
The whiche, as Guydo lyst to specefie,	*chose*
Helde the lordschipe and the regallye	*kingship*
Of this yle as governour and kyng,	*island*
Of whiche the pepil, by record of writyng,	
Myrmidones were called in tho dawes,	*those*
Of whom Ovyde feyneth in his sawes,	*Ovid invents in his tales*
Methamorphoseos, where as ye may rede	
How this peple sothfastly in dede,	*truly*
So as myn auctor maketh mencioun,	
Were brought echon to destructioun	*each one*
With sodeyn tempest and with fery levene	*sudden storms; bright flames*
By the goddys sent down from the hevene;	*gods*
For they of ire, withoute more offence,	*wrath*
With the swerde and stroke of pestilence	
On this yle whylom toke vengaunce,	*once*
Lyche as it is putte in remembraunce.	*Just*
For this peple distroied were serteyn	*certainly*
With thonder dent and with haiel and reyn	*thunderbolt; hail*
Ful unwarly, as Guydo list discryve;	*unexpectedly; chose to describe*
For ther was noon of hem lefte alyve	
In al the lond that the violence	
Escape myghte of this pestilence,	
Excepte the kyng, the whiche went allone	*who*
Into a wode for to make his mone	*forest; complaint*
Sool by hymsilfe, al disconsolate,	*Alone*
In a place that stood al discolat,	*deserted*
Wher this kyng, roomyng to and fro,	
Compleynynge ay of his fatal woo	*Lamenting*
And the harmys that he dide endure —	

Til at the laste, of caas or aventure, *by chance*
35 Besyde an holt he sawe wher stode a tre *wood*
Of ful gret heght and large of quantité, *size*
Holwe by the rote, as he kowde knowe, *Hollow*
Where as he sawe by the erthe lowe
Of amptis crepe passyng gret plenté, *A large number of ants creeping*
40 With whiche syghte he felle doun on his kne
And made his preyer in his paynym wyse *pagan manner*
To the goddes with humble sacrifyse
Upon his wo and gret adversité
Only of mercy for to have pyté,
45 To turne thise amptis into forme of man. *ants*
Thus gan he praye with colour pale and wan
His lond t'enhabite whiche stondeth disolat, *to populate*
And he alone, awaped and amaat, *dejected and dismayed*
Confortles of any creature,
50 Hym to releve of that he dide endure.
And as Ovide maketh mencioun,
That Jubiter herde his orisoun *Jupiter; prayer*
And hath swiche rowth on hym at the laste *pity*
That he anoon fulfilled his requeste, *immediately*
55 And of his myghte, whiche that is devine, *with his power*
His grace he made from hevene for to schyne
Benyngnely unto the erthe doun,
That a sodeyn transmutacioun
Was made of amptis to forme of men anon,
60 Whiche on her feet gonne streght to goon *began*
To Thesalye and salue ther the kyng *salute*
And lyche his liges token her dwellynge *vassals; their residence*
Withinne a cité called tho Egee, *Aigion*
As in Ovide ye may beholde and see.
65 The whiche peple for her worthines, *prowess*
For her strenthe and grete hardynes
Myrmidones so longe have boor the name *borne*
(As in the lyfe ye reden may the same
Of Seynt Mathewe, how thei be called soo, *St. Matthew*
70 Where the apostel so mochel hadde adoo)
Whiche for wisdam and prudent advertence, *attention to the future*
Besy labour and wilful dilligence,

	By forseynge and discrecioun,	*foresight*
	As I suppose in myn opinioun,	
75	That this fable of amptis was contreved,	*invented*
	Whiche by her wysdam han so myche achevid	*their*
	Thorugh her knyghthod, whoso list to loke,	*Through*
	Her manly dedis thoroughout *Troie Boke*.	
	In al meschef so wel thei han hem born	*misfortune*
80	That thei ful wysly provided wern toforn	*were before*
	Or that it fil, bothe in werre and pees;	*Before it happened; war; peace*
	For of no slouthe thei wer nat rekeles,	*they were not negligent for laziness*
	But as the ampte t'eschewen ydelnesse	*ant to avoid*
	In somer is so ful of besynesse	
85	Or wynter com, to saven hir fro colde	*Before*
	Sche toforne astored hath hir holde.	*beforehand has provided for her nest*
	But in this mater I holde no sermoun,	
	I wil no longer make digressioun,	
	Nor in fables no more as now sojourne,	
90	But there I lefte I wyl agayn retourne,	
	Of Pelleus ferther to procede.	
	Whiche kyng forsothe, in story as I rede	*truly*
	And as myn auctor lysteth to endyte,	*is pleased to compose*
	Had a wyf that called was Tedite;	*who; Thetis*
95	Of whiche two, platly this no les,	*plainly this is no lie*
	The manly man, the hardy Achilles,	
	So as Guydo lesteth to termyne,	*wishes to declare*
	Descended was, sothly as be lyne,	*by lineage*
	Most renomed of manhood and of myght	
100	Amonges Grekis and the beste knyght	
	Iholde in sothe thorughoute al her lond,	*Regarded in truth*
	In worthines preved of his hond.	
	Whos cruelté Troiens sore abought	
	So passynge merveilles in armys ther he wrought	*great; performed*
105	Duryng the sege, as ye schal after lere,	*siege (of Troy); learn*
	Paciently yif ye liste to here.	*if you wish*
	But Pelleus, that I spak of aforne,	*whom; before*
	A brother hadde of o moder born	*one*
	That hyghte Eson, so fer yronne in yeris,	*was named Aeson; grown old*
110	That he of luste hath lost al his desyris,	*pleasure*
	So fer he was ycropen into age	*had crept*

That al his witte was turned to dotage; *mind; feebleness*
For bothe mynde and memorial *memory*
Fordulled wern and dirked so at al *Were dulled and clouded*
115 That verrailly his discrecioun
Was hym birafte, in conclusioun. *taken from him*
Wherfor the regne and lond of Thesalye,
Croune and septre with al the regalye, *Crown*
He hath resygned his brother for to queme, *please*
120 Estate royal and also diademe:
Bycause he was croked, lame, and blynde
And to governe loste bothe wit and mynde,
So febled was his celle retentif *memory*
And fordirked his ymaginatif *darkened; faculty of imagination*
125 That lost were bothe memorie and resoun;
For whiche he made a resygnacioun
To his brother, next heyr by degré *heir by descent*
And next allye of his affinité. *relation*
But as somme auctours in her bokys seyn,
130 To youthe he was restored new ageyn
By crafte of Medee, the gret sorceresse, *Medea*
And renewed to his lustynesse; *liveliness*
For with hyr herbes and hir pociouns, *potions*
Sotyl wyrchyng of confecciouns, *drugs*
135 By quentyse eke of hir instrumentys, *subtle craft*
With hir charmys and hir enchauntementys, *spells*
Sche made a drynke, in bokys as is tolde,
In whiche a yerde that was drye and olde *branch*
Withoute abod anoon as she it caste *Immediately as soon as*
140 To blosme and budde it began as faste,
Turne grene and fresche for to beholde.
And thorugh this drinke sche hath fro yeris olde
Eson restored unto lusty age
And was of witte and resoun eke as sage *wise*
145 As ever he had his lyve ben aforn.
The whiche Eson of his wyfe yborn
Hadde a son, and Jason was his name,
In wirk of whom Nature nas to blame; *was not*
For sche hir crafte platly and konnyng *skill plainly; shrewdly*
150 Spent upon hym hooly in wirkyng, *wholly*

40

Whan sche hym made with herte, wil, and thought,

That of hir crafte behynde was ryght nought.   *nothing was omitted*

To rekne his schap and also his fayrnes,

His strenthe, his bewté, and his lyflynes,

155   His gentilles and wyse governaunce,

How large he was, and of dalliaunce   *speech*

The moste goodly that men koude knowe,

In al his port bothe to hyghe and lowe,   *behavior*

And with al this avise and tretable —   *prudent*

160   That of konnyng God wot I am nat able

For to discreye his vertues by and by.   *make known*

For as myn auctor telleth feithefully,

He was beloved so of old and yonge

That thorugh the londe is his honour spronge;

165   But for that he was but yonge and sklender,   *because; tender*

Of age also inly grene and tender,   *extremely*

He was committed to the governaille   *governance*

Of Pelleus, to whom withoute faille

In everythyng he was as servisable,

170   As diligent in chambre and at table,

As evere was any childe or man

Unto his lorde, in al that ever he can

Devise in herte of feithful obeyschaunce;   *Will; obedience*

So that in chere nor in countenaunce,   *expression*

175   Inwarde in herte nor outwarde in schewyng,

To his uncle ne was he nat grucchyng;

Albe he had holly in his hande   *wholly*

The worthi kyngdam and the riche lande

Of this Jason and the eritage,

180   Only for he was to yonge of age.   *because*

Unto whom Pelleus dide his peyne

Ageynes herte falsely for to feyne,   *dissemble*

To schewen other than he mente in herte,

And kepte hym cloos that nothing hym asterte,   *kept strictly silent; escape*

185   Lyche an addre under flouris fayre,

For to his herte his tonge was contrarie:

Benyngne of speche, of menyng a serpente,

For under colour was the tresoun blente   *concealed*

To schewe hym goodly unto his allye;

41

190	But inwarde brent of hate and of envie	
	The hoote fyre, and yit ther was no smeke,	*smoke*
	So covertly the malys was yreke,	*hidden*
	That no man myght as by sygne espie	*discover*
	Toward Jason in herte he bare envie.	
195	And merveil noon, for hit was causeles,	*let no one wonder*
	Save he dradde that he for his encres	*gain*
	And for his manhood likly was t'ateyne	*reach*
	For to succede in his faders reigne,	
	Whiche Pelleus unjustly ocupieth;	
200	And day be day cast and fantasieth	
	How his venym may be som pursute	*by; assault*
	Uppon Jason be fully execute.	
	Heron he museth every hour and tyme,	*ponders*
	As he that dradde to sen an hasty pryme	*see; an early season*
205	Folowen a chaunge, as it is wont to done,	
	Sodeynly after a newe moone;	
	He caste weyes and compasseth sore,	*contrives*
	And under colour alwey more and more	
	His felle malys he gan to close and hide,	*cruel ill will; enclose*
210	Lyche a snake that is wont to glyde	
	With his venym under fresche floures;	
	And as the sonne is hoot afore thise schoures,	*before*
	So of envie hattere bran the glede.	*hotter burned the coal*
	Upon a tyme he sought to procede	
215	To execute his menynge everydel,	*wholly*
	In porte a lambe, in herte a lyoun fel,	*demeanor; cruel*
	Dowble as a tygre slighly to compasse,	*cunningly contriving*
	Galle in his breste and sugre in his face,	
	That no man hath to hym suspecioun,	
220	Howe he purveieth the destruccioun	*plans*
	Of his nevewe and that withinne a whyle,	
	Pretendyng love, albe the fyn was gyle.	*even though; aim; guile*
	His malys was ischette so under keye	*locked*
	That his entent can no man bewreye;	*reveal*
225	It was conceled and closed in secré,	
	Under the lok of pryvé enmyté,	*personal*
	And that in soth greved hym the more:	
	Upon hymsilf the anger frat so sore,	*tormented so deeply*

	Abydyng ay til unto his entent	
230	He fynde may leyser convenient	
	Upon his purpos platly to procede	*intention; plainly*
	For to parforme it fully up in dede.	
	Wherof Jason hath ful lytel rought —	*took no heed*
	His uncle and he wer not in o thought —	
235	Of whos menyng was no convenience,	*accordance*
	For malys was coupled with innocence;	*joined with*
	And grownde of al, as I can divise,	
	Was the ethik of false covetise,	*covetousness*
	Whiche fret so sore falsly for to wynne,	*burns so deeply; gain*
240	As crop and rote of every sorowe and synne,	*branch and root*
	And cause hath ben, sythen goo ful yore,	*since a long time ago*
	That many a rewme hath abought ful sore	*kingdom; suffered dearly for*
	The dredful venym of covetyse, allas!	
	Lat hem be war that stonden in this caas	*careful; circumstance*
245	To thinke aforne and for to have in mynde	
	That al falshed draweth to an ende:	
	For thoughe it bide and last a yer or two,	
	The ende in soth schal be sorwe and wo	*truth*
	Of alle that ben false and envious.	

[*Peleus learns of a ram with golden fleece in the kingdom of Colchos, which is ruled by Cethes (Aetes). The ram is protected by wild bulls, a serpent, and men who spring from the serpent's teeth and fight one another when the teeth are sown in the ground. Anyone trying to win the fleece has to survive all these tests. Peleus schemes to have Jason undertake the adventure, and at a council he flatters him and then asks him to try to win the fleece. Not suspecting Peleus's treachery, Jason accepts the challenge and gathers his companions, among them Hercules who performed twelve labors. The heroes set out for Colchos but after a difficult passage land on the Trojan coast to rest (lines 250–722).*]

	Whan Hercules and Jasoun on his hond	*at his side*
	Out of hir schip taken han the lond	*their; have*
725	And with hem eke her knyghtes everychon	*them also their; each one*
	That fro the see ben to londe goon,	*shore*
	Forweried after her travaille;	*Exhausted; their labor*
	And thei in sothe come to arivaille	*arrived at*
	At Symeonte, an havene of gret renoun,	
730	That was a lyte bysyde Troye town —	

And thei wer glad to ben in sikirnesse — *safety*
From storm and tempest after werynesse; — *fatigue*
For thei ne ment tresoun, harm, nor gyle — *intended*
But on the stronde to resten hem a while; — *shore*
735 To hynder no wyght, of no maner age, — *injure; person*
Nor in that ile for to do damage
To man or beste, wherevere that thei goo, — *beast*
But for to abyde ther a day or two — *rest*
Hem to refresche and repeire anoon — *depart immediately*
740 Whan that the rage of the see wer goon.
And whiles thei on the stronde leye, — *shore*
Thei nothyng dide but disporte and playe — *divert themselves*
And bathe and wasche hem in the fresche ryver
And drank watrys that were swote and clere, — *sweet*
745 That sprange lyche cristal in the colde welle,
And toke right nought but it were to selle. — *on sale (paid for)*
It was no thing in her entencioun — *not at all*
Unto no wyghte to done offencioun, — *person; offense*
For to moleste or greven ony wyght; — *aggrieve anyone*
750 But the ordre of Fortunys myght
Hath evere envy that men lyve in ese, — *Is always jealous*
Whos cours enhasteth unwarly to dissese. — *hastens unexpectedly to discomfort*
For sche was cause, God wotte, causeles, — *God knows; with justification*
This gery Fortune, this lady reccheles, — *fickle; imprudent*
755 The blynde goddesse of transmutacioun,
To turne her whele by revolucioun
To make Troyens unjustly for to wene — *think*
That Grekys werne arived hem to tene, — *harm*
So that the cause of this suspecioun
760 Hath many brought unto destruccioun.
Ful many worthi of kynges and of princes
Thorughoute the worlde, rekned in provinces, — *mentioned one after another*
Werne by this sclawnder unto deth brought, — *Were; false statement*
For thing, allas, that was never thought. — *Because of something*
765 For it was cause and occasioun
That this cité and this royal town
Distroied was, as it is pleynly fownde, — *seen*
Whos walles highe wer bete down to grounde. — *beaten*
And many man and many worthi knyghte

770	Were slawe ther, and many lady bryghte	
	Was wydowe made by duresse of this werre,	*severity; war*
	As it is kouthe and reported ferre;	*known; far and wide*
	And many mayde in grene and tender age	
	Belefte wer sool in that grete rage,	*alone*
775	Behynd her fadris, allas, it falle schulde!	*fathers*
	And for nothing but that Fortune wolde	*for no reason except*
	Schewen her myght and her cruelté,	
	In vengaunce takyng upon this cité.	
	Allas, that evere so worthi of estate	
780	Schulde for lytel fallen at debate!	*in strife*
	Whan it is gonne, it is not lyght to staunche:	*easy to stop*
	For of griffyng of a lytel braunche	*grafting*
	Ful sturdy trees growen up ful ofte;	*very often*
	Who clymbeth hyghe may not falle softe;	*land softly*
785	And of sparkys that ben of syghte smale	
	Is fire engendered that devoureth al;	
	And a quarel, first of lytel hate,	
	Encauseth flawme of contek and debate	*Causes; discord and strife*
	And of envie to sprede abrod ful ferre.	*very far*
790	And thus, allas, in rewmys mortal werre	*kingdoms deadly war*
	Is first begonne, as men may rede and see,	
	Of a sparke of lytel enmyté	*By*
	That was not staunchid first whan it is gonne.	*extinguished*
	For whan the fyre is so fer yronne	
795	That it enbraseth hertis by hatrede	*encompasses*
	To make hem brenne, hoot as any glede,	*glede*
	On outher party thorugh his cruel tene,	*either; malice*
	Ther is no staunche but scharpe swerdys kene,	*check*
	The whiche, allas, consumeth al and sleth;	*slays*
800	And thus the fyne of enmyté is deth.	*end*
	Though the gynnyng be but casuel,	*circumstantial*
	The fret abydyng is passyng cruel	*continuing torment; exceedingly*
	To voide rewmys of reste, pees, and joye,	*empty*
	As it fil whilom of this worthi Troye.	*once*
805	It doth me wepe of this case sodeyne;	*causes me to; unforeseen case*
	For every wyght oughte to compleyne	
	That lytel gylte schulde have swyche vengaunce,	
	Except parcas thorugh Goddys purvyaunce	*perhaps; God's foresight*

45

	That this mescheffe schulde after be	*misfortune; afterwards have*
810	Folwyng perchaunse of gret felicité.	*Outcome*
	For Troye brought unto destruccioun	
	Was the gynnyng and occasioun,	*beginning*
	In myn auctor as it is specified,	
	That worthi Rome was after edefied	*built*
815	By the ofspryng of worthi Eneas,	*Aeneas*
	Whilom fro Troye whan he exiled was.	*long ago*
	The whiche Rome, rede and ye may se,	
	Of al the worlde was hed and chef cité	
	For the passyng famous worthinesse.	
820	And eke whan Troye was brought in distresse	*also*
	And the wallis cast and broke down,	
	It was in cause that many regioun	*for this reason*
	Begonne was and many gret cité:	
	For this Troyan, this manly man Enee,	
825	By sondri sees gan so longe saille,	*various*
	Til of fortune he com into Ytaille	*by; Italy*
	And wan that lond, as bookes tellen us;	*conquered*
	With whom was eke his sone Askanius,	*Ascanius*
	That after Enee next began succede	*Who*
830	The lond of Ytaille justly to possede;	*possess*
	And after hym his sone Silvius,	
	Of whom cam Brute, so passyngly famus;	*Brutus (founder of England)*
	After whom, yif I schal nat feyne,	*if; lie*
	Whilom this lond called was Breteyne,	*Britain*
835	For he of geauntys thorugh his manhood wan	*giants*
	This noble yle and it first began.	
	From Troye also with this ilke Enee	*same Aeneas*
	Cam worthi Francus, a lord of highe degré	
	Whiche upon Rone, t'encressen his renoun,	*the Rhone, to augment his fame*
840	Bilt in his tyme a ful royal toun,	
	The whiche sothly, his honour to avaunce,	
	After his name he made calle Fraunce;	
	And thus began, as I understond,	
	The name first of that worthi lond.	
845	And Anthenor, departyng from Troyens,	*Antenor*
	Gan first the cité of Venycyens;	*the Venetians*
	And Sycanus withinne a lytel while	

	Gan enhabite the lond of Cecyle.	*Sicily*
	And after partyng of this Sycanus,	
850	His worthi brother, called Syculus,	
	So as I fynde, regned in that yle;	
	And after hym it called was Cecille.	
	But Eneas is to Tuscy goon,	*Tuscany*
	It t'enhabite with peple right anoon;	*his followers*
855	And in Cecille he Naplis first began,	*Naples*
	To whiche ful many Neopolitan	
	Longeth this day, ful riche and of gret myght.	*Belong as citizens*
	And Diomedes, the noble worthi knyght,	
	Whan Troye was falle with his toures faire,	*towers*
860	As to his regne he cast to repaire,	*kingdom; return*
	His leges gan to feynen a querele	*subjects; invent*
	Ageynes hym and schop hem to rebelle;	*prepared*
	And of malys and conspiracioun,	*conspiracy*
	Thei hym withhilde bothe septer and croun,	
865	Her dueté and her olde lygaunce	*allegiance*
	And hym denye trouthe and obeissance.	
	Wherfor anoon, so as bokes telle,	
	With al his folke he went for to dwelle	*followers*
	Unto Callabre and gan it to possede.	*Calabria (southern Italy)*
870	And ther the knyghtes of this Dyomede	
	That fro Troye han him thider swed	*followed as subjects*
	To forme of briddes wern anon transmwed	*birds; transformed*
	By Cyrces crafte, doughter of the sonne,	
	And in the eyr to fleen anoon thei gonne	*fly*
875	And called ben, in Ysidre as I rede,	*Isidore of Seville*
	Amonges Grekys briddes of Dyomede.	
	But as som bokys of hem ber witnesse,	
	This chaunge was made be Venus the goddesse	
	Of wrath sche had to this worthi knyghte;	*Because of*
880	Only for sche sawe hym onys fyghte	*once*
	With Eneas, hir owne sone dere.	
	At whiche tyme, as thei faught ifere	*together*
	And Diomede with a darte igrounde	*sharp*
	Gan hame at hym a dedly mortal wounde,	*aim*
885	His moder Venus gan anoon hym schroude	*cover*
	Under a skye and a mysty cloude	

47

	To saven hym that tyme fro meschaunce.	*misfortune*
	And for this skyl Venus took vengaunce:	*by this means*
	Into briddes to turne his meyné.	*followers*
890	And in that forme fro yer to yer thei fle	
	Unto his towmbe, wher that he is grave.	*tomb; buried*
	So upon hym a mynde yit thei have,	*memory*
	That of custom for a remembraunce	
	A rite thei holde and an observaunce	
895	At his exequies thise briddes everychon	*funeral rites*
	A dayes space and thennys nought ne gon.	*and do not leave*
	And overmore, as it to hem is dwe,	*appropriate to them*
	Thei love Grekis, and platly thei eschewe	*avoid*
	Latyns alle, for ought that may betyde:	*whatever may happen*
900	For thei present, anoon thei flen aside;[1]	
	And eche from other, as bokys us assure,	
	This briddes knowe only of nature	*instinctively*
	Grekys and Latyns kyndely assonder,	*how to distinguish*
	Whan thei hem seen: the whiche is swiche a wonder	
905	Unto my witte that I can nought espie	*mind; discover*
	The causys hid of swiche sorcerye.	*hidden source; magic*
	But wel I wot, though my wit be blent,	*But I know well, though my mind is dulled*
	That rote of al was fals enchauntement.	*cause*
	But of our feithe we oughte to defye	*reject*
910	Swiche apparencis schewed to the eye,	*false appearances*
	Whiche of the fende is but illusioun —	*devil*
	Herof no more. And thus whan Troye toun	
	Eversed was and ibrought to nought,	*Overthrown*
	Ful many cité was ibilt and wrought,	*made*
915	And many lond and many riche toun	
	Was edified by th'ocasioun	*built because of the accident*
	Of this werre, as ye han herde me telle.	
	Whiche to declare now I may not dwelle	
	From point to point, lyche as bokis seyn,	
920	For to Jason I wil resorte ageyn	*return*
	That londed is with worthi Hercules	
	At Symeonte, the havene that thei ches,	*chose*

---

[1] *If they (Latins) are present, they (the birds) immediately fly off*

As I have tolde, to reste hem and counforte,
And for not elles but only to disporte.   *anything else*
925 But to the kyng regnyng in Troye town
That was that tyme called Lamedown,   *Lamedon*
Of fals envy reported was and tolde   *malicious ill will*
How certeyn Grekis wern of herte bolde   *were*
To entre his lond, the whiche thei nat knewe,   *whom they (the Trojans)*
930 Wel arrayed in a vessel newe.
Whiche to arryve hadde no lycence   *They*
And hem purpose for to doon offence   *intend to do harm*
Be liklyhed and his lond to greve: *harm*
For thei of pryde withouten any leve   *permission*
935 Or safcondyte han the stronde ytake;   *safeconduct; shore*
And swiche maistries on the lond thei make,   *free actions*
As in her power wer alle maner thyng,   *As if*
Havyng no rewarde pleynly to the kyng;   *gift*
Of his estat take thei noon hede.
940 Of swyche straungeris gretly is to drede,
Yiffe men be laches outher necligent   *If; careless or*
Fully to wit what is her entent,   *know*
But furthe prolong and no pereil caste.   *delay and foresee no peril*
Swyche sodeyn thing wolde be wist as faste   *unforeseen; should*
945 And nat differrid til the harme be do;   *deferred*
It wer wisdam that it wer seie to:
Men may to long suffryn and abyde
Of necligence for to lete slyde   *delay*
For to enqueren of her governaunce.   *intentions*
950 This was the speche and the dalyaunce   *conversation*
Everyche to other by relacioun   *Each one to each other in turn*
In every strete thorughoute Troye toun.
Somme rounyng and somme spak abrood;   *whispering; openly*
And this speche so longe ther abood
955 From on to another, sothly, that the soun
Reported was to Kyng Lamedoun,
As ye han herde, the whiche of wilfulnesse,
Without counsail or avisenesse,   *foresight*
To hastily maked hath his sonde   *message*
960 To wit how thei wern hardy for to londe   *To learn; bold*
Besyde his leve, of presumpcioun.   *Without*

49

Wherfore he bad in conclusioun
Withoute abood sone to remwe, *delay; remove themselves*
Or finally thei schulde nat eschewe *avoid*
965 To be compellid, maugre who seith nay. *despite*
And so the kyng upon a certeyn day
In haste hath sent his embassatour
Unto Jason, of Grekys governour,
That nouther thought harme nor vylonye *neither*
970 But innocent with his companye
Disported hym endelong the stronde *along the full length*
And ever hath do sethen he cam to londe. *since*
And of the charge that he on hym leyde
And word by word to Jason how he seide,
975 As in effecte with every circumstaunce,
This was the somme pleinly in substaunce. *gist; essence*
"The wise, worthi, moste famus of renoun,
The myghty kyng, the noble Lamedoun
Hath unto yow his message sent,
980 Of whiche th'effect, as in sentement, *purpose; meaning*
Is this in sothe: that he hath mervaille *truth*
Into this londe of your arivaille,
Bryngyng with yow Grekys nat a fewe,
And have no condyte for yow to schewe, *safeconduct*
985 Proteccioun, pleynly, nor lycence, *permission*
In prejudise of his magnificence. *defiance*
Wherfore he hath on me the charge leyde
And wil to yow that it be platly seyde *openly*
That ye anoon, withoute more delay,
990 Withoute noyse, or any more affray *disturbance*
Of Troye lond the bowndis that ye leve; *boundaries*
Or yow and youres he casteth for to greve. *intends; punish*
And bet it is with ese to departe *better*
Than of foly your lyves to juparte *foolishly; risk*
995 In any wyse, for lak of providence
Ageyns his wille to make resistence
Outher of pride or of wilfulnesse, *Either out of*
For to be bolde withoute avisenesse *forethought*
To interrupte his felicité;
1000 For he desyreth in tranquillité

	To holde his regne withoute perturbaunce.	
	In whos persone is made swyche aliaunce	
	Atwen his manhood and royal magesté	
	That thei nyl suffre noon of no degré	*will not*
1005	T'enpugne his quiete in any maner wyse;	*assail*
	Wherfore I consaille, as ye seme wyse,	
	To taken hede unto that I seye	
	And his byddyng noght to disobeie,	
	Liste ye offende his kyngly excellence.	*Lest*
1010	For ye schal fynde in experience	
	Withoute feynyng sothe al that I telle:	*truth*
	Take hede therfor; I may no lenger dwelle	
	From poynt to poynt, syth ye be wis and sage;	*since*
	For this is hool th'effecte of my massage."	
1015	Whan Jason herd of the massanger	*from*
	Thise wordes alle, he gan chaunge cher	*appearance*
	And kepte hym cloos with sobre contenaunce	
	And was nat hasty for ire nor grevaunce;	
	For no rancour he caughte of his tale,	
1020	Save in his face he gan to wexe pale;	*grow*
	Long abydyng or ought he wolde seyn	*before he said anything*
	And or he spak any worde ageyn	
	Unto hym that from the kyng was sent,	
	He gan disclose the somme of his entent	*reveal; gist*
1025	Unto his foolke stondyng ronde aboute;	
	For unto hem he discurede oute	*revealed*
	The message hool, firste whan he abreide,	*whole; began to speak*
	And worde by worde thus to hem he seyde:	
	"Sirs," he seyth, "to yow be it knowe —	
1030	Taketh hede, I praye, both hygh and lowe —	
	How Lamedoun, that is Kyng of Troye,	
	Hath sent to us a wonderful envoye,	*strange*
	Chargynge in haste to hyye oute of his lond;	*hie*
	And axeth how we upon the stronde	*inquires*
1035	For to arive hadden hardinesse	
	Withoute leve: seth here his gentillesse	*Without permission; see*
	And his fredam, the whiche is nat a lite!	*nobility (or generosity)*
	How lyche a kyng that he can hym quite	*behave*
	Unto straungerys that entren in his ile	

1040	For nought, God wot, but for a litel while	*For no reason*
	Hem to refresche and departe anoon,	
	Lyche as ye can recorden everychon	*remember*
	And bere witnes, bothe alle and somme.	*one and all*
	Allas, fredam, wher is it now becom?	
1045	Where is manhood and gentilnesse also,	
	Whiche in a kyng togidre bothe two	
	Schulde of custom han her restyng place?	
	And wher is honour, that schulde also enbrace	
	A lordis hert, whiche of knyghtly ryght,	
1050	Of manly fredam, with alle his fulle myght,	
	Schulde straungeris refresche and reconforte,	
	That aftirward thei myght of hym reporte	
	Largesse expert, manhood, and gentillesse	*Well-schooled generosity*
	That thei han founden in his worthinesse.	
1055	For yiffe noblesse wer of his allye	*if*
	And fredam eke knyt with his regalye	*joined; rule*
	(So as longeth to honour of a kyng),	*is appropriate to*
	He schulde have chargid first of alle thing	*instructed*
	His worthi liges with al that myghte plese	
1060	To have schewed the comfort and the ese	
	With al hir myght and her besy cure	*concern*
	Unto straungeris that of aventure	*by chance*
	Wern in the see dryven and dismaied	*disheartened*
	And of our comfort nat ben evel payed.	*badly disposed*
1065	For yif that he in any cas semblable,	*similar*
	Outher by fortune that is variable,	
	By sort or happe, that may not be withstonde,	*chance or luck (see note)*
	Arived had into Grekys londe,	
	More honestly, lyche to his degré,	*appropriate to his standing*
1070	He schulde of us have resseived be,	
	Lyche as it longeth unto genterie.	
	But syth that he, for ought I can espie,	*understand*
	Hath fredam, honour, and humanité	
	Atonys made oute of his courte to fle,	*At once*
1075	Chose dishonour and late worschip goon —	*good name*
	Ther is no more. But we schal everychon	*each one of us*
	That he hath chosen helpe to fulfille	*What (see note)*
	Whan power schal nat be lyke his wille:	*to his advantage*

52

This to seyne — and sothe it schal be founde —	*truth*
1080	That his dede on hymsilfe schal rebounde,	
	Sith of malys he hath this werke begonne,	*Since*
	Paraventure or the somer sonne	*Perhaps before*
	The sodiak hath thries gon aboute.	*zodiac*
	For late hym trust and no thing ben in doute,	*let; in no way*
1085	We schal hym serve with swyche as he hath sought;	*repay*
	For yif I lyve it schal be dere abought,	*paid for dearly*
	Albe therof I sette as now no tyde.	*Although*
	And in this lond I nyl no lenger byde	
	Til I have leiser better to sojorne."	
1090	And with that worde he gan anoon to turne	
	With manly face and a sterne chere	*fierce countenance*
	Sodeynly unto the massangere	
	That fro the kyng unto hym was sent;	
	And in this wyse he scheweth his entent:	
1095	"My frende," quod he, "I have wel understande	
	The massage hool that thou toke on honde	*whole*
	Of thi kyng to bryngen unto us	
	Right now unwarly; and syth it standeth thus,	*without warning; since*
	That I have his menyng everydel	
1100	From point to point and understonde it wel —	
	For word by worde I have it plein conseived	
	And the giftes that we han resseived	
	On his byhalve in our grete nede —	*behalf*
	I wil remembre and take right gode hede	
1105	To everything that thou hast us brought.	
	For truste wel that I foryete it nought	
	But enprente it surly in my mynde	*imprint; securely*
	And with al this, how goodly that we fynde	
	The gret bounté in al maner thing	
1110	Within this lond of Lamedoun the Kyng:	
	His wolcomyng and his grete cher	
	And the goodly sond that thou bryngist her,	*message*
	Nat accordyng unto oure entent;	
	For God wel wot that we never ment	
1115	Harme unto hym nor pleinly no damage	
	To noon of his of no maner age.	
	And heruppon the goddis inmortal	*gods*

	That of kynde ben celestial	*naturally*
	Unto recorde with al myn hert I take;	*I promise*
1120	And touchyng this my borwys I hem make,	*pledge*
	In witnessyng we mente noon offence	
	Ne toke nat, as by violence,	
	Within his rewme of womman, child, nor man;	
	And so thou maist reporte yif thou can —	
1125	But for that we, fordriven in the se,	
	Compellid wern of necessité	
	For to arive, as thou haste herd me seyn,	
	Only to reste us her upon the pleyn,	
	Withoute more, unto a certeyn day	
1130	And afterward to holde furthe our way	
	Upon our jorneye and make no tariyng,	
	Liche as thou maist recorde to thi kyng —	
	And seye hym eke he schal the tyme se	
	That he paraunter schal mow thanked be,	*by chance may well be repaid*
1135	Whan tyme comyth, by us or by som other:	
	Go furthe thi waye and seie hym thus, my brother."	
	And than anoon, as Jason was in pes,	*quiet*
	The manly knyght, the worthi Hercules,	
	Whan he had herd this thing fro poynt to point,	
1140	He was anoon brought in swyche disjoint	*agitation*
	Of hasty rancour and of sodeyn ire,	
	The whiche his hert almost set afire,	
	That sodeynly, as he abreyde abak,	*start out of silence*
	Of high disdeyn even thus he spak	*scorn*
1145	With cher askoyn unto the messanger	*sidelong glances*
	And seide, "Felaw, be no thing in wer	*doubt (do not worry about)*
	Of our abidyng but be right wel certeyn	
	That or Tytan his bemys reise ageyn	*before*
	We schal depart and to schippe goon;	
1150	That of oure men ther schal nat leven oon	*not one be left*
	Withinne this lond and, God toforn, tomorwe.	*before God (an oath)*
	And herupon have her my feith to borwe;	*here; to be sure*
	For we no lenger schal holden her sojour,	
	For elleswher we schal make our retour	*return*
1155	Tomorwe erly in the dawenyng	
	Up peyne of repref; and so go seie the kyng.	*blame*

And or thre yere, yif God us graunte lyf,
Maugre who gruccheth or maketh any strif,   *Despite*
Unto this lond we schal ageyn retourne
1160   And caste anker a while to sojourne.   *anchor*
Take hede therfore and note wel the tyme:
A newe chaunge schal folwen of this pryme,   *follow from this beginning*
And thanne his power schal not so large strecche;
Of his saufconduit lytel schal we recche.   *safeconduit; reckon*
1165   I seie the platly, as is oure entent,   *tell you plainly*
We wil not have to his maundement   *orders*
But lytel reward, and we that day abide;   *concern, if we see that day*
For takyng leve schal be set asyde
Because he hath now begonne a play
1170   Which we schal quite — be God, yif that I may —
That torne schal into his owne schame;
And spare nought to seie the kyng the same."
This massanger than gan ageyn replye
And seide, "Syr, ye may me not denye
1175   Of honesté my massage to declare;
Avise yow, for I wil not spare   *Reflect carefully; fail*
The kynges sonde pleynly for to telle.   *message*
And wherso be ye lyst to goon or dwelle,
Ye may yit chese, whoso be lefe or lothe;   *happy or sad*
1180   Ye have no cause with me to be wroth;
For it sit not unto your worthines,   *it does not befit*
Yffe ye take hede be weye of gentilnes,
Of manassyng swyche arwes for to schete;   *to shoot such menacing barbs*
For more honest it were youre thretyng lete   *threatening forego*
1185   And kepe secrete til ye ben at your large.   *at liberty*
For certeinly no parcel of my charge
Is for to strive with yow or debate.
But bet it is bytymes than to late   *before it is too late*
That ye be war for harme that myghte fale.
1190   And for my parte, I saie unto yow alle,
It were pité that ye distroied were
Or any man hyndre schulde or dere   *injure or harm*
So worthi persones in any maner wise
Whiche ben so likly to be discret and wise;

1195 And list with wordis as now I do you greve, *lest*
     I saye no more. I take of yow my leve."

[Jason and his men leave Trojan territory and sail to Colchos. They march in splendor to Cethes's palace, and the king receives them courteously. Jason asks for permission to undertake the tests to gain the fleece. Cethes, wary of being blamed, explains the dangers but grants permission. A feast is prepared, to which Cethes summons Medea, his daughter and heir. Medea has been educated in the liberal arts and exercises great powers over nature. Cethes seats Medea next to Jason (lines 1197–1822).]

     But O, allas, ther lakked high prudence, *was lacking*
     Discret avis of inward providence, *forethought*
1825 Wisdam also with pereil caste afore *peril foreseen*
     To trust a maide of tendre yeres bore, *born*
     Of unhappy fonned wilfulnes. *unfortunate infatuated*
     For this kyng of his gentelnes
     Comaunded hath to his confusioun, *destruction*
1830 To his dishonour and destruccioun
     His owne doughter, born to be his eyr,
     That was also so wommanly and fair,
     So sodeynly doune to descende —
     Considered nat the meschef of the ende.
1835 Allas, why durst he in hir youthe affie *trust*
     To make hir sytten of his cortesie
     Wher sche myght by casuel mocioun
     Ful lightly cacche or han occasioun *seize*
     To don amys; allas, whi dide he so?
1840 Why list hym nat taken hede therto *did he not wish*
     Nor to adverte in his discresioun, *turn aside*
     Wysly to caste aforn in his resoun *foresee*
     The unwar chaunge that is in wommonhed, *unexpected*
     Whiche every man oughte for to drede?
1845 For who was ever yit so mad or wood *insane*
     That ought of resoun conne aright his good *know his well being*
     To yeve feith or hastily credence *give*
     To any womman withoute experience
     In whom is nouther trust ne sikernesse? *neither; certainty*
1850 Thei ben so double and ful of brotilnesse *brittleness*
     That it is harde in hem to assure; *have faith*

For unto hem it longeth of nature   *it is natural for them*
From her birth to haven alliaunce   *their*
With doubilnes and with variaunce.
1855   Her hertes ben so freel and unstable,   *frail*
Namly in youthe so mevynge and mutable
That so as clerkis of hem liste endite   *wish to write*
(Albe that I am sori it to write)
Thei seyn that chawng and mutabilité
1860   Appropred ben to femynynyté —   *Are characteristic of*
This is affermed of hem that were ful sage.
And speciali while thei be tender of age   *especially*
In her wexyng and whan that thei be yonge,   *growing*
Whos herte acordeth ful selde with her tonge.
1865   For if the trouthe inwardly be soughte
With the surpluse and remnaunte of her thoughte,
Men may ther the trewe patron fynde
Of inconstaunce, whos flaskisable kynde   *inconstant nature*
Is to and fro mevyng as a wynde,   *moving like*
1870   That Hercules wer nat strong to bynde
Nouther Sampson, so as I bileve,   *Nor*
Wommannes herte to make it nat remeve.   *alter*
For as the blase whirleth of a fire,   *flame*
So to and fro thei fleen in her desire   *fly*
1875   Til thei acomplische fulli her delite.   *fully*
For as matere by naturel appetit,
Kyndely desyreth after forme   *Naturally*
Til he his course by processe may performe,
So this wommen restreynen hem ne can
1880   To sue her lust ay fro man to man.   *follow*
Thei wil not cesse til al be assaied;   *tried*
But wolde God, as mater is apaied   *pleased*
With o forme and holdeth him content,
Whan of his boundys he hath the terme went   *reached*
1885   And not desyreth ferther to procede
But stille abitte and wil it nat excede,   *waits*
That by ensample alle wommen wolde
Resten in on, as duelly thei schulde,   *properly*
And holde hem peyde and stille ther abide.   *satisfied*
1890   But unsure fotyng doth hem ofte slide,   *support; causes*

	For thei be nat content with unité:	
	Thei pursue ay for pluralité,	
	So of nature to mevyng thei be thewed,	*disposed*
	Although amonge, by signes outward schewed,	*from time to time*
1895	Thei pretende a maner stabilnes;	
	But under that is hid the dowbilnes	
	So secretly that outward at the eye	
	Ful harde it is the tresoun to espie.	*discover*
	Under curteyn and veil of honesté	
1900	Is closed chaunge and mutabilité,	*hidden*
	For her desyr is kepte ful cloos in mewe	*concealment*
	And thing thei hadde levest for to sewe	*would wish most to pursue*
	Only outward for to have a laude,	*praise*
	Thei can decline with feynyng and with fraude.	*dissimulation*
1905	Wherfore, Cethes, thi wit was to bareyne	*mind*
	That thou aforne by prudence naddist seyne	*did not foresee*
	What schulde folwe of this unhappy caas.	
	Whi wer thou bolde for to suffre, allas,	
	Thin owne doughter, so fair and fresche of hewe,	
1910	With straunge gestis entred but of newe	*foreign; lately*
	So folily for to lete hir dele,	*associate*
	Wherthorugh thin honour, thi worschip, and thin hele	*health*
	Was lost in haste, and sche to meschef brought	
	In straunge londe with sorwe and myche thought.	
1915	Wheras sche to grete sclaunder of the	*you*
	In gret miserie and adversité	
	An ende made and thou wer lefte al sool,	*alone*
	Thou myghtest wel compleyne and make dool.	*lament; complaint*
	Allas the while, yif in thi prudent syght	
1920	Thou haddest grace to remembre aright	
	And to have cast by discret purvyaunce,	
	And weied wysely by mesour in balaunce	
	The fraude of wommon and the freelté,	*frailty*
	In whom ful selde is any sikerté,	*seldom; stability*
1925	As in his Latyn Guydo doth expresse.	
	Wherfor, thou Cethes, of verray reklesnesse	
	Thou hast attonys in augment of thi woo	*at once; woe*
	Without recure bothe two forgoo:	*remedy*
	Firste thi tresour and thi doughter dere,	

1930	That was to the so passyngly entere,	*exceedingly dear*
	And eke thin ayre; for whan that sche was goon,	*heir*
	As seithe myn auctor, other was ther noon	
	After thi day for to occupie	
	Thi royal septre nor thi lond to guye.	*guide*
1935	But what was worth the grete providence,	
	The wakir kepyng, or besy diligence	*wakeful watch*
	Of myghti Mars, that god is of bataile?	
	What myght it help, diffende, or availe	
	Ageyn the wit of womman or the sleighte	
1940	Whos fraudes arn of so huge a weighte	*are*
	That as hem list ay the game gothe,	*as they wish*
	Her purpos halt, whoso be lefe or lothe —	*intention held; happy or sad*
	Thei ben so slighe, so prudent, and so wyse!	
	For as this story plainly doth devise,	
1945	This Medea by hir engyne and crafte	*ingenuity*
	From hir fader his tresour hath berafte	*taken*
	Thorugh the werchyng of hir sleighty gyle,	*crafty*
	As ye schal her withinne a lityl while.	
	For as sche sat at mete in that tyde	*time*
1950	Next hir fader and Jason by hir syde,	
	Al sodeinly hir fresche rosen hewe	
	Ful ofte tyme gan chaunge and renewe	
	An hondrid sythe in a litel space.	*times*
	For now the blood from hir goodly face	
1955	Unto hir hert unwarly gan avale,	*began to drop*
	And therewithal sche wexe ded and pale;	*grew*
	And efte anoon, who that can take hed,	*soon afterwards*
	Hir hewe chaungeth into a goodly red.	*hue*
	But evere amonge t'ennwen hir colour,	*to shade*
1960	The rose was meynt with the lillie flour;	*mingled*
	And though the rose stoundemele gan pase,	*from time to time; pass away*
	Yit the lillie abideth in his place	
	Til nature made hem efte to mete.	*again*
	And thus with colde and with sodein hete	
1965	Was Medea in hirsilfe assailled	
	And passyngly vexed and travailed.	*distressed*
	For now sche brent, and now sche gan to colde,	*burned*
	And ay the more that sche began beholde	*always*

	This yong Jason, the more sche gan desyre	
1970	To loke on hym, so was sche sette afire	
	With his bewté and his semlynesse;	*attractiveness*
	And everything sche inly gan enpresse	*notice*
	What that sche sawe, bothe in mynde and thought;	
	Sche al enprenteth and forgat right nought;	*remembers; nothing*
1975	For sche considereth every circumstaunce	
	Bothe of his port and his governaunce:	*behavior; demeanor*
	His sonnelyche here, crisped liche gold wyre,	*sunny hair*
	His knyghtly loke and his manly chere,	*face*
	His contenaunce with many noble signe,	
1980	His face also, most gracious and benigne,	
	Most acceptable unto hir plesaunce;	
	For, as sche thought, it was sufficiaunce	
	Withouten more unto hir allone	
	To considre and loke on his persone.	
1985	For in that tyme withouten any drede	
	Of mete or drinke sche toke but litel hede,	
	For sche of food hath loste hir appetit;	
	To loke on hym sche hath so gret delite —	
	He was so prented in hir remembraunce.	*imprinted*
1990	Love hath hir caught so newli in a traunce	
	And ymarked with his firy brond	*marked; arrow*
	That sche may nought eskapen fro his hond	
	Nor eschewe his strok in special;	*avoid*
	For sche was yolde body, herte, and al,	*given up*
1995	Unto Jason platly for to seye,	*plainly*
	And evere among on hym sche cast hir eye,	*at the same time*
	Whan that sche fonde a leyser oportune.	*opportunity*
	But of wisdam sche wolde nat contune	*persist in*
	Hir loke to longe, list men dempte amys;	*lest; judge amiss*
2000	But as the maner of this wommen is,	*these*
	Sche kepte hir cloos and wonderly secree,	*herself*
	That by hir chere no man myghte see	*appearance*
	What that sche ment by noon occasioun.	*by no opportunity*
	Sche put hem out of al suspeccioun,	
2005	For openly ther was no tokne sene.	*token*
	Sche caste rather that men schulde wene	*thought; believe*
	That th'enchesoun of hir abstinence	*cause*

60

	And why that sche satte so in silence —	
	How that it was only of wommanhede,	
2010	Of honest schame, and of chaste drede,	
	That togidre in hir herte mette;	
	The whiche tweyn so this maide lette	*kept*
	Fro mete and drink, as it wolde seme.	*food and drink*
	Thus of wisdam sche made hem for to deme	*judge*
2015	And so to cast in hir opinioun;	*believe; their*
	And thus sche blent hem by discrecioun,	*deceived them*
	For hir chere koude everything excuse.	*expression; explain*
	Sche gaf no mater folis for to muse;	*to foolish people to ponder*
	No cher unbridled that tyme hir asterte;	*expression unguarded; escaped*
2020	For ther was oon enclosed in hir herte	
	And another in her chere declared.	
	For maidenes han ofte sythes spared	*often times*
	To schewen oute that thei desyre in dede;	*reveal*
	As it falleth, whoso can take hede,	*Since it happens, as anyone can see*
2025	That whil thei flouren in virginité	
	And for youthe have no liberté	
	To specifie that her herte wolde,	
	Thei kepe hem cloos, for thei be nat bolde	
	To schewen out the somme of her sentence.	*reveal; whole; meaning*
2030	And thus Medea, kepyng ay silence,	
	Ne lete no worde by hir lippis passe,	
	But covertly with sobre chere and face	
	What sche ment scheweth with hir eye	
	So secretly that no man koude espie	
2035	The hoote fire in hir breste yreke;	*hot; concealed*
	And in hirself right thus sche gan to speke,	
	As sche in sothe that so moche can:	*knows*
	"So wolde God, this yonge lusty man,	
	Whiche is so faire and semly in my sighte,	
2040	Assured were to be myn owne knyghte.	
	Whiche is to me most plesaunt and entere	*beloved*
	With berd ysprong, schyning liche gold were,	*growing; wire*
	So wel ilemed and compact by mesure,	*well-built*
	Wel growe on heighte and of gode stature;	*good*
2045	And lyketh me in every part so wel	*it pleases me*
	That by assent of Fortune and hir whele	

I ewred were to stonden in his grace.   *destined*
For as me semeth, on his knyghtly face
It is to me an hevene to byholde,
2050   Albe therwith myn hert I fele colde;
And yit in soth it may noon other be.   *truth*
Allas! whi nadde he upon my wo pité   *did he not have*
Or, at the leste, he knewe in his entente
How moche trowth to hym that I mente!   *faithfulness*
2055   Of whiche, allas, he taketh no maner hede,
Albe for hym I brenne as doth the glede   *Although; burn; coal*
And to be ded I dar not me discure.   *allow to be seen*
Allas! my pitous and woful aventure
Is to rewful and my mortal peyne   *pitiable*
2060   So to be mordred, and dar me not compleyne *tormented*
To frende nor foo of my chaunce, allas,
To finden help or socour in this caas.
And trewely, yit as I schal devise,
I nothing mene but in honest wise,
2065   Liche as it schal openly be fownde;
For I desire to be knet and bounde   *joined*
With hym in wedlok and never fro hym twynne; *part*
For my menyng is withowten synne,   *intention*
Grounded and set upon al clennes,
2070   Withoute fraude or any doubilnes —
So clene and pure is myn entencioun!"
Loo, ay the maner and condicioun
Of this wommen, that so wel can feyne   *dissemble*
And schewen on, though thei thinke tweyne; *one thing; another*
2075   And covertly, that nothing be seyn,
With humble chere and with face pleyn
Enclose her lustis by swyche sotilté   *subtlety*
Under the bowndis of al honesté
Of hir entent, though the trecherie
2080   With al the surplus under be ywrye. *rest underneath; hidden*
And though that thei feith aforn pretende
And can her fraude with florissyng wel diffende *fine words; vindicate*
And flaterie, only the worlde to blende,   *blind*
With dowbilnes enclosed in the ende,
2085   Yit ay deceyt is benethe ment

Undre the sugre of feyned clene entent,

As it were soth in verray existence;   *truth*

But, trust me wel, al is but apparence.

Thei can schewe on and another mene,   *one thing*

2090   Whos blewe is lightly died into grene;   *easily turned*

For under floures depeint of stabilnes,   *colored with*

The serpent dareth of newfongilnes.   *lies hidden; novelty*

So pleyne thei seme with wordis faire glosed,   *clothed with specious adornments*

But undernethe her covert wil is closed;   *hidden intention*

2095   For what thing be most unto ther pay   *liking*

Thei wil denye and rathest ther swere nay.   *deny it; quickly*

Thus liketh Guydo of wommen for t'endite.   *write about*

Allas, whi wolde he so cursedly write

Ageynes hem or with hem debate?

2100   I am right sory in Englische to translate

Reprefe of hem or any evel to seye;   *Reproach*

Lever me wer for her love deye.   *I would rather*

Wherefore I preye hem to take in pacience;   *bear*

My purpos is nat hem to done offence;

2105   Thei ben so gode and parfyte everechon,   *each one*

To rekne alle, I trowe ther be nat on   *judge; one*

But that thei ben in wille and herte trewe.

For though amonge thei chese hem lovis newe,   *from time to time*

Who considreth, thei be no thing to blame;   *Who thinks about it will see; not at all*

2110   For ofte tyme thei se men do the same.   *often*

Thei most hem purveie whan men hem refuse;   *provide for themselves*

And yif I koude, I wolde hem excuse.

It sitteth nat a womman lyve alone;   *It is not fitting*

It is no stor but thei have more than oon.   *of no account*

2115   Preying to hem for to do me grace,

For as I hope, to hem is no trespas

Though my makyng be the same in al,   *versifying*

As Guydo wryt in his original —

Where he mysseyth, late hym bere the wyte.   *take the blame*

2120   For it sit wel that the vengaunce byte   *it is appropriate*

On hym that so this wommen hath offendid;

And yif I myght, it schulde ben amendid.

He schulde reseyve duely his penaunce;   *duly*

For yif he died withoute repentaunce,

2125	I am dispeired of his savacioun,	*despair; salvation*
	Howe he schulde ever have remissioun,	*forgiveness for sins*
	But he were contrite his synne to redresse;	*Unless; to atone*
	It may not ben, as clerkys bere wytnesse.	
	And be my trouthe, and he were alyve —	*by; if*
2130	I mene Guydo — and I schulde hym shryve,	*confess him*
	So bitter penaunce pleynly he schulde have	
	That to the tyme that he were igrave	*buried*
	He schulde remembre and platly not asterte	*escape*
	For to repente hym with al his hole herte	
2135	That he so spake to his confusioun.	*misfortune*
	I wil no lenger make digressioun	
	Fro my matere, but let Guydo be	
	And telle forthe the worching of Medee,	
	That hath licence of hir fader nome	*permission to withdraw; taken*
2140	And to hir chaumbre is allone ycome,	
	Whan oute of halle withdrawen was the pres	*crowd*
	And whan Jason and also Hercules,	
	Liche as the kyng after mete bad,	*commanded*
	To her chaumbres conveied wern and lad,	*their; were; led*
2145	Ful rially arrayed and beseyn;	*appointed*
	For every wal was cured in certeyn	*overspread*
	With clothe of golde in ful statly wyse.	

[*At the end of the feast, Medea retires to her chamber alone. She has fallen in love with Jason but is held back by modesty and the fear of shame. Fortune eventually resolves the conflict of love and shame when Cethes sends Medea to entertain Jason and Hercules. Medea seizes the chance to speak privately to Jason. She tries to dissuade him from trying to win the fleece. When he perseveres in his intention, she offers him her help, which is his only chance to survive and prevail. Jason in return promises to obey her and be her knight. She tries again to dissuade him, but Jason asserts that he would rather perish than suffer the shame of abandoning his goal. Medea says she will put aside her lineage and birthright, if Jason will marry her. Jason agrees, and the two are bound by their pledges to each other. Medea says she will send a go-between to bring him to her chamber that night. At midnight she calls for an old woman, experienced in love's tactics, to bring Jason (lines 2148–2812).*]

Whan that the cok, comoun astrologer,	*rooster, public*
The mydnyght hour with his vois ful clere	

2815	Began to sowne and dide his besy peyne	*sound; endeavored*
	To bete his brest with his wyngys tweyne	*two*
	And of the tyme a mynute wil not passe	*go beyond*
	To warnen hem that weren in the place	
	Of the tydes and sesoun of the nyght,	*time*
2820	Medea to wayten upon hir knyght	*await*
	Ful redy was the entré for to kepe,	
	As sche that list ful litel for to slepe;	*wished*
	For that ne was no parcel of hir thought.	
	And whan Jason was to hir chambre brought	
2825	Without espying of eny maner wight,	*being seen*
	Than sche anoon conveyeth hym ful right	
	Into hir closet in al the hast sche may,	*private room*
	Ful wel beseyn with gret and riche araye,	
	Where by hir side sche made hym take his se.	*seat*
2830	And first of alle this ilke lees of thre,	*leash of three*
	By hir that was moste expert in this cas,	*in these matters*
	Was sodeynly turned to a bras;	*brace (a pair)*
	For the vekke to stare upon the mone	*old woman; moon*
	Is walked out and hath hem lefte allone.	
2835	And whan Medea the dores hadde schet,	*shut*
	Down by Jason anoon sche hath hir set.	
	But first I fynde with al hir besy myght	
	Aboute the chamber that sche sette up light	
	Of grete torches and cyrges ful royal	*candles*
2840	Aboute on pilers and on every wal,	
	Whiche yaf a light liche the sonne schene.	*gave; sunshine bright*
	And to a cheste wrought of cristal clene	*clear crystal*
	First of al sche taketh hir passage,	*goes*
	Out of the wiche sche toke a rich ymage	
2845	Of pured gold, ful lusty to beholde,	*pleasing*
	That by custom of this rytes olde	
	To myghti Jove, eterne and increat,	*self-existent*
	Ihalwed was and also consecrat.	*Holy; consecrated*
	The whiche ymage, devoutly as sche oughte,	
2850	With humble herte to Jason first sche broughte	
	And made hym lowly theron take his othe	
	Unto his laste, outher for lefe or lothe,	*Unto death; happy or sad*
	That he hir schulde take unto his wife	

Fro that day forth duryng al his life
2855 With hert unfeyned and feith inviolat   *sincere*
And cherischen hir liche to hir estat.
For to that tyme, I fynde how that sche
Hadde ever floured in virginité;
And as myn auctor wel reherse can,   *report*
2860 Ay kepte hir clene from touche of any man
In thoughte and dede and never dide amys:
For sche of herte so hooly yoven is   *given*
Unto Jason and that for evermo.
And he anoon hath put his honde therto
2865 And sworne fully, as ye han herde me say,
Al hir requestes withoute more delay
To kepen hem whil his life may laste.
But, O allas, how sone he overcaste   *soon; threw over*
His heste, his feith, with whiche he was assured,   *promise; guaranteed*
2870 And hadde his fraude with flaterie ycured   *concealed*
So covertly that hir innocence,
Hir trewe menyng, and hir diligence,
And al that ever sche devise can
Deseyved was by falshed of this man!
2875 And though that trouthe was apparent above,
Doubilnes so slighly was in schove,   *Duplicity; cunningly; introduced*
As though he hadde sothly ben allied
With trewe menyng, and so nothing espied
Under faire chere was feynyng and fallas.   *deception*
2880 For what myght sche ha wrought more in this cas   *have done more*
Than for thi sake, septre and regalye,
And alle the lordis eke of hir allye
Forsoke attonys and toke of hem noon hede;   *Forsaken at once*
And of pité and verray goodlyhede
2885 Loste hir frendes and hir goode fame,
Only, Jason, to save the fro schame;   *you*
And yit, moreovere, forsoke hir heritage,
Sche that was born of so highe parage   *lineage*
And schulde have ben by successioun
2890 Eyre by dissent of that regioun.   *Heir by descent*
But wommanly for sche wolde hir quite,   *as a woman; please herself*
Of al yfere sche sette nought a myte,   *everything together; set at nothing*

	But at oon hour al sche hath forsake,	
	And unto the sche hath hir hooly take:	*you*
2895	Only for truste thou schuldest have be kynde.	*naturally*
	Riches and honour sche hath yleft byhynde	
	And ches in exil with the for to goon	*chose; you to go*
	From al hir kyn, this cely maide allone.	*simple maiden*
	Allas, I wepe for thin unkyndenes!	*unnaturalness*
2900	What, hath sche nat fro deth and fro distresse	
	Preserved the, and yit thou takest noon hede,	
	That schust adeyed, nadde sche ben thin rede!	*Who should; had she not; help*
	Of thi conqueste sche was the verray cause!	
	That I may nat schortly in a clause	*Since*
2905	Writen hir bounté nor brefly comprehende	*encompass*
	Effectuelly parformed to the ende,	*given to the fullest extent*
	At wordes fewe it may nat be tolde.	*In*
	Thorugh whom thou hast the riche flees of golde	*fleece*
	Manly conquered, whiche withoute doute	
2910	Unlikly was the to have brought aboute;	
	For whan thou were of helpe destitut,	
	Sche was thi counfort and singuler refut.	*succour*
	And with al this, thou maist it nat deneye,	
	Al erthly honour how sche gan defye	*renounce*
2915	The to conserve out of hevenes;	*preserve from grief*
	And hir fader sche hath of his riches	
	So emporisched that pité is to here:	*impoverished*
	Be exaumple of whiche wommen myght lere	*learn*
	How thei schulde truste on any man.	
2920	Allas, Medea, that so moche can	*knows*
	Bothe of sterris and of astronomye!	
	Yet sawe sche nat aforn hir destenye:	*beforehand*
	Love hadde hir put oute of governaille,	*self-control*
	That al hir crafte ne might hir not availle.	
2925	Sche was to slowe by calculacioun	*too*
	To cast aforn the constellacioun	
	Of hir birthe and hir woful fate;	
	For rekleshed sche sawe it al to late.	*Through recklessness; too*
	But I suppose hir konnynge was fallible;	
2930	For douteles, me semeth nat credible,	
	That yif sche hadde wist of it tofore,	*before*

67

So pitously sche hadde nat be lore,   *brought to ruin*
As ye schal seen hereafter hastely,
So as the story reherseth by and by,   *recounts*
2935 Howe it befel of Jason and Medee.
But first ye schul the ordre and maner se
How sche wrought after he was swore: *acted*
The same nyght, allas, sche hathe forbore   *parted with*
Hir maidenhed, and that was grete pité.
2940 And yet sche ment nat but honesté;   *meant nothing wrong*
As I suppose, sche wende have ben his wyfe;   *thought she was*
But touching that, I holde as now no strife.   *regarding; make no demur*
And yit o thing I dar afferme and seyne,
That the menyng of this ilke tweyne   *two*
2945 Ne was nat on but wonder fer atwene;   *Was not the same; exceedingly far apart*
For al that sche trewely gan mene,
Of honesté thinkyng noon outerage,   *harm*
Liche a maide innocent of age,
He to acomplische his fleschely fals delite   *pleasure*
2950 And to parforme his foule appetite   *satisfy*
Wrought everything to hir entent contrerie.   *Did*
Allas, that sche was so debonaire   *kindly*
For to trust uppon his curtesye
Or to quite hir of hir genterie,   *repay; courtesy*
2955 So hastely to rewe upon his smerte: *quickly to pity his distress*
But wommen ben of so tender hert
That thei wil gladly of routhe and pité,   *compassion*
Whan that a man is in adversité,
Saven his life rather than he deye.
2960 And so Medea, schortly for to seye,
Castyng no pereil after that schal falle,   *Foreseeing*
His desyris and his lustis alle
Hooly obeyeth with al hir ful myght;
And that so longe almost that the nyght
2965 Hath his cours rounde aboute goon.
At whiche tyme to hir spake Jason
And lowly seide, "My lady, it is tyme
That we arise, for sone it wil be pryme: *dawn*
Ye may se wel the day begynneth springe,
2970 For we may here how the briddes singe.   *birds*

	Preying to yow in al my beste wyse,	
	How I schal wirke that ye list devise	*do; wish set forth*
	And ceryously everything dispose,	*in due order; prepare*
	I yow beseche, O goodly fresche rose,	
2975	Myn emprise to bringen to an ende;	*undertaking*
	And thanne at erst hennes wil I wende,	*not until then hence*
	Save that I thinke first with you to trete	*discuss*
	In what wyse this contré ye schal lete	*abandon*
	And into Grece repeire ageyn with me,	*return*
2980	Whiche is a londe of gret felicité.	
	For trusteth wel, and beth no thing in drede,	*have no worry*
	Into that regne with me I schal you lede	
	After my conquest, yif so be that I wynne.	*prevail*
	Wherfore, I praye you goodly to begynne,	
2985	How I schal werke, in al the hast ye may,	
	For in good feith anoon it wil be day."	

[*To aid Jason in his quest to gain the fleece, Medea gives him a silver image, ointment to protect him against fire, an agate ring that will destroy poison and make him invisible, a document to read before touching the ram, and a container of liquid to glue the bulls' jaws shut. Jason leaves and goes to Cethes shortly after dawn. Fearing blame should Jason die, Cethes again tries to dissuade him from undertaking the adventure, but Jason persists in his determination (lines 2987–3200).*]

	Whan Titan had with his fervent hete	*burning*
	Draw up the dewe from the levis wete	*Drawn; wet leaves*
	Toward mydmorwe, as I can diffyne,	*state*
	Upon the hour whan the cloke is nyne,	*clock*
3205	Jason ful manly and ful lyke a knyght,	
	Armed in steel, of chere ful glad and lyght,	
	Gan dresse him forth, what hap that ever falle,	*Went forth, whatever may happen*
	And seide adieu unto his feris alle,	*companions*
	He in the bot and thei upon the stronde.	*boat; shore*
3210	And al allone, whan he cam to londe	*land*
	And in the water had his vessel lafte,	*left*
	He first of al remembring on the crafte	
	Of Medea, with al the circumstaunces	
	And how he schulde kepe his observaunces	*follow instructions*
3215	In everything and had it wel in mynde —	

And thanne anoon ful manly, as I fynde, — *immediately*
He schope him forthe and wente a knyghtly pas — *set forthe; bravely*
Toward the bolis, that forget wer of bras. — *bulls; forged; brass*
But at the point whan he his jorné gan — *undertaking began*
3220 For hym Medea wexe ful pale and wan,
So sore agast that nothing myght hir glade, — *terrified; please*
A routh it was to se what wo sche made: — *pity; woe*
For the teris on hir chekis tweyne,
Ful pitously doun distille and reyne, — *trickle down*
3225 That al fordewed wern hir wedis blake. — *bedewed; black clothes*
And ay this sorwe sche made for his sake
Liche a womman ferful and in doute,
While he his armys ful manly brought aboute. — *feats of arms*
To sobbe and syghe sche can not ben in pees, — *peace*
3230 List he for hast were oughte rekeles — *Lest; careless*
From point to point to don liche as sche bad. — *instructed*
This was the life that sche for hym hath lad.
And for to seen how he schulde hym defende,
Sche gan anoon by greces to ascende — *stairs*
3235 Of a tour into a highe pynacle — *turret*
Ther as sche myght have noon obstacle
Nor lettyng nouther, for to han a sighte — *no hinderance; have*
Of hym that was hir owne chose knyghte. — *chosen*
And ever among with wordis out sche brak — *now and then*
3240 And stoundemel thus to hir silf sche spake: — *from time to time; self*
"O thou Jason, my sovereyn hertis hele, — *well being*
Yif thou knewe what wo for the I fele, — *you*
Sothly, I trowe, it schuld the nat asterte — *Truly; think; fail*
For to be trewe with al thin hoole herte. — *whole*
3245 And God, I praye, this journé at the leste — *undertaking; least*
May this tyme tornen for the beste,
And kepe the sauf and sounde in every membre, — *you safe*
And yif the myght fulli to remembre, — *give you the power*
As I the taught and in the same forme, — *manner*
3250 Everything fully to parforme,
Only this day thin honour to avaunce,
Whiche for to sen wer al myn hool plesance. — *see*
For certeyn, Jason, yif the fil ought amys, — *if anything happened to you*
Farewel myn helthe and al my worldly blis,

3255	And my welfare, my fortune, and my grace,	
	And farewel thanne my myrthe and my solace,	*happiness*
	And al attonys myn hertly sufficiance!"	*at once*
	Lo, this for him was hir governaunce	*command*
	From the tyme that he the lond hath nome.	*has taken (arrived)*
3260	And first of al, whan that he was come	
	Where as the bolis, fel and dispitous,	*bulls; cruel; pitiless*
	Out caste her fire and flawme furious	
	At her mowthes, wonder large and huge,	*their mouths*
	Ageyn the whiche, for his chefe refuge,	*remedy*
3265	Hym to save that he wer nat brent	*burned*
	He was enoynt with an oignement	*anointed; ointment*
	On his body, that kepte hym fro damage	
	Of thilke fire, that was so ful of rage,	*that same; fury*
	And the smokys, dirke and ful horrible,	
3270	Whiche to eskape was almost impossible	
	For any man, of what estat he be,	
	Withoute comfort and conseil of Medee,	
	By whos doctrine Jason can so wirke	*act*
	That he is skapid from the mystis dirke	*escaped*
3275	Of the fire with his blases blake,	*its blazes*
	That al the eyre so cloudy dide make.	*air*
	Sche had hym made so discrete and sage	
	Only by vertu of thilke ymage,	*that same*
	Which that he aboute his nekke bare,	*bore*
3280	Wherby he was so prudent and so war	*alert*
	That, whan the bolis han most fersly gaped,	*have; fiercely opened their mouths*
	He hath her malis avisely eskapid.	*their venom wisely escaped*
	For th'enfeccioun of hir troubled eyr	*poison; their murky air*
	He hath venquesched and was in no dispeire;	*desperation*
3285	For in effecte, ageyn the foule fume,	*against the foul smoke*
	That wolde a man unto the deth consume,	
	The ymage was a preservatif,	*safeguard*
	Hym to defende and to save his life.	
	And more surly to kepe hym oute of drede,	*danger*
3290	Ful ofte sythe the writ he dide rede;	*often; document*
	For the vertu of that orisoun	*power; prayer*
	Was unto hym ful proteccioun,	
	That he nat fil into no distresse.	*danger*

	And after that, for more sikernesse,	*security*
3295	Hym to preserve in this mortal caas,	*deadly*
	He toke the licour that in the viol was	*liquid; vial*
	And therwithal, ful like a manly man,	
	Al attonis, he to the bolys ran	*at once*
	And forgat nat so warly it to caste;	*carefully; throw*
3300	And therwithal her chaules wer made faste	*jaws*
	And by the vertu so myghtely englewed	*closed together with glue*
	That he therthorugh hath outterly eschewed	*escaped*
	Th'enfeccioun of the smoky levene.	*poison; seething flame*
	And whan the eyr gan cleryn and the hevene	*air*
3305	And the mystis wern wastid hym toforn,	*had disappeared before him*
	With manly hert he raughte by the horn	*seized*
	The sterne bolis; and by violence	*fierce*
	He drowe hem forthe, in whom was no diffence,	*resistance*
	And yoketh hem, so as the maner was;	*yokes*
3310	And with the plowe he made hem gon a pas	*go forward*
	Nowe up, now doun and to ere the lond.	*plow*
	And at his lust so buxum he hem fonde	*obedient; found*
	That the soil, smothe, bare, and pleyn,	
	Thei maked han redy to bere greyn,	*have; produce grain*
3315	And on rengis it torned upsodoun:	*furrows; over*
	For tho in hem was no rebellioun	*then*
	But humble and meke and redy at his wille,	*But [they were] (see note)*
	Alle his desires pleynly to fulfille.	
	And Jason thanne liche a champioun	
3320	Gan hym inhast towarde the dragoun,	*hurry*
	That was a beste gret and monstruous,	*beast*
	Foule and horrible and right venymous,	
	And was enarmed in skalis large and thikke,	*scales*
	Of whom the brethe more perillous and wikke	*injurious*
3325	Was than the eyr of any pestelence;	*breath*
	For his venym was of swiche violence	
	That it was ful dedly and mortal.	
	And at his throte ther issed oute withal	*from; issued*
	A flawme of fire, as of a fournes mouthe	*furnace*
3330	Or liche the levene that doun by the southe	*lightning*
	Out of the est is wont in tempest smyte:	*storm to strike*
	Right so the dragoun, sothly for to write,	*truly*

	Out of his mouthe had a flaume blasid.	*blew fire*
	Wherof Jason first a litel masid	*frightened*
3335	Was in his hert of that dredful thing,	
	But whan that he remembrid on his ring,	
	Al fer and drede was leide asyde and goon;	*fear*
	For in that ring ther was sette a stoon,	*stone*
	Ful riche and noble and right vertuous,	*powerful*
3340	The whiche, as techith gret Ysydorus	*Isidore*
	And myn auctor also, as I fynde,	
	Most comounly cometh out of Ynde,	*India*
	And mot be kepte chast and wonder clene,	*pure*
	And of colour surmounteth every grene.	*is superior to*
3345	Whos vertu is al venym to distroye	
	And to withstonde that it may nat anoye,	*disable*
	Of dragoun, serpent, adder and of snake.	
	And specialy, yif that it be take	
	And yholden in the opposyt	*held; before*
3350	Of any werm, even ageyn the syght,	*snake; in front of the eyes*
	Withoute abood, in sothe, he may not chese:	*delay; choose*
	Of his venym the force he moste lese,	*lose*
	How strong it be or violent of rage.	*fury*
	But to the stoon it doth ful gret damage;	
3355	For whan he hath his vertu don, as blyve	*power exercised, as quickly*
	On pecis smale it gynnyth al to rive	*It begins to shatter in small pieces*
	And in itsilf hool abit no while.	*whole remains*
	For in the londe that called is Cecyle	*Sicily*
	Ther is a worme that Bufo bereth the name;	*serpent*
3360	And whan men wil of malis make him tame	*malice; docile*
	And his venym outerly represse,	*bring under control*
	Thei take a squille, myn auctor bereth witnes,	*quill*
	Whan thei wil wirke, or a large canne,	*reed*
	And in the ende the ston thei sette thanne,	
3365	And lyne right ageyn the wormes hed	*straight against; snake's*
	Thei holden it, til that he be ded.	
	For that is sothly his vertu of nature,	*its natural power*
	That no venym may lasten nor endure	
	In the presence of this riche stoon.	
3370	And as I fynde, this Bufo right anoon	
	Thorugh myght therof bresteth even on tweyne	*breaks in two*

Only by kynde, whiche no man may restreyne.   *naturally*
For the goddesse that called is Nature,
Whiche nexte hir lord hath al thing in cure,   *charge*
3375   Hath vertu yove to herbe, gras, and stoon,   *power given*
Whiche no man knoweth but hirsilf allon;   *only*
The causis hid ben closed in hir honde,   *hand*
That wit of man can not understonde
Openly the myght of hir wirkynge.
3380   And so Jason by vertu of this ring
And thorugh his ston, that myght him most avaunce,   *aid*
Hath the dragoun brought unto uttraunce.   *overcome completely*
In whom he fonde no maner resistence
Hym to withstonde, force nor diffence,
3385   Nouther be venym nor noon other strif;   *Neither by; other danger*
Wherfor he hath berefte hym of hys life
In manly wise and in the felde outraied.   *overcome*
And Jason than, ful glad and wel apaied,   *satisfied*
Hath with his swerd spent on him many stroke
3390   And leied on him as men hewe on an oke;   *oak*
His brighte squamys wern so harde and dure   *scales were; tough*
That wel onethe he ne myght endure   *scarcely*
Hym to dismembre and smyten of his hed.   *off*
And than anoon in the stede of sed   *in place of seed*
3395   He gan his teth out of his hed arrace,   *remove*
And right forthewith in the silfe place   *same*
He gan hem sowe, liche as men do corn,   *plant, just as; grain*
Upon the lond that ered was aforn.   *plowed*
Of whiche sede ther sprang a wonder greyn,   *fruit*
3400   Bright armed knyghtes stondyng on the pleyn,
The whiche anon with scharpe swerdis grounde   *keen*
Everyche gan other for to hurte and wounde,
Til eche his felawe hath cruelly yslawe: *slain*
This of hir fate was the fynal lawe,   *requisite*
3405   That noon of hem schulde be victorie   *in*
The deth rejoische of other by memorie;
For alle yfere thus thei made an ende.   *all together*
And after this Jason gan to wende   *went*
Unto the ram with al his dilligence,
3410   In whiche he fonde no power nor diffence,   *resistance*

	No maner strife nor rebellioun;	
	And myghtely the ram he draweth doun	
	And sette on hond upon every horn	*a hand*
	And slowe it first; and than he hath it schorn	*slew*
3415	Out of his flees of gold so passyng riche,	
	That in this world ther was no tresour liche.	
	And after that he made no delay	
	To take his bote as faste as he may	*boat*
	And roweth forthe into the tother yle,	*other island*
3420	Wher Hercules, al the mene while	
	Upon the brinke with many another mo,	*bank; many others*
	Abod Jason til he hadde do.	*Waited for; finished*
	And everychon I fynde that as blive,	*everyone; happy*
	Only for joye whan he dide aryve,	
3425	Thei gan to thanke to her goddes alle	
	So graciously that it hath yfalle	*for what happened*
	And that the flees he hath so knyghtly wonne,	
	That schon as clere as the somer sonne,	*brightly; summer sun*
	Whiche that he brought with hym unto londe,	
3430	His feris alle abyding on the stronde.	*companions; waiting; shore*

[*Jason returns to Cethes, who is inwardly distressed that Jason has won the fleece but covers his disappointment with a show of good cheer that Jason takes as genuine. Medea tells Jason to come secretly to her chamber at night, where they make love. She agrees to go with him to Greece, and they sail off together with much of her father's treasure. Later when Jason has satisfied his desires with her, he abandons her. Guido says no more about her, but the rest of her story can be found in Ovid. Meanwhile, Jason and Hercules return to Thessaly, where King Peleus receives them, feigning happiness at Jason's success. Peleus restores the kingdom that Jason should rightfully inherit. Jason is still angry at King Lamedon's treatment when he landed in Troy, and he secures money and men from Peleus to pursue his vengeance. Hercules enlists Castor and Pollux, then King Telamon and Nestor. The Greeks set forth for Troy and land at Symeonte. Peleus convenes a council in his tent, where he explains the aims of the expedition, which are to forestall Greek losses, to destroy their foes, and to win victory and riches (lines 3431–4019).*]

4020	And also faste as the kyng was stille,	*just as soon as*
	The noble knyghte, the strong Hercules	
	In the presence of that worthi pres	*crowd*
	Seide his counseil was heghly to commende,	*greatly to be valued*

For wis begynnyng is preysed be the ende:

4025 "But to effecte our purpos for to bryng, *conclusion*

My counseil is, in the morwenyng *morning*

Toforne or we discured ben be day, *Before; revealed; by*

That we us arme in al haste we may

And on this felde that we do oure peyne

4030 For to devyde oure meyné into tweyne; *divide; force; two*

And of the ton schal Kyng Thelamoun *the one*

Be governour for his highe renoun, *because*

And of the tother Kyng Pelleus schal have *other*

The governaunce, wysly hem to save;

4035 And I mysilfe and Jason here my brother

Schal secrely go with alle the tother *the others*

Under the cité, or the sonne schynes, *Below; before*

And in the bruschail and the thikke vynes *underbrush; vines*

We schal us hyde and kepe us ther ful koye; *quite still*

4040 For Lamedoun, that is Kyng of Troye, *who*

Anon as he may heren and espie *As soon as*

Of the Grekis, with his chevalrye *knights*

Out of the cité wele issen oute anoon *sally out immediately*

With yow to fighte and venge him of his foon; *take revenge; foes*

4045 But whan he cometh to our schippis ward, *toward our ships*

Nestor the duke schal in the firste ward *division*

Metyn with hym, and Castor schal also,

Whan he seth tyme, knyghtly have ado

To help Nestor, yif that it be nede.

4050 The thridde warde Pelleus schal lede; *third*

And whiles ye thus hym occupie,

Jason and I schal us faste hye *go*

To the cité, unwiste of hem echon; *unbeknownst to them*

I doute nat we schal it wynne anoon. *conquer*

4055 Doth be counseil, and it wil yow availe; *Follow; serve*

And her my trouthe, ye ne may not fayle *hear my pledge*

For to conquere the cité yonde afore;

This al and some — ye gete of me no more."

And thei acorde with al her strenthe and myghte *agree*

4060 And armen hem in stele that schon ful brighte *themselves in steel armor*

Ageyn the sonne amorwe whan he riseth, *in the morning; it*

And wrought fully as Hercules deviseth. *did; planned*

And Lamedoun, whan he herde telle

Of her comyng, hym lyst no lenger dwelle, *wished*

4065 But out he went with many a noble knyghte,

Flourryng in youthe and desirous to fyghte,

And alle tho that myght armes bere, *those; bear*

Or koude schete or durste handle a spere. *knew how to shoot; were so bold as to*

And whan thei were assemblid in the felde,

4070 Everyche his armes depeynt uppon his scheld, *blazon displayed*

Brouded or bete upon his cote armure, *Inlaid or embossed; surcoat*

Than Lamedoun with al his besy cure *Then; complete attention*

Set hem in ordre and his wardes maketh, *divisions*

And in the felde furthe his weye he taketh

4075 Towardis the Grekis, as eny lyne righte, *straight as a line*

Fully purposyng to abide and fighte.

He was nat war of hem that were behynde; *aware*

He nat adverteth nor casteth in his mynde *noticed; foresaw*

The grete sleighte nor the trechery

4080 That hym was schape: he koude it nat espie; *was prepared for him*

But furthe he went with his wardis set. *divisions*

And the Grekis anoon with hym han met

With herte bolde, astonyed nat at al. *amazed*

Duke Nestor firste, sturdy as a wal,

4085 In whos manhod was never founde lake, *lack*

Ful knyghtly than uppon horse bake, *back*

To hert his men and his knyghtes eke, *exhort; also*

Gan presen in with many worthi Greke,

With Lamedoun sturdely to mete.

4090 At whiche tyme thei felte ful unswete,

And in the frountel ful many manly man *first battle-line*

With scharpe speris first togidre ran;

And with swerdis scharpe and kene grounde

Was thilke day yoven many wounde; *given*

4095 Ther as thei mette upon every syde,

Thorugh plate and mayle her woundis bledde wyde. *armor plate; chain mail*

And basenettis thei riven to the crowne; *helmets; cut through to the head*

The noise of strokis in the eyr gan sowne; *strokes; air did sound*

And of the blood that was schad of newe

4100 The grene soile chaunged hath his hewe:

For it was died playnly into red, *dyed*

77

Upon the whiche ful many man lay ded

And many worthi loste ther his lif. *nobleman*

And certeynly in this mortal strif,

4105 The Grekis had discomfetid ben echon, *would have been defeated*

Nadde Castor socored hem anoon; *Had not; supported them immediately*

Thei of Troye so manly han hem bore *themselves borne*

That many knyght of Grekis were ilore: *lost*

But whan Castor entreth in batail

4110 With his knyghtes, so sore he dide assayl *assault*

The worthi Troyans that with spere and scheld *spear; shield*

Grekis ageyn recured han the felde, *regained have*

That many oon lyth slayen on the grene,

Girt thorugh the body with scharp speris kene, *Pierced*

4115 That thai of Troye in this mortal stour *combat*

Were drive abak, til ther cam socour

To hem in hast of worthi Lamedoun, *from*

Whiche entred in liche a wood lyoun *raging lion*

And made weye upon every syde.

4120 And where as he made his swerde to glide,

Ther was but deth, so manly he hym bare

That wel unnethe was ther non that dar *scarcely no one dare*

Abide his stroke; for ridyng up and doun,

He made weye aboute hym enviroun. *all around*

4125 In the rengis he hath his foon oute sought; *ranks; foes*

That day in armys merveiles he hath wrought, *arms*

That by his manhod and his worthines

He Grekis hath brought in swiche distres *misfortune*

That thei his swerde fledden as the deth,

4130 Merciles so many of hem he sleth.

Of whiche slaughter the Grekis wer confus,

Til Pelleus cam to her rescus, *their rescue*

Iros and wood, as he wer falle in rage. *Wrathful and angry; fury*

He thought he wolde the grete pompe aswage *pride lessen*

4135 Of hem of Troye, and so he dide anoon;

For he unhorseth of hem many oon

And felly slowe al that stood hym aforne, *cruelly; before*

And many harnes he hath that day totorne *armor; torn to pieces*

And made scheldes for to rive asoundre, *shields split apart*

4140 That to beholde it was a verray wonder,

	Til Lamedoun his peple sawe goo bake,	
	For Pelleus brought hem so to wrake.	*destruction*
	Wherof he felt in hert ful gret peyne,	
	Besechyng hem to repeyre ageyne	*return*
4145	And kythe her myght and lyche as men endure;	*show their*
	And so the felde he made hem to recure,	*regain*
	Til duke Nestor knewe that Lamedoun	
	Amyd the felde was Kyng of Troye town.	
	And right anoon withoute more abood	*delay*
4150	Ageynes hym a ful gret pas he rood;	*swiftly*
	And whan the kyng dide hym first espie,	*see*
	Of highe dispit, of rancour and envie,	*great hatred; anger; enmity*
	In knyghtly wyse gan to torne ageyn,	*turn*
	No thing agast but of highe disdeyn,	*In no way afraid; scorn*
4155	With irous hert enbollid al with pride,	*wrathful heart swollen*
	His hors fersly gan takyn in the syde,	*struck (with spurs)*
	Til ther ran out the verray rede blood;	
	And to Nestor, liche as he were wood,	*crazy*
	He rood anoon, and his spere brake;	
4160	But he ful knyghtly kepte his horse bak	
	And ful deliverly, hym ageyn to quyte	*nimbly gave him in return*
	With a spere ful scharpe whet to byte,	*honed to cut*
	Thorugh schelde and breste gaf hym swiche a wounde	*shield; breast*
	That from his hors he felde him doun to grounde.	*dropped*
4165	Of whiche fal the kyng no thing aferde	*did not fear at all*
	But ros hym up and pulled out a swerde,	
	So anger fret hym at his herte rote	*gnawed at; deeply in his heart*
	That he unhorsed feghte muste on fote;	*fight; foot*
	Wherof he was in parti ful confus,	*did not know which way to turn*
4170	Til oon Cedar cam to his reskus,	
	That was made knyghte the silfe same yere,	*very*
	Yong, fresche, and lusty, and of noble chere,	*lively*
	Sitting that tyme on a noble stede.	
	And whan that he gan to taken hede	
4175	And sawe the kyng on fote at meschef fighte,	*foot; distress*
	He gan to prike in al the hast he myghte	*ride fast*
	Toward Nestor and with a spere hym hitte,	
	From his sadel that he made hym flitte	*fall*
	Down to the grounde afore Kyng Lamedoun.	*before*

4180	But he anon liche a champioun	*immediately*
	Recured up and hymsilfe diffendeth;	*Got up and regained himself*
	And many strok eche on other spendeth	
	With scharpe swerdis, kene for to bite;	
	Everyche at other gan to foyne and smyte,	*thrust*
4185	Til Lamedoun with a dispitous chere	*pitiless*
	From his face raced his visere	*slashed through; visor*
	And by force al at onys smet	*with strength all suddenly smote*
	A riche cercle from his basenet,	*ornamental band; helmet*
	Of large perle goyng enviroun —	*gems going all around*
4190	With creste and al, he fersly bette adoun:	*plumes; fiercely*
	That whiles Nestor thus aforn him stood,	
	His face was al depeynt with blood,	*covered*
	That certeynly, the sothe to conclude,	
	Had nat Grekis with gret multitude	
4195	Reskewed hym, he hadde of Lamedoun	*Rescued*
	Be slaye as faste; for he was bore doun	*cast*
	Unto the erthe among the horse feet.	
	But Castor thoghte that he nolde leet	*hesitate*
	To be his helpe, as he behelde afeer;	*from afar*
4200	And irously he toke a myghty speer,	
	And to Cedar, that I spak of late,	*recently*
	He gan to ride and priken in gret hate:	*charge; enmity*
	But or he cam to hym, douteles,	*before*
	A Troyan knyght, callid Segnerides,	
4205	Cosyn to Cedar, whan he hath this seen,	*kinsman*
	On a courser rood anoon between;	*steed*
	And with a spere he smete Castor so	
	That with the stroke he brake evene atwo.	
	To whom Castor withoute more areste	*hesitation*
4210	Hath with a spere amyddes of the breste	
	Segnerides yove a mortal wounde,	*given*
	That likly was never for to sounde.	*never to heal*
	Wherof Cedar caughte swiche envie	*felt such anger*
	That he anoon, of malencolye	*rage*
4215	And of dispit boilyng in his herte,	*disdain*
	Segnerides whan he sawe so smerte,	*suffer from wounds*
	Maugre who gruccheth, amyddes of the feld	*Despite opposition*
	Of verray myght from Castor toke his scheld	*shield*

80

	And thorugh viser, of rancour and of rage,	*visor*
4220	He wounded hym amyddes the visage;	*face*
	And his hors from hym also he caughte,	
	And to his squier manfully it raughte:	*carried off*
	That certeynly he stood in swiche disjoynt,	*turmoil*
	This worthi Castor, that he was in poynt	*about*
4225	To have ben take of hem of Troye tho;	*taken by; then*
	For he on fote with hem moste have go,	
	Nadde Pollux with many manly knyght,	
	Mo than sevene hundrid in stele armyd bright,	
	The rather com Castor to reskewe;	*The sooner; rescue*
4230	Whiche after hem so sore gan to sewe	*follow*
	That maugre hem, Castor whan he fond,	*despite them*
	Of force he toke hym fre out of her hond	*released him*
	And to his hors restorid hym ageyn.	*returned*
	And after that, this Pollux in certeyn,	
4235	Of verray angre and of fervent ire,	*true*
	Agein Troyens with rancour set afire,	
	That al attonis he uppon hem set;	*at once*
	And in his mood, by fortune as he met	
	A Troyan knyght, called Eliatus,	
4240	In armys yong, fresche, and desirous,	
	Wonder semly and but tender of age,	*handsome*
	The Kynges sone also of Cartage	*Carthage*
	And nevewe eke unto Lamedoun,	*nephew*
	Whom Pollux hath lyche a ferse lyoun	
4245	Withoute routhe, pité, or mercy,	
	In the rengis slawen cruelly —	*battle-lines*
	That Lamedoun, whan he gan take hede,	
	Of inward dool felte his herte blede,	*sorrow; bleed*
	Whan he hym sawe evene uppon the deth	
4250	Ful pitously yelden up the brethe	*yield*
	Upon the playn, as he lay hym beforn.	*plain*
	For whiche anoon he made sowne an horn,	*sound*
	At whiche ther cam a ful riche array,	*mustering of an army*
	Sevene thowsand knyghtes, in al hast thei may	
4255	Upon his deth avenget for to be.	
	Whiche mercyles, of grete cruelté,	
	The Grekis han here and ther igrounded:	*struck to earth*

Here lith on ded, ther another wounded,   *lies one*
So that thei myght have with hem no tak. *hold their own against them*
4260 So mortally thei made hem gon abak,
That al gan turne to her confusioun;   *misfortune*
And finaly that day with Lamedoun
The tryumphe had and the felde ygoon, *won the field*
Save that, allas, oute of the toun anoon
4265 Unto the kyng ther cam a messager   *messenger*
That hath hym tolde with a ful pitous chere *sorrowful face*
How the Grekis han the cité take.
Than for to se the wo he dide make
It wolde have made a pitus hert as blyve *sympathetic; as quickly*
4270 Of verray dool asondre for to rive, *sorrow apart to break*
So sore he gan within hymsilfe to morne. *mourn*
He wiste nat what party he myght turne; *did not know where*
But in a were he abydynge longe   *uncertainty*
Aforn hym sawe the myghty Grekis stronge *before*
4275 And in the cyté another host behynde: *armed force*
Almost for wo he went out of his mynde;
And sodenly, bacward as he behilde
Toward the cité, he sawe com in the felde
First Hercules and with hym Jason,
4280 That by her sleyght wonen han the toun. *treachery have won*
And in al hast this cruel Hercules,
The myghty geaunt of force pereles, *giant; unmatched*
Liche a lyoun wood and dispitous   *mad; merciless*
Or a tigre in rage furious,
4285 Gan of newe hem of Troye assaille
And with his swerde perce plate and mail, *armor plate; chain mail*
Whiche of labour wer ful mate and feynt *exhausted; feeble*
And of long fighte with werynes atteynt. *weariness affected*
And he cam in, lusty, fresche, and grene,
4290 That thei his force myghte nat sustene;
For as he rod among hem here and yonder,
In cruel wyse he severed hem asonder *divided their ranks*
And put hem holy in this highe meschaunce *in great disorder*
Oute of rewle and of governaunce; *discipline; control*
4295 So that the kyng, oppressed al with dool, *sorrow*
Of his wardis destitute and sool, *guardians; alone*

	At meschef lefte and al infortunat,	*misfortune*
	And of comfort fully disconsolat —	
	This Hercules with a dispitous look	
4300	With scharpe spors his stede felly toke	*cruelly spurred on*
	And cruelly rod til Lamedoun,	
	And to the erthe fersly bare hym doun,	*fiercely bore*
	And upon hym, in al the hast he myghte,	
	Downe of his hors sodeinly alyghte,	*off; alighted*
4305	And myghtely rent of his basenet,	*tore off; helmet*
	And with a swerde scharpe grounde and whet	
	Smot of his hede — ther was noon other grace —	*Cut off*
	And caste it furthe in the silve place	*same*
	Among the hors by cruel violence,	
4310	Withoute pité or any reverence;	
	And in a rage raghte his hors ageyn	*remounted*
	And lyche a lyoun rengyng on the playn	*moving to and fro*
	Bar downe and slowe what cam in his weye.	*whatever*
	And many Troyan that day made he deye,	
4315	That liche to schepe wer forskatered wyde,	*sheep; scattered*
	Al destitute of governour or guyde,	*Without; leader*
	Ne can no rede, schortly to conclude;	*[They] can take no counsel*
	For the Grekis with double multitude	
	Gan hem enchace to the deth ful blyve,	*pursue; at once*
4320	That wel unnethe ther left noon alyve.	*hardly any were left*
	The feld thei han and ben that day victours;	*gain*
	And with tryumphe, liche as conquerours,	
	To the cité thei take her weye after	
	And rende doun bothe sparre and rafter;	*tear; beam*
4325	And al the tresour and riches of the toun	
	Thei toke anoon to her pocessioun,	
	Who ever grucche or be lef or lothe;	
	What thei founde, pleynly with hem gothe.	
	In the temples thei dide gret offence,	
4330	To the goddis doyng no reverence;	*homage*
	For al thei spoyle, withoute drede or fere,	*despoil*
	And unto schip everything thei bere;	
	And merciles on croked, olde, and lame,	
	Her swerde thei made cruelly atame;	*put to the sword*
4335	And children soukyng at the moder brest	

Thei mordre and sle withoute more arest;   *hesitation*
And yong maydenes, wepyng in distresse,
Ful gentil born and of gret fayrnesse,
With hem thei ladde and may hem nat excuse   *keep from*
4340   Her fresche bewté falsly to mysuse.   *abuse*
Thei waste and brenne and consumen al,   *burn*
And withoute thei brake adoun the wal.   *outside*
And Exione, the kynges doughter dere,   *Hesione*
That was to hym passyngly entere   *beloved*
4345   By his lyve — I mene Lamedoun —
Meke and benyng of condicioun,   *meek*
Hercules hath anoon hir take,
That for drede pitously gan quake,   *shake*
And hir delivered unto Thelamoun,
4350   For he entrede first into the toun.   *Because*
And he his gifte reseyved hath at gre   *with pleasure*
Because sche was surmountyng of bewté   *of surpassing beauty*
And tretid hir after as he wolde,   *wished*
Nat lyche as he a kynges doughter schulde.
4355   For syth he gat hir that day be victorie
For his worschip and his owne glorie,
Havyng rewarde to hir highe degré,
He schulde rather of kyngly honesté
And of knyghthood have weddid hir therfore,
4360   Syth that sche was of blood so gentil bore,   *born*
Than of fals lust, ageyn al godlyhede
Used hir bewté and hir womanhede
Dishonestly, and in synful wyse —
Of royal blood nat liche the highe emprise,   *intent*
4365   Nor the doctrine of naturis right,   *Nature's*
Nor liche the norture of a gentil knyght: *upbringing*
Considered first hir birthe and hir kynrede,
Hir grene youthe, and hir maydenhed,
So gode, so fayre, so womanly therto.
4370   A kynges doughter of birth sche was also;
To have wedded hir it had be no schame.
Now, Thelamoun, in soth thou wer to blame;   *truly you*
For thorugh the errour of thi governaunce,   *behavior*
Ther kyndled was of ful hyghe vengaunce

84

4375	So hoot a sparke after of envye	*hatred*
	That thorugh the worlde the fyr gan multiplie,	
	Whiche was nat liche to quenchyn of his hete.[1]	
	For hatred olde to brenne can nat lete	*stop*
	With newe flawme, whoso taketh hede;	
4380	Yif it nat smeke, it is the more to drede,	*If; smoke; fear*
	As in the story herafter schal be knowe.	*known*
	And whan this toun was brent and broughte lowe,	
	Bothe tour and wal with the soil made pleyn,	*made even with the ground*
	And nothing stood, allas, that may be seyn,	*seen*
4385	(So outterly the Grekis hem oppresse,	*completely; destroy them*
	Makyng al waste liche a wyldernesse),	*barren*
	For good and tresour and riches infinyt,	
	With many jowel ful plesyng of delyt	*jewel*
	To her schippis out of the toun thei lede,	*went*
4390	And in schort tyme homward thei hem spede	
	With tresour stuffid and haboundance of good.	*abundance*
	And whan thei seye that the wedir stood,	*weather*
	The wynde also at her lust thei hadde,	*wishes*
	Thei gan to saille, and with hem hom thei ladde	
4395	Exyona and many a mayde mo,	*Hesione; more*
	That out of Troye into Grece goo.	
	And seyling forthe, within a lytel space	
	Thei ben eskapid fro the se by grace	
	And unto lond aryved merily.	
4400	At whos commyng the Grekis outerly	
	So joyful ben of her goode spede;	
	And specialy, in Guydo as I rede,	
	Her schippes wern with golde and tresour lade;	*laden*
	Wherof in herte thei wexe wonder glade.	*became*
4405	And for thei hadde out so wel hem born	*done so well*
	To conquere Troye and so fewe lorne	*lost*
	Of her meiné, thei thanke her goddes alle	*their retinue (of warriors)*
	And of the grace that to hem is falle.	*befell*
	For with the tresour that thei han hom brought	*home*
4410	Ful many pore was made up of nought;	*Many poor people were raised from penury*

---

[1] *Which was not likely to be extinguished because of its heat*

85

Thorughout the lond there was swiche aboundance,
So moche good, and so gret sufficiaunce
That no wight had amonges hem no nede.
And many day this blisful lyfe thei lede
4415   From yer to yer by revolucioun;   *Through the cycle of the years*
And for her manhood and her highe renoun
Her honour ran rounde the worlde aboute,
That hem t'offende every londe hath doute,   *people hesitates*
For her knyghthod and for thei wer so wyse.   *Because of; because*
4420   And til the story liste ageyn devyse   *pleases*
In this mater ferther to procede,
With the favour of youre goodlyhed
I wil me reste for a litel space
And than, upborn with support of your grace,   *then*
4425   Forthe acomplische as I undertook.
And here an ende of the firste book
I make now with quakyng hond for drede,   *shaking*
Only for fer of yow that schal it rede,   *fear*
Liste ye, allas, of hasty mocyoun   *Lest; inward impulse*
4430   Ne wil not have no compassioun,
Pyté, nor routhe upon my rudenesse;   *lack of skill*
Lowly beseching to your gentilnes
Of mercy only bothe neghe and ferre   *near*
Where ye fynde that I fayle or erre,
4435   For to correcte or ye ferther flitte,   *before; proceed*
For to your grace I holy al commytte.   *wholly*

Book 2

	The envious ordre of Fortunas meving,	*Fortune's*
	In worldly thing fals and flekeryng,	*changeable*
	Ne wil not suffre us in this present lyf	
	To lyve in reste withoute werre or striffe;	*war*
5	For sche is blinde, fikel, and unstable,	
	And of her cours fals and ful mutable.	

[*Fortune brings those who sit highest to ruin. She gives some renown and victory, and humbles others. She overthrows all who trust her, just as she did King Lamedon. Thus I advise every man to take heed before starting a dispute. Be warned by Lamedon's example and show kindness to strangers. Old Troy was destroyed, the people were led into exile, and Hesione was given to Telamon because of Lamedon's unkindness. Great war and destruction can be caused by small events (lines 7–133).*]

	Allas, whi nyl thei taken better hede?	*will they not*
135	For olde Troye and afterward the newe	
	Thorughe smal enchesoun, who the trouthe knewe,	*cause; truth*
	Wer finally brought to distruccioun,	
	As olde bokes maken mencioun,	
	And many worthi and many noble knyght	
140	Slayn in the feld by dures of that fight;	*hardship*
	Kynges, princes at that sege ded	*siege died*
	Whan Antropos tobrak hir lyves thred,	*broke (see note)*
	That for to telle the meschef and the wo	
	I wante connynge and I fele also	*lack skill; feel*
145	My penne quake and tremble in my hond,	
	List that my lord, dredde on see and lond,	*Lest; feared*
	Whos worthines thorugh the world doth sprede,	
	My makyng rude schal beholde and rede,	*humble composing*
	Whiche of colour ful nakyd is and bare:	*rhetorical figures*
150	That but yif he of his grace spare	*unless*
	For to disdeyne and list to have pité,	*wish*
	For fere I tremble that he schuld it se.	

But only mercy, that dothe his hert embrace,
Byt me preswme fully in his grace,   *Bids*
155 Seynge in hym, most vertuous and good,   *Seeing*
Mercy anexid unto royal blood,   *joined to*
As to a prince longeth nyghe and ferre,   *is due near and far*
Ay tofore ryght pité to preferre.   *Always before*
For thorughe the support of his highe noblesse
160 Sowpowailled, I wil my stile dresse   *Aided; writing instrument prepare*
To write forthe the story by and by
Of newe Troye in ordre ceriously   *consecutively*
As myn auctor in Latyn, Guydo, writ,
Preying the reder wher any word myssit,   *is inappropriate*
165 Causyng the metre to be halte or lame,
For to correcte, to save me fro blame:
Late hym nat wayte after coryousté,   *elaborateness*
Syth that in ryme Ynglysch hath skarseté.   *scarcity*
I am so dulle, certeyn, that I ne can
170 Folwen Guydo, that clerke, that coryous man,   *elegant writer*
Whiche in Latyn hath be rethorik
Set so his wordis that I can nat be lyke.
To sewe his stile in my translacioun   *follow his stylus (writing instrument)*
Word by word lyche the construccioun
175 After the maner of gramariens   *grammarians*
Nor lyke the stile of rethoricyens,
I toke nat on me this story to translate;   *did not undertake*
For me to forther Clyo cam to late,   *Clio (muse of history)*
That in swyche craft hath gret experience;
180 I leve the wordis and folwe the sentence.
And trouth of metre I sette also asyde,   *correctness*
For of that arte I hadde as tho no guyde   *then*
Me to reducyn whan I went awrong;   *lead back*
I toke non hede nouther of schort nor long   *short or long [syllables]*
185 But to the trouthe and lefte coryousté   *elaborateness*
Bothe of makyng and of metre be,
Nat purposyng to moche for to varie
Nor for to be dyverse nor contrarie
Unto Guydo, as by discordaunce,
190 But me conforme fully in substaunce,
Only in menyng to conclude al on;

Book 2

	Albe that I ne can the weye goon	*way*
	To swe the floures of his eloquence	*follow*
	Nor of peyntyng I have noon excellence	
195	With sondry hewes noble, fresche, and gay,	
	So riche colours biggen I ne may;	*construct*
	I mote procede with sable and with blake.	*the color black*
	And in enewyng wher ye fynde a lak,	*shading*
	I axe mercy or I fro yow twynne;	*depart*
200	And with your favour anon I wil begynne	*immediately*
	And in al haste my style furthe directe;	
	And where I erre, I praye yow to correcte.	*err*

[*At the time Old Troy was destroyed and Lamedon killed, his son Priam and his family were besieging a castle. Priam performed great deeds of arms, risking his life in battle. He had five sons and three daughters. The oldest son was Hector, the root and stock of chivalry, who excelled everyone in knighthood. Paris was Hector's next brother, and he was the most handsome man alive. Deiphebus, a brave and wise man, was the third son. The fourth was Helenus, a man known for his learning in the liberal arts. Troilus was the fifth son, and he was called "Hector the secounde" (line 288) because of his manliness. Vergil records that Priam had two other sons. Polydorus was sent from Troy by Priam to a king he trusted, but the king cut the boy's throat and buried him in a hidden grave. The other son, Ganymede, was carried off by Jupiter who made him his butler. Priam's oldest daughter was Creusa, who married Aeneas, son of Anchises by the goddess Venus. Priam's second daughter was Cassandra, who had the power of prophecy. His third daughter was Polyxena, a maiden whom Pyrrhus, the son of Achilles, eventually slew. Priam also had thirty natural sons, all of them noble and hardy in arms.*

While Priam was besieging the castle, he was told of the fall of Old Troy, his father's death, and the fate of Hesione. Sorrow overcame him; he dressed in black, raised the siege, and returned to Troy. He found a wilderness and lamented for three days, at the end of which he resolved to rebuild Troy (lines 203–478).]

	The sorwe aswaged and the syghes olde	*lessened*
480	By longe processe, liche as I yow tolde,	
	This worthi kyng, callyd Priamus,	
	Is in his herte nowe so desyrous	
	Upon the pleyn that was so waste and wylde,	*plain*
	So strong a toun of newe for to bilde,	
485	At his devyse a cité edefye,	*By his direction; to build*

	That schal th'assautys outterly defye	*assaults; entirely*
	Of alle enmyes and his mortal foon	*foes*
	With riche tourys and wallys of hard stoon.	*towers*
	And al aboute the contrés enviroun	*surrounding*
490	He made seke in every regioun	*made to be sought*
	For swiche werkemen as were corious,	*ingenious*
	Of wyt inventyf, of castyng merveilous,	*understanding; planning*
	Or swyche as coude crafte of gemetrye,	*such as knew; geometry*
	Or wer sotyle in her fantasye;	*were subtle; imagination*
495	And for everyche that was good devysour,	*planner*
	Mason, hewer, or crafty quareour;	*quarrier*
	For every wright and passyng carpenter	*builder; excellent*
	That may be founde, owther fer or nere;	
	For swyche as koude grave, grope, or kerve;	*carve; incise; sculpt*
500	Or swiche as werne able for to serve	*were; build*
	With lym or stoon for to reise a wal	
	With bataillyng and crestis marcial;	*battlements; warlike cresting*
	Or swiche as had konyng in her hed,	*knowledge; head*
	Alabastre, owther white or redde,	
505	Or marbil graye for to pulsche it pleyn	*polish it smooth*
	To make it smothe of veynes and of greyn.	*vein-like roughnesses; rough surfaces*
	He sent also for every ymagour,	*sculptor*
	Bothe in entaille, and every purtreyour	*patterns; portrait painter*
	That coude drawe, or with colour peynt	
510	With hewes fresche, that the werke nat feynt;	*lose color*
	And swiche as coude with countenaunces glade	
	Make an ymage that wil nevere fade —	
	To counterfet in metal, tre, or stoon	*To imitate; wood*
	The sotil werke of Pigmaleoun	*subtle; Pygmalion*
515	Or of Appollo, the whiche as bokis telle	*Apollo (Appelles; see note)*
	In ymagerye alle other dide excelle;	*painting images*
	For by his crafty werkyng corious,	
	The towmbe he made of Kyng Daryus	*Darius*
	Whiche Alysaundre dide on heyghte reise,	*Alexander the Great*
520	Only for men schuld his fame preise	*praise*
	In his conquest by Perce whan he went.	*Persia*
	And thus Priam for every maister sent,	
	For eche kerver and passynge joignour	*wood worker*
	To make knottis with many corious flour,	*knobs beautifully wrought*

525	To sette on crestis withinne and withoute	*cresting inside and out*
	Upon the wal the cité rounde aboute;	
	Or who that wer excellyng in practik	*practice*
	Of any art callyd mekanyk	*mechanical*
	Or hadde a name flouryng or famus	*reputation distinguished*
530	Was after sent to come to Priamus.	
	For he purposeth, this noble worthi kyng,	*intended*
	To make a cité most royal in byldyng —	
	Brod, large, and wyde — and lest it wer assailled,	*attacked*
	For werre proudly aboute enbatailled.	*war; furnished with battlements*
535	And first the grounde he made to be sought,	*examined by probing*
	Ful depe and lowe, that it faille nought	
	To make sure the fundacioun;	
	In the place where the olde toun	
	Was first ybilt he the wallis sette;	*built*
540	And he of lond many myle out mette	*measured*
	Aboute in compas for to make it large,	
	As the maysters that toke on hem the charge	*themselves*
	Devysed han the settyng and the syyt,	*Planned; site*
	For holsom eyr to be more of delyt.	*air*
545	And whan the soille, defoulit with ruyne	*soil strewn*
	Of walles old, was made pleyn as lyne,	*level as a line*
	The werkmen gan this cité for to founde	
	Ful myghtely with stonys square and rounde,	
	That in this world was to it noon lyche	
550	Of werkmanschip nor of bildyng riche	
	Nor of crafte of coryous masounry.	*elegant masonry*
	I can no termys to speke of gemetrye;	*I know*
	Wherfore as now I muste hem sette asyde,	*for now*
	For douteles I radde never Euclide	*read*
555	That the maister and the foundour was	
	Of alle that werkyn by squyre or compas	*square*
	Or kepe her mesour by level or by lyne;	
	I am to rude clerly to diffyne	*too unlearned*
	Or to discrive this werk in every parte	
560	For lak of termys longyng to that arte.	*pertaining to*
	For I dar wel of trouthe affermyn here,	*affirm*
	In al this world ne was ther never pere	*equal*
	Unto this cité, and write it for a sothe,	*truth*

As in this boke my mayster Guydo doth.
565 And that it myght in prosperité,
In hyghe honour and felicité,
From al assaut perpetuelly contune,   *endure*
It reysed was in worschip of Neptune   *built*
And namyd Troye, as it was aforn,   *before*
570 Lyche the firste that was thorugh Grekis lorn.   *Like; lost*
The lenthe was, schortly to conclude,
Thre dayes journé, lyche the latitude,
That never I herd make mencioun
Of swiche another of fundacioun
575 So huge in compas nor of swiche larges,   *in circuit; size*
Nor to counte so passyng of fayrnes,   *reckon*
So edyfied or lusty to the syght.
And, as I rede, the walles wern on highte   *were in height*
Two hundrid cubites, al of marbil gray,   *cubits (c. 300 feet)*
580 Maskowed withoute for sautis and assay;[1]
And it to make more plesaunt of delyt,
Among the marbil was alabaster white
Meynt in the walles, rounde the toun aboute,   *Mixed*
To make it schewe withinne and withoute
585 So fresche, so riche, and so delitable,
That it alone was incomperable   *incomparable*
Of alle cités that any mortal man
Sawe ever yit sithe the world began.   *since*
And at the corner of every wal was set
590 A crowne of golde with riche stonys fret   *adorned*
That schone ful bright ageyn the sonne schene;   *shone; sun's shining*
And every tour bretexed was so clene   *furnished with battlements*
Of chose stoon that wer nat fer asondre,   *chosen; apart*
That to beholde it was a verray wonder.
595 Therto this cité compassed enviroun   *circled around*
Hadde sexe gatis to entre into the toun: *six*
The first of al and strengest eke with al,
Largest also and most principal,
Of myghty bildynge allone peerles,   *unequalled*

---

[1] *With openings to the outside for [thwarting] assaults or probes*

600	Was by the kyng callyd Dardanydes;	
	And in story, lyche as it is fownde,	
	Tymbria was named the secounde;	
	And the thridde callyd Helyas;	
	The fourte gate hight also Cethas;	*was called*
605	The fyfte Troiana; the syxte Anthonydes,	
	Strong and myghty bothe in werre and pes,	
	With square toures set on every syde.	
	At whos corners, of verray pompe and pride,	*true glory*
	The werkmen han with sterne and fel visages,	*fierce and cruel gargoyles*
610	Of riche entaille, set up gret ymages	*carving*
	Wrought out of ston, that never ar like to fayle,	
	Ful coriously enarmed for batayle.	
	And thorugh the wal, her fomen for to lette,	*their foes to hinder*
	At every tour wer grete gunnys sette	*catapults*
615	For assaut and sodeyn aventurys;	*assaults; events*
	And on tourettis wer reysed up figurys	*turrets*
	Of wylde bestis, as beris and lyouns,	*bears*
	Of tigers, bores, of serpentys and dragouns	
	And hertis eke with her brode hornes,	*harts*
620	Olyfauntes and large unicornes,	*Elephants*
	Buglis, bolys, and many grete grifoun,	*Wild oxen, bulls*
	Forged of brasse, of copur and latoun,	*latten (brass-like alloy)*
	That cruelly by sygnes of her facys	
	Upon her foon made fel manacys.	*foes; evil threats*
625	Barbykans and bolewerkys huge	*Double towers over gates; ramparts*
	Afore the toun made for highe refuge,	*Before; [were] made; shelter*
	Yiffe nede were, erly and eke late;	*If*
	And portecolys stronge at every gate,	*portcullises (iron grating)*
	That hem thar nat non assailyng charge;	*dissuade (see note)*
630	And the lowkis thikke, brode, and large,	*bars and bolts*
	Of the gatys al of yoten bras;	*cast*
	And withinne the myghty schittyng was	*inside; shutting*
	Of strong yrne barres square and rounde	*iron*
	And gret barrerys picched in the grounde	*barriers*
635	With huge cheynes forged for diffence,	*defense*
	Whiche nolde breke for no violence,	*would not*
	That hard it was thorugh hem for to wynne.	*to force one's way*
	And every hous that was bilt withinne,	*inside*

93

	Every paleys, and every mancioun	
640	Of marbil werne thoroughout al the toun,	*was*
	Of crafty bildyng and werkyng most roial.	
	And the heght was of every wal	
	Sixty cubites from the grounde acountid;	*measured*
	And ther was non that other hath surmountid	*exceeded in height*
645	In the cité, but of on heght alyche,	*one same height*
	In verray sothe, bothe of pore and riche,	
	That it was harde of highe estat or lowe	
	Hous or palys asounder for to knowe,	*distinguish from one another*
	So egaly of tymbre and of stoon	
650	Her housis wern reysed everychon.	*were each raised (built)*
	And if I schulde rehersen by and by	*recite*
	The korve knottes by crafte of masounry,	*carved knobs*
	The fresche enbowyng with vergis right as linys,	*arches; shafts of columns straight*
	And the vowsyng ful of babewynes,	*vaulting; grotesque figures*
655	The riche koynyng, the lusty tablementis,	*corner work; pleasant cornices*
	Vynettis rennynge in the casementis;	*Ornamental leaves; hollow mouldings*
	Though the termys in Englisch wolde ryme,	
	To rekne hem alle I have as now no tyme	*account for them*
	Ne no langage pyked for the nonys,	*chosen for the occasion*
660	The sotil joynyng to tellen of the stonys,	*subtle*
	Nor how thei putten in stede of morter	
	In the joynturys copur gilt ful clere	*joints; bright*
	To make hem joyne by level and by lyne	
	Among the marbil, freschely for to schyne	*reflect off*
665	Agein the sonne, whan his schene lyght	
	Smote in the gold that was bornyd bright,	*burnished*
	To make the werke gletere on every syde.	*glitter*
	And of the toun the stretis large and wyde	
	Wer by crafte so prudently provided	
670	And by werkemen sette so and devided	
	That holsom eyr amyddis myght enspire	*blow in gently*
	Erly on morwe to hem that it desyre;	
	And Zephirus, that is so comfortable	*advantageous*
	For to norysche thinges vegetable,	
675	In tyme of yere thoroughoute every strete,	
	With sugred flavour, so lusty and so swete,	*lively*
	Most plesantly in the eyr gan smyte,	*penetrate*

The cytezeyns only to delyte,	*inhabitants*
And with his brethe hem to recomfort,	*refresh*
680 Whan thei list walke hemsilven to disport.	*wished; entertain*
And thorugh the toun by crafty purviaunce,	*arrangement*
By gret avys and discret ordynaunce,	*plan; disposition*
By compas cast and squared out by squires,	*compass; carpenter's squares*
Of pulsched marbil upon strong pilleris	*polished; pillars*
685 Devised wern, longe, large, and wyde,	
In the frountel of every stretis syde	*facade*
Fresche alures with lusty highe pynacles	*covered passages; turrets*
And moustryng outward riche tabernacles,	*outward facing; shrines*
Vowted above like reclinatories,	*Vaulted; canopied beds (see note)*
690 That called werne deambulatories,	*covered walks*
Men to walke togydre tweine and tweyne	*two by two*
To kepe hem drie whan it dide reyne	
Or hem to save from tempest, wynde, or thonder,	
Yif that hem list schrowde hemsilve therunder.	*protect*
695 And every hous cured was with led;	*roofed*
And many gargoyl and many hidous hed	*gargoyle*
With spoutis thorugh and pipes as thei ought	
From the stonwerke to the canel raught,	*masonry; gutter extended*
Voyding filthes low into the grounde	*Emptying*
700 Thorugh gratis percid of yren percid rounde;	*gratings perforated; iron punctured*
The stretis paved bothe in lengthe and brede	*breadth*
In cheker wyse with stonys white and rede.	*Like checkerboard*
And every craft that any maner man	*kind of*
In any lond devise or rekene can	*imagine; name*
705 Kyng Priamus, of highe discrecioun,	*sound judgment*
Ordeyned hath to dwellyn in the toun	*Decreed*
And in stretis severyd her and yonder,	*separated*
Everyche from other to be sette asonder	*apart*
That thei myght for more comodité	*convenience*
710 Eche be hymsilfe werke at liberté:	
Goldsmythes first; and riche jowellers;	*jewelers*
And by hemsilf crafty browdereris;	*themselves; embroiderers*
Wevers also of wolne and of lyne,	*woolen; linen*
Of cloth of gold, damaske, and satyn,	*silk cloth*

715	Of welwet, cendel, and double samyt eke,[1]	
	And every clothe that men list to seke;	*wish*
	Smythes also that koude forge wele	
	Swerdis, pollex, and speris scharp of stele,	*battle ax*
	Dartis, daggeris, for to mayme and wounde,	*maim*
720	And quarel hedis scharp and square grounde.	*crossbow bolts; pointed (see note)*
	Ther wer also crafty armoureris,	
	Bowyers, and fast by fleccheris,	*Bowmakers; arrow makers*
	And swyche as koude make schaftes pleyn,	*could; smooth*
	And other eke that dide her besy peyn	*effort*
725	For the werre to make also trappuris,	*trappings for horses*
	Bete baners and royal cote armuris,	*Pound; surcoats*
	And by devise stondardis and penowns,	*banners; pennons*
	And for the felde fresche and gay gytouns.	*small standards*
	And every crafte that may rekned be,	*mentioned*
730	To telle schortly, was in this cité.	
	And thorugh this toun, so riche and excellent,	
	In the myddes a large river went,	*middle*
	Causyng to hem ful gret commodité;	*convenience*
	The whiche on tweyne hath partid the cité,	
735	Of cours ful swyft, with fresche stremys clere;	
	And highte Xanctus, as Guydo doth us lere.	*it was named; inform*
	And as I rede, that upon that flood,	
	On eche asyde many mylle stood,	*many a mill*
	Whan nede was her grayn and corn to grinde,	
740	Hem to sustene, in story as I fynde.	
	This river eke, of fysche ful plenteuous,	*plentiful*
	Devided was by werkmen corious	*ingenious*
	So craftely, thorugh castyng sovereyne,	*matchless planning*
	That in his course the stremys myght atteyn	
745	For to areche, as Guydo doth conjecte,	*be able; conjecture*
	By archis strong his cours for to reflecte	*curves; divert*
	Thorugh condut pipis, large and wyde withal,	*water pipes*
	By certeyn meatis artificial,	*channels*
	That it made a ful purgacioun	*purification*
750	Of al ordure and fylthes in the toun,	*refuse*

---

[1] *Of velvet, sendal (thin, rich silken material), and double fine silken cloth also*

	Waschyng the stretys as thei stod a rowe	*all together*
	And the goteris in the erthe lowe,	
	That in the cité was no filthe sene;	
	For the canel skoured was so clene	*gutter*
755	And devoyded in so secré wyse	*discharged; hidden*
	That no man myght espien nor devyse	
	By what engyn the filthes, fer nor ner,	*device*
	Wern born awey by cours of the ryver —	
	So covertly everything was cured.	
760	Wherby the toun was outterly assured	
	From engenderyng of al corrupcioun,	*producing*
	From wikked eyr and from infeccioun,	
	That causyn ofte by her violence	
	Mortalité and gret pestilence.	
765	And by example of this flode ther was	
	Made Tibre at Rome and wrought by Eneas,	*devised*
	The whiche also departeth Rome on two,	
	Myn auctor seith, I not wher it be so.	*do not know whether*
	And to enabite this royal chef cité	*populate*
770	Kyng Priam hath aboute in the contré	
	Made for to serche with al his hool entent	
	And in provinces that werne adjacent,	
	In borwys, townys, and in smale villages,	*boroughs*
	Igadred out of al maner ages,	*Gathered from*
775	And of thropis folkys ful divers;	*hamlets*
	And swiche as wern vacaunt and dispers	*dispersed*
	Aboute Troye in many regioun;	
	He maked hath to entre into the toun	
	Gret multitude, what of yong and olde,	
780	It to enhabite, as ye han herde me tolde.	
	And hem that wern afore to hym foreyns	*strangers*
	He hath in Troye maked citezeyns,	
	Ful discretly, liche as it is founde.	*prudently*
	And whan thei gan with peple to abounde,	
785	Kyng Priamus of highe affeccioun	
	After the bildyng of this myghty toun	
	Hath in his hert caught a fantasye	
	His newe cité for to magnyfye.	*glorify*
	And it to put the more in remembraunce	

790	He cast fully to do some observaunce	
	To myghty Mars, sterne and ferse of hewe;	*color*
	And specialy with certeyn pleies newe,	*games*
	On horse and fote, in many sondry wyse,	
	To yeve his men in knyghthod excersyse,	
795	Everyche to putten other at assaye	*to the test*
	In justis, bordis, and also in tornay,	*tilting; tournament*
	To preve her force whan thei happe mete.	*chance*
	The whiche pleies wer fondid first in Crete,	*games*
	And in that lond of highe and lowe estat	
800	In Martys honour thei wer dedicate.	*Mars's*
	And in palestre at wakys on the nyght	*athletic practice fields; watches*
	Wern other pleies men t'assay her myght,	*test*
	Only on fote with many sotil poynt;	*much subtlety*
	And some of hem wer nakyd and anoynt;	*covered with oil*
805	To wynne a prys thei dide her ful entent.	*prize*
	And ther was founde by clerkys ful prudent	
	Of the ches the pleye most glorious,	*chess (see note)*
	Whiche is so sotil and so mervelous	
	That it wer harde the mater to discryve;	
810	For thoughe a man stodied al his lyve,	*studied*
	He schal ay fynde dyvers fantasyes	*ideas*
	Of wardys makyng and newe juparties:	*protective moves; problems*
	Ther is therin so gret diversité.	
	And it was first founde in this cité	
815	Duryng the sege, liche as seyth Guydo;	
	But Jacobus de Vitriaco	
	Is contrarie of oppynioun:	
	For, like as he makyth mencioun	
	And affermeth fully in his avys,	
820	How Philometer, a philysofre wys,	
	Unto a kyng, to stynte his cruelté,	*stop*
	Fond first this pleie and made it in Caldé;	*originated; Chaldea*
	And into Grece from thense it was sent.	
	Also in Troye by gret avysement	
825	The pleye was first founde of dees and tables	*dice; backgammon*
	And of castyng the chaunces deceyvables,	*deceptive*
	That han be cause ofte of gret debat:	
	For yif that on be nowe fortunat	*one*

	To wynne a while be favour of his chance,	
830	Or he be war be sodeyn variaunce	*by*
	Unhappely he is putte abak	*is overthrown*
	And another, that stood upon the wrak	*was near ruin*
	And of losse was plounged in distresse,	
	Thei reysed han unto hyghe ryches;	
835	Gladnes of on is to another rage.	*one*
	Adevaunte, hasard, and passage —	*(see note)*
	Yif on have joye, another suffereth wo,	
	Liche as the bonys renne to and fro;	*dice*
	An hundrid sythe in a day thei varie,	*times*
840	Now blaundisschyng and now thei be contrarie;	*favorable*
	No man with hem assured is in joye.	
	And first also I rede that in Troye	
	Wer song and rad lusty fresche comedies	
	And other dites that called be tragedies.	*verse compositions*
845	And to declare schortly in sentence	
	Of bothe two the final difference:	
	A comedie hath in his gynnyng,	
	At prime face, a maner compleynyng	
	And afterward endeth in gladnes;	
850	And it the dedis only doth expres	
	Of swiche as ben in povert plounged lowe;	*poverty*
	But tragidie, whoso list to knowe,	
	It begynneth in prosperité	
	And endeth ever in adversité;	
855	And it also doth the conquest trete	
	Of riche kynges and of lordys grete,	
	Of myghty men and olde conquerouris,	
	Whiche by fraude of Fortunys schowris	*onset*
	Ben overcast and whelmed from her glorie.	*thrown*
860	And whilom thus was halwed the memorie	*made sacred*
	Of tragedies, as bokis make mynde;	
	Whan thei wer rad or songyn, as I fynde,	
	In the theatre ther was a smal auter	*altar*
	Amyddes set that was half circuler,	
865	Whiche into the est of custom was directe;	*east*
	Upon the whiche a pulpet was erecte,	
	And therin stod an awncien poete	

	For to reherse by rethorikes swete	*in elegant expressions*
	The noble dedis that wer historial	
870	Of kynges, princes for a memorial	*record*
	And of thes olde, worthi emperours,	
	The grete emprises eke of conquerours,	*undertakings also*
	And how thei gat in Martis highe honour	
	The laurer grene for fyn of her labour,	*laurel as a reward for their*
875	The palme of knyghthod disservid by old date	
	Or Parchas made hem passyn into fate.	*Before*
	And after that with chere and face pale,	
	With stile enclyned gan to turne his tale,	
	And for to synge after al her loos	*reputation*
880	Ful mortally the stroke of Antropos,	
	And telle also, for al her worthihede,	
	The sodeyn brekyng of her lives threde:	
	How pitously thei made her mortal ende	
	Thorugh fals Fortune, that al the world wil schende;	*destroy*
885	And howe the fyn of al her worthines	*intent*
	Endid in sorwe and highe distresse	
	By compassyng of fraude and fals tresoun,	
	By sodeyn mordre or vengaunce of poysoun,	
	Or conspiringe of fretyng fals envye;	*corrosive*
890	How unwarly that thei dide dye;	
	And how her renoun and her highe fame	
	Was of hatrede sodeynly made lame;	
	And how her honour drowe unto decline;	*approached*
	And the meschef of her unhappy fyne;	*death*
895	And how Fortune was to hem unswete —	
	Al this was tolde and rad of the poete.	
	And whil that he in the pulpit stood	
	With dedly face al devoide of blood,	
	Singinge his dites with Muses al torent,	*verses; torn furiously*
900	Amydde the theatre schrowdid in a tent	
	Ther cam out men gastful of her cheris,	*dreadful; expression*
	Disfigurid her facis with viseris,	*visors (see note)*
	Pleying by signes in the peples sight,	*facial expressions*
	That the poete songon hath on hight;	
905	So that ther was no maner discordaunce	
	Atwen his dites and her contenaunce:	

100

For lik as he alofte dide expresse
Wordes of joye or of hevynes,
Meving and cher, bynethe of hem pleying   *Movement; facial expression*
910   From point to point was alwey answering.
Now trist, now glad, now hevy, and now light,   *sad*
And face chaunged with a sodeyn sight,
So craftili thei koude hem transfigure,
Conformyng hem to the chaunteplure,   *mixture of joy and sadness*
915   Now to synge and sodeinly to wepe,
So wel thei koude her observaunces kepe.
And this was doon in April and in May,
Whan blosmys new bothe on busche and hay   *hedges*
And flouris fresche gynne for to springe;
920   And the briddis in the wode synge
With lust supprised of the somer sonne,
Whan the pleies in Troye wer begonne
And in theatre halowed and yholde.   *sanctified; performed*
And thus the ryyt of tragedies olde
925   Priamus the worthi kyng began.
Of this mater no more telle I can.
But I wil furthe of this story wryte
And on my maner boistusly endyte,   *roughly compose*
How Priamus was passyng dilligent,
930   Right desyrous, and inwardly fervent,
Yif he myght among his werkes alle
To bilde a paleys and a riche halle   *palace*
Whiche schulde ben his chose chef dongon,   *chosen; palace*
His royal se and sovereyn mansioun.
935   And whan he gan to this werke aproche,
He made it bilde highe upon a roche   *ordered it to be built; rock*
(It for t'assure in his fundacioun)
And callyd it the noble Ylyoun,
The sight of whiche, justly circuler,   *exactly*
940   By compas cast rounde as any spere.
And who that wold the content of the grounde
Trewly acounten of this place rounde
In the theatre he most first entre,
Takyng the lyne that kerveth thorugh the centre
945   By gemetrie, as longeth to that art,

101

	And treblid it with the seventhe part;	*multiplying it by three and one seventh*
	He fynde myght by experience	
	The mesour hool of the circumference,	
	What lond also withinne the stronge wal	
950	Contened was pleynly eke with al —	
	The creste of whiche, wher it lowest was,	
	Hadde in hight ful sixe hundred pas,	
	Bilt of marbil, ful royal and ful strong,	
	And many other riche stoon among;	
955	Whos touris wern reysed up so highe	*built*
	That thei raght almost unto the skye;	*extended*
	The werk of whiche no man myght amende.	*improve*
	And who that list by grecis up ascende,	*stairs*
	He myghte seen in his inspeccioun	
960	To the boundis of many regioun	*limits*
	And provincys that stond rounde aboute.	
	And the wallys, withinne and withoute,	
	Endelong with knottis grave clene,[1]	
	Depeynt with azour, gold, ginopre, and grene,	*cinnabar*
965	That verraily, whan the sonne schon,	
	Upon the gold meynt among the stoon,	*mixed*
	Thei yaf a light withouten any were	*wire*
	As Phebus doth in his mydday spere —	*orbit (sphere)*
	The werke of wyndowe and fenestral,	*window pane*
970	Wrought of berel and of clere cristal.	
	And amyddys of this Ylyoun,	
	So fresche, so riche of fundacioun,	
	Whiche clerkys yit in her bokis preyse,	
	Kyng Pryam made an halle for to reyse,	
975	Excellyng alle in bewté and in strenthe,	
	The latitude acordyng with the lengthe.	*as long as it was wide*
	And of marbil outeward was the wal;	
	And the tymbre, most nobil in special,	
	Was halfe of cedre, as I reherse can,	
980	And the remenant of the riche eban,	*ebony*
	Whiche most is able, as I dar specefye,	

---

[1] *Carved all along their length with embossed ornaments [were]*

With stoon to joyne by craft of carpentrie;

For thei of tymbre have the sovereynté.

And for to telle of this eban tre,

985 Liche in bokys sothly as I fynde,   *truly*

It cometh out of Ethiope and Ynde,

Blak as is get; and it wil wexe anoon,   *jet (lignite); grow*

Whan it is korve, harde as any stoon,   *carved*

And evermore lasten and endure,

990 And nat corrupte with water nor moysture.

And of his halle ferther to diffyne,

With stonys square by level and by lyne

It pavid was with gret diligence

Of masownry and passyng excellence.

995 And al above, reysed was a se,   *royal throne (see)*

Ful coriously of stonys and perré,   *precious jewels*

That callid was, as chefe and principal,

Of the regne the sete moste royal.   *throne*

Tofore whiche was set by gret delyt

1000 A borde of eban and of yvor whyt,   *table*

So egaly joyned and so clene   *perfectly*

That in the werk ther was no rifte sene;

And sessions wer made on every syde,   *places for sitting*

Only the statis by ordre to devyde.   *estates (classes/ranks)*

1005 Eke in the halle, as it was covenable,   *appropriate*

On eche party was set a dormont table   *table fixed to the floor*

Of evor eke and this eban tre;   *ivory; ebony*

And even ageyn the kynges royal see,

In the party that was therto contrarie

1010 Ireised was by many crafty stayre

Highe in the halle in the tother syyt,   *other*

Right as any lyne in the opposyt,

Of pured metal and of stonys clere

In brede and lengthe a ful riche auter.   *altar*

1015 On whiche ther stood of figure and visage

Of massé gold a wonderful ymage,   *pure*

To ben honoured in that highe sete,

Only in honour of Jubiter the grete.   *Jupiter*

And the statue, for al his huge weghgte,

1020 Fiftene cubites complet was of heighgte,   *cubits (c. 25 feet); height*

A crowne of gold highe upon his hed
With hevenly saphirs and many rubé red
Fret enviroun with other stonys of Ynde;   *Richly adorned*
And among wer medled, as I fynde,   *mixed*
1025 Whyte perlis — massyf, large, and rounde;
And for most chefe al dirkenes to confounde,
Was a charbocle, kyng of stonys alle,   *carbuncle*
To recounfort and gladyn al the halle
And it t'enlumyn in the blake nyght
1030 With the freschenes of his rody light.   *its ruddy*
The valu was therof inestimable
And the riches pleynly incomperable,
For this ymage by divisioun   *in design*
Was of schap and of proporcioun
1035 From hed to foot so maisterly entayled
That in a point the werkeman hath nat failed
It to parforme by crafty excellence.
Whom Priamus with drede and reverence
Honoured hath above the goddys alle,
1040 In al meschef to hym to clepe and calle;   *beseech*
For in hym was his hool affeccioun,
His sovereyn trust and devocioun,
His hope also and his affyaunce,   *faith*
His heile, his joye, and his assuraunce;   *health*
1045 And his welfare and prosperité
He hath commytted to his deité,
Wenyng in hert wonder sekerly   *Thinking; confidently*
To ben assured from al meschef therby,
And diffended in eche adversité,
1050 And hold his regne in highe felicité,
And in honour continuelly to schyne,
Whil Jubiter thorugh his power divyne
Hym and his hath in proteccioun —
This was his trust and ful oppinioun.
1055 And thus this werke finally acheved,
Wherof Priam with joye ful releved
That he his cité and noble Ylyoun
Hath fully brought unto perfeccioun,
Liche his entent whan that he began.

Book 2

1060 And thus Priam, this kyng, this worthi man,	
Ful many day in his newe Troye	
With his liges lad his lyf in joye,	*vassals*
Wher I hym leve in his royal sete	
Sovereynly regnynge in quiete,	
1065 Procedyng forthe, yif ye liste to here,	*hear*
Unto the effect anoon of my matere.	

[*Anger and malice continue to stir Priam to seek vengeance on the Greeks. Though Hector is away, Priam calls a council in Troy to announce his intent to seek revenge. Before starting a war, however, he will seek peaceful redress, and he decides to ask that Hesione be returned. Antenor is chosen as an ambassador; he sails to Thessaly where King Peleus receives him graciously but then orders him to leave when he reveals Priam's demand to return Hesione. Antenor sails next to King Telamon, who holds Hesione. Telamon listens to Antenor's message, derides him and Priam, and orders him to leave. Antenor sails to Achaia where Castor and Pollux angrily reject the demand. His final visit is to Pylos where King Nestor can barely control his anger when Antenor delivers his message. After a terrifying storm at sea, Antenor reaches Troy and reports to Priam. Driven by his anger, Priam decides to risk war by sending a fleet to attack the Greeks (lines 1067–1796).*]

But seye, Priam, what infelicité,	*unhappiness*
What new trouble, what hap, what destyné,	*chance*
Or from above what hateful influence	
1800 Descendid is by unwar violence	*unforeseen*
To meve the — thou canst not lyve in pes!	*move you*
What sodeyn sort, what fortune graceles,	*fate*
What chaunce unhappy, withoute avisenes,	*prudence*
What wilful lust, what fonnyd hardynes	*foolish*
1805 Han putte thi soule out of tranquillité,	
To make the wery of thi prosperité!	
Whi hast thou savour in bitter more than swete,	
That canst nat lyve in pes nor in quyete?	
Thou art travailed with wilful mocions,	*tormented; impulses*
1810 Overmaystred with thi passiouns,	
For lak of resoun and of highe prudence	
Dirked and blind from al providence,	*Clouded*
And ful bareyn to cast aforne and see	*dull; judge*
The harmys foloyng of thin adversité!	
1815 Thou wer to slow wisely to consydre;	

105

For want of sight made the to slydre,   *slip*
Thorugh myst of errour falsely to forveye   *go astray*
By pathis wrong from the righte weye,
To voyde resoun of wilful hastynes!
1820 Wher was thi guyde, wher was thi maistres
Discrecioun, so prudent and so sad,
Avisely that schulde the have lad   *Wisely; you*
From the tracis of sensualité,   *lower nature*
Though it ful selde in mannys power be
1825 By suffraunce hymsilven to restreyne,
Whan sodeyn ire doth his herte streyne?
Thou schust aforn bet ha cast thi chaunce,   *have*
Wrought by counseil, and nat put in balaunce
Thi sikernes — allas, whi distow so? —
1830 And have symuled somdel of thi wo,   *feigned*
And cast thi chance wel afore the prime
To have forgoten wrongis of old tyme,
And thought aforn in thin advertence   *consideration*
That ofte falleth in experience
1835 That whyles men do most besynes   *are busiest*
Vengably her wrongis to redres,
With double harme, or that thei ar ware,   *before; aware*
Thei falle ageyn in a newe snare;
And damages that wer foryete clene   *forgotten entirely*
1840 By fals report of rumour fresche and grene
Renewed ben, thorugh the swifte fame   *rumor*
That fleth so fer to hindre a lordis name;   *takes to flight; slander*
Namly, whan thei to a purpos wende   *intention suppose*
Only of hed and se nat to the ende.   *carelessly*
1845 For of pride and of sodeyn hete   *fervor*
Thei voide hemsilf out of al quiete,   *withdraw themselves from*
Adverting nat to wirke avisely   *Considering; prudently*
Nor the proverbe that techeth commounly,
"He that stant sure, enhast hym not to meve";   *hasten him; move*
1850 For yif he do, it schal hym after greve;
And he that walkyth surly on the pleyn,   *surely*
Yif he stumble, his wit is but in veyn;
But if so be he list of his foly   *wishes*
Be necligent to putte hym wilfully

1855	In aventure and of hymsilf ne reche	*take heed*
	T'eschewen perel, I hold he be a wreche.	*peril*
	For sothly, Priam, thou wer to rekles	*too*
	For to comytte thi quiete and thi pes	
	So dredfully, duryng by no date,	
1860	To cruel Fortune or to fikel Fate;	
	Whos maner is of costom comounly	
	That whan a man trusteth most sovereynly	
	On this goddesse, blind and ful unstable,	
	Than sche to hym is most deceyveable,	
1865	Hym to abate from his royal stalle,	*cast down; station*
	And sodeynly to make hym doun to falle,	
	And with a trip throwe hym on the bake —	
	Who that geynstryveth schal have litel tak.	*resists; power of resistance*
	Sche is so sleighty with hir gynny snare	*tricky; cunning*
1870	That sche can make a man from his welfare	
	With hir panter, that is with fraude englued,	*net*
	Whan he lest weneth for to be remewed.	*least expects*
	Therfor, no man have noon affyance,	*trust*
	In Fortune nor in hir variaunce;	
1875	Ne late no wight his ese more jupart —	*let; person; risk*
	List that the pleye wil afterward departe —	*Lest; be stopped*
	To turne his chaunce outher to wel or wo:	*happiness or grief*
	For selde in oon sche doth the gamen go,	*seldom; lets an undertaking go*
	As ye may se be example of Priamus	
1880	That of foly is so desyrous	
	To wirke of hede and folwe his oune wille,	
	To trouble, allas, the calm of his tranquille —	
	As in this boke hereafter schal be founde —	
	Hym and his cité platly to confounde	*plainly to ruin*
1885	And outterly to his confusioun;	
	That afterward by long successioun	
	It schal be rad in story and in fable	*read*
	And remembrid with dites delytable	*verses*
	To do plesaunce to hem that schal it here:	
1890	That be example thei may be war and lere	
	Of hasty lust or of volunté	*will*
	To gynne a thing which in nounsureté	*uncertainty*
	Dependeth ay, as strif, werre, and debate;	

	For in swiche pley unwarly cometh chekmate;	*unexpectedly*
1895	And harme ydone to late is to amende,	
	Whos fyn is ofte other than thei wende —	*suppose*
	In this story as ye schal after seen.	
	And late Priam alwey your merour ben,	*pattern*
	Hasty errour be tymes to correcte.	
1900	For I anoon my poyntel wil directe	*pen*
	After the maner of his tracis rude	*its crude verses*
	Of this story the remnaunte to conclude.	

[*Priam summons lords from every part of the town to a parliament at which he discloses the Greeks' rejection of Antenor's mission. He reminds his men of the need for unity and proposes to send a force by ship to attack Greek towns and lay waste to their fields. Mindful of Fortune's instability, he thinks it may now be time for her to favor the Trojans over the Greeks who have been lifted up so high. Priam then recesses parliament and calls for his sons to gather in council, where he can reveal his intention to seek vengeance for the death of their ancestors, the destruction of Old Troy, and the outrage to Hesione. He calls first on Hector to carry out his purpose, and Hector answers with soft, courteous speech (lines 1903–2182).*]

	"Myn owne lord and my fader dere,	
	Benignely yif ye list to here,	*if you wish*
2185	After the force and the grete myght	
	And the somme of naturis right,	*whole*
	Whiche everything by kynde doth constreyne	*keep in bounds*
	In the boundis of hir large cheyne,	
	It fittyng is, as sche doth enspire,	*animate*
2190	And acordyng that every man desyre	
	Of wrongis don to han amendement	
	And to hir law right convenient;	
	Namly, to swiche that with nobilité	
	Kynd hath endewed and set in highe degré;	*Nature; invested*
2195	For to swiche gret repref is and schame	
	Whan any wrong be do unto her name;	
	For eche trespas mote consydered be,	
	Justly mesurid after the qualité	
	Of hym that is offendid and also	
2200	After the persone by whom the wrong is do;	
	Be it in werre, in contek, or debate.	*war; strife*

For gretter gref is to highe estate
To suffre an harme, of cas or aventure,
Or any wrong unjustly to endure,
2205   Or injuries compassed of malys   *ill will*
Is more offence by discret avys   *on competent opinion*
To hem that ben famous in manhod,
Renomed, and born of gentyl blood,   *Renowned*
Than to swiche on that holde is but a wreche.   *one*
2210   Wherfore, we most gretly charge and reche   *are anxious*
Only of knyghthod oure worschip for to eke,   *increase*
Of wrongis don amendis for to seke,
Oure staat consydered and oure highe noblesse
And in what plyte we stonde of worthines,   *state*
2215   Whan that bestis of resoun rude and blinde   *unskilled*
Desire the same by instynt of kynde.   *instinct*
And for my part trusteth in certeyn,
Ye have no sone that wolde halfe so feyn   *glad*
Upon Grekis avenged ben as I:
2220   For here my trouth I seye yow feithfully,
For ire of hem I brenne as doth the glede;   *burn; hot coal*
I thurst her blood more than other mede;   *anything else*
For right as I eldest am of age
Among your sonys, so am I most with rage
2225   Ifret withinne, justly of knyghthood,   *Tormented*
With my right hond to schede the Grekys blod,
As thei schal fynd paraunter or thei wene: *before they think*
Whan tyme cometh, the sothe schal be sene.
But first I rede, wysely in your mynde   *advise*
2230   To cast aforn and leve nat behynde,
Or ye begynne, discretly to adverte   *reflect*
And prudently consyderen in your herte
Al, only nat the gynnyng but the ende   *not only*
And the myddes, what weie thei wil wende,
2235   And to what fyn Fortune wil hem lede: *end*
Yif ye thus don, amys ye may nat spede.
For that counseil in myn oppinioun
Is worthi litel by discrecioun
To have a pris that cast nat by and by   *benefit*
2240   The course of thinges by ordre ceryously,   *one after another*

What weye thei trace to wo or to delite;
For though a gynnyng have his appetite,
Yet in the ende, pleynly this no fable,   *invented story*
Ther may thing folwe whiche is nat commendable.
2245   For what is worthe a gynnyng fortunat,
That causeth after strif and gret debat?   *later; contention*
Wherfor in sothe principles are to drede,   *truth; beginnings; to be feared greatly*
But men wel knowe what fyn schal succede;
For a gynnyng with grace is wel fortunyd,   *given good fortune*
2250   Whan ende and myddes aliche ben contunyd.   *remain alike*
But whan that it in wele ne may contene,   *persist*
It is wel bet bytymes to abstene   *better*
Than put in doute that stant in sureté;
For whoso doth hath ofte adversité.
2255   But humblely to your estat royal
Of hert I praye, lat nat offende at al,
That I am bolde to seie my mocioun;   *express my view*
For in good feith, of noon entencioun
I no thing mene yow to don offence;   *in no way*
2260   But only this — that your magnificence
Procede nat of hede wilfully   *without care*
Ne that no spirit you meve folyly
To gynne thing that after wil you schende,   *begin; bring to ruin*
For lak that ye se nat to the ende
2265   Nor taken hede in youre advertence   *judgment*
To consydere by good providence
How Grekis han in her subjeccioun
Europ and Aufrik with many regioun
Ful large and wyde, of knyghthod most famus,
2270   And of riches wonder plentevous,   *abundant*
Right renomed also of worthines.   *renowned*
With your support that I dar wel expresse,
Ful perlous is displese hem or disturbe;
For yif that we oure quiete now pertourbe,   *if*
2275   Whiche stant in pes, gretly is to drede;   *peace*
For though al Asye help us at our nede,
Yif it be lokid on every part aright,
Thei be nat egal unto Grekis myght;
And though also myn aunte Exioun   *Hesione*

110

2280	Ageyn al right be holde of Thelamoun,	*Telamon*
	It is nat good for hir redempcioun	*deliverance*
	To putte us alle to destruccioun.	
	I rede nat to bien hir half so dere;	*advise; redeem her*
	For many of us in hap that sitten here	*by chance*
2285	And other mo myghten for hir sake	*more*
	Deth underfonge and an ende make;	*receive*
	Whiche were no wisdam, liche as semeth me.	
	And it may happen also how that sche	
	In schort tyme hir fatal cours schal fyne,	*end*
2290	Whan Antropos the threde atwo schal twyne.	*in two; part*
	What had we wonne thanne and sche wer go	*if she*
	But enmyté, thought, and sorow and wo,	*care*
	Slaughter of oure men, deth and confusioun!	
	Wherfore I rede, by dissymulacioun,	*feigning*
2295	Withoute more that we oure wo endure	
	And nat to putte ouresilf in aventure —	*at risk*
	This hold I best — and wirkyn as the wyse.	
	But douteles for no cowarddyse	
	I seie nat this in youre highe presence.	
2300	But for cause I hold it no prudence	
	To Fortune, ful of doubilnes	*duplicity*
	(Sith we be sure) to putte oure sikernes:	*Seeing that; security*
	This al and som, th'effect of al my wille."	
	And with that worde Hector held hym stille.	
2305	And whan Hector by ful highe prudence	
	Concluded hath the fyn of his sentence,	*end*
	Ful demurly he kepte his lippis cloos.	*closed*
	And therwithal Parys up aroos	
	And gan his tale thus afore the kyng.	
2310	"My lord," quod he, "so it be lykyng	
	To youre highnes for to taken hede,	
	As me semeth, we schuld litel drede	
	In knyghtly wyse for to undirtake	
	Upon Grekis a werre for to make,	
2315	Al attonys her pride to confounde;	*destroy*
	Sith that we passyngly habounde	
	Of chivalrie here withinne our toun	
	And have plenté and pocessioun	

111

Of eche thing that may to werre aveile,
2320 Stuf in oursilf and ryal appareile
Of al that longeth to assautis marcial,   *pertains to*
And with al this, more in special,
Help and socour of many regioun
With us to werke to her destruccioun,
2325 The pompe and pride manly to abate   *put down*
And of Grekis the malis for to mate;   *overcome*
For al that thei of herte ben so stoute,
Me semeth schortly that we dar nat doute   *fear*
Nor on no part for to be dismaied.
2330 Wherfor I rede, lat nat be delaied   *advise*
Our schippes first redy for to make;
And I mysilf wil fully undirtake,
So it to you be lykyng and plesance,   *Providing it be to your*
Of this emprise hoolly the governaunce,   *undertaking*
2335 And yow assuren and putte in certeyn
Exyona to recure ageyn.   *get back again*
And in what forme that it schal be wrought
I have a weye founden in my thought
That likly is hereafter to be don,
2340 Whiche unto yow I wil declare anoon.
First, I have cast with strong and myghty hond   *determined*
For to ravysche som lady of that lond   *carry off*
Of heyghe estat, and make no tarying,   *delay*
And myghttyly into Troye hir bring,
2345 Maugre her myght, for this conclusioun: *Despite; resistence*
That ye may have restitucioun
Be eschange of hir that ye desyre so.
And hereupon schal be no long ado,
I you behete, for al the Grekis strong.   *promise*
2350 And for that I schal yow nat prolonge,
I wil yow seyn excludyng every dout   *expelling*
How this avis schal be brought aboute: *design*
First, how that I schal this purpos fyn   *accomplish*
The goddis han thorugh her power devyne
2355 Schewed unto me be revelacioun;
For theruppon I had a visioun
But late agoon, as I ley and slepe,

112

	Unto the whiche, yif ye taken kepe,	*heed*
	Ye may not faile nor be in no dispeire	*despair*
2360	To han recur of hir that is so faire,	*recovery*
	For whom ye have now so moche care.	
	And the maner hol I wil declare	*entire*
	Of this drem to your magnificence,	
	Yif it so be ye yeve wil credence	*If; give*
2365	To my tale; for I schal nat dwelle	
	Ceriously in ordre for to telle	*Point by point*
	The trouthe pleyn and no fable feyn	
	To yow that ben my lord most sovereyn.	
	First, yif that ye remembryn in your mynde,	
2370	This other day whan I was last in Ynde	
	By your avis and commaundement	
	For a mater whiche in your entent	
	Was specialy had in cherité,	*Was dear to you*
	As it is kouthe atwixe you and me,	*known between*
2375	Of whiche I toke upon me the charge	
	In the boundis of that lond ful large,	
	The same tyme your desyre to spede —	*advance*
	Whan that Tytan with his bemys rede	*beams*
	From Gemmyny drof his chare of gold	*drove; chariot*
2380	Toward the Crabbe for to take his holde,	
	Whiche named is the paleys of Dyane,	
	The bente mone that wexe can and wane;	*curved moon*
	Whanne halwed is the sonnys stacioun	*observed; sun's*
	Nighe the myddes of the moneth of Jun —	*Near*
2385	At whiche sesoun erly on a morwe,	
	Whan that Phebus to voide nyghtes sorwe	*to do away with*
	Doth Pirrous hys wayn ageyn up drawe	*chariot*
	And Aurora estward doth adawe,	*awake*
	And with the water of hir teris rounde	
2390	The silver dewe causeth to abounde	
	Upon herbis and on floures soote	
	For kyndely norissyng bothe of crop and rote;	
	Then out I roos of my bedde anoon	
	Ful desyrous on huntyng for to goon,	
2395	Priked in hert with lusty fresche plesance	*Stirred*
	To do to Love some due observaunce	

113

	And Lucyna that day to magnifie,	*the moon*
	Which callid is lady of venarye;	*of the chase*
	And duely oure rytis to observe,	
2400	Cithera and hire for to serve,	*Cytherea (Venus)*
	I and my feris, oure hertis to releve,	*companions*
	Cast us fully til it drowe to eve,	*Determined; darkness fell*
	In the forest to pley us and disport	
	And plesauntly us to recomfort,	
2405	As it longeth to love of lustines.	*pertains*
	For thilke day to Venus the goddes	
	Isacrid was by ful gret excellence,	*Dedicated*
	With gret honour and due reverence	
	Doon unto hir, bothe of on and alle;	*one*
2410	And on a Fryday this aventure is falle,	
	Whan we gan hast us to the wodis grene	
	In hope that day som game for to sene,	
	With gret labour rydyng to and fro,	
	Til we hadde ful many buk and do	*buck and doe*
2415	By strengthe slaw, as we myght hem fynde,	*slain*
	The hert ichasid with houndis and the hynde	*hart hunted; hind*
	Thorugh the downys and the dalys lowe,	*dales*
	Til brighte Phebus of his daies bowe	*sun's semicircular course*
	Amyd the arke was of meridyen,	
2420	Whan his bemys ful hote wern and schene,	*bright*
	And we most besy wern upon the chas,	
	Than me byfil a wonder divers cas.	*strange event*
	For of fortune it happed sodeynly,	
	Whil I was severyd fro my company	*parted*
2425	Sool be mysilf among the holtis hore	*Alone; grey (aged) woods*
	To fynde game desyrous evermore,	
	Or I was war, thorugh thikke and thinne,	
	A ful gret hert I sawe afore me renne	*run*
	Doun by the launde and the walys grene	*glade*
2430	That I in soth myghte nat sustene,	
	He was so swyft, for to nighe hym ner;	
	Albe that I priked my courser	*Although; spurred*
	Nighe to the deth thorugh many sondri schaw,	*thickets*
	Out of my sight so fer he gan withdrawe,	
2435	For al that ever that I sewen myght,	*follow*

	That I anoon lost of hym the sighte	
	In a wode that Ida bare the name.	
	And I so feynt gan wexen of that game,	*weary became*
	And myn hors on whiche I dide ryde,	
2440	Fomyng ful whit upon every syde	
	And his flankis al with blood disteyned —	*discolored*
	In my pursute so sore he was constreyned	*driven*
	With my sporis, scharp and dyed rede —	
	After the hert so priked I my stede	
2445	Now up, now doun, with a ful besy thought;	
	But my labour availed me right nought,	
	Til at the last among the bowes glade	
	Of aventure he caught a plesaunt slade,	*By chance; reached; dell*
	Ful smothe and pleyn and lusty for to sene	
2450	And soft as welwet was the yonge grene —	*velvet*
	Wher fro myn hors I alight as faste	
	And on a bowe I his reyne cast,	
	So feynt and maat of werynes I was	*exhausted; weariness*
	That I me laide doun upon the gras,	
2455	Upon a brink, schortly for to telle,	*bank*
	Besyde a river and a cristal welle.	
	And the water, as I reherse can,	
	Like quiksilver in his stremys ran,	
	Of whiche the gravel and the brighte stoon	
2460	As any gold ageyn the sonne schon.	
	Wher right anon for verray werynes	*true weariness*
	A sodeyn slep gan me so oppresse	
	That fro tyme that I first was born	
	I never was aslepe so toforn;	
2465	And as I ley I hadde a wonder swevene.	*dream*
	For methought highe doun fro hevene	
	The wynged god wonderful of cher,	
	Mercuryus, to me dide appere,	*Mercury*
	Of whom I was first somdel aferde;	*somewhat*
2470	For he was girt with his crokyd swerde,	*equipped*
	And with hym brought also in his honde	
	His slepy yerde, plyaunt as a wonde,	*stick; wand*
	With a serpent goyng enviroun.	*around*
	And at his fete also lowe adoun	

2475	Me sempte also that ther stood a cok,	*It appeared to me*
	Singyng his houris trewe as any clok.	
	And to the mouthe of this god Mercurie	
	Wer pipes sette that songe wonder merye,	
	Of whiche the soote sugred armonye	*sweet*
2480	Made in myn eris swiche a melodye	*ears*
	That me sempte tho in myn avis	*opinion*
	I was ravasched into paradys.	*carried off*
	And thus this god, divers of liknes,	*strange in appearance*
	More wonderful than I can expresse,	
2485	Schewed hymsilf in his apparence	
	Liche as he is discrived in Fulgence,	*Fulgentius*
	In the book of his *Methologies*,	*Mythologies (see note)*
	Wher be rehersed many poysyes	*poetic narratives*
	And many liknes, liche as ye may se.	*symbolic meanings*
2490	And for to take the moralité,	
	His longe yerde, right as is a lyne,	*long stick, true*
	Whiche on no syde wrongly may decline,	
	Signefieth the prudent governaunce	
	Of discret folke that thorugh her purviaunce	
2495	Cast a perel or that it befalle;	*Foresee peril before*
	And his pipes, loude as any schalle,	*schawm (instrument like oboe)*
	That thorugh musik ben entuned trewe	
	Betokeneth eke, with many lusty hewe,	*Signifies also*
	The sugred dites by gret excellence	*sweet verses*
2500	Of rethorik and of eloquence,	*rhetoric*
	Of whiche this god is sovereyn and patroun;	
	And of this cok the soote lusty soun	*sweet lively sound*
	That justly kepeth the houris of the night	
	Is outerly th'avise inward sight	*absolutely the guide for insight*
2505	Of swiche as voide by waker dilligence	*such; vigilant*
	Oute of her court slouthe and necligence;	
	And his swerd, whiche croketh so ageyn,	*curves*
	That is nat forget nor ymade in veyn,	
	Is to revoke to the righte weye	*bring back*
2510	Swiche as wrongly fro trouthe do forveye;	*go astray*
	And the serpent, whiche that I of tolde,	
	Whiche wrinkled is, as ye may beholde,	*coiled*
	Upon the yerde and aboute goth,	

116

	Signefieth that falshede wood and wroth	*mad; angry*
2515	Lith in aweyt by many sleighty weye,	
	With his gynnes trouthe to werreye.	*deceits; attack*
	And this god, of elloquence kyng,	
	Brought with hym eke in his commyng	
	Cithera, whom loveres serve,	
2520	Juno, and Pallas, that callid is Minerve.	
	And this Venus, her legis to delite,	*followers*
	Aboute hir hed hadde dowes white,	*doves*
	With loke benigne and eyen deboneyre,	*eyes mild*
	Ay flikeryng with snowy wyngys fayre,	
2525	For to declare schortly in sentence	
	By the dowes verray innocence	
	Of hem in love that but trouthe mene,	*only*
	And that her grounde schulde honest be and clene,	
	Itokenyd is, clerly be witnes,	
2530	Without soillyng or any unclennes;	*staining*
	And the fairnes of the roses rede,	
	That in somer so lustyly do sprede	
	And in wynter of her colour fade,	
	Signyfieth the hertly thoughtis glade	
2535	Of yonge folkis that ben amerous,	
	Fervent in hope, and inly desyrous,	*inwardly*
	Whan love gynneth in her hertis flour	
	Til longe proces maketh hem to lour	*look dull and feeble*
	With the wynter of unweldy age,	*feeble*
2540	That lust is pallid and dullid with the rage	*weakened; onslaught*
	Of febilnes whan somer is agoon,	
	As folkys knowe, I trowe mo than on;	
	And therfor Venus fleteth in a se	*floats*
	To schewe the trowble and adversité	
2545	That is in love and his stormy lawe,	
	Whiche is beset with many sturdy wawe,	*wave*
	Now calm, now rowe, whoso taketh hede,	*rough*
	And hope assailled ay with sodeyn drede.	
	And next Venus, Pallas I behelde,	
2550	With hir spere and hir cristal schelde	*shield*
	And a raynbowe rounde aboute hir hed,	
	That of colour was grene, blew, and red;	

And aforn hir, as I can discryve,
Sche growyng had a grene fresche olyve;   *olive tree*
2555 And theruppon with his browes fowle
In the brawnchis I sawe sitte an owle.
And first the scheld of Pallas the goddes
Signified, as I can expresse,
In vertu force, by manly highe diffence   *virtue strong*
2560 Ageyns vices to maken resistence;   *Against*
And hir spere, scharp and kene grounde,
By just rygour was forged to confounde   *destroy*
Hem that be false and to putte abake;
And for that mercy schal medle with the wrak,   *mingle; vengeance*
2565 The schaft in soth schave was ful pleyn,   *scraped smooth*
List merciles that right ne wrought in veyn;   *Lest*
And after werre to make a ful reles
Ther was the olyve that betokneth pes;
The owle also, so odyous at al,
2570 That songis singeth at festis funeral
Declareth pleynly the fyn of every glorie
Is only deth, who hath it in memorie;
And the raynbow grene, red, and pers   *blue*
Signifieth the changis ful divers
2575 That ofte falle in werre and bataille,
Now to wynne and sodeynly to faille,
Now stable as blew, chaunging now as grene;
For Pallas pley is alwey meynt with tene.   *mixed; woe*
And alderlast, as I have in mynde,   *last of all*
2580 With hir nymphes Juno cam behynde,
Whiche of custom, as Fulgense tellis,
Abide in flodis and in depe wellis.
And this Juno, as poetis seyn,
A mayden is and of frute bareyn;   *offspring*
2585 And the pecok to this fresche quene
Isacrid is with his fetheris schene,
Splayed abrod as a large sail   *Spread out*
With Argus eyen enprented in his tail.   *stamped*
The water rennyng in river and in flood
2590 Is the labour that men have for good,
The grete trouble and the besynes

That day and nyght thei suffre for ryches;
That who that ever in this flodis rowe,
Lat hym be war, for ay after the flowe
2595 Of nature, right as it is dewe,
Folwyng the mone ther mote an ebbe sewe;   *moon; must an ebb tide follow*
The moste drede is ay uppon the fulle,
List Fortune the fresche fetheris pulle   *Lest*
Of riche folke that schyne in gold so schene,
2600 Sith sche of chaunge lady is and quene.
And Argus eyen that ar sette behynde
In nygard hertis be oft sythes blynde,   *miserly*
Whiche nat adverte of goodis to the ende,   *do not foresee the end*
That liche an ebbe sodeynly wil wende,
2605 Whyche thei no thing consydren in her sight;   *in no way*
For as the faire lusty fetheris bright
Of a pecok unwarly falle awey,
Right so riches schortly at a day
Wiln her maister sodeynly forsake,   *Will*
2610 Seyn adieu, and her leve take.
And as Juno bareyn is of frute,
Right so nakid, bare, and destitute
Ar thes gredy hertis covetous,
Whiche to gadre ben so desyrous
2615 That in nothing can have sufficiaunce;
The fret of drede hem putte in swiche meschaunce,   *gnawing*
Ymagenyng that the world wil faille;
And in her fere ageyn the wynd thei saille   *fear*
Til attonys thei mote go ther fro.
2620 And thus of good ay the fyn is wo,   *end*
Namly of hem that so pynche and spare: *are miserly and niggardly*
For this no drede, as clerkis can declare,
The frute of good is to spende large;
And who is manful, set but litel charge   *he has no scruples*
2625 To parte frely his tresour in comoune,
Whan he discretly seth tyme oportune.
He hath no joye to put his good in mwe;   *hiding*
For an hert that fredam list to sewe   *generosity*
Of gentilnes taketh noon hed therto.
2630 And in this wyse, Pallas and Juno

With fresche Venus ben adoun descended,

Liche as I have schortly comprehended,   *described*

Under the guying of Mercurius,   *guidance*

Whiche unto me gan his tale thus.

2635 "Parys," quod he, "lifte up thin eye and se!

Loo, this goddesses here in noumbre thre,

Whiche fro hevene with her eyen clere

So diversly unto the appere,   *wonderfully*

Wern at a fest, as I the tellyn schal,

2640 With alle the goddis above celestial

That Jubiter held at his owne borde.   *table*

Was non absent only save Discord;

And for dispit sche was not ther present,

To be avenged sche sette al hir entent

2645 And in hir wittes many weyes sought,

Til at the last evene thus sche wrought,

Of poetis liche as it is tolde:

Sche toke an appil rounde of purid gold   *apple*

With Greke lettris graven up and doun

2650 Whiche seide thus, in conclusioun,

Withoute strife that it were yove anon   *given*

To the fairest of hem everychon.

And of Discord this lady and goddes,

As sche that is of debat maistres,   *mistress*

2655 Hath this appil, passyng of delit,

Brought to this fest, of malis and despit,   *out of*

And cast it doun among hem at the bord

With deyvious chere, spekyng not a word;   *devious*

But on hir weye faste gan hir hiye.   *hasten*

2660 And sodeynly so privé gret envie

Into the court this appil hath in brought,

So gret a werre and swiche a contek wrought   *dissension*

In the hertis of this ilke thre

That after long may not staunched be;   *extinguished*

2665 Among hemsilf so thei gan disdeyn

Whiche in bewté was most sovereyn

And whiche of hem hath best title of right

For to conquere this bornyd appil bright.   *burnished*

And first thei gan thus for bewté strive,

120

2670	That for rancour her hertis almost ryve	*split*
	To wit of right who schuld it first possede —	*possess*
	Loo, yit envye regneth in womanhede,	
	That on is fayrer than another holde;	
	For eche woman of hir kynde wolde	
2675	Have on som part pris above another;	*preeminence*
	In eche estat, in soth it is noon other.	
	And eche of hem in her owne avis	*opinion*
	Hath joye in bewté for to han a pris;	*place of honor*
	For non so foule doth in a myrour prye	*peer*
2680	That sche is feir in hir owne eye.	
	But liche a fool he hymsilf doth quite	*behave*
	That awmber yelwe cheseth for the white.	*prefers to*
	A gowndy eye is deceyved sone,	*bleared*
	That any colour cheseth by the mone;	*moon*
2685	For som colour is with fir made fyn,	
	And som encresid with spicis and with wyn,	
	With onymentis and confeccions;	
	And on nyght by false illusiouns	
	Somme appere wonder fresche and faire,	
2690	That loke dirke a daylight in the eyre.	*air*
	Ther is no pref but erly by the morwe	*proof*
	Of swiche as nede no bewté for to borwe	
	But as Nature hath hirsilf disposed.	
	Therfore fastyng, or boystis ben unclosyd,	*boxes [of cosmetics] are opened*
2695	Make thi choyse, liche as bit Ovide,	*bids*
	Whan every drogge and pot is set asyde,	*drug*
	List that thou be, after his sentence,	*Lest*
	Deceyvid lightly by fals apparence;	
	For nowadayes swiche craft is ful rife.	
2700	And in this wyse thus began the stryf	
	Betwixe Juno, Venus, and Pallas	
	That be descendid for this sodeyn caas,	*unexpected happening*
	By on assent, towching her bewté,	*one*
	The dom therof comitted unto the.	
2705	I speke to the, that callid art Parys,	*you; Paris*
	And holdyn art right prudent and right wys;	
	Be avysed how thi dom schal fyne;	*judgment shall end*
	For thei ne may to nor fro declyne	

	But obeie, alle, by oon assent	
2710	Withoute strif to thi jugement.	
	But herke, frist, or that thou procede,	*first, before*
	Of eche of hem what schal be thi mede;	*reward (bribe)*
	Considere aright, and take good hede therto:	
	Yif thou the appil graunte unto Juno,	
2715	Sche schal the yef plenté of riches,	*give you*
	Highe renoun, of fame eke worthines,	
	With habundaunce of gold and of tresour,	
	And do the reise to so highe honour	
	That thou allone alle other schalt excelle	
2720	For thi guerdoun, liche as I the telle.	*reward*
	And yif to Pallas, goddesse of prudence,	
	The liste the fyn conclude of thi sentence	*You wish*
	That sche may lady of the appil be,	
	For thi mede sche schal assure the	*reward; you*
2725	That of witte and of sapience	
	Thou schalt hooly han the excellence,	
	And of wisdam and discrecioun,	
	To discerne by clernes of resoun;	*clarity*
	Also fer as Phebus cast his light,	
2730	Ther schal nat be a more prudent knyght,	
	Nor in this world, sith that it began,	
	Of just report a manlier man,	*By right account*
	Nor to thi name noon equipolente.	*equal in value*
	And yif to Venus of trew and clene entent	
2735	The list to graunt in conclusioun	
	Of the appil to have pocessioun,	
	The fresche goddes that sit so highe above	
	Schal the ensure to have unto thi love	*insure that you have*
	The fairest lady that is or was tofore	
2740	Or in this world ever schal be bore;	
	And in Grece thou schalt hir knyghtly wynne.	
	Now be avised or that thou begynne	*before*
	Justly to deme and for nothing spare."	*judge*
	And I anoon gan loken up and stare,	
2745	Gretly astoned what me was best to do,	*bewildered*
	Til at the last I spake Mercurye to,	
	And seide, certeyn, that I ne wolde there	

	Yeven no dom but thei naked were,	*Give no judgment unless*
	So that I myght have fully liberté	
2750	Everyche of hem avisely to se	*carefully*
	And consyderen every circumstaunce	
	Who fairest wer unto my plesaunce	*was*
	And goodliest, to speke of womonhede,	
	And after that to my doom procede.	*judgment*
2755	And thei anoon, as ye have herde me seie,	
	To my desyre mekely gan obeie	
	In al hast to don her besy cure	*exert themselves*
	Hem to dispoille of clothing and vesture,	*Themselves to strip; garments*
	Liche as the statut of my dom hem bonde:	*obligated*
2760	In a poynt, thei nolde it not withstonde	*refuse*
	That I myght have ful inspeccioun	
	Of forme and schap and eche proporcioun,	
	For to discerne, as I can remembre,	
	Avisely by ordre every membre	
2765	And thanne at erst to jugen after right.	*at first*
	But whanne that I of eche had a sight,	
	I yaf to Venus the appil right anoon,	*gave; immediately*
	Because sche was fairest of echon	
	And most excellyng, sothly, in bewté,	
2770	Most womanly and goodly on to se,	*to look upon*
	As I dempte pleynly in my sight.	*judged*
	For the stremys of hir eyen bright	*(see note)*
	Iliche glade and egal evene of light	*Equally*
	Wern to that sterre that schewith toward nyght,	
2775	Whiche callid is Esperus so schene,	*Hesperus; bright*
	Venus hirsilf, the fresche lusty quene.	
	The whiche anon, this hevenly emperesse,	
	After my doom, of hertly highe gladnesse,	
	That of the appil sche hooly hath the glorie	
2780	And wonyn hit justly by victorie	*gained*
	Rejoysched hir more than I can telle,	
	That sche hir feris in bewté dide excelle.	*companions*
	And sche in hast, of trewe affeccioun,	
	Concluded hath fully for my guerdoun,	*reward*
2785	Ful demurly, lowe and nat alofte,	
	To Mercurye with sobre wordis softe,	

	Devoide bothe of doubilnes and slouthe,	*duplicity*
	Liche hir behest holde wil hir trouth.	*promise*
	And sodeynly without more injurye	*wrongs*
2790	Thei disapered, and the god Mercurie	
	Streght to hevene the righte weye toke;	
	And I anon out of my slepe awoke.	
	Wherof, my lord, whom I most love and drede,	
	Yif ye adverte and wysly taken hede	*consider*
2795	That this behest, affermyd in certeyn,	*promise confirmed*
	Was unto me assured nat in veyn	
	Of goodly Venus, liche as I have tolde,	
	Wherfore, I rede ye ben of herte bolde	*advise*
	Me for to sende with strong and myghty hond	
2800	Withoute abood into Grekis lond	*delay*
	After the forme that I have yow seyde.	
	And, I hope, ye schal be wel apayde,	*satisfied*
	Whan I have sped, as Venus hath behight,	*promised*
	And hom retourned with my lady bright:	
2805	So schal ye best, me list nat speke in veyn,	*I do not wish to speak*
	Beschaunge of hir your suster wynne ageyn,	*By exchanging*
	Whom Thelamoun withholden hath so yore.	*for so long*
	Lo, this is al; I can seye you no more	
	Towching th'effect hooly of myn avis."	*wholly*

[*After Paris recounts his dream, Deiphebus speaks in favor of sending him to capture a prisoner to exchange for Hesione, but Helenus, who has the power of prophecy, warns that Troy will be destroyed if Paris is sent. Troilus then speaks in favor of the expedition, urging the Trojans not to rest idly nor to presume to know God's hidden intents. The parliament recesses, and when it resumes the next day the mission is confirmed, despite further warnings by Pentheus and Cassandra. In May, Paris sets out with 3,000 knights and 22 ships. Along the way he happens across Menelaus who is sailing to visit Nestor, but the two proudly sail past each other, neither deigning to greet the other. Paris arrives at the harbor of Cythera, an island sacred to Venus (lines 2810–3434).*]

3435	Now in this ile of passyng excellence
	Ther was a temple of gret reverence
	That bilded was of olde fundacioun
	And most honoured in that regioun
	Thorughoute the lond bothe fer and ner —

3440	The feste day ay from yer to yer,	
	Liche as it fil by revolucioun,	*by yearly repetition*
	Repeyryng theder of gret devocioun,	*Returning*
	In honour only of Venus the goddes,	
	Whom the Grekis with al her besynes	*their*
3445	Honoured most of every maner age	
	With giftes bringyng and with pilgrimage,	
	With gret offeryng and with sacrifyse,	
	As usid was in her paynym wyse.	*observed; pagan custom*
	For in this phane, as thei knele and wake	*temple; keep vigil*
3450	With contrit hert and her prayer make,	
	The statue yaf of every questyoun	
	Pleyn answer and ful solucioun,	
	With cerymonyes to Venus as thei loute;	*bow*
	Of everything that thei hadde doute	
3455	Thei hadde ful declaracioun.	
	And thus the Grekis upon Cytheroun	*on the island of Cythera*
	Halwyn this fest with riche and gret array,	*Observe*
	With rytis due, as ferforthe as thei may,	*to the extent that*
	In hope fully the better for to thrive.	
3460	And of fortune, whan he dide aryve	
	Upon the lond by aventure or cas,	*chance*
	The same tyme this feste halwed was	
	Of many Greke commyng to and fro	
	From every cost that to the temple go	*country*
3465	On pilgrimage her vowes to acquyte,	*fulfill*
	Of the place the reliques to vesyte.	*visit*
	And whan Paris dide this espie,	
	He gadred out of his companye	
	The worthiest that he chesen may;	
3470	And to the temple he taketh the right waye	
	Ful wel beseyn and in knyghtly wyse,	
	And dide his honour and his sacrifyse	
	Ful humblely to the Grekis liche;	
	With many nowche and many jouwel riche,	*clasp*
3475	With gold and silver, stonys and perré	*precious stones*
	He spendeth ther, liche to his degré,	
	And quit hym manly in his oblaciouns;	
	And devoutly in his orisouns	*prayers*

He hym demeneth, that joye was to se.   *behaves himself*

3480   Now was Parys of passyng gret bewté

Amonges alle that ever werne alyve:

For ther was non that myght with hym strive,   *contend*

Troyan nor Greke, to speke of semlyhede,

Wonder fresche and lusty, as I rede,

3485   And in his port ful lik a gentil knyght.   *bearing*

Of whos persone for to han a sight

Thei gan to prese bothe nyghe and fere,

So ryally he had hym in his gere,   *royally*

And coveyte of highe estat and lowe   *[they] desire*

3490   What he was gretly for to knowe;

And of his men thei aske besely

Fro when he cam and the cause why

Of his comyng, enqueryng on by on.

But prudently thei kepte hem everychon,

3495   That nothing was openly espyed

In her answere; so thei han hem guyed   *conducted themselves*

That everything kepid was secré;

Everyche of hem was so avisee;   *cautious*

Albe that somme oppenly declare

3500   What that he was and ne list not spare

But tolde pleynly the cause of his commyng

And how Priam, the stronge myghty kyng,

His fader was, most royal of renoun,

And how he cam also for Exyoun.   *Hesione*

3505   Thus eche of hem gan with other rowne   *whisper*

At pryme face whan he cam to towne,

And therupon wer ymagynatyf,   *filled with speculation*

Sore musyng and inquisytif,

Eche with other be suspecioun

3510   Demyng therof liche her oppinioun,

And rathest thei that nothing ne knewe,   *most readily*

As folkis don of thinges that be newe.   *novel*

And whiles thei of this mater trete

In sondry wyse amonge her wordes grete,

3515   The fame of hem gan anoon atteyne

To the eris of the Quene Eleyne,

Nighe besyde in that regioun.

126

	And whan sche herd be relacioun	
	And by report of hem that cam bytwene,	
3520	This faire Eleyne, this fresche, lusty quene,	
	Anon as sche the sothe undirstood	*Soon; truth*
	Withoute tarying or any more abood	*delay*
	Sche hasteth hir to this solempnité,	
	The fresche folke of Frigye for to se —	*Phrygia*
3525	Wel mor, God wot, in hir entencioun	
	To se Parys than for devocioun.	
	Under colour of holy pylgrymage	*pretext*
	To the temple sche taketh hir viage	*makes her way*
	With gret meyné and ryal apparaille,	*entourage*
3530	Parys to sen for sche wil nat faille.	
	But, O allas, what lusty newe fyre	
	Hath hir hert enflawmyd be desyre	
	To go to vigiles outher to spectaclis!	
	Noon holynes to heryn of myraclis	
3535	Hath mevid hir, that ther schal befalle;	*moved*
	But as the maner is of women alle	
	To drawe thedir, platly to conclude,	*thither, plainly to say*
	Where as thei be sure that multitude	
	Gadrid is at liberté to se,	
3540	Wher thei may finde opportunyté	
	To her desyre, ful narwe thei awaite,	
	Now covertly her eyne for to baite	*feast [the eyes]*
	In place wher as set is her plesaunce,	
	Now prively to have her daliaunce	
3545	Be som sygne or castyng of an eye	
	Or toknes schewyng in herte what thei drye,	*drew*
	With touche of hondis stole among the pres,	*crowd*
	With arm or foot to cache up in her les	*their snare*
	Whom that hem list, albe he fre or bonde,	*Whomever places them*
3550	Of nature thei can hym holde on honde —	
	Ageyn whos sleight availeth wit nor myght:	
	For what hem list, be it wrong or right,	
	Thei ay acheve, who seyth ye or nay,	
	Ageyn whos lust diffende him no man may.	
3555	Thus Guydo ay of cursid fals delit	
	To speke hem harme hath kaught an appetit	

Thorughoute his boke of wommen to seyn ille,
That to translate it is ageyn my wille.
He hath ay joye her honour to transverse;   *speak against*
3560   I am sory that I mote reherse   *must*
The felle wordis in his boke yfounde.   *cruel*
To alle women I am so moche bounde:
Thei ben echon so goodly and so kynde,
I dar of hem nat seyen that I fynde
3565   Of Guydo write thorughout *Troye Book*;
For whan I radde it, for fer myn herte quoke;   *fear*
And verrailly my wittis gonne faille,
Whan I therof made rehersaille.
Liche his decert lat Guydo now be quit;   *As he deserves; requited*
3570   For ye schal here anon how that he chit   *chided*
The Quene Eleyne, for cause that sche went
With devoute hert hir offring to present
To the temple of Venus the goddes;
Thus, word by word, he seith to hir expres:
3575   "O mortal harme that most is for to drede!
A, fraude ycast be sleight of wommanhede!
Of every wo gynnyng, crop, and rote,   *beginning, root, and branch*
Ageynes whiche helpe may no bote.   *be remedy*
Whan lust hath dryve in her hert a nail,
3580   Ay dedly venym sueth at the tail,   *follows*
Whiche no man hath power to restreyne;
Recorde I take of the Quene Eleyne
That hoote brent, allas, in hir desires   *burned hotly*
Of newe lust to dele with straungeris   *associate with*
3585   Whom sche knewe nat ne never saw aforn,
Wherthorugh, allas, ful many man was lorn,   *lost*
Of cruel deth embracid in the cheyne
Withoute pité. Now, sey, thou Quene Eleyne,
What gost or spirit, allas, hath mevid the
3590   Sool fro thi lord in swiche ryalté   *Alone*
Oute of thin house to gon among the pres?   *crowd*
Whi were thou wery to live at home in pes   *peace*
And wentist out straungeris for to se,
Takyng noon hed unto thin honesté?
3595   Thou schust a kepte thi closet secrely   *have stayed in; room*

And not have passed out so folily
In the abscence of thi lorde, allas!
Thou wer to wilful and rakil in this cas | *too; hasty*
To sen aforn what schuld after swe; | *foresee; follow*
3600 For al to sone thou wer drawe out of mwe, | *hiding*
That koudist nat kepe at home thi boundis.
Thou wentist out as hare among houndis
For to be caught of verray wilfulnes,
And thi desyre koudist not compesse; | *restrain*
3605 For thou thi lust list nat to refreyne. | *control*
O many woman hath kaught in a treyne | *trap*
Her goyng oute swiche halwes for to seke; | *saints to seek*
It sit hem bet hemsilven for to kepe
Clos in her chaumbre and fleen occasioun: | *temptation*
3610 For never schip schulde in pereil drown,
Nor skatre on rok, nor be with tempest rent, | *shatter*
Nor with Karibdis devourid nor yschent, | *Charybdis; destroyed*
Nor gon to wrak with no wedris ille, | *weathers*
Yif it wer kepte in the havene stille. | *If; harbor*
3615 For who wil not occasiouns eschewe
Nor dredith not pereil for to swe, | *pursue*
He most among of necessité,
Or he be war, endure adversité; | *Before*
And who can nat hir fot fro trappis spare, | *foot; avoid*
3620 Lat hir be war or sche falle in the snare: | *Let; before*
For harme ydon to late is to compleine.
For yif whilom the worthi Quene Eleyne
Hirsilven had kepte at home in clos,
Of hir ther nadde ben so wikke a loos | *would not have been; reputation*
3625 Reported yit, grene, fresche, and newe;
Whos chaunce unhappi eche man oughte rewe,
That cause was of swiche destruccioun
Of many worthi and confusioun
Of hir husbonde and many other mo
3630 On Grekis syde and on Troye also,
In this story as ye schal after rede."
And so this quene, as fast as sche may spede,
To the temple hath the weye nome | *taken*
Ful rially; and whan that sche was come

129

3635	Ful devoutly withinne Cytheroun,	
	Made unto Venus hir oblacioun	*offering*
	In presence and sight of many on,	
	With many jowel and many riche stoon.	
	And whan Parys hadde this espied,	
3640	To the temple anon he hath hym hyed	*hastened*
	Ful thriftely in al the hast he myght;	*worthily*
	And whan that he hadde first a sight	
	Of the goodly, faire, fresche quene,	
	Cupidis dart, that is whet so kene,	*sharpened*
3645	Or he was war, hathe hym markid so	*Before; aware*
	That for astonyed he nist what to do,	
	So he merveileth hir gret semlynes,	
	Hir womanhed, hir port, and hir fairnes:	
	For never aforne wende he that Nature	*thought*
3650	Koude have made so faire a creature;	
	So aungillyk sche was of hir bewté,	
	So femynyn, so goodly on to se	
	That he dempte, as by liklynes,	*judged*
	For hir bewté to be som goddes.	
3655	For his hert dide hym ay assure	
	That sche was no mortal creature;	
	So hevenly faire and so celestial	
	He thought sche was in party and in al	
	And considereth ful avisely	
3660	Hir feturis in ordre by and by	
	Ententifly withinne in his resoun,	
	Everything by good inspeccioun:	
	Hir golden her lik the schene stremys	*hair; bright*
	Of fresche Phebus with his brighte bemys,	
3665	The goodlyhed of hir fresche face,	
	So replevished of bewté and of grace,	*full*
	Evene ennwed with quiknes of colour	*Evenly shaded; living reality*
	Of the rose and the lyllie flour,	
	So egaly that nouther was to wyte	
3670	Thorugh noon excesse of moche nor to lite.	
	Withinne the cerclyng of hir eyen bryght	
	Was paradys compassid in hir sight,	*contained*
	That thorugh a brest the bewté wolde perce.	

	And certeynly, yif I schal reherse	*if*
3675	Hir schap, hir forme, and feturis by and by,	
	As Guydo doth by ordre ceryously,	*one by one*
	From hed to foot, clerly to devise,	
	I han non Englysche that therto may suffyse;	
	It wil nat be — oure tonge is not lyke.	*appropriate*
3680	I want flouris also of rethorik	
	To sue his florischyng or his gey peynture,	
	For to discrive so fayre a creature;	
	For my colours ben to feble and feynt,	
	That nouther can ennwe wel nor peint;	*shade*
3685	Eke I am nat aqueintid with no mwse	
	Of alle nyne: therfore I me excuse	
	To you echon, nat al of necligence	
	But for defaut only of eloquence,	
	And you remitte to Guydo for to se	*refer*
3690	How he discriveth bi ordre hir bewté;	
	To take on me it were presumpcioun.	
	But I wil telle how Parys up and doun	
	Goth in the temple, and his eye cast	
	Toward Eleyne, and gan presen fast,	*push fast*
3695	As he that brent hote in Lovys fyre,	
	That was enflawmed gretly be desyre.	
	And oft he chaungeth countenaunce and chere,	
	And ever he neieth to hir ner and nere,	*draws close*
	Idarted thorugh with hir eyen tweyne.	
3700	And ageynward the fresche Quene Eleyne	*in return*
	As hote brent in herte pryvely,	
	Albe no man it outward koude espie;	*Although; discern*
	For sche thought sche had never aforn	
	Of alle men that ever yet wer born	
3705	Sey non so fair nor like to hir plesance;	
	On hym to loke was hir sufficiaunce.	
	For in the temple sche toke hede of right nought	
	But to compasse and castyn in hir thought	
	How sche may cachen opportunyté	
3710	With hym to speke at good liberté:	
	This holly was al hir besynes.	*effort*
	For hym sche felt so inly gret distres	

131

That ofte sche chaungeth countenaunce and hewe.   *color*
And Venus hath marked hem of newe
3715 With hir brondes fired by fervence   *ardor*
And inflawmed be sodeyn influence,
That egaly thei wer brought in a rage.   *equally*
And save the eyen atwen was no message:
Eche on other so fixe hath cast his sight   *steadily*
3720 That thei conseive and wisten anon right   *knew*
Withinne hemsilfe wat her herte ment.
And nere to hir ever Parys went
To seke fully and gete occasioun
That thei myght by ful relacioun
3725 Her hertis conceit declare secrely.   *thought*
And so bifel that Paris neigheth nyghe   *moves nearer*
To the place wher the Quene Eleyne
Stood in her se, and ther atwen hem tweyne   *seat*
Thei broken out the somme of al her hert   *revealed; their*
3730 And yaf issu to her inward smerte.   *suffering*
But this was don, list thei werne espied,   *lest; discovered*
Whan the peple was most occupied
In the temple for to stare and gase,   *gaze*
Now her, now ther, as it wer a mase.   *maze*
3735 Thei kepte hem clos, that no worde asterte;   *might escape*
Ther was no man the tresoun myght adverte   *perceive*
Of hem tweyn ne what thei wolde mene;
But at the last, Paris and this quene
Concluded han with schort avisement
3740 Fully the fyn of her bothe entent   *object of their mutual*
And sette a purpos atwix hem in certeyn
Whan thei cast for to mete ageyn.   *plan*
But list men had to hem suspecioun,
Thei made an ende withoute more sermoun
3745 And depart, albe that thei wer lothe.
And sobirly anoon this Paris goth
Out of the temple, his hert in every part
Wounded thorughout with Lovys fyré dart;
To his schippis he halt the righte way.   *he went directly*

Book 2

[Paris gathers his men, and that night they rob the temple sanctuary of its jewels, killing all who oppose them and carrying off many Greeks as slaves. Paris goes to Helen, who accompanies him to his ship without a struggle. He then returns to plundering the island and sails back to Troy. Priam prepares a feast in honor of Paris's return. Helen meanwhile grows distraught as she realizes how isolated she is from her family and homeland. Paris comforts her and proposes to marry her. Helen accepts the fate the gods have prepared for her. Paris ceremoniously leads Helen into Troy, guiding her horse by the reins. The next day they are married in Pallas's temple. At the marriage feast, Cassandra foretells the destruction of Troy and names Helen as the cause. To end Cassandra's disruption, Priam casts her in prison. While the Trojans enjoy their good fortune, Menelaus hears word of the sack of the island, the slaughter of its defenders, and the abduction of his wife. Nestor sends for Agamemnon, Menelaus's brother, to comfort him (lines 3750–4336).]

	"O brother myn, what wo, what hevynes,	
	What dedly sorwe thus inly may oppres	
	Your knyghtly hert or trouble youre manhede,	
4340	More furiously ywis than it is nede;	*certainly*
	For though that right requered outerly	
	Yow for to sorwe and had cause why,	
	Yet, me semeth, by juste providence	
	Ye schulde lightly dissymble youre offence:	*feign; grievance*
4345	Sith eche wiseman in his adversité	*Since*
	Schulde feyne cher and kepen in secré	
	The inward wo that bynt hym in distresse,	*bound*
	Be manly force rathest ther compesse	*By; contain*
	The sperit of ire and malencolie,	
4350	Where the peple it sonest myght espie.	
	It is a doctrine of hem that be prudent	
	That, whan a man with furie is torent,	*torn apart*
	To feyne chere til tyme he se leyser	
	That of vengaunce he kyndle may the fer;	*fire*
4355	For sorwe outeschewid, yif I shal nat feine,	*outwardly visible; lie*
	Whoso take hede, it doth thinges tweyne:	
	It causeth frendis for to sighe sore,	
	And his enymyes to rejoische more.	
	Thi frende in hert is sory of nature;	
4360	Thin enemy glad of thi mysaventure.	
	Wherfore in hert, whan wo doth most abounde,	
	Feyne gladnes thin enmy to confounde	*confuse*

133

And schewe in cher as thou roughtist nought   *appearance as if you did not care*
Of thing that is most grevous in thi thought.
4365 And wher thou hast most mater to compleyne,
Make ther good face and glad in port the feine;   *bearing; dissemble*
For into teris, though thou al distille   *dissolve*
And rende thisilfe, as thou woldest the spille,   *tear apart; kill yourself*
It helpith nat to aleggen thi grevaunce: *alleviate*
4370 For nouther honour nor pursut of vengaunce
With sorwe makyng mow ben execut —   *may be carried out*
Though it last ay, ther cometh thereof no frut.
Men seyn how he that can dissymble a wrong,   *conceal*
How he is slighe and of herte stronge;
4375 And who can ben peisible in his smerte,   *peaceful; sorrow*
It is a tokene he hath a manly herte
Nat to wepen as wommen in her rage,
Whiche is contrarie to an highe corage.   *great spirit*
With word and wepyng for to venge oure peyne
4380 Be no menys to worschip to attayne;   *honor; gain*
Lat us with swerde and nat with wordis fight;
Oure tonge apese, be manhod preve oure myght:
Word is but wynde, and water that we wepe;
And though the tempest and the flodis depe
4385 Of this two encresen everemo,
Thei may nat do but augmente oure wo;
And to oure foon, therof whan thei here
Bothe of oure dool and of oure hevy chere,   *sorrow*
Al is to hem but encres of joye.
4390 Wherfore, brothir, a while dothe acoye   *calm*
The cruel torment that byndeth yow so sore;
For in proverbe it hath ben said ful yore
That the prowes of a manly knyght
Is preved most in meschef, and his myght:
4395 To ben assured in adversité,
Strongly sustene what wo that it be,
Nat cowardly his corage to submitte
In every pereil, nor his honour flitte   *waver*
Thorugh no dispeire, but hopen alwey wel   *despair*
4400 And have a trust, trewe as any stel,
T'acheven ay what he take on honde.

Book 2

	For finally I do you undirstonde	*make*
	That of hymsilfe who hath good fantasie	
	To sette upon and putte in jupartie	
4405	What that befalle (hap what happe may),	
	Takyng what chaunce wil turnen on his play,	
	The fyn of whiche gladly is victorie,	*end*
	Thei feile selde of the palme of glorie.	*seldom*
	And tyme is now, to speke in wordis fewe,	
4410	O brothir myn, manhod for to schewe,	
	To pluk up herte and you to make strong;	
	And to venge your damages and youre wronge,	
	We schal echon help and leye to honde —	
	Kynges, dukes, and lordis of this londe —	
4415	And attonys done oure besynes,	*immediately; purpose*
	I you behete, your harmys to redresse.	*promise*
	And in dispit of whom that evere us lette,	*hindered us*
	We schal us loge and oure tentis sette	*camp*
	Evene in the felde afore Troye toun	
4420	And leyne a sege to her distruccioun,	
	Albe herof I sette as now no day.	
	But, brothir, first, in al the haste we may,	
	Lete make lettris, withoute more sermoun,	
	To alle the lordis of this regioun,	
4425	Of this mater touching youre villenye,	*the wrong done to you*
	To come togidre and schape remedie —	
	This is th'effect of al that I can seyn."	

[*Menelaus follows Agamemnon's advice and dispatches letters to his kinsmen and allies. Achilles, Patroclus, Diomede, and others come to his aid. In open parliament they agree to be governed by Agamemnon. In the meantime, Helen's brothers, Castor and Pollux, take it upon themselves to avenge her abduction and set forth for Troy. A storm destroys their ship at sea and all hands drown, except the two brothers; one was sent to heaven and the other to hell, though some poets make up the story that they were made into stars. Dares the Phrygian, who passed between the camps during times of truce, wrote descriptions of all the principal characters; he says the following about Criseyde (lines 4428–4676).*]

	And overmore, to tellen of Cryseyde	*moreover*
	Mi penne stumbleth, for longe or he deyde	*before*
	My maister Chaucer dide his dilligence	

135

4680	To discryve the gret excellence	
	Of hir bewté, and that so maisterly,	
	To take on me it were but highe foly	
	In any wyse to adde more therto;	
	For wel I wot, anoon as I have do,	*know*
4685	That I in soth no thanke disserve may	*truth*
	Because that he in writyng was so gay —	
	And but I write, I mote the trouthe leve	*unless I write a book; depart*
	Of *Troye Boke,* and my mater breve,	*shorten*
	And overpasse and nat go by and by,	
4690	As Guydo doth in ordre ceryously.	*point by point*
	And thus I most don offencioun	
	Thorughe necligence or presumpcioun:	
	So am I sette evene amyddes tweyne!	*between the two*
	Gret cause have I and mater to compleyne	
4695	On Antropos and upon hir envie	
	That brak the threde and made for to dye	
	Noble Galfride, poete of Breteyne,	
	Amonge oure Englisch that made first to reyne	*rain down*
	The gold dewedropis of rethorik so fyne,	
4700	Oure rude langage only t'enlwmyne.	
	To God I pray that He his soule have,	
	After whos help of nede I moste crave	
	And seke his boke that is left behynde	
	Som goodly worde therin for to fynde	
4705	To sette amonge the crokid lynys rude	*crude, rough lines*
	Whiche I do write; as by similitude	*comparison*
	The ruby stant, so royal of renoun,	
	Withinne a ryng of copur or latoun,	*brass alloy*
	So stant the makyng of hym, douteles,	
4710	Among oure bokis of Englische pereles:	
	Thei arn ethe to knowe, thei ben so excellent;	*easy to know*
	Ther is no makyng to his equipolent;	*equal in value*
	We do but halt, whoso taketh hede,	*limp*
	That medle of makyng, withouten any drede.	
4715	Whan we wolde his stile counterfet,	
	We may al day oure colour grynde and bete,	
	Tempere oure azour and vermyloun:	*Mix [with oil]*
	But al I holde but presumpcioun —	

	It folweth nat; therfore I lette be.	*It does not follow as a consequence*
4720	And first of al I wil excuse me	
	And procede as I have begonne	
	And thorugh his favour certeyn, yif I konne,	
	Of *Troye Boke* for to make an ende;	
	And ther I lefte ageyn I wil now wende	
4725	Unto Cryseyde; and though to my socour	
	Of rethorik that I have no flour	
	Nor hewes riche, stonys nor perré —	*jewels*
	For I am bare of alle coriousté	*artfulness*
	Thorugh crafty speche to enbroude with her sleve —	*embroider*
4730	Yet for al that, now I wil not leve	
	But ben as bolde as Baiard is, the blynde,	
	That cast no peril what wey that he fynde;	*foresees no trouble*
	Right so wil I stumble forthe on hede	*rashly*
	For unkonnyng and take no better hede,	*lack of skill*
4735	So as I can, hir bewté to discrive.	
	That was in soth of alle tho on lyve	
	On the fayrest, this Calchas doughter dere;	*One of*
	Therto of schap, of face, and of chere,	
	Ther myghte be no fairer creature	
4740	To highe nor to lowe, but mene of stature —	*Too tall*
	Hir sonnysche her, liche Phebus in his spere,	*hair; sphere*
	Bounde in a tresse, brighter thanne golde were,	*wire*
	Doun at hir bak, lowe doun behynde,	
	Whiche with a threde of golde sche wolde bynde	
4745	Ful ofte sythe of acustummaunce;	
	Therto sche hadde so moche suffisaunce	
	Of Kyndes wirke withouten any were,	*Nature's; doubt*
	And save hir browes joyneden yfere,	*except that; joined together*
	No man koude in hir a lake espien.	*fault discover*
4750	And, ferthermore, to speken of hir eyen,	
	Thei wer so persyng, hevenly, and so clere,	
	That an herte ne myght hymsilfe stere	*govern*
	Ageyn hir schynyng, that thei nolde wounde	
	Thorughout a brest, God wot, and biyonde.	
4755	Also sche was, for al hir semlynes,	*beauty*
	Ful symple and meke and ful of sobirnes,	
	The best norissched eke that myghte be,	*educated*

137

Goodly of speche, fulfilde of pité,   *compassion*
Facundious, and therto right tretable,   *Eloquent; capable of discussion*
4760 And, as seith Guydo, in love variable —
Of tendre herte and unstedfastnes
He hir accuseth, and newfongilnes.   *fond of novelty*

[*Dares tells how the King of Persia, a tall, fat, red-headed man with warts on his face, came to aid the Greeks; and then he turns to the Trojans, describing Priam and Hector before coming to Troilus (lines 4763–4860).*]

But Troylus schortly yif I schal discryve,   *describe*
Ther was of hert non manlier on lyve
Nor more likly in armys to endure: *prevail*
Wel woxe of heighte and of good stature,   *grown*
4865 Yong, fresche, and lusty, hardy as a lyoun,
Delivere and strong as any champioun,   *Agile*
And perigal of manhod and of dede   *worthy*
He was to any that I can of rede
In doring do, this noble worthi knyght,   *derring-do*
4870 For to fulfille that longeth to a knyght.
The secunde Ector for his worthines
He callid was and for his highe prowes
Duryng the werre, he bare hym ay so wel;
Therto in love as trewe as any stele,
4875 Secré and wys, stedefast of corage,   *heart*
The moste goodly also of visage
That myghte be, and benigne of cher,   *gracious*
Withoute chaunge, and of on hert entere.   *sincere*
He was alwey feithful, just, and stable,
4880 Perseveraunt, and of wil inmutable
Upon what thing he onys set his herte,
That doubilnes myght hym nat perverte;   *duplicity*
In his dedis he was so hool and pleyn;
But on his foon, the sothe for to seyn,   *against his foes; truth*
4885 He was so fers thei myght him nat withstonde
Whan that he hilde his bloodly swerde on hond: *held*
Unto Grekis deth and confusioun,
To hem of Troye help and proteccioun.
And his knyghthod schortly to acounte,

138

4890	Ther myght in manhod no man him surmounte	*excel*
	Thorugh the worlde, though men wolde seke	
	To reknen al, Troyan nouther Greke,	*nor*
	Noon so namyd of famus hardynes,	
	As bokis olde of hym bere witnes;	
4895	Excepte Ector, ther was nat swiche another.	

[*Dares continues his portraits with descriptions of Paris, Aeneas, Antenor, and other warriors and with descriptions of the Trojan women — Hecuba (man-like in appearance but the true example of femininity), Andromache, Cassandra, and Polyxena. These are all he described at this point, and I shall hurry on to the story of the war. In February, the Greeks assemble their ships at Athens. My author, Guido, gives a catalogue of which heroes came and how many ships they brought with them. Agamemnon calls a council and advises that Apollo be consulted at Delos. The Greeks send Achilles and Pirithous, and an explanation of the origin and history of idolatry is offered. Apollo tells Achilles that after ten years the Greeks shall conquer Troy and slay Priam's family. At that moment, Calchas, sent by Priam to consult the god, also appears, and he is advised not to go back to Troy but to join the Greeks. Returning to Athens, Achilles conveys the god's prophecy, and the Greeks accept Calchas. At the feast that Priam holds the next day, Calchas advises the Greeks to strike immediately. They set out in fair weather, but a storm soon strikes and Calchas uses his powers to assuage it. He explains that Diana must be appeased; she is angry at their setting out without first sacrificing to her. Putting in at Aulus, Agamemnon prepares to sacrifice his daughter, Iphigenia, in the temple, but Diana sets a hart in her place. The Greeks reach the boundaries of Troy and destroy the castle Sarobona, before landing at Tenedos, six miles from Troy. The Greeks lay siege to Tenedos and conquer it by force of their numbers. Agamemnon convokes the lords and kings to distribute the plunder according to their merits, and he addresses them as a body (lines 4896–6516).*]

	"Sirs," quod he, "ful worthi of degré,	
	Of verray right and necessité	
	We be compelled, bothe highe and lowe,	
6520	With al oure myght, liche as ye wel knowe,	
	To redresse a thing that is amys:	*wrong*
	For thorugh the world, as it reportid is,	
	We ben of force, of power, and of myght,	
	Of worthines in every wighttes syght	*person's*
6525	Most renomed and most worschipable,	*honorable*
	And idempte and juged for most able	*thought*
	Of alle peples, and likliest to stonde	

139

	For to parforme what we take on honde,	*undertake*
	Who that evere gruccheth or seyth nay.	*complains*
6530	Yit me semeth, yif it be to your pay,	*satisfaction*
	Thilke power most is acceptable	
	Unto goddis and lengest stondeth stable	
	That is devoide of surquidie and pride;	*arrogance*
	For it is kouthe uppon every syde,	*known*
6535	In eche lond, bothe of oon and alle,	
	How many harmys and grevis han befalle	
	Thorugh rancour only, pride and wilfulnes,	
	So importable, as I coude expresse,	*unbearable*
	That thorugh pride is ther don offence;	
6540	The highe goddis make resistence	
	To alle tho that be surquedous,	*excessively proud*
	Whiche is a vice so contrarius	
	That it may in no place abide.	
	And in good feith, manhood is no pride:	
6545	For who that hath any acqueintaunce	
	Outher by frenschip or by alyaunce	
	With a prowde man, to be confederat	
	With hym in herte, of highe or lowe estat,	
	He nedis muste, whatever that he be,	
6550	To many other of necessité	
	Be lothsom first, enmy, and contraire;	*hateful*
	For nothing may a man so moche apaire	*damage*
	As pride, in soth, in highe or lowe degré.	
	Wherfore, I rede pleinly how that we	
6555	This foule vice oute of our hert arrace,	*tear*
	That our quarel may have the more grace;	
	And specially that oure dedis alle	
	Conveied ben, however that it falle,	
	Be rightwesnesse more than volunté:	
6560	For yif trouthe oure sothfast guyde be,	
	Us to directe by his rightful lyne,	
	Than oure quarel schal ay in honour schine	
	And contune eke in ful felicité.	*remain*
	And ferthermore, this knowen alle ye,	
6565	How we ar come for to do vengaunce	
	With oure frendschip and oure alliance	

Upon Priam for wrongis don of olde
By hym and hyse, as I have ofte tolde;
And hereupon we han his grounde itake,   *captured*
6570   And some of his maked to awake
With manful honde, and his castellis strong
Ibete doun, that stonden have so longe,   *Demolished*
And take there the riches that we founde,
And slawe his men with many blody wounde,   *slain*
6575   And harmys mo don in his contré
That I wot wel, yif her enmyté   *if their*
Was unto us gret and moche afore,
I dar seie now it is in double more;
That yif that thei avenged myghte be
6580   On us echon, anon ye schulde se
Her gret ire, so cruel and so huge,
Ben execute withoute more refuge.   *carried out; remedy*
And yit, in soth, I wote thei han espied   *truth; know*
Oure beyng here; though we be nat askried   *challenged*
6585   Of hem as yit, I dar seyn outterly
Thei are wel war that we ar faste by;
And overmore, this wote I wel also,   *moreover*
Of the harmys that we han hem do,
The whiche as yit ben but fresche and grene,
6590   Yif thei wer strong and myghti to sustene,   *If*
A werre on us anon thei wolde gynne.
And yit the cité whiche thei ben inne
Is wallid strong and tourid rounde aboute,   *defended by towers*
That thei wene fully, oute of doute,   *think*
6595   With the meyné that thei have gadrid inne   *troops*
Of her alies, that we schal nat wynne
Of hem but smal in werre nor in strif:
For he in sothe hath a prerogatyf   *truth; privilege*
And avauntage, that in his contré
6600   Hymsilfe diffendith; namly, yif that he
Be stuffid strong of frendis hym beside   *supplied*
And of allies, where he doth abyde;
Like as the raven with his fetheres blake
Withinne his nest wil ofte tyme make
6605   Ageyn the faukon — gentil of nature —   *Against*

	Ful harde diffence whiles he may dure,	*as long as he can*
	Or that he be venquissched and outtraied.	*Until; overcome*
	And yit som while the faukon is delaied,	
	Whils the raven besyde his nest doth fle	*fly*
6610	Withinne his covert at his liberté;	*shelter*
	As every foule is froward to arest	*threatening; seize*
	For to be daunted in his owne nest.	*overcome*
	And yit this wordis to you I nat sey	
	In any wyse to putten in affray	*to alarm*
6615	Youre knyghtly hertis, so manly and so stable,	
	Nor that to you it schulde be doutable,	
	But the Troiens that we schal confounde	*destroy*
	And her cité, in whiche thei habounde,	
	Pleinly distroie, although that it be strong,	
6620	And thei and alle that ben hem among	
	Schal finally consumpte be with deth,	
	Thorugh Grekis swerde yelden up the breth.	
	But the cause, withouten any drede,	
	Why I seye thus is that ye take hede	
6625	For any pride or presumpcioun	
	To adverte in youre discrecioun	*notice*
	So prudently that resoun in this nede	
	For any hast may oure bridel lede	
	And so ordeyn, or we hennes wende,	*go hence*
6630	That laude and pris aftir in the ende	*praise; worthiness*
	May be reported, as I have devised:	*explained*
	For many man that hath nat ben avised	*thoughtful*
	In his pursut, for lak of providence	
	To sen toforn in his advertence	*consideration*
6635	What schulde falle, to deth it hath him broght:	
	Swiche wilful hast wer good to be thoght	
	Of us aforn be examynacioun	
	And wel decut by revolucioun	*ripened by thought (see note)*
	Of thingkyng ofte, that we nat repente.	
6640	And first remembrith how that Priam sente	
	To us but late only for Exyoun,	
	That is yit holde of Kyng Thelamoun,	
	Whiche was of us withoute avisement	*reflection*
	Undiscretly denyed by assent;	

142

6645	Whiche hath to us be non avauntage
	But grounde and rote of ful gret damage.
	For yif that we thorugh wys purviaunce
	Of hir had maked delyveraunce,
	The harmys grete hadde ben eschewed,
6650	That aftir wern of Parys so pursewed
	In the temple of Cytherea,
	That bilded is beside Cirrea.
	The tresour gret also that he hadde,
	And jowellis that he with hym ladde
6655	Thene to Troie, and the gret riches,
	The slaughtre of men, and the hevynes
	That yit is made for the Quene Eleyne
	Thorughoute Grece, and the grete peyne
	Of Menelay — al had ben unwrought,
6660	Yif we hadde seyn this in oure thought
	Wisely aforn and Exyoun restored.
	Than had nat the harmys be so morid
	On us echon in verray sothfastnes,
	Nor spent oure labour so in ydelnes,
6665	Tresour nor good wasted so in veyn,
	Nor come so fer for to fecche ageyn
	The Quene Eleyne with costis importable,
	Withoute harmys, now ineschuable:
	And for al this yit ne wite we
6670	Whether to joye or adversité
	The thing schal turne that we be aboute,
	Sith ofte sithe dependent and in doute
	Is fatal thing, unsiker and unstable;
	And fro the gynnyng ofte variable
6675	The ende is seyn. Fortune can transmewe
	Hir gery cours, and therfore, to eschewe
	The harmys likly possible to falle,
	My conseil is, here among yow alle,
	Upon travail traveil to eschewe
6680	In this mater or we ferther swe:
	To Priamus withouten any more
	To sende first ageyn for to restore
	The Quene Eleyne, as right and resoun is,

Glosses:
- 6659 *all would not have been done*
- 6662 *increased*
- 6667 *unbearable*
- 6668 *unavoidable*
- 6669 *know*
- 6672 *Since often times*
- 6675 *change*
- 6676 *fickle; avoid*
- 6677 *occur*
- 6680 *before; pursue*

And other harmys don eke be Parys,
6685 Aftir his trespas and offencioun
Justly to make restitucioun.
Than may we alle in worschip and honour
Retournen hom withoute more labour,
Yif thei assent to don as we require;
6690 And oure axyng yif hem list nat here
But folily of her wilfulnes
Refusen it, than oure worthines
Is double assured on a siker grounde, *certain*
By juste title Troyens to confounde. *destroy*
6695 With thinges two we schal ben underpight: *upheld*
First oure power, borne up with our right,
Schal for us fight our quarel to dareyne, *to settle by combat*
In balaunce to weye atwixe us tweyne
To fyn that we schal be more excusid;
6700 For thei toforn han wilfully refusid *earlier*
Oure just proferes made to hem afore; *proposals*
And we schal be thorugh the world, therfore,
Withoute spot of trespace or of blame,
Of mysreport in hyndring of our name, *slandering*
6705 Wher thei of foly schal ynoted be
Of wilful wodnes, pleinly, wher that we *madness*
Schal stonde fre oure power for to use;
And every man schal us wel excuse,
Though that we doon execucioun
6710 Be takyng vengaunce for her offencioun
Of man and childe, of eche sect and age, *sex*
That schal of deth holde the passage
And be the swerd withouten mercy pace, *under; pass*
Oon and other — ther is no better grace.
6715 But yit toforn, I conseil taketh hede
That ye to hem alle mesour bede: *moderation offer*
This hold I best and most sikirnes;
And werketh now be good avisenes *caution*
Among yoursilf, and no lenger tarie."

[*Ulysses and Diomede are chosen to carry Agamemnon's message to Troy, and they present the Greek demands with a rudeness calculated to offend Priam. Though himself driven to*

144

Book 2

anger, Priam restrains his men, who wish to punish the messengers on the spot. After the ambassadors return, Agamemnon sends Achilles and Telephus to secure provisions from the island of Mysia. During the ensuing battle Telephus prevails on Achilles to spare the mortally wounded King of Mysia, Teuthras, who names Telephus as his heir because Telephus's father, Hercules, originally helped him secure the kingship. The book next recounts the kings and lords who come to the aid of Troy: Dares says that 32,000 knights and lords, besides those of India, flocked to Priam's city. King Palamedes, delayed earlier by illness, joins the Greeks at Tenedos. Diomede urges that the Greeks attack Troy immediately. When the Greeks arrive in force the next day, the Trojans sally forth to oppose their landing. The Greeks have no choice but to fight or be thrown back into the sea. Battle rages back and forth with terrible slaughter. First one side and then the other holds the advantage as heroes like Hector and Achilles enter the battle at decisive points and subsequently retire. At length, the Greeks are able to land their main force. Agamemnon decides on a place to establish the Greek camp, oversees the fortification, and sets a watch to guard the camp while his men rest in their tents before Troy (lines 6720–8702).]

	And thus eche thing disposid as it ought,	*arranged*
	I wil procede to telle how thei wrought,	
8705	Ceriously withoutyn and withinne,	*In due order*
	With youre support the thridde boke begynne.	

145

Book 3

Whan Aurora, with hir pale light,
Under the mantel of the mirké nyght
And the curtyn of her hewes fade   *colors*
Ischroudid was in the dirke schade,
5   Abasched rody, as I can diffyne,   *Blushing red; say*
Only of fer that is femynyne,   *fear*
Foraschamyd durste nat be seyn   *Greatly ashamed*
Because sche had so longe abedde leyn
With fresche Febus, hir owne chose knyght,   *Phoebus; chosen*
10   For whiche sche hidde hir sothly out of sight   *truly*
Til his stede that callid is Flegonte
Enhasted hym above oure orizonte;   *Hastened; horizon*
And Appollo with his bemys clere
Hath recounforted hir oppressid chere —   *soothed her troubled mood*
15   This to seyne, aftir the dawenyng,
Whan Titan was in the est rysyng,
Of his hete atempre and right softe   *mild*
Her emyspery for to glade alofte —   *hemisphere*
The same hour the Troyan champioun,
20   Governour of werris of the toun,   *Commander in chief*
Worthi Ector, whiche in the cité
Next Priam had of alle sovereinté
The toun to guye be knyghtly excellence,   *direct*
For his manhod and his sapience   *wisdom*
25   Of Troyan knyghtes lord and eke chefteyn,
Whiche hath commaunded in a large pleyn,   *Who*
To highe and low, he exceptyng noon,
Kynges, princes, and lordis everychon,
The same morwe for to mete ifere,   *together*
30   In hir array to moustre and appere,   *gather for inspection*
Like as thei were of name and of estate,
Besyde a temple whilom consecrate
To the goddes that callid is Dyane,

146

	Moste honoured in that riche fane —	*temple*
35	Ther to arraye hem, in al the haste thei can,	
	Lik the devis of this knyghtly man.	*To the liking*

[*Hector supervises the arming of all the Trojans and sets the order of battle. He divides the forces into nine divisions, each led by his legitimate and natural brothers in addition to foreign kings. He assigns a rearguard to Priam, with special orders to stay between the main troops and the city. The women of Troy watch from the walls as the troops move forward (lines 37–535).*]

	And of Grekis furthe I wil yow telle,	
	Yif so be ye list abide a whyle,	*If; wish*
	For now most I my fordullid stile	*greatly dulled stylus*
	Ageyn directe to Agamenoun.	
540	Wel may I make an exclamacioun	
	On ignoraunce, that stant so in my light,	
	Whiche causeth me with a ful cloudy sight	
	In my makynge to speken of the werre.	*war*
	For lak of termys I mote nedis erre	*must; wander*
545	Connyngly my wordis for to sette;	*Skillfully*
	Cruel Allecto is besy me to lette,	*to hinder me*
	The nyghtes doughter, blindid by dirknes,	
	Be craft of armys the trouthe to expresse	
	In ordre due a feld to discryve.	
550	And Chaucer now, allas, is nat alyve	
	Me to reforme or to be my rede	*instruct; help*
	(For lak of whom slougher is my spede),	*dilatory; speed in writing*
	The noble rethor that alle dide excelle;	*rhetorician*
	For in makyng he drank of the welle	*poetic composition*
555	Undir Pernaso that the Musis kepe,	*Parnassus; Muses*
	On whiche hil I myghte never slepe —	
	Onnethe slombre — for whiche, allas, I pleyne.	*Hardly; lament*
	But for al this, ther is no more to seyne.	
	Though my wede be nat polymyte,	*garment; many colored*
560	Colourles, forthe I wil endyte	*Without rhetorical colors; compose*
	As it cometh evene to my thought,	
	Pleinly to write how the kyng hath wrought,	
	The manly knyght, gret Agamenoun,	
	Lyk as the Latyn maketh mencioun.	

565	What! Trowe ye that he in his entent	*Do you know*
	Was founde sloughe outher necligent	
	On Grekis half his wardis for to make?	*divisions*
	Nay, nay, nat so; for hym list to wake	*he wished*
	That tyme more, sothly, than to slepe,	
570	Ful lik a kyng that day the feld to kepe.	
	Nor necligence myght his herte sade,	*[make] his heart indifferent*
	For in that day I fynde that he made	
	Six and twenty wardis by and by,	
	So wel devised and so prudently	*arranged*
575	That no man myght amende his ordinaunce.	
	And of the first he yaf governaunce	
	To the manful noble Patroclus	
	That with hym ladde (myn auctour telleth thus)	
	Mirmidones, so myghti and so stronge,	
580	With alle the folke that to Achilles longe,	*belong*
	Besyde thilke that wern of his meyné	*those; retinue*
	Whiche that he brought out of his contré	
	At his comyng to the sege of Troye;	
	And he rood furthe with hem on his woye	*way*
585	Into the feld and made no delaye.	
	Now fille it so on the same day	
	That Achilles kepte hym in his tente	
	And for seknes that day oute ne wente;	
	For his lechis made hym to abstene,	*physicians; withhold himself*
590	For his woundes fresche wern and grene	*unhealed*
	That he kaught on the day tofore,	*before*
	Whiche for to hele of her akyng sore	
	He be counseil kepte hym silfe cloos	*removed*
	And from his bed that day nat ne roos,	
595	In hope only the bettre to endure	
	Whan that he was restored unto cure.	*health*
	But alle his men he toke to Patroclus,	*transferred to*
	Whiche was in armys passyngly famus	
	And be discent come of gret kynrede,	
600	And was also — of hym as I rede —	
	Habundaunt of gold and of riches,	*Generous*
	And fer comendid for his gentilles,	*widely praised*
	And hadde a name of highe discrecioun.	

	Now was ther evere swiche affeccioun	
605	Of entere love, trouthe, and feithfulnes,	*complete*
	So gret desyre and inward kyndenes,	
	Besy thinkyng, and so gret fervence,	*ardor*
	So moche frendeschip and thoughtful advertence,	*attention*
	So huge brennyng, passyng amerous,	
610	Betwixe Achilles and this Patroclus	
	That her hertis were lokkid in o cheyne.	
	And whatsoever, if I schal nat feyne,	
	The ton hath wrought, as brother unto brother,	*The one*
	In hert it was confermyd of the tother;	*sanctioned; other*
615	For wil and godys bothe were commune,	
	And to the deth thei evere so contune —	*remain*
	Withoute chaunge her love so abood.	*persisted*
	And Patroclus furthe amonge hem rood	
	Into the feld with Myrmidones,	
620	And in his tent abideth Achilles.	

[*Agamemnon, like Hector, disposes his troops in divisions led by heroes and kings. The Greeks move forward, with their banners and devices signaling their burning desire for battle, and they confront the Trojans. Patroclus leads the first division in place of Achilles, whose physicians prevail on him not to take the field because of the wounds he suffered the day before (lines 621–743).*]

	The first, asondre but a litel space,	*apart*
745	Began to approche with al her ful myght;	
	And Hector tho lik a doughty knyght	*powerful*
	Formest of alle on the side of Troye,	*First*
	The ire of whom no man myght acoye	*appease*
	But lik a lyoun in his hungri rage,	
750	Issed oute, furious of visage,	*Sallied forth; in appearance*
	Toward Grekis on his myghti stede,	*steed*
	That with his sporis made his sides blede:	*spurs*
	His knyghtly hert so inly was totorn	*torn to pieces*
	Of mortal ire. And as he rood toforn,	
755	Brennynge ful hote in his malencolye,	*anger*
	The whiche thing whan Grekis gan espie,	
	Patroclus withoute more abood	*delay*
	Of surquedie afore the wardis rood	*pride; troops*

	Oute al toforn, in bothe hostis sight,	*before all*
760	For to encontre pleinly, yif he myght,	
	With worthi Hector whan he him saw afer,	
	And as right lyne as is diameter,	*as straight as the line of diameter*
	Rood unto hym in his hatful tene;	*rage*
	And with a spere scharpe grounde and kene	
765	Thorughoute his schelde, of envious rage,	
	He smote Hector withoute more damage,	
	Except only that the hed of stele	
	That was toforn, forged and whet ful wele,	*sharpened*
	Thorugh plate and maile myghtely gan glace,	*penetrate*
770	But to the skyn for no thing myght hit trace:	*in no way; cut through*
	Albe it cam of passyng violence,	*Although*
	Yit to Hector it dide noon offence,	
	Oute of his sadel onys hym to flitte.	*momentarily; shift position*
	For though that he sturdely hym hitte,	
775	He myghte nat bakward bow his chyne	
	Nor on no parti make hym to enclyne;	*bend*
	But fatally to his confusioun	*ruin*
	This myghti man, this Troyan champioun,	
	In his ire ay brennynge more and more,	
780	Upon hym the hate frat so sore,	*consumed*
	Lefte his spere, myn auctor writeth thus,	*Left*
	And with a swerd rood to Patroclus,	
	Avised fully that he schal be ded,	*Determined*
	And furiously gan hamen at his hed,	*aimed a blow*
785	And rof hym doun — ther was no maner lette —	*cut; hindrance*
	Into the brest thorugh his basenet,	*headpiece*
	As seith Guydo, with so gret a peyne	
	That with the stroke he partid hym on tweyne.	
	His mortal swerde whettid was so kene	*sharpened*
790	That Patroclus myghte nat sustene	
	Upon his hors but fil doun to grounde,	
	As he that kaught his laste fatal wounde,	
	Beyng present his knyghtes everychon.	
	And delyverly upon hym anon	*quickly*
795	Worthi Hector from his stede adoun	
	Discendid is lik a wode lyoun,	*mad*
	Of hatful ire brennynge as the fire,	

	Havinge in hert inly gret desire	
	To spoilen hym of his armure anoon,	*strip*
800	In whiche ther was ful many riche stoon,	
	Bothe of rubies and saphiris Ynde:	*blue*
	For thilke daies, pleinly as I fynde,	
	Kynges, lordis, and knyghtes (this no nay)	
	To bataille went in her best array.	
805	And sothly Hector, whan he first gan se	
	The multitude of stonys and perré	*jewelry*
	On Patroclus, so orient and schene,	*lustrous and shining*
	Upon his arme he hynge his horse rene,	*rein*
	The menewhile whil he of hool entent	*All the while*
810	To cacche his praye was so dilligent	*prey*
	Of covetyse in ther alder sightes,	*sight of all*
	Til Merioun with thre thousand knyghtes	
	Armed in stele rounde aboute hym alle	
	Is sodeynly upon Hector falle,	
815	The dede cors of Patroclus to save,	*dead body*
	That his purpos Hector may nat have	
	At liberté the riche kyng to spoille,	*plunder*
	Whiche caused hym in anger for to boille.	
	To whom the kyng callid Merion,	
820	Irous and wood, seide among echon:	*among them all*
	"O gredy lyoun, O wolfe most ravenous,	
	O hatful tygre, passyng envious	
	Of avarice, O beste insaturable	*insatiable*
	And of desire sothly unstaunchable,	
825	Upon this pray thou schalt the nat now fede;	*prey*
	Go elliswhere to swe for thi mede:	*seek after your reward*
	For truste well, in conclusioun,	
	Fifti thousand to thi distructioun,	
	Of oon entent, pleinly wil nat faille	
830	Thin hatful pride attonys for to assaille!"	*at once*
	And sodeinly with speris scharpe whette	
	On every half thei gonne hym besette,	*side*
	Maugre his force, his myght, and his manhede,	*Despite*

151

	Enforcyng hem t'arevid him his stede,[1]	
835	That sothfastly of gret violence	*So that*
	He constreyned, for al his strong diffence,	*was compelled (see note)*
	As seith Guydo, to falle upon his kne;	
	But thorugh his myght and magnanymyté,	
	He of manhood hath his hors recurid	*recovered*
840	And among Grekis is so moche assurid	
	In his strengthe and his grete myght	
	That he recurid lik a worthi knyght	*regained*
	His stede ageyn amiddes alle his foon.	*foes*
	And right as lyne he rood to Merion,	*straight*
845	Ful desyrous avengid on hym to be	
	In his furye of hasty cruelté;	
	For theruppon was sette al his delit,	
	That in his mortal blody appetit,	
	In verray soth, he hadde hym slaw anon,	
850	Save that the kyng which callid was Glacon	*Except that*
	Cam to rescue hym with Kyng Theseus	
	And his sone that hight Archilagus,	
	As I have tolde, Merion to rescue.	
	And thre thousand knyghtes gan hym swe,	*pursue*
855	Ful assentid attonis in bataille	
	For lyf or deth Hector to assaille,	
	In await unwar on hym to sette.	*ambush unexpected*
	But al this whyle with whom that ever he mette,	
	With his swerde he kylleth and bare doun,	
860	That finally ther gayneth no raunsoun;	*no price paid*
	For any Greke that durst wyth hym mete	
	At departyng felte ful unswete:	*At the exchange of blows*
	He made a weye aboute hym everywhere,	
	That thei fledde hym as the deth for fere,	*fear*
865	For where he rod he made a path ful pleyn.	
	And as I rede, to Patroclus ageyn	
	He is repeired to spoille hym, yif he myght,	*returned*
	Amyd the feld in the Grekis sight,	
	As he that wolde his praye nat lightly lete,	*prey; abandon*

---

[1] *Exerting themselves to rob him of his steed*

870	Til Ydwme cam, the worthi Kyng of Crete,	*Idomeneus*
	With two thousand clad in plate and maille,	
	Worthi knyghtes, Hector to assaille	
	Whyles that he was so desirous,	
	As I have tolde, to spoille Patroclus,	
875	And new ageyn to his confusioun,	
	Lyk as I fynde, cam Kyng Merioun;	
	And or Hector myghte taken hede,	
	Thei of force reften hym his stede,	*deprived*
	That sothly he (ther was noon other bote)	*remedy*
880	Compellid was for to fight on fote.	
	And of knyghthod his herte he reswmeth;	*took heart again*
	And with his swerde aboute hym he conswmeth	
	Al that withstood, bothen hors and man;	
	And furiously this Troyan knyght began	
885	Armys, leggis, schuldris, by the boon,	*bone*
	To hewen of amyd his mortal foon,	*off*
	That Grekis myght aforn him nat sustene	
	And, as I rede, that he slowe fiftene	
	Of hem that were besy hym to take,	
890	And swiche a slawghter he gan among hem make,	
	That thei ne durste abide aforn his face.	
	And Merion in the silfe place	
	This menewhile toke up Patroclus	
	With hevy chere and face ful pitous;	
895	And on his stede he leide it hym beforn;	
	And to his tent anon he hath it born,	
	Alwey Grekis in her cruel mood	*All the time*
	Aboute Hector, furious and wood,	
	Felly abood, fightynge upon fote.	*Cruelly*

[*The Greeks continue their furious assault on Hector, but the Trojans rush to his support and force the Greeks to retreat. Hector remounts his horse and resumes his slaughter of the Greeks (lines 900–75).*]

	For thilke day the lyoun pleyed he,	*that same*
	Upon Grekis his manhod for to haunte;	*employ*
	For he her pride so mortally gan daunte	*subdue*
	That thei hym fled, whereso that he rood,	

980	Makyng al hoot the stremys of her blood	
	Endelonge to renne upon the grene,	*At full length on*
	Til the tyme the duke of grete Athene	
	That callid was whilom Menesteus	
	With thre thousand knyghtes ful famous,	
985	Of whiche he was bothe lord and guyde,	*commander*
	The feld hath taken upon the lefte side,	
	For a deceyt, in ful secré wyse,	
	Where Troylus was with the folke of Fryse	
	Whiche hath that day, whoso liste to seke,	*wants*
990	By his knyghthod kylled many Greke.	
	Liche a tigre gredy on his pray,	*prey*
	Troylus bar hym al the longe day,	
	Sleynge of Grekis many worthi knyght.	
	And while that he was besiest in fight	
995	Ageyn his foon with Kyng Antipus	*foes*
	And the kyng that highte Alcanus,	*was called*
	Upon Grekis elyche fresche and newe,	*alike*
	Makynge her sydes al of blody hewe,	
	By oon assent, this thre thorugh her manhede —	
1000	And specially uppon his baye stede	
	Whersoever that this Troylus rood,	
	Every Greke that his swerd abood	*met*
	Sodeinly he made for to sterve,	*die*
	Thorugh her platis so depe he dide kerve.	*cut*
1005	And this contuneth til duke Meneste	*continues*
	Of Troylus sawe the grete cruelté	
	And the slawghtre that he on Grekis made —	
	Of hasty ire, with face pale and fade,	*dim*
	Hent a spere and threwe it in the reste	*[He] seized*
1010	And Troylus smet evene amyd the breste	*smote*
	So sternely that maugre his renoun	*despite*
	To the erthe anon he bare hym doun	
	In the myddis of his mortal foon	*foes*
	That cruelly hym besette anoon	*Who*
1015	And him to treyne leide out hoke and laas	*snare; line*
	Rounde aboute in maner of compas,	
	With spere and darte and swerdis forgid bright.	
	But he hymsilf diffendith like a knyght,	

	With gret manhod his honour to avaunce,	
1020	Albe his lif was honged in balaunce	
	Where he stood and felte ful unswete,	
	In poynt of deth amonge the horse fete,	
	With gret await of duke Meneste	*watchfulness*
	How this Troylus myght have take be	
1025	Of mortal hate castyng in his thought,	
	At meschef take that he eskape nought.	
	On every half he was so besette	*side*
	With swerdis rounde, kene gronde and whette,	*around him*
	Allone, allas, mortally bestadde;	*hard pressed*
1030	Thei sesid hym, and furthe thei han hym ladde,	
	Til Miseres, a worthi knyght of Troye,	
	Gan to crye as he stood in the woye,	*way*
	Forabassched, in right furious wyse:	*Greatly disconcerted*
	"O ye noble worthi men of Fryse!	
1035	Manly knyghtes, ay preved in the feld,	*tested*
	Most renomed bothe with spere and scheld,	
	Considereth now unto your highe fame	
	And adverteth the glorie of youre name,	*think of*
	How this day thorugh youre necligence,	
1040	By the power and myghti violence	
	Of the Grekis Troylus is itake	*taken*
	Sool in the feld. For ye han hym forsake,	*Alone*
	That schal rebounde to youre alder schame:	*all your*
	For ye in soth gretly are to blame,	
1045	Yif he that is of worthinesse flour	*If*
	Be take of Grekis for lak of socour,	*support*
	That, but yif ye taken hasty wreche,	*unless; vengeance*
	Schamful report your honour schal apeche	*cast a slur on*
	Perpetuelly and seide therof amys	*speak ill of*
1050	In youre defaute that Troylus taken is,	*Through your fault*
	Whiche named be so worthi and famus."	
	And with that word the Kyng Alcamus	
	Of malencolye felt his herte ryve,	*anger; break*
	And in his ire hent a spere blyve,	*quickly*
1055	And prikynge after enhasteth what he might,	*riding; hurries*
	Til he of hem pleinly had a sight	
	That besy wern Troylus for to lede.	

155

And he ful knyghtly sittyng on his stede
Ran oon thorugh, that he fil doun ded;
1060   And eft ageyn, pale and no thing red,   *not at all*
In his rancour no lenger wolde lette,   *hinder*
But a Greke, the firste that he mette,
Thorugh the body smette he with a spere,
That men myghte se the poynt afere,   *come through*
1065   By brest and plate thorugh the scholder-bon,
That to the grounde he fil doun ded anoon.
And therwithal the worthi Freses alle
Cam flokmel doun and on Grekis falle   *by companies*
So myghtely that, maugre her diffence,   *despite*
1070   Thei sette upon with so gret violence
That Troylus is from al daunger fré;
And thorugh her knyghtly magnanymyté   *fortitude*
Thei maden hym to recure his stede.   *regain*
And specially helpyng in this nede
1075   Was Zantipus, the stronge manly kyng,
Whiche of disdeyn at his incomyng
On Meneste gan his spere grate,   *strike*
And thorugh his scheld, mail, and thikke plate,
So sore he smot that this Menestee
1080   Had be ded, nadde his armour be;   *had not*
Whiche for ire gan to tremble and schake   *Who*
That Troylus was from his hondis take
And eskaped to be prisoner,
Dispit his berd and maugre his power.   *In spite of anything he can do*
1085   Wherfor he gan of hasti hoot envie
On his knyghtes furiously to crye
That wer so myghti, renomed, and stronge,
To peynen hem for to venge his wronge   *exert themselves*
Upon Troyens, to mete hem in the face.
1090   And thei in hast gan myghtely enbrace   *lay hold of*
Her scharpe speris, grounde for to bite,
And felly foyne, and togidre smyte.   *thrust*
For tho began the grete mortal werre:
The fire brast out, schene as any sterre,   *bright*
1095   On basenettis and her platis bright,   *helmets*
That thorugh the feld flawmeth the light;

Book 3

	To lyf nor deth thei toke tho non hede;	
	And doun the playn, bothe in lengthe and brede,	
	The wardis gan proudly to avale;	*divisions; descend*
1100	And with lokis of envie pale,	
	Thei aproche and assemble ifere,	*together*
	In hate brennynge that no man may stere,	*control*
	And gan hurtle with spere, swerd, and darte,	
	And mortally upon every parte	
1105	The slaughter gan gretly for to rewe.	*was greatly to be regretted*

[*As the wholesale battle begins, Hector kills many Greeks and the Trojans seize the advantage. When he advances alone in the fray, the Greek King Theseus, moved by admiration and his sense of gentility, warns him not to risk his life foolishly. Hector later returns the noble gesture by prevailing on the Trojans to allow Theseus to escape. Nestor arrives with more Greek troops, but Aeneas advances from Troy with reinforcements. As Aeneas and Ajax fight, Ulysses joins the battle, driving back the Trojans and nearly killing Paris, who is rescued by Troilus. Hector eventually calls on Priam to commit the reserves, and he fights Ajax. Greek and Trojan heroes ride to each other's rescue, and in the battle Hector confronts King Merion, who rescued Patroclus's body after Hector had slain him (lines 1106–1888).*]

	And as I rede, amyd of his victorie	
1890	Hector mette under a tentorie	*tent*
	Amonge Grekis Merioun the Kyng,	
	To whom he spake withoute more tariyng:	
	"O thow traytour, the hour aprocheth faste,	
	For thow arte come sothly to thi laste;	
1895	Thi fatal day hath his cours ironne.	
	For truste wel, or westring of the sonne	*before the setting*
	I cast pleinly to quite the thi mede	*to repay you*
	And with my swerd in haste thi blood to schede:	
	For thou so bolde were on me today	
1900	To lettyn me of my riche praye	*hinder me from; prey*
	At the spoilynge of Kyng Patroclus —	*plundering*
	That for cause thou were presumptuous	*Because*
	Me to distourbe, thou schalt anon be ded."	
	And doun he stirte, and smote of first his hed,	*off*
1905	And hym to spoille also gan hym haste;	
	But Meneste cam on hym as faste,	

157

Whan he behilde traverse at his bake,   *from behind*
And with a spere, in whiche was no lake,
Smot hym in with grete violence,
1910   Withoute sight, or any advertence   *warning*
Of worthi Hector, or any takynge hede,
The wounde of whom sore gan to blede.
But out he went and made it faste bynde;   *had it bound up*
And Meneste stale aweye behynde,
1915   Nat in purpos sothly, yif he may,
To mete Hector of al that ilke day.
But whan that he was ybonde sore,
His wounde staunche that it bled no more,   *was dressed so that*
More furious than evere he was toforn,
1920   Repeired is, with anger al totorne   *Returned*
(So ay the ire on his herte fret),   *gnawed*
That he bar doun al that evere he met,
Sleth and kylleth — he was so mercyles —
Alle tho that put hemsilf in pres   *combat*
1925   Or hardy wern with hym for to mete.
For in his boke lik as writ Darete   *Dares*
For verray soth and in the stori seith
(Yif it be so that men may yeve feyth   *give*
And credence of possibilité,
1930   As in Guydo clerly ye may se),
Aftir that he caught his lattre wounde,
Finally Grekis to confounde   *destroy*
(So as it is affermed in certeyn),
A thousand knyghtes with his hond wer slayn,
1935   Withoute hem tho that I spak of rath.   *just now*
And newe alweye he gan his swerd to bathe
In Grekis blod, that sodeinly thei be
So overlayn thorugh his cruelté   *overwhelmed*
That Greke was noon, of highe nor lowe estat,
1940   That he ne was awhaped and amaat   *amazed and stupified*
Of his knyghthod and manly excellence:
For ther was non to make resistence
Nor outterly that durste take on honde   *utterly; undertake*
Of al that day Hector to withstonde.
1945   And as it is made also mencioun,

Book 3

	Thilke day Kyng Agamenoun,	*That same day*
	As seith Guydo, cam nat in the felde;	
	For causes gret his presence he withhelde	
	On Grekis side, that al goth upsodoun:	*goes badly*
1950	Hector on hem so pleyeth the lyon	
	That to her tentes thei fled for socours.	*relief*
	And thei of Troye, proudly as victours,	
	Sued aftir by tracis of her blood;	*Followed*
	And ther thei wan tresour and gret good,	*possessions*
1955	And spoiled hem in ful gret distresse	*plundered*
	Of her armour and of her richesse,	
	And felle on hem or that thei were ware,	*before; ready*
	And home to Troye al the good thei bare.	
	For finally that day with meschaunce	
1960	Grekis had be brought unto outtraunce,	*ruin*
	Withoute recure in soth for everemore;	*remedy*
	On every parte thei were beleyn so sore	*set upon*
	Thorugh the manhod of Hector and the myght,	
	With helpe of many other worthi knyght,	
1965	That so felly ageyn Grekis wrought:	*cruelly*
	For to swiche meschef pleinly thei hem brought	
	That nadde ben her owne pitous slouthe,	*were it not; sloth*
	Of pride only and of foly routhe,	*pity*
	Thei had of hem at her volunté	
1970	That day for evere hadde the sovereynté	
	And recured thorugh her highe renoun	*obtain*
	Lordschip of hem and domynacioun,	
	Whiche schuld have laste and be contynuel,	
	Victoriously and perpetuel	
1975	Have endurid; save cruel Fate	
	Is redy ay with Fortune to debate	*contest*
	Ageyn thinges that gynne in welfulnes,	
	To make hem fyne ay in wrechidnes	
	Thorugh her envious disposicioun	
1980	Of sodeyn chaunge and revolucioun	
	And unwar tournyng of hir false whele,	*unforeseen*
	That wil nat bide whan a thing is wele —	
	Allas, freel, devoide of sikernesse.	*changeable; certainty*
	The cause was dymmed with dirknesse,	

1985	That hath Troyens thorugh false oppinioun	
	Iblended so in her discresioun	*Blinded*
	And specially fordirked so the sight	*obscured*
	Of worthi Hector, the prudent manly knyght,	
	To sen aforn what schuld after swe,	*follow*
1990	Be good avis the meschef to eschewe	*prudence; trouble; avoid*
	That folwid hem at the bak behynde.	
	Allas, thei wern wilfully made blynde	
	The same day, whan thei wer set softe	
	Be victorie on the hille alofte,	
1995	That thei nat koude of necligence se	
	The aftirfal of her felicité,	*consequences*
	So put abak was her advertence	*attention*
	For lak of resoun and of highe prudence:	
	For thei her hap han voided and her grace,	*chance; emptied*
2000	That presently were sette afore her face.	
	For in a man is nat commendable	
	Yif Fortune be to hym favourable	*If*
	And blaundischinge with a forhede clere	
	To smyle on hym with a plesaunt chere,	
2005	Only of favour for to help hym oute,	
	Whan he in meschef is beset aboute,	
	Yif he refuse his hap of wilfulnes,	*out of*
	Fortune avoidynge thorugh unkyndnes	*unnaturalness*
	Whan sche mynystreth to hym of hir grace:	
2010	Another tyme he schal hir nat embrace,	*grasp*
	Whan he hath nede to hir helpe at al,	
	To socour hym or he cacche a fal;	
	But rather than for his ingratitude	
	Frowardly with mowes hym delude,	*Perversely; derisive grimaces*
2015	Whan he best weneth stond in sikernes.	*thinks to; certainty*
	Fortune is ay so ful of brotulnes,	*frailty*
	Remewable, and redy for to flitte	*Fickle; take away*
	Hir welful hour that who list nat amytte	*wish to consent*
	With hir favour for to ben allied,	
2020	Another tyme it schal be denyed,	
	Whan he wer levest finde hir favourable:	*most glad to find*
	For in some hour, sothly this no fable,	
	Unto som man sche graunteth his desires,	

That wil nat after in a thousand yeres,

2025 Paraventure, onys condiscende *By chance; agree*

Unto his wil nor his lust hym sende, *desire*

As it hath falle this day unhappily *happened*

To worthi Hector that so wilfully

Wrought of hede Grekis for to spare, *Took care*

2030 Fatally whan thei were in the snare.

For he of hem like a conqueroure,

With victorie, triumphe, and honour

Might have brought, thorugh his highe renoun,

The palme of conquest into Troye toun,

2035 Whiche he that day reffusid folily.

For as he rood, this Hector, cruelly

Amonge Grekis slowe and bar al doun, *slain; overthrown*

Casuely he mette Thelamoun,

I mene Ajax, nyghe of his allye, *near [to him] in kinship*

2040 That of hate and cruel hoot envie

To Hector rood, like as he were wood,

Albe to hym that he was nyghe of blod;

Yit for al that, this yonge lusty knyght *Yet*

Dide his power and his fulle myght

2045 Withoute feynyng to have born hym doun *overcome*

(Whos fader hight also Thelamoun,

That hym begat, the stori telleth thus,

Of Exioun, suster to Priamus). *Hesione*

And this Ajax, flourynge in yonge age,

2050 Fresche and delyver and of gret corage,

Sette on Hector of knyghtly highe prowes;

And as thei mette, bothe in her wodnes, *fury*

On her stedis, this manly champiouns, *these*

Everyche on other lik tigers or lyons

2055 Began to falle, and proudly to assaille,

And furiously severe plate and maille —

First with speris, longe, large, and rounde,

And aftirwarde with swerdis kene grounde.

And fightyng thus longe thei contune, *continue*

2060 Til it befil of cas or of fortune, *happened by*

Tokne or signe, or som apparence,

Or by Naturis kyndly influence,

161

Whiche into hertis dothe ful depe myne,   *penetrate*
Namly of hem that born ben of o lyne,   *lineage*
2065 Which cause was, paraunter, of this tweyne,
Naturelly her rancour to restreyne,
And her ire for to modefie —
Only for thei so nyghe were of allye,   *kinship*
Unwist of outher and therof unsure,   *Unknown to*
2070 Til thei wer taughte only of Nature:
For naturelly blod wil ay of kynde   *nature*
Draw unto blod, wher he may it fynde,
Whiche made Hector kyndly to adverte   *turn his attention*
To be mevid and sterid in his herte,
2075 Bothe of knyghthod and of gentilnes,
Whan he of Ajax sawe the worthines,
Spak unto hym ful benygnely
And seide: "Cosyn, I seye the trewely,   *to you*
Yif thou list Grekis here forsake   *If; wish*
2080 And come to Troye, I dare undirtake   *promise*
To thin allyes and to thi kynrede
Thou schalt be there withouten any drede
Ful wel receyved, in party and in al,
Of hem that ben of the blood royal
2085 Sothly discendid and hyest of degré,
That it of right schal suffise unto the,
And kyndely be to the plesaunce   *you*
For to repeire to thin allyaunce —   *return; kinsmen*
To gentil herte sith nothing is so good
2090 As be confederid with his owne blood;   *joined*
For I conceyve be the worthines,   *perceive*
Whiche Nature doth in the expresse,   *you*
Of Troyan blood that thou arte descendid,
Whiche of Grekis long hath be offendid:
2095 Wherfore I rede to leve hem outterly."   *advise; altogether*
And he answered ageyn ful humblely
That, sithen he of berthe was a Greke,
And was of youthe amonge hem fostered eke
From the tyme of his nativité,
2100 And taken had the ordre and degré
Of knyghthood eke amongis hem aforn,   *also*

	And, over this, bounde was and sworn	
	To be trewe to her nacioun	
	(Makyng of blood noon excepcioun),	
2105	He swore he wold conserven his beheste;	*keep his promise*
	And to Hector he made this requeste:	
	That yif that he of manful gentilnes	
	Wolde of knyghthood and of worthines	
	Shewe unto hym so gret affeccioun	
2110	To make hem that wer of Troye toun	
	Only withdrawe Grekis to pursewe,	*stop pursuing*
	And fro her tentis make hem to remewe,	
	And resorte ageyn unto the toun,	*return*
	Of knyghtly routhe and compassioun,	
2115	Withoute assailyng or any more affray	
	Made on Grekis for that ilke day,	*same*
	Sith unto hem ought inowgh suffice	
	That of the felde, in so knyghtly wyse,	
	Thei were of manhood fully possessours	
2120	And of her fomen finally victours,	
	Lyk as toforn fully is diffinyd.	*described*
	To whos requeste Hector is enclyned	
	(Allas the while) of hasty wilfulnes	*out of*
	And made anoon withoute avysenes	*forethought*
2125	Mid the felde a trompet for to blowe,	
	Wherby Troyens fully myghte knowe	
	That be his wil thei schulde hem withdraw	
	Aftir the custom, pleynly, and the lawe,	
	And the usaunce, bothe nygh and ferre,	
2130	Amongis hem that ben expert in werre,	
	Whan thei were moste fervent for to fight,	
	Upon Grekis for to preve her myght,	
	And had hem chacid lowe to the stronde,	*shore*
	That thei wer weyke of power to withstonde:	
2135	For thei of Troye, alle of o desire,	*one*
	Gan settyn on with schot of wylde fire	
	To brenne hir schippis and of highe meschaunce	
	Finally to putte hem at outtraunce.	*to ruin*
	And so thei had, this the verray trouthe,	*they would have*
2140	Nadde Hector had uppon hem routh,	*If Hector had not; compassion*

163

	Makynge Troyens repeire to the toun	*return*
	Ungraciously, to her confusioun,	*Unfortunately; destruction*
	As the story schal aftir specefie.	
	For tho he putte, allas, in juparté	
2145	Life and deth, whiche myght have be sure,	*might have been secure*
	The whiche ageyn thei nevere schal recure.	*recover*
	Thei han mater to compleyne sore:	
	For fro that day, farewel for everemore	
	Victorie and laude fro hem of the toun,	*praise*
2150	To hem denyed by disposicioun	
	Of mortal fate, whiche was contrarie —	
	In this mater me liste no lenger tarie.	
	For thei of Troye ben entrid her cyté	
	And schet her gatis for more sureté;	*shut*
2155	For of that day, lyk as made in mynde,	
	This was the ende, in Guydo as I fynde —	
	Thei wende have do paraunter for the beste.	

[*The Trojans are prepared to renew battle the next day, but the Greeks ask for an eight days' truce, during which they bury their dead and Achilles constructs a tomb for Patroclus and for Protesilaus. The Trojans tend to their wounded, while Priam mourns for his natural son Cassibellan, whom he buries in a rich tomb in the temple of Venus. During the funeral rite, Cassandra prophesies the fall of Troy (lines 2158–2237).*]

	In whiche thing, whan that Cassandra	
	Withinne hirsilfe considered and beheld	
2240	And saw up offrid his helm and his sheld,	
	His swerd also, and unto Mars his stede,	
	Of inward wo sche felt hir herte blede,	
	Herynge the noise and the pitous crye,	
	The tendre weping and sorwynge outterly	
2245	Of hem of Troye, and the lamentacioun	
	Whiche for her frendis, thorughoute al the toun,	
	Thei gan to make, that wer slawe afore.	*slain before*
	With sodeyn rage her herte was totore,	*torn*
	So inwardly sche myght hir nat restreyne	
2250	Furiously to cryen and compleine,	
	And seide, "Allas" ful ofte and "Wellawey":	
	"O woful wrecchis that ye be this day,	

	Unhappy eke and graceles also,	*too*
	Infortunat and inly wobego!	*wretched*
2255	How may ye suffre the grete harmys kene	
	Whiche ye ar likly herafter to sustene	
	Durynge the sege in this toun beloke,	*shut up*
	Seynge your foon, redy to be wroke,	*avenged*
	Aboute you, beset on every side,	*besieged*
2260	To be vengid on youre grete pride?	
	I wot right wel ye may hem nat eschewe,	*know*
	That thei ne schal unto the deth pursewe	
	You everychon, besegid in this place,	
	Withoute mercy, pité, or any grace.	
2265	Allas, allas, whi nil ye besy be,	*will you not*
	Ye woful wrechis schet in this cité,	*shut*
	With the Grekis for to seken pes,	
	Or the swerd of vengance merciles	*Before*
	On highe and lowe do execucioun?	
2270	And or this noble, worthi, royal toun	
	Eversid be and ybrought to nought,	*Overthrown*
	Why list ye nat consideren in your thought	*do you not wish*
	How the modres with her childre smale	
	In stretis schal, with face ded and pale,	
2275	Lyn mordred here thorugh Grekis cruelté	
	And yonge maydenes in captivité	
	Bewepen schal in myserie and in wo	
	Her servytude; and this toun also,	
	So famous ryche — allas, it is pité —	
2280	With Grekis fire schal distroied be	
	In schort tyme, sothly this no were.	*doubt*
	Eleyne of us, allas, is bought to dere,	
	Sith for hir sake we schul everychon,	
	Pore and riche, I excepte noon,	
2285	An ende make woful and pitous:	
	The ire of hem schal be so furious	
	Upon us alle, ther is noon other mene	*means*
	Sauf only deth us to go betwene."	*to mediate between us*
	This was the noise and the pitous cry	
2290	Of Cassandra that so dredfully	
	Sche gan to make aboute in every strete	

	Thorugh the toun, whomever sche myght mete,	
	Lyk as sche had ben oute of hir mynde,	
	Til Priamus faste made hir bynde	*had her bound*
2295	And schettyn up — it was the more roughth;	*pity*
	Sche was nat herde, albe sche seide troughth:	*truth*
	For nouther wisdam nor discrecioun,	
	Counseil nor wit, prudence nor resoun,	
	Trouth nor rede — withouten any lye —	
2300	Nor the spirite of trewe proficye,	*prophecy*
	Availeth nat nor al swiche sapience	
	In place wher ther is noon audience.	
	For be a man inly nevere so wys	
	In counseillynge or in hyghe devys,	*advice*
2305	In werkynge outher in elloquence,	
	Eche thing to sen in his advertence	*foresight*
	Or it be falle, aforn in his resoun,	*Before*
	Amyd the eye of his discreccioun,	*(see note)*
	Yet for al this (it is the more dool),	*sorrow*
2310	Withoute favour he holde is but a fool:	*is thought*
	For unfavored, wysdam availeth nought	
	Nouther trouth, how dere that it be bought,	
	Liche as Cassandra for al hir wyse rede	*advice*
	Dispised was, and taken of noon hede	
2315	Of hem of Troye, to her confusioun,	*destruction*
	But cruelly ythrowen in prisoun,	
	Where a whyle I wele leve hir dwelle	
	And of Grekis furth I wil you telle.	

[*In the Greek camp, King Palamedes complains about the selection of Agamemnon as their leader, but others intervene to mollify him for the moment. When battle resumes, Achilles and Hector fight one another, and then in succession Diomede and Troilus, and Menelaus and Paris confront each other. When Prothenor, Achilles's cousin, tries to attack Hector from behind, Hector cuts him in two. Hungry for vengeance, Achilles tries to rally the Greeks for an attack on Hector, but Hector and the Trojans drive the Greeks from the field and return to Troy in glory. The Greek chieftains meet to consider what they should do about Hector (lines 2319–2666).*]

	Whan Esperus, the faire brighte sterre,	
	Ageynes eve caste his stremys ferre	*far*

	And in the weste rathest gan appere,	*most readily did*
2670	Whan the twylyght with a pale chere,	
	In maner morneth the absence of the sonne	
	And nyght aprocheth with his copis donne,	*dark copes*
	The same tyme whan Titan toke his leve	
	That clerkis calle crepusculum at eve —	*dusk*
2675	Whiche is nat ellis but the mene light	*intermediate*
	Of Phebus absence and the dirke nyght,	
	And twylight hatte (for it is a mene	*is called; midpoint*
	Of day and nyght, departinge hem betwene,	
	Fully nouther but of bothe meynt,	*mixed*
2680	Or the hevene be clustryd and depeynt	*Before; painted*
	With brighte sterris in the evenynge) —	
	At whiche tyme Agamenoun the Kyng	
	For his lordis sodeinly hath sent	
	To come anon echon into his tent.	*at once each one*
2685	And whan thei wern assemblid alle yfere,	*together*
	Triste and hevy with a sorful chere,	*Sorrowful*
	Thei gan the slaughter of Hector to compleine,	*lament*
	Affermynge playnly thei myght never ateyne	
	Unto victorie while he were on lyve:	
2690	Wherefore thei gan to conspire blive	*at once*
	The deth of hym in many sondry woye	
	Echon concludynge, while he wer in Troy,	
	It was nat likly Grekis for to wynne;	
	For he alone of hem that were withinne	
2695	Was chef diffence and protectioun,	
	And sovereynly upholder of the toun,	
	Her myghty castel and her stronge wal,	
	And unto Grekis dedly fo mortal:	
	For thei ne myght his grete force endure	
2700	Nor never aright ageyn her foos be sure,	
	He stondyng hool (thei seide) in no degré	
	Nor whil he floureth in felicité.	
	Wherfor, echon of oon entencioun,	*each one being*
	Thei condiscende to this conclusioun:	*agree*
2705	That be som sleight of await lying,	*ambush*
	Whan he were most besy in fightynge	
	Amongis hem in meschef or distresse,	

That Achilles do his besynes
With al his myght unwarly him to assaille,   *without warning*
2710 That hym to slen for no thing that he faille.   *slay; in no way*
And Grekis alle gan her prayer make
To Achilles for to undirtake
Of this emprise fynally the swt,   *pursuit*
Thorugh his manhod that it be execut —
2715 The hasty deth of her mortal foo.
And Achilles withoute wordis moo   *more*
Her requeste assenteth to parforme   *Their*
And to her lust gan holly hym conforme.   *wishes*
Fro that tyme late hym be war, I rede,
2720 To be to hasty this journé for to spede,   *combat*
Upon Hector his power for to kythe,   *show*
List Fortune awronge hir face writhe,   *Lest; wrongly; turn away*
To loke on hym with a froward chere,   *unfavorable face*
Hym to bringe unto the hondis nere
2725 Thorugh sort or hap, of Hector, folily
To put his lif of deth in juparty,   *jeopardy*
List unto hym it happe evene lyche   *alike*
To falle hymsilfe in the same dyche
That he for Hector compassid hath and shape: *planned*
2730 For it is wonder yif that he eskape,   *if*
Sith Hector hadde withouten any drede   *Since*
As brennyng ire and as grete hatrede
To Achilles his deth for to purvey,
Yif he hym founde or in place sey
2735 Convenient for execucioun.
I trow ther schuld hym gayne no raunsoun,
Nor other mede his herte to quyete,   *reward*
But only deth, whan so that thei mete:
This the ende and fyn of this mater,
2740 As in this boke after ye schal here.
And thus Grekis maked han an ende
Of her counseil, and anoon thei wende,
Everyche of hem, hom to her loggynge,   *their dwellings*
And toke her reste til the morwenynge.

168

Book 3

[Hector leads the Trojans out, eager to finish the fight. In the individual confrontations, Hector battles Agamemnon and Achilles, Diomede and Aeneas resume their hatred, and Menelaus wounds Paris. When Thoas and Achilles fight later in the day, Hector is wounded but is able to cut off half of Thoas's nose. Thoas is captured and carried off to Troy. Paris shoots Menelaus with a poison arrow. After the surgeons care for his wound, Menelaus returns to battle and finds Paris unarmed. Aeneas intervenes and sends Paris back to Troy as the Trojans force the Greeks back to their camp before retiring. On the next morning, Priam calls his counselors to him (lines 2745–3102).]

	Til on the morwe that the rowes rede	*red beams*
	Of Phebus carte gonne for to sprede	*chariot*
3105	Aforn his upriste in the orient,	*rising*
	At whiche tyme Kyng Priamus hathe sent	
	For swiche as werne with him moste prevé	*such; intimate*
	And of his counseille inwardly secré;	
	And specialy he sente for be name	
3110	For worthi Hector, that grettest was of fame,	
	For Paris eke, and for Dephebus,	*also*
	And for Troylus, freshe and desirous,	*eager*
	For Anthenor, and for Pollydamas,	
	And for the Troyan called Eneas:	
3115	For he that day cast him nat to goon	*meant*
	Into the felde to mete with his foon.	
	And whan thei wern to his paleis come,	
	The lordis han the righte weye nome	*came directly*
	Unto the kyng withinne his closet;	*inner chamber*
3120	And whan the hussher hath the dore shet,	*usher; shut*
	And everyche hadde liche to his degré	*according*
	His place take and his dewe see,	*appropriate seat*
	This worthi kyng, as made is mencioun,	
	Gan to declare his hertis mocioun,	
3125	And his menynge aforn hem specifie,	
	And seide: "Sirs, in whom I moste affie,	*trust most*
	To yow is knowe how Kyng Thoas is here	*known*
	In this cité taken prisoner,	
	And is as yet beloken in prisoun	
3130	Whiche evere hath be unto Troye toun	*Who*
	An enmy gret, unto his power,	
	And us offendid bothe fer and nere	

	In many wyse (albe we litel reche)	*take little notice*
	As fer as he his force myghte streche;	
3135	And now with Grekis cam to sege our toun,	*beseige*
	As he that wilneth oure distruccioun,	
	And thereuppon hath done his besynes:	
	Wherfore, of doom and of rightwysnes,	*judgment*
	Bothe of resoun and of equyté,	
3140	I seie pleynly, as semeth unto me,	
	So that it be to yow acceptable	*Providing*
	And that ye think my counseil comendable,	
	Liche as he hath caste oure deth and shape,	
	I holde rightful that he nat eskape	
3145	But that of deth he resseyve his guerdoun.	*receive; reward*
	For right requereth and also good resoun,	
	That deth for deth is skilful guerdonynge,	*reasonable reward*
	Unto my wit, and right wel sittynge:	*appropriate*
	Seth your avis pleynly in this cas."	*State*
3150	And first of alle tho spake Eneas	
	And seide: "Lord, so it be noon offence	
	To youre highnes to yeve me audience,	*give*
	Thorugh supporte here of hem that be ful wys,	
	I shal reherse pleynly my devys,	*explain; advice*
3155	What is to werken as in this matere:	*to be done*
	Me semeth first, my lege lorde so dere,	
	That youre noble, royal excellence	
	Consydre shulde, with ful highe prudence,	
	In every werke and operacioun	
3160	To caste aforn, in conclusioun,	*foresee*
	The final ende that may after swe;	*follow*
	For to a wysman only is nat dewe	*necessary*
	To se the gynnynge and the endynge noght,	
	But bothe attonis peisen in his thought	*at once contemplate (weigh)*
3165	And weien hem so justly in balaunce	*weigh*
	That of the fyn folwe no repentaunce.	*from the outcome*
	Whi I seie this and platly whi I mene	*express my opinion*
	Is for that ye oughten for to sene	
	How Kyng Thoas is oon the principal	
3170	Amonge Grekis and of the blood royal,	
	Yif ye considre descendid as be lyn;	*If*

170

	Wherfore, yif he have thus foule a fyn	*end*
	To be slawe while he is in presoun,	*slain*
	It myght happen, in conclusioun,	
3175	That ye and yours that therto assente	
	Hereafterwarde sore to repente.	
	I preve it thus: that yif by aventure	*demonstrate (the point)*
	Or fortune, that no man may assure,	
	Some of youre lordis were another day	
3180	Of Grekis take, as it happe may,	*By; taken*
	Or of youre sonys, so worthi of renoun,	
	Or of kynges that ben in this toun,	
	Trusteth me wel that swiche gentilnes	*such*
	As ye schew to hem in her distres	
3185	Thei wil you quyte, whan in cas semblable	*return*
	Fortune to hem thei finde faverable,	
	The whiche no man constreyne may nor binde.	
	Wherfore, my lorde, have this thing in mynde:	
	For yif Thoas, of short avisement,	*reflection*
3190	Shal nowe be ded thorugh hasty jugement,	
	Another day Grekis wil us quyte,	*repay*
	And of rigour make her malis byte	*ill will bite*
	On some of youris, whoevere that it be,	
	And nouther spare highe nor lowe degré,	
3195	Though he were paraunter of youre blood;	*by chance*
	The whiche thing, for al this worldis good	
	It myghte falle that ye nolde se.	*would not want to see it happen*
	Wherfore I rede, lete Kyng Thoas be	*advise*
	Honestly keped in prisoun	
3200	Lyche his estate stille here in this toun,	*According to his social rank*
	List, as I seide, that another day	*Lest*
	Somme lorde of youris, as it happe may,	
	Casuelly were take of aventure:	*By chance*
	Be eschaunge of hym ye myghte best recure	*By; recover*
3205	Withoute strif youre owne man ageyn.	
	In this mater I can no more seyn,	
	But finally this is my fulle rede."	*advice*
	To whiche counseil Hector toke good hede,	
	And for it was accordynge to resoun,	*because*
3210	He hit commendith in his oppinoun.	*praises*

But Priam, evere of oo entencioun,
Stode alweie fix to this conclusioun,
Pleinly affermynge: "Yif Grekis may espie
That we this kyng spare of genterye,   *because he is noble*
3215 Thei wil arrette it cowardyse anoon,   *attribute*
That we dar nat venge us of oure foon
For verray drede, havyng noon hardines
Nor herte nouther to do rightwisnes;
Yet, nevertheles, after youre assent   *agreement*
3220 That he shal leve, I wele in myn entent
To youre desire fully condescende."   *agree*
And of this counseil so thei made an ende
Withoute more, save Eneas is go
And Troylus eke and Anthenor also
3225 Into an halle, excellynge of bewté,
The Quene Eleyne of purpos for to se,
With whom was eke Eccuba the Quene,   *also*
And other ladyes goodly on to sene,
And many mayde that yonge and lusti was.   *pleasing*
3230 And worthi Troilus with this Eneas
Dide her labour and her besy peyne
For to counforte the faire Quene Eleyne,
As sche that stood for the werre in drede;
But for all that, of verray wommanhede
3235 Thilke tyme with al hir herte entere,   *The same*
As she wel koude, maked hem good chere,
Havynge of konnynge inly suffisaunce   *skill*
Bothe of chere and of dalyaunce.   *mood; conversation*
And Eccuba, beyng in this halle
3240 Verray exaumple unto wommen alle,
Of bounté havynge sovereyn excellence,   *goodness*
In wisdam eke, and in elloquence,
Besoughte hem tho wonder wommanly
And counsaillede eke ful prudently,
3245 For any haste, bothe nyghe and ferre,
Avisely to kepe hem in the werre,   *cautiously*
And nat juparte her bodies folily,   *risk*
But to adverte and caste prudently   *consider*
In diffence knyghtly of the toun,

172

3250	Hem to governe by discrecioun:	
	She spake of feith and koude no thinge feyne.	*in no way*
	And thanne of hir and after of Eleyne	
	Thei toke leve and no lenger dwelle	
	But went her wey.	

[*The Greeks mourn their losses, and during the night a high wind blows down the tents in their camp. But the damage is repaired by dawn, and Achilles leads their forces into the field, where he kills the giant Hupon. The centaur Epistrophus, a skilled archer, slays many Greeks, but he is killed by Diomede. During the fighting Achilles and Hector meet again and Antenor is captured by the Greeks. In the next day's battle, the Trojans suffer many losses and must retire to the city. In the morning, the Greeks send Ulysses and Diomede to Priam to ask for a three months' truce, which everyone in Priam's council, except Hector, endorses. During the truce, it is agreed to exchange Thoas for Antenor (lines 3255–3663).*]

	And while the trewe dide thus endure,	*truce*
3665	Thei fil in trete and in comwnynge	*negotiation; conversation*
	Of Anthenor and Thoas the Kyng:	
	That Anthenor delyvered shulde be	
	For Kyng Thoas to Troye the cité	
	And Thoas shulde to Grekis home ageyn,	
3670	Only be eschaunge, as ye han herde me seyn,	*exchange*
	Oon for another, as it accorded was.	
	And in this while the byshope, he, Calchas,	
	Remembrid hym on his doughter dere	
	Callid Cryseide, with hir eyen clere,	
3675	Whom in Troye he had lefte behynde	
	Whanne he wente, as the boke makith mynde:	
	For whom he felte passingly gret smert,	*grief*
	So tendirly she was set at his herte	
	And enprentid, bothe at eve and morwe.	
3680	And chefe cause and grounde of al his sorwe	
	Was that she lefte behynde hym in the toun	*was left*
	Withoute comforte or consolacioun,	
	As he caste, sothly in his absence	
	And specially for his grete offence	
3685	That he hath wrought ayens hem of Troye;	*against*
	And as hym thought, he never shulde han joye	
	Til he his doughter recurid hath ageyn.	*recovered*

Wherfore Calchas, the story seith certeyn,

In his wittes many weies caste — *mind*

3690 Howe that he myght, while the trew doth laste,

Recure his doughter by som maner way; — *Regain*

And as I fynde, upon a certeyn day

In his porte wonder humblely, — *appearance*

With wepynge eye, wente pitously

3695 In compleynynge, of teris al bereyned, — *lamenting; wet*

(Whos inwarde wo sothly was nat feined);

And on his knees anoon he falleth doun

Tofore the grete Kyng Agamenoun, — *Before*

Besechynge hym with al humilité,

3700 Of verray mercy and of highe pité,

With other kynges sittinge in the place,

To have routhe, and for to don hym grace,

And on his wo to have compassioun,

That he may have restitucioun — *return*

3705 Of his doughter whom he loved so,

Preyinge hem alle her dever for to do, — *to do their best*

That thorugh her prudent medyacioun

For Antenor that was in her prisoun

With Kyng Thoas she myght eschaunged be,

3710 Yif that hem liste of her benignyté — *If; kindness*

To his requeste goodly to assente.

And thei him graunte; and forthe anoon thei sente

To Kyng Priam for to have Cryseide

For Calchas sake; and therwithal thei leide

3715 The charge for hir wonder specially — *duty*

On hem that wente for this enbassatrie — *embassy*

To Troye toun and to Kyng Priamus,

To whom Calchas was so odyous,

So hateful eke thorughoute al the toun

3720 That this reporte was of him up and doun:

That he a traytour was and also false,

Worthi to ben enhonged be the halse — *neck*

For his tresoun and his doublenes. — *duplicity*

And, overmore, thei seiden eke expresse

3725 That he disserved hath be right of lawe

Shamfully firste for to be drawe — *drawn*

174

And afterward the most orrible deth — *horrible*
That he may have, to yelden up the breth
Liche a treytour in as dispitous wyse — *pitiless*
3730 As any herte can thenke or devyse,
Everyche affermynge as by jugement
That deth was noon ffully equipolent — *equivalent*
To his deserte nor to his falsenes, — *appropriate punishment*
As yonge and olde pleinly bar witnes,
3735 Concludynge eke for his iniquité
That thei wolde assent in no degré
Unto nothinge that myght his herte plese
Nor of Cryseide, for to don hym ese,
Thei caste nat to make delyveraunce —
3740 Lever thei hadden to yeve hym meschaunce, — *They would prefer; disaster*
Yif thei hym myght have at goode large. — *at liberty*
But finally th'effecte of al this charge — *effort*
Is so ferforthe dryven to the ende
That Priamus hath graunted sche shal wende
3745 With Kyng Thoas — shortly, ther is no more —
Unto hir fader for Daungh Anthenor: — *Lord*
Whoevere gruche, the Kyng in parlament
Hath theruppon yove jugement — *given*
So outterly it may nat be repellid; — *completely; rescinded*
3750 For with his worde the sentence was asselid — *confirmed*
That she mot parte with hir eyen glade. — *must; bright*
And of the sorwe pleinly that she made
At hir departynge heraftir ye shal here,
Whan it ageyn cometh to my matere.
3755 The trew affermyd, as ye han herd devise,
On outher side of hem that wer ful wyse
And ful assentid of hem everychon
Til thre monthes come be and goon,
Liche as I rede, on a certeyn day,
3760 Whan agreable was the morwe gray,
Blaundisshinge and plesant of delit,
Hector in herte caughte an appetite
(Like as Guydo liketh for to write)
The same day Grekis to vesite
3765 Ful wel beseyn and wounder richely — *good looking*

    With many worthi in his company,

    Of swiche as he for the nonys ches.   *such; occasion chose*

    And to the tent first of Achilles,

    I fynde, in soth this worthi Troyan knyght

3770 Upon his stede toke the weie right,

    Ful liche a man, as made is mencioun.

    Now hadde Achilles gret affeccioun

    In his herte bothe day and nyght

    Of worthi Hector for to han a sight:

3775 For never his lyve by non occasioun

    He myght of hym han non inspeccioun

    Nor hym beholde at good liberté;

    For unarmyd he myght him never se.

    But wonder knyghtly bothe in port and chere   *bearing and mood*

3780 Thei had hem bothe as thei mette in fere   *together*

    And right manly in her countenaunce,

    And at the laste thei fille in dalyaunce.   *conversation*

    But Achilles firste began abreide   *cry out*

    And unto hym evene thus he seide.

3785 "Hector," quod he, "ful plesynge is to me

    That I at leiser nakid may the se,   *without armor*

    Sith I of the nevere myght have sight   *thee*

    But whan thou were armyd as a knyght;

    And now to me it schal be ful grevous,

3790 Whiche am to the so inly envious,   *you*

    But thou of me — ther is no more to seyne —

    Be slaie anon with myn hondis tweyne:

    For this in soth wer hoolly my plesaunce,

    By cruel deth to take on the vengaunce;

3795 For I ful ofte in werre and eke in fight

    Have felt the vertu and the grete myght

    Of thi force thorugh many woundis kene,

    That upon me be ful fresche and grene

    In many place be shedynge of my blood.

3800 Thou were on me so furious and wood,   *mad*

    Ay compassynge to my distruccioun: *contriving*

    For many a mail of myn haberion   *habergeon (shirt of mail)*

    Thi sharpe swerd racid hathe asonder   *cut*

    And cruelly severed here and yonder,

176

3805	And mortally, as I can signes shewe,	
	My platis stronge percid and ihewe;	*cut*
	And myn harneis, forgid bright of stele,	*armor*
	Might nevere assured ben so wele,	
	In thin ire whan thou liste to smyte,	*wished*
3810	That thi swerd wolde kerve and bite	
	Into my fleshe ful depe and ful profounde,	
	As shewith yit be many mortal wounde	
	On my body, large, longe, and wyde	
	That yit appere uppon every syde	
3815	And day be day ful sore ake and smerte.	
	For whiche thing me semeth that myn herte	
	Enbolleth newe, now whan I the se,	*Swells*
	Of highe dispit avengid for to be —	
	So am I fret of envious rage	*consumed*
3820	That it may never in my brest aswage	*diminish*
	Til the vengaunce and the fatal sut	*pursuit*
	Of cruel deth be on the execut.	*performed*
	And of o thing moste is my grevaunce,	
	Whan I have fully remembraunce	
3825	And in my mynde considre up and doun —	
	How thou madist a divisioun	
	Of me, allas, and of Patroclus,	
	So yonge, so manly, and so vertuous.	
	Whom I loved, as it was skyl and right,	*reasonable and just*
3830	Right as mysilf with al my ful myght,	
	With as hol herte and inly kyndenes	*affection*
	As any tonge may tellen or expres.	
	Now hast thou made a departisioun	*separation*
	Of us that werne by hool affeccioun	
3835	Iknet in oon of hertly allyaunce,	*Joined*
	Withoute partynge or disseveraunce —	*separation*
	So outterly oure feithful hertis tweyen	*absolutely*
	Ilacid werne and lokkid in o cheyne,	*Fastened together*
	Whiche myghte nat for noon adversité	
3840	Of lyf nor deth assonder twynned be,	*severed*
	Til cruelly thou madest us departe,	
	Whiche thorugh myn hert so inwardly darte	*pierce*
	That it wil never in soth out of my thought.	

	And trust wel, ful dere it shal be bought	
3845	The deth of hym and be no thing in were,	*do not doubt it*
	Paraventure or endid be this yere:	*before*
	For upon the only for his sake	
	Of cruel deth vengaunce shal be take,	
	I the ensure, withouten other bond;	*assure*
3850	Yif I may lyve, with myn owne hond	*If*
	I shal of deth don execucioun,	
	Withoute abood or long dylacioun.	*waiting*
	For right requereth withouten any drede	
	Deth for deth for his final mede;	*reward*
3855	For I mysilfe theron shal be wroke,	*avenged*
	That thorugh the world herafter shal be spoke	
	How Achilles was vengid of his foo	
	For Patroclus that he loved so.	
	And though that I be to the envious	*you ill willed*
3860	And of thi deth inly desirous,	
	Ne wyte me nat, ne put on me no blame;	*reproach*
	For wel I wote thou arte to me the same,	*know*
	And haste my deth many day desyred,	
	And therupon inwardly conspired:	
3865	And thus shortly, as atwen us two,	
	Ther is but deth withoute wordis mo;	
	Whan Fortune hath the tyme shape,	
	I hope fully thou shalt nat eskape —	
	Truste noon other, I seie the outterly."	
3870	To whom Hector nat to hastely	
	Answerid ageyn with sobre countenaunce,	
	Avised wel in al his daliaunce,	*Considered*
	As he that was in no thing rekeles;	*in no way*
	And evene thus he spake to Achilles:	
3875	"Sir Achilles, withouten any faille	
	Thou aughtest nat in herte to mervaille	
	Though with my power and my fulle myght,	
	With herte and wylle, of verray due right	
	Day be day I thi deth conspire,	
3880	And ever in oon compasse it and desire,	*contrive*
	And do my labour erly and eke late	
	To pursue it by ful cruel hate.	

Thou oughteste nat to wondren in no wyse	
But fully knowe, by sentence of the wise,	
3885 In no maner, whoso taketh hede,	
Of rightwysnes it may nat procede	
That outher I or any other wight	*person*
Shulde hym love that with al his myght	*who*
My deth pursuweth and destruccioun,	
3890 And over this, to more confusioun,	*destruction*
Hath leide a sege aboute this cité	
On my kynrede and also uppon me,	
And therupon felly doth preswme	*cruelly*
With mortal hate of werre to conswme	
3895 Us everychon. Iwis, I can nat fynde	
In myn herte, as by lawe of kynde,	*nature*
Swiche on to love of right nor equité	
Nor have hym chere sothly in no degré:	*love*
For of werre may no frendlyhede	
3900 Nor of debate love aright procede;	*strife*
For sothly love moste in special	
Of feithfulnes hath his original,	*source*
In hertis joyned by convenience	
Of oon accorde, whom no difference	*Of one accord*
3905 Of doubilnes may in no degré,	*duplicity*
Nouther in joye nor adversité,	
For lyf nor deth assounder nor dissevere;	*sunder*
For where love is, it contuneth evere;	*continues*
But of hate al is the contrarie.	
3910 Of whiche sothly from hertis whan thei varie,	
Procedeth rancour, at eye as men may se,	*as men may plainly see*
Debat, envye, strife, and enmyté,	
Mortal slaughter, bothe nyghe and ferre,	
Moder of whiche in sothfastnes is werre,	
3915 The fyn wherof, longe or it be do,	*result; long before it is gone*
Severith hertis, and frendship kut atwo,	
And causeth love to be leide ful lowe.	
But for al this, I wil wel that thou knowe	
Thi proude wordis, in herte nor in thought,	
3920 In verray soth agaste me right nought;	*frighten*
And yif I schal ferthermore outebreke	*break out [into speech]*

179

Withoute avaunte the trouthe for to speke,   *boast*
I seie the pleinly, hennes or two yere,
Yif I may live in this werris here
3925   And my swerde of knyghthod forthe acheve,
I hope in soth so mortally to greve   *harm*
The Grekis alle, whan I with hem mete,
That thei and thou shul fele ful unswete,   *feel*
Yif ye contynewe and the werris haunt: *pursue*
3930   I shal your pride and surquedie adaunte   *arrogance subdue*
In swiche a wyse with myn hondis two
That, or the werre fully be al do,   *all done*
Ful many Greke sore shal it rewe.
For wel I wote of olde and nat of newe
3935   That ye Grekis gadred here in on   *together*
Of surquedie are fonned everychon,   *infatuated*
Only for want of discresioun
To undirtaken of presumpcioun
So highe a thing — a sege for to leyn —   *seige*
3940   And youresilfe to overcharge in veyn   *overburden*
With emprises whiche, withouten fable,   *lie*
Bene of weight to you inportable,   *too heavy*
And the peis of so gret hevynes   *burden*
That finally it wil you alle oppres   *bear down*
3945   And youre pride avalen and encline,   *send downwards; overthrow*
The berthen eke enbowe bak and chyne   *bend down*
And unwarly cause you to falle   *suddenly*
Or ye have done, I seie to oon and alle.
And, overmore, be ful in sureté —
3950   Thou, Achilles, I speke unto the —
That fatal deth first schal the assaille
Toforn thi swerde in anything availle
Ageynes me for al thi worthines.
And yif so be that so gret hardines,
3955   Corage of wil, vigour, force, or myght
Meven thin herte be manhod as a knyght
To take on the, as in dorynge do,   *desperate courage*
For to darreyne here betwene us two   *settle by combat*
Thilke quarel, howso that befalle,
3960   For the whiche that we striven alle,

I wil assent pleinly to juparte   *risk*
Til that the deth oon of us departe.
Ther is no more but that thes lordis here,
Kynges, princes wil accorde ifere   *together*
3965   That it be do fully be oon assent
And holde stable of herte and of entent,
Within a felde only that we tweyne,
As I have seide, this quarel may dareyne   *settle by combat*
And it finyshe, be this condicioun:
3970   That yif it hap thorugh thin highe renoun
Me to venquyshe or putten at outraunce,   *bring to ruin*
I wil you maken fully assuraunce
That firste my lord, Priamus the Kyng,
Shal unto Grekis in al maner thing,
3975   With septre and crowne, holly him submitte
And in a point varie nouther flitte,   *nor waver*
Fully to yelde to youre subjectioun
Al his lordshipe withinne Troye toun;
And his legis in captivité   *liege lords*
3980   Shal goon her weye oute of this cité
And leve it quit in youre governaunce,   *clear*
Withoute strif or any variaunce.
And hereupon to maken sureté,
To devoyde al ambiguyté   *do away with*
3985   Tofore the goddis be othe and sacramente
We shal be swore in ful good entent;   *sworn*
And, overmore, oure feith also to save,
To assure you in plegge ye shal have   *pledge*
The menewhile to kepe hem on your syde
3990   At youre chois hostagis to abide
From Troye toun, of the worthieste   *noblest*
That ye liste chese and also of the beste,   *please*
So that ye shal of no thing be in were   *in no way; doubt*
Of al that evere that I seie you here.
3995   And, Achilles, withoute wordes mo,
Yif that thou liste accorde ful therto
That I have seide, thin honour to encrese,
To make this werre sodeinly to sese
That likly is for to laste longe

181

4000	Betwene Troyens and the Grekis stronge,	
	Thou shalt nat only with honour and with fame	
	Thorughoute the world getyn the a name	
	But therwithal — and that is nat a lyte —	*little*
	Thorugh thi knyghthod to many man profite	
4005	That fro the deth shal eskape alyve	
	And to his contré hol and sounde aryve	
	That likly arn by cruel aventure	
	For to be ded, yif the werre endure.	
	Come of, therfor, and late nat be proloigned,	
4010	But lat the day atwen us two be joyned,	*agreed on*
	As I have seide, in condicioun,	
	Yif in diffence only of this toun	
	I have victorie by fortune on the,	
	I axe nat but anoon that ye	*immediately*
4015	Breke up sege, and the werre lete,	*end*
	And suffreth us to lyven in quiete,	
	Into Grece hom whan ye ar goon."	
	To the whiche thing Achilles anon,	
	Hoot in his ire and furious also,	
4020	Brennynge ful hote for anger and for wo,	
	Assentid is with a dispitous chere;	*pitiless*
	And gan anoon to Hector dresse him nere;	*turn to*
	And seide he wolde delyvere him outterly	*commit himself*
	Fro poynt to point his axyng by and by;	
4025	And therin made noon excepcioun,	
	But of hool herte and entencioun	
	His requeste accepted everydel,	
	And, as it sempte, liked it right wel.	*seemed*
	And for his parte, he caste a glove doun	
4030	In signe and tokene of confirmacioun	
	For lyfe or deth that he wil holde his day	
	Ageyn Hector, hap what happe may,	*whatever may happen*
	Unto the whiche Hector lifly sterte	*quickly leapt*
	And toke it up with as glad an herte	
4035	As evere dide yit man or knyght	
	That quarel toke with his foo to fight.	
	Ther can no man in soth aright devyse	*describe*
	How glad he was of this highe emprise,	*undertaking*

182

Of whiche the noise and the grete soun
4040 Ran to the eris of Agamenoun;
And he anoon cam doun to her tent
With alle the lordis of his parlement
Where Achilles and Hector wern ifere,   *together*
To wit her wille as in this matere: *know*
4045 Wher thei wolden assenten finally
To putte the quarel ful in juparty   *hazard*
Of outher part atwene these knyghtes tweyne,
As ye han herde, it fully to darayne.   *settle by single combat*
And with o vois Grekis it denye
4050 And seide thei nolde of swiche a companie   *would not*
Of kynges, dukis, and lordis eke also
Bothe life and deth juparten atwene two
Nor to the course of Fortune hem submitte,
That can hir face alday chaunge and flitte.   *turn*
4055 And some of Troye, in conclusioun,
Juparte nolde her lyves nor her toun,
In the hondis only of a knyght   *of a single knight*
To putten al in aventure of fight,
Priam except, whiche sothly in this caas
4060 Within hymsilf fully assentid was
Pleinly to have put and set in juparté
Holy the honour of his regalye,   *Entirely; kingship*
Supposynge ay, as maked is memorie,
That Hector shuld have had the victorie
4065 Of this emprise, yif it he toke on honde.   *undertook*
But for Priam myghte nat withstonde
Ageyn so many of oon entencioun
That were contrarie to his oppinioun,
Bothe of Grekis and on Troye side,
4070 He helde his pes and lete it overeslyde.   *pass*
And so the Grekis parted ben echon;
And Hector is from Achilles goon
Home to Troye, where I him leve a while,
Whiles that I directe shal my stile   *writing instrument*
4075 To telle of Troylus the lamentable wo,
Whiche that he made to parte his lady fro.   *because he had to part from*
    Allas, Fortune, gery and unstable   *fickle*

And redy ay to be chaungable
Whan men most triste in thi stormy face,   *trust*
4080   Liche her desire the fully to embrace,
Thanne is thi joye aweye to turne and wrythe,   *draw away*
Upon wrechis thi power for to kithe.   *show*
Record on Troylus that fro thi whele so lowe   *Remember; wheel*
By fals envie thou hast overthrowe,
4085   Oute of the joye which that he was inne,
From his lady to make him for to twynne   *separate*
Whan he best wende for to have be surid.   *thought; pledged*
And of the wo that he hath endured
I muste now helpe hym to compleyne,   *lament*
4090   Whiche at his herte felt so gret a peyne,
So inward wo, and so gret distresse,
More than I have konnynge to expresse;   *ability*
Whan he knew the partynge of Cryseide,
Almoste for wo and for peyne he deyde
4095   And fully wiste she departe shal   *knew*
By sentence and jugement fynal
Of his fader, yove in parlement.   *given*
For whiche with wo and torment al torent,   *torn up*
He was in point to have falle in rage,   *ready to go mad*
4100   That no man myght apese nor aswage   *ease; soothe*
The hidde peynes which in his breste gan dare: *hidden; lurk*
For lik a man in furie he gan fare   *behaved*
And swiche sorwe day and nyght to make,
In compleyninge only for hir sake.
4105   For whan he sawe that she schulde aweie,
He lever had pleinly for to deye   *preferred; die*
Than to lyve behynde in hir absence:
For hym thought, withouten hir presence
He nas but ded — ther is no more to seine.   *was nothing except; say*
4110   And into terys he began to reyne,   *weep*
With whiche his eyen gonne for to bolle,   *swell*
And in his breste the sighes up to swolle
And the sobbyng of his sorwes depe,
That he ne can nat but rore and wepe,   *cry*
4115   So sore love his herte gan constreyne;   *distress*
And she ne felt nat a litel peyne,

But wepte also, and pitously gan crye,
Desyring ay that she myghte dye
Rather than parte from hym oute of Troye,
4120 Hir owne knyght, hir lust, hir lives joye,
That be hir chekis the teris doun distille, *trickle*
And fro hir eyen the rounde dropis trille, *flow*
And al fordewed han hir blake wede; *wetted through; clothes*
And eke untressid hir her abrod gan sprede, *her hair*
4125 Like to gold wyr, forrent and al totorn, *torn*
Iplukked of, and nat with sheris shorn. *Pulled out; shears*
And over this, hir freshe rosen hewe,
Whilom ymeint with white lilies newe, *mixed*
With woful wepyng pitously disteyned, *discolored*
4130 And like herbis in April al bereyned *bedewed*
Or floures freshe with the dewes swete,
Right so hir chekis moiste wern and wete
With cristal water, up ascendyng highe
Out of her breste into hir hevenly eye;
4135 And ay amonge hir lamentacioun,
Ofte sithe she fil aswone doun, *Many times*
Dedly pale, fordymmed in hir sight, *made dull*
And ofte seide: "Allas, myn owne knyght,
Myn owne Troylus, allas, whi shal we parte?
4140 Rather late Deth with his spere darte *let*
Thorugh myn hert, and the veynes kerve,
And with his rage do me for to sterve. *die*
Rather, allas, than fro my knyght to twynne! *part*
And of this wo, O Deth, that I am inne,
4145 Whi nyl thou come and helpe make an ende?
For how shulde I oute of Troye wende, *go*
He abide, and I to Grekis goon, *go*
Ther to dwelle amonge my cruel foon? *foes*
Allas, allas, I, woful creature,
4150 Howe shulde I ther in the werre endure —
I, wreche woman, but mysilf allone
Amonge the men of armys everychon!"
Thus gan she cryen al the longe day;
This was hir compleint with ful gret affray, *outburst*
4155 Hir pitous noyse, til it drowe to nyght, *approached*

185

That unto hir hir owne trewe knyght,

Ful triste and hevy, cam ageynes eve,   *sad; toward*

Yif he myght hir counforte or releve.

But he in soth hath Cryseide founde

4160 Al in a swowe, lyggynge on the grounde;   *swoon; lying*

And pitously unto hir he wente

With woful chere, and hir in armys hent,   *took*

And toke hir up: and than atwen hem two

Began of new swiche a dedly wo   *such*

4165 That it was routhe and pité for to sene:

For she of cher pale was and grene

And he of colour liche to ashes dede;

And fro hir face was goon al the rede

And in his chekis devoided was the blod,   *emptied*

4170 So wofully atwene hem two it stood.

For she ne myght nat a worde speke,

And he was redy with deth to be wreke   *avenged*

Upon hymsilfe, his nakid swerd beside;

And she ful ofte gan to grounde glide   *slip*

4175 Out of his armys, as she fel aswowne;

And he hymsilf gan in teris drowne.

She was as stille and dowmb as any ston;

He had a mouthe, but wordis had he non;

The weri spirit flikerit in hir breste

4180 And of deth stood under arreste,   *in custody*

Withoute meinpris sothly as of lyf.   *ransom*

And thus ther was, as it sempte, a strif,   *seemed*

Whiche of hem two shulde firste pace;   *pass away*

For deth portreied in her outher face

4185 With swiche colour as men go to her grave.

And thus in wo thei gan togidre rave,   *talk wildly*

Disconsolat, al the longe nyght,

That in gode feith, yif I shulde aright

The processe hool of here bother sorwe   *course; both their sorrows*

4190 That thei made til the nexte morwe,

Fro point to point it to specefie,   *relate in detail*

It wolde me ful longe occupie

Of everythinge to make mencioun,

And tarie me in my translacioun,   *delay*

4195	Yif I shulde in her wo procede.	
	But me semeth that it is no nede,	
	Sith my maister Chaucer heraforn	*Since*
	In this mater so wel hath hym born	
	In his *Boke of Troylus and Cryseyde*	
4200	Whiche he made longe or that he deyde,	
	Rehersinge firste how Troilus was contrarie	*unwilling*
	For to assendyn up on Lovis steire,	
	And how that he, for al his surquedie,	*pride*
	After becam oon of the companye	
4205	Of Lovis folke for al his olde game,	
	Whan Cupide maked hym ful tame	
	And brought him lowe to his subjeccioun	
	In a temple as he walked up and doun,	
	Whan he his ginnes and his hokis leide	*traps*
4210	Amyd the eyen cerclid of Cryseyde,	*round eyes*
	Whiche on that day he myghte nat asterte:	*escape*
	For thorugh his brest percid and his herte,	
	He wente hym home, pale, sike, and wan.	
	And in this wise Troylus first began	
4215	To be a servaunt, my maister telleth thus,	
	Til he was holpe aftir of Pandarus,	*helped*
	Thorugh whos comforte and mediacioun	
	(As in his boke is maked mencioun)	
	With gret labour firste he cam to grace	
4220	And so contuneth by certeyn yeris space,	*continues*
	Til Fortune gan upon hym frowne,	
	That she from hym must goon oute of towne	
	Al sodeynly and never hym after se.	
	Lo, here the fyn of false felicité!	
4225	Lo, here the ende of worldly brotilnes,	
	Of fleshly lust! Lo, here th'unstabilnes!	
	Lo, here the double variacioun	
	Of wordly blisse and transmutacioun —	*worldly*
	This day in myrthe and in wo tomorwe —	
4230	For ay the fyn, allas, of joie is sorwe!	
	For now Cryseide with the Kyng Thoas	
	For Anthenor shal go forthe, allas,	
	Unto Grekis and ever with hem dwelle.	

	The hoole story Chaucer kan yow telle,	
4235	Yif that ye liste — no man bet alyve —	*no better man is alive*
	Nor the processe halfe so wel discryve.	*course of events*
	For he owre Englishe gilte with his sawes,	*gilded; tales*
	Rude and boistous firste be olde dawes,	*Unpolished; rough; days*
	That was ful fer from al perfeccioun	
4240	And but of litel reputacioun,	
	Til that he cam and thorugh his poetrie	
	Gan oure tonge firste to magnifie	*make greater in importance*
	And adourne it with his elloquence:	
	To whom honour, laude, and reverence	
4245	Thorughoute this londe yove be and songe,	*given; sung*
	So that the laurer of oure Englishe tonge	*laurel*
	Be to hym yove for his excellence,	*given*
	Right as whilom by ful highe sentence,	*meaning*
	Perpetuelly for a memorial,	
4250	Of Columpna by the cardynal	
	To Petrak Fraunceis was yoven in Ytaille —	
	That the report nevere after faille	*reputation; lack*
	Nor the honour dirked of his name,	
	To be registred in the house of fame	
4255	Amonge other in the higheste sete,	
	My maister Galfride, as for chefe poete	*Geoffrey*
	That evere was yit in oure langage,	
	The name of whom shal passen in noon age	
	But ever ylyche withoute eclipsinge shyne.	
4260	And for my part, I wil never fyne,	*end*
	So as I can, hym to magnifie	*glorify*
	In my writynge pleinly til I dye;	
	And God, I praye, his soule bring in joie.	
	And where I lefte I wil ageyn of Troie	
4265	The story telle and first how that Guydo	
	Within his boke speketh Troylus to,	
	Rebukyng hym ful uncurtesly	
	That he so sette his herte folili	
	Upon Cryseide, ful of doubilnes:	*duplicity*
4270	For in his boke as Guydo list expresse	
	That hir teris and hir compleynynge,	
	Hir wordis white, softe, and blaundyshynge,	

	Wer meynt with feynyng and with flaterie	*mixed*
	And outward farsed with many a fals lye;	*seen from the outside stuffed*
4275	For under hid was al the variaunce,	
	Cured above with feyned contenaunce,	*Concealed; appearance*
	As wommen kan falsly teris borwe —	*borrow*
	In her herte though ther be no sorwe —	
	Lik as thei wolde of verray trouthe deie.	
4280	Thei can think oon and another seie,	
	As a serpent under floures faire	
	His venym hydeth, where he doth repaire —	*return*
	The sugre aforn, the galle hid behynde,	
	As approprid is unto hir kynde	
4285	To be dyvers and double of nature,	
	Rathest deceyvynge whan men most assure.	*Soonest; pledge their troth*
	For under colour everything thei wirke,	
	The faire above, the foule in the dirke	
	Thei hide so, that no man may espie;	
4290	And though so be that with a woful eye	
	Thei can outward wepyn pitously,	
	The tother eye can laughe covertly —	*secretly*
	Whos sorwes alle are temprid with allaies.	*alloys*
	And her colour is meynt ever with raies;	*mixed; streaks*
4295	For upon chaunge and mutabilité	
	Stant hool her trust and her sureté,	
	So that thei ben sure in doubilnes	
	And alwey double in her sikernes,	
	Semynge oon whan thei best can varie,	
4300	Likest to acorde whan thei be contrarie;	
	And thus thei ben variaunte in acorde,	
	And holest seme whan ther is discord.	
	And Guydo seith how ther are fewe or noon	
	That in her herte apaied is with oon;	*satisfied*
4305	And yit thei can, be it to oon or tweyne,	
	To thre or foure, in her speche feyne	
	Like as thei wern to oon and to no moo	
	Hool in her love, for wele and eke for wo,	
	That everyche shal of hymsilfe deme	*think*
4310	That he be next, lik as it doth seme.	
	And thus in hope stant eche of hem alle,	

189

The trewest ay redyest to falle;
Who serveth best, nexte to ben appaired: *injured*
And thus in chaunge al her love is feired.   *involved*
4315 Farwel tomorwe, though it be sure today;
Lat no man trust but cache whan he may;
The faire of chaunge lasteth over yere,   *market; long*
But it is foly for to byen to dere   *buy*
Thilke tresour, whiche harde is to possede
4320 But fleeth aweye whan men therof most nede.
And yif it hap that no chapman be   *merchant*
(As seith Guydo), yit al day men may se
It shewed oute at large fenestrallis,   *windows*
On chaumbres highe, and lowe doun in hallis,
4325 And in wyndowes eke in every strete;
And also eke men may with hem mete
At pilgrymages and oblaciounes,   *offerings*
At spectacles in cytés and in townys
(As seith Guydo), and al is for to selle:
4330 But after hym I can no ferther telle.
And eke he seith in his sentament   *judgment*
Ther is no fraude fully equipollent   *equivalent*
To the fraude and sleighty compassyng   *contriving*
Of a womman nor like in worchynge:
4335 For who that set al his feithfulnes,
Wenynge in hem to fynde stabilnes,   *Thinking*
He shal hem fynde stedefaste as the mone,   *moon*
That is in point for to chaunge sone.
Yif he be yonge, thei cast hym in a rage;   *frenzy*
4340 Yif he be olde, he falleth in dotage;   *feebleness of mind*
"Wherfore, my counseil is to bothe two:
Cast of the bridel, and lightly lete hem go."   *off*
Thus techeth Guydo, God wot, and not I,   *knows*
That hath delyt to speke cursidly
4345 Alwey of wommen thoroughout al his bok,
As men may se, whoso list to loke.
To hem he had envie in special,   *hatred*
That in good feith I am right wrothe with al   *angry*
That he with hem list so to debate;   *wished; quarrel*
4350 For ire of whiche, the Latyn to translate

	Inwardly myn herte I felte blede,	
	Of highe dispit his clausis for to rede	*sentences*
	That resownede, in conclusioun,	
	Only of malys to accusacioun	
4355	Of this women — ful evel mote he thrive —	*let him have bad fortune*
	So generally her secte to discryve,	*describe*
	Whiche made nat, thorugh indiscrecioun,	
	Of good nor badde noon excepcioun.	
	He was to blame — foule mote hym falle —	*befall*
4360	For cause of oon for to hindren alle:	*slander*
	For I dar wel affermen by the rode	*cross*
	Ageyn oon badde ben an hundrid gode;	
	And though som oon double be and newe,	
	It hindreth nat to hem that be trewe.	*disparages*
4365	And be exaumple, also, though he shewe	
	That som oon whilom was a shrewe,	*scoundrel*
	Thei that be gode take shal noon hede,	
	For it noon hindrynge is to wommanhede,	
	Though two or thre can be double and feyne:	*be duplicitous*
4370	For ther ageyn sothly at Coleyne	
	Of virgines, inly ful of grace,	
	Ellevene thousand in that holy place	
	A man may fynde and in oure kalendere	
	Ful many maide parfit and entere,	
4375	Whiche to the deth stable wern and trewe.	
	For somme of hem with the rosen hew	
	Of martirdom the blisse of hevene wonne;	
	And somme also, as bokis telle konne,	*can*
	With the lillye of virginité	
4380	And violettis of parfit chastité,	
	Ascendid ben above the sterris clere	
	And the cercle of the nynthe spere,	*(see note)*
	Where joie is evere and gladnes eterne.	
	Wherefor in soth, as I can discerne,	*recognize*
4385	Though som clerkis of shrewis have myssaid,	*scoundrels; slandered*
	Lat no good womman therof be myspaid:	*displeased*
	For lak of oon, alle are nought to blame,	*failing in one*
	And eke of men may be seide the same.	
	For to the trewe it is no reprefe,	

4390	Though it so be another be a thefe;	
	For what is he the werse in his degré,	
	Though the tother be honged on a tre?	
	Nor unto wommen hindring is it noon,	*harm*
	Among an hundrid though that ther be oon	
4395	Of governaunce that be vicious.	*wicked*
	For ther ageyn a thousand vertuous,	
	Yif that ye liste, lightly ye may fynde.	
	And though Guydo writ thei han of kynde	*naturally*
	To be double, men shulde it goodly take	
4400	And ther ageyn no maner grucching make:	*complaining*
	Nature in werkynge hath ful gret power,	
	And it wer harde for any that is here	
	The cours of hir to holden or restreyne,	
	For she wil nat be guyed be no reyne,	*guided; rein*
4405	To be coarted of hir due right.	*restrained from*
	Therfore, eche man with al his fulle myght	
	Shulde thanke God and take paciently;	
	For yif wommen be double naturelly,	
	Why shulde men leyn on hem the blame?	
4410	For though myn auctor hindre so her name	*reprove*
	In his writinge, only of Cryseide,	
	And upon hir swiche a blame leide,	
	My counseil is, lightly overpasse	
	Wher he mysseith of hir in any place —	*slanders*
4415	To hindre wommen outher eve or morwe.	
	Taketh noon hede, but late him be with sorwe,	
	And skippeth over wher ye list nat rede,	
	Til ye come where that Dyomede	
	For hir was sent into Troye toun,	
4420	Where ceriously is maked mencioun	*in due order*
	First how that she to hym delyvered was	
	For Anthenor and the Kyng Thoas;	
	And how Troilus gan hir to conveie	
	With many other to bringe hir on the weie;	
4425	And after this how that Dyomede	
	By the weie gan hir bridel lede	
	Til he hir brought to hir fadres tent;	
	And how that Calchas in ful good entent	

	Received hir, logged ther he lay,	*lodged*
4430	And of hir speche duryng al that day,	
	And al the maner hool and everydel.	
	Al is rehersid ceriously and wel	*recounted point by point*
	In *Troylus Boke*, as ye han herd me seyn;	
	To write it efte, I holde it wer but veyn.	*again*
4435	But Guydo seith, longe or it was nyght	*before*
	How Cryseyde forsoke hir owne knyght	
	And yaf hir herte unto Dyomede	*gave*
	Of tendirnes and of wommanhede,	
	That Troilus wexe in hir herte as colde,	*grew*
4440	Withoute fire as ben these asshes olde.	
	I can noon other excusacioun	*know; excuse*
	But only Kyndes transmutacioun,	*(see note)*
	That is appropred unto hir nature,	
	Selde or never stable to endure,	
4445	Be experience as men may ofte lere.	
	But now ageyn unto my matere	
	I mut resort, though that I be ferre,	*must*
	As I began to writen of the werre.	*war*

[*After the truce, Hector leads the Trojans out to battle. He is wounded in the face, and the Trojans are thrown back before the walls of Troy, where Hector sees Helen, Hecuba, Polyxena, and the other women watching the battle. Fearing shame before them, he rallies the Trojans, cuts King Merion in two (he has earlier killed him by cutting his head off), and nearly kills Achilles. During the battle, Diomede captures Troilus's horse, which he sends to Criseyde as a gift. Criseyde says she cannot refuse a gift from someone kind and generous to her in a strange place. Later Polydamas unhorses Diomede and takes his mount to Troilus, who has been fighting on foot and is bathed in Greeks' blood. Hector again nearly kills Achilles. After this the battle rages for thirty days, during which the Greeks suffer many loses, six of Priam's natural sons are killed, and Hector is wounded. Priam asks for a six months' truce. He prepares the burial of his sons, and Hector recovers from his wounds. Diomede meanwhile has fallen in love with Criseyde (lines 4449–4819).*]

4820	And al that tyme sike laie Diomede,	*sick*
	With Lovys dart woundid to the herte,	
	As he that felt inwardly gret smerte	*pain*
	Of woful sighes, wiche in his brest abraide	*rise*
	Ful ofte a day for love of Cryseyde;	

193

4825   For he was shake with a fevere newe
       That causid him to be ful pale of hewe
       And to wexe bothe megre and lene;   *grow*
       For pitously he gan hym to abstene
       Fro mete and drinke and from al solace,
4830   As it was sene in his dedly face;
       And ofte a day to hir he wolde pleyne   *lament*
       Of his dissese and his mortal peyne,
       Preiynge of grace that she wolde se
       Upon his wo for to han pité
4835   And of mercy for to taken hede
       Of hir servaunt, only of wommanhede,
       Or pleinly elles — ther is no more to seie —
       For hir sake he seide he wolde deye.
       But konnyngly and in ful sleighty wyse,   *skillfully*
4840   To kepe hym lowe under hir servyse,
       With delaies she hilde hym forthe on honde
       And maked hym in a were to stonde,   *state of uncertainty*
       Ful unsur betwene hope and dispeire.
       And whan that grace shulde have had repeire   *come to him*
4845   To putte hym oute of al hevynes,
       Daunger of newe brought hym in distresse;   *Resistance*
       And with disdeyn to encrese his peine,
       Of double were she brought hym in a treyne,   *uncertainty; trap*
       As wommen kan holde a man ful narwe,
4850   Whan he is hurt with Cupides arwe,
       To sette on hym many fel assaies,   *cruel tests*
       Day be day to putte hym in delaies,
       To stonde unsur betwixe hope and drede,
       Right as Cryseyde lefte Diomede
4855   Of entent to sette hym more afire,
       As this wommen kyndely desyre,
       Whan thei a man have brought in a traunce,
       Unevenly to hange him in balaunce,
       Of hope and drede to lynke hym in a cheyne,
4860   Ay of the fyn unsure of bothe tweyne,   *ending*
       To dryve him forthe yeres hem to serve
       And do no force wher he lyve or sterve: *take no heed whether; die*
       This is the fyn of Lovis fyri rage.

And for she wolde have hym in servage,
4865 She lokkid hym under swiche a keye
That he wot nat wher to lyve or deye;   *did not know*
And in doute thus I lete hym dwelle,
And forthe I wil of the story telle
And to my mater eke resorte ageyn.

[*After the truce ends, fighting renews for twelve days. Because of heat and infection,
however, plague sweeps the Greek camp. Agamemnon must ask for another thirty days' truce,
which Priam immediately grants (lines 4870–88).*]

Whan the moreyn and the woful rage   *plague*
4890 Of pestilence began for to swage   *abate*
And the trews were wered oute and goon,
The Grekis cast to mete with her foon   *planned*
Upon a day in platis armyd clene
Whan Phebus shon with his bemys shene
4895 Ful plesauntly and gan to shede his lyght.
But, as I fynd, toforne the silfe nyght
Andronomecha, the feithful trewe wyf   *Andromache*
Of worthi Hector, hym lovynge as hir lyf,
Be whom he had gete childre two,
4900 Wonder semly, and inly fair also —   *handsome*
And Lamedonte callyd was the ton,   *the one*
So yonge the tother that hit ne myghte goon   *the other*
And Astronanta, I rede, that he hyght,   *was named*
Fetured wel, and passynge fair of sight,
4905 And, as Guydo listeth to endite,   *record*
Of his moder at the pappis white
For verray yong that tyme was soukynge,
And with his armys hir brestis embrasynge.
And she that nyght, as made is mencioun,
4910 Hadde in hir slepe a wonder visioun;
I not in soth what I may it nevene —   *do not know; name*
Outher a dreme or verraily a swevene,
Or fro above a revelacioun,
(As whilom had the Kyng Scipioun)
4915 Or a shewynge, outher an oracle,
Or of goddis a warnyng be myracle.

For in sothnes slepynge as she lay,   *truth*
Hir thoughte pleynly, yif the nexte day
Hector went his fomen for to assaille,   *attack*
4920 As he was wont, armyd in bataille,
That he ne shulde eskapen outterly,
In Fatis hondis to falle finally;   *Fate's*
And, overmore, Antropos shal fyne   *end*
For evermore his lyves threde to twyne   *cut*
4925 And shewe the force of hir felle myght,
Whan the parodie of this worthi knyght   *term of life*
Aprochen shal withouten wordis mo,
Into the feld pleynly yif he go —
Of whiche astonyd, streit and short of breth,   *astonished, winded and*
4930 Wher as she lay, abreid upon the deth,   *frightened*
And with a sighe stinte for to slepe,   *woke up*
And pitously braste oute for to wepe   *burst*
For the constreint of hir hertly sorwe.   *pressure*
And specially on the woful morwe,
4935 Whan that she sawe this stok of worthines,
As he was wont, manfully him dresse   *prepare*
To armyn hym in stele bornyd bright,   *steel burnished*
This Troyan wal, Hector, this worthi knyght,
She can no more but at his fete fil doun,   *fell*
4940 Lowly declarynge hir avisioun,
With quakynge herte of verray wommanhede.
Whereof, God wote, he toke litel hede
But therof hadde indignacioun,
Platly affermyng that no discrecioun   *Plainly*
4945 Was to trest in swiche fantasies   *trust*
In dremys shewid, glady meynt with lyes,   *mixed*
Ful of japis and illusiouns,   *tricks*
Of whiche pleynly the conclusiouns
Be nat ellis but folkis to delude,
4950 Albe it so that this peples rude
Therin somwhile han affeccioun
To juge and deme in her oppinioun
Diversly what thei may pretende,
And ofte falle and happen as thei wende,
4955 And folweth like in conclusioun.

	For drede of whiche the lamentacioun	
	Encrese gan of Andronomecha,	
	And in hir swowe first she cried, "A,"	
	Seiyng, "Allas, myn owne lord so dere,	
4960	Your trewe wif, allas, whi nyl you here,	
	Whiche of so feithful hool affeccioun	
	Desireth ay youre savacioun!"	
	And up she roos deedly of visage;	*deadly pale*
	And like a womman caught with sodein rage	
4965	To Kyng Priam and Eccuba the Quene	*Hecuba*
	In haste she wente, hirsilfe to bemene,	*bemoan*
	And of hir wyfly herte, trewe as stele,	
	Ceriously declarid everydele	*Point by point*
	Hir pitous dreme, whiche thorugh oracle	
4970	To hir only, be devyne myracle,	
	Ishewed was thorugh Goddes purvyaunce;	*Shown; foresight*
	And tolde hem eke the final ordinaunce	
	Of Fortunes fals disposicioun,	
	Fully purveied to destruccioun	
4975	Of hir lord withoute more delay,	
	Into the felde yif he go that day.	
	Wherfore, she preieth with a dedly hewe	
	Unto the kyng of mercy for to rewe,	
	Upon hir wo to have compassioun,	
4980	For to ordeyne by discrecioun	
	Of his lordship and sovereinté	
	That hir lord nat distroyed be	
	Of rekleshede nor of wilfulnes;	
	And with that worde of verray kyndenes,	
4985	In whom was ay so moche love founde,	
	Tofore the quene aswowne fil to grounde	*in a faint*
	And seide, "Allas" with a ful pale chere,	
	"Helpe in this cas, myn owne moder dere,	
	Of wommanhed and routhe doth me grace,	
4990	That my lord into the feld ne pace	*go*
	And doth your dever of moderly pité	*duty*
	Benignely and goodly for to se	
	To his knyghthod and his highe prowes,	
	For to restreyne his renomed noblesse,	

197

4995 Thilke day to handle spere nor shelde,
Nor that he go armyd into the felde."
And bothe tweyne assente for the beste
And condescende unto hir requeste,   *agree*
Finally accordynge into oon
5000 That whan the wardis wer redi everychon   *divisions*
On issinge oute, and Troylus first of alle,
And Paris next, on Grekis for to falle,
And after hym the Troyan Eneas,
Kyng Sarpedoun, and Pollydamas,
5005 Kyng Eroys, and Kyng Epistrophus,
And eke the kyng ycalled Forcius,
In plate and mail everyche armed clene;
And alderlaste cam Kyng Philomene
With alle the kynges and lordes of renoun
5010 That in diffence comen of the toun,
With the Grekis knyghtly to debate.   *contend*
And Priamus sothly to the gate
Conveied hem at her oute goyng,
And sette her wardes, this noble worthi kyng,   *placed their divisions*
5015 Ful prudently thorugh his sapience,
And after yaf hem congé and licence   *gave them permission*
Upon Grekis for to kythe her myght,   *make known their*
Ageynes whom ful redy for to fight
Her fomen wern with royal apparaille
5020 Amyd the feld abidynge the bataille.
But Priamus in this menewhile,
Lyke as Guydo remembrith in his stile,
For thilke fyn that ye han herd me seyn
To worthi Hector repeired is ageyn,   *returned*
5025 Hym contermaundynge that he ne shold gon   *ordering*
Thilke day to fight ageyn her foon.
For whiche thing of highe dispit he brent,   *burned*
Whan that he sawe other lordis went
Oute at the gate and he allone abood;
5030 For whiche he wexe furious and wood,   *grew; mad*
Hooly the cause arrettynge to his wif,   *ascribing*
That was of cherté so tendir over his lyf,
Puttinge on hir fully the occasioun

Of his abidynge that day in the toun,
5035 In prejudise of his worthines   *To the detriment of*
And disencresse of his highe prowes.   *diminution*
And list thorugh tongis to his highe estat,   *lest*
Thorugh fals report it were derogat,   *derogatory*
He caste anoon of a ful knyghtly herte
5040 For lyf nor deth it shuld him nat asterte   *escape*
Withinne the feld that day to be founde,
Though it so wer with many mortal wounde
He shulde on pecis hewe be asoundre,   *cut*
Upon the pleyn dismembrid here and yonder;
5045 So hool in manhod was his herte sette
That he anoon withoute lenger lette   *delay*
Ageyn to arme hym was ful dilligent,
Agein the precepte and commandement
Of his fader, and rood forthe on his weie.
5050 For fer of whiche, as she wolde deie,
His wif of newe crie gan and shoute,
And with hir pappis also hanging oute,
Hir litel childe in hir armys tweyne,
Aforn hir lord gan to wepe and pleyne,
5055 Besechinge hym of routhe and pité,
Yif he nolde to hir sorwe se,
At the leste for hir wifly trouthe
That he of manhod have in herte routhe
Upon hir child and on hir also,
5060 Whiche that she bar in hir armys two,
And nat myght him fro criynge kepe,
Whan he sawe his woful moder wepe.
And knelyng doun, unto hym she seide,
In hir sobbynge as she myght abreide: *burst out*
5065 "Myn owne lorde have mercy now on me
And on this litel child whiche that ye se
So pitously afore you wepe and crye.
Have mercy lord on us or we deye.   *before*
Have mercy eke upon this cyté,   *also*
5070 Myn owne lorde. Have mercy or that we
By cruel deth passe shal echon,
For lak of helpe, allas, whan ye ar goon."

This was the crie of Andronomecha,
With whom was eke hir suster Cassandra,
5075   Eccuba, and faire Polycene,   *Polyxena*
And Eleyne, the lusty freshe quene,   *Helen*
Whiche alle attonys fellen hym beforn,   *at once*
With heer untressid and wepinge al totorn,   *hair*
And loude gan to crien in the place,
5080   Besechinge hym of mercy and of grace
For thilke day to abiden in the toun
And in his herte to have compassioun
On her compleint and her woful mone,   *moan*
Sith al the trust of the toun allone   *Since*
5085   In hym abode and al the resistence:
For ageyn deth he was her chef diffence;   *their*
And in hym hooly was her affiaunce,   *faith*
Her sureté, and her suffisaunce,
In eche thing that hem myghte greve.   *injure*
5090   And yif al this ne myght his herte meve
For to abide, yit of goodlyhede
Thei hym besought to her wommanhede
He wolde enclyne his harded herte of stele, *bend*
That thei myght a litel drope fele
5095   Only of pité on her wo to rewe,
That likly was to moren and renewe   *increase and grow afresh*
Finally to her distruccioun;
For of the cité sothly and the toun
His unhap were endeles ruyne.   *misfortune would be*
5100   But yit al this myght hym nat encline
That he nold oute in conclusioun,   *would not*
So indurat and hertid as lyoun   *obstinate*
He was alweie, contunynge in his rage,
Whos herte myght asofte nor aswage   *soothe*
5105   Nouther praier nor waymentacioun, *lamentation*
Hym to restreyne from his oppinioun:
For every pereil he leide tho aside;   *dismissed*
And on his weie gan anoon to ryde.
Wherthorugh his wif noon other bote can *remedy*
5110   But in hir rage to the kyng she ran,
So amased in hir mortal wo   *confused*

	That she unethe myghte speke hym to,	*scarcely*
	So diffacid and ruful of hir sight	*disfigured; pitiable*
	That by hir hewe knoweth hir no wight;	
5115	For lost she had bothe myght and strengthe,	
	And plat she fil to the grounde alengthe	*flat; prostrate*
	Tofore the kyng, that routhe was to sene,	
	Besechynge hym of entent ful clene	
	Of his grace to consider hir wo:	
5120	For but he help, Hector is ago.	*unless; dead (a goner)*
	And he, seinge hir faithful wommanhede,	
	At hir requeste raught anoon his stede,	*seized*
	And priked after, only for hir sake,	*rode fast*
	In so gret haste that he hath overtake	
5125	Worthi Hector withinne the cyté,	
	And hent his reyne with gret difficulté,	*snatched*
	And maugre hym made him tourne ageyn	*despite*
	In swiche wyse he durst it nat withseyn,	*dared; refuse*
	Albe that he was ful lothe therto;	*Although; unwilling*
5130	So that by force and praier also	
	From his stede he made hym alight,	
	The areste of whom eschewen he ne myght,	*halting; avoid*
	For he ne wolde ageyn his fader strive,	*against*
	Albe that he felte his herte rive	*Although; split*
5135	Of malencolie, and of hertly ire,	
	And of disdeyn newe sette afire.	*scorn*
	So inwardly sterid was his blod	
	That like a tigre or a lyoun wood	*mad*
	That wer deprived newly of his praye,	*prey*
5140	Right so firde he al that ilke day,	*acted*
	Or liche a bore that his tusshes whette,	*tusks sharpened*
	While the Grekis and thei of Troye mette,	
	Furiously walkynge up and doun.	
	And in diffence sothly of the toun,	
5145	Troylus first on his baye stede	
	Of aventure mette Diomede,	*By chance*
	And eche at other, surquedous of pride,	
	With sharpe speris gan togidre ryde;	
	And Guydo seith, withouten any dred,	
5150	Oon or bothe had anoon be ded,	

201

Nadde Menelay knyghtly go betwene.   *Had not*

And after that in a furious tene,   *rage*

He smet his hors in ful knyghtly wyse;

And Meryem, the myghty Kyng of Frise,

5155 Menelaus markid hath ful wel;

And with his swerd, ful sharpe ground of stel,

Unhorsid him and threwe him on the grene;

For he the strok ne myghte nat sustene,

This Menelay was on him so wood   *furiously*

5160 That it was likly, evene ther he stood,

With the lif he shulde nat eskape.

For the Grekis ful hastily hem shape

This Meriem, as ye han herde me seyn,

For to besette rounde aboute the pleyn

5165 And to sese hym by the aventaille   *protective covering for lower face and neck*

On every part and cruelly to assaille,

Al destitut in this dredful cas.

But hym to helpe cam Pollydamas

With his knyghtes and gan to neighen ner   *drew near*

5170 Whan he hym sawe take prisoner;

And maugre alle that uppon hym sette,   *despite*

From her hondis Pollydamas him fette,   *took*

At whos reskus ther was so gret a strif   *rescue*

That many on therfore lost his lyf: *many a one*

5175 For Grekis rather than he shulde eskape

From her hondis in that hasti rape   *seizure*

Caste hem pleynly that he shal be ded,   *planned*

Fully in purpos to have hadde his hed —

He stood of meschef in so gret disjoynt.   *harm; peril*

5180 But hym to helpe evene uppon the point

Cam Troylus in, most knyghtly of aray,

And of his manhod made swiche affray   *wreaked such havoc*

Amongis hem in reskus of this kyng

That maugre hem at his incomyng   *despite*

5185 Delyvered was this worthi lord of Frise

From cruel deth, as ye han herd devyse.

But theruppon cam Thelamonius,

Proude in armys, and evere surquedous   *arrogant*

With thre thousand, ful worthi everychon;

5190	And he unhorseth Pollydamas anoon	
	Among his knyghtes and proudly bar him doun;	
	But Troylus hath thorugh his highe renoun	*valor*
	Mid of his foon get hym his hors ageyn.	*In the middle; foes*
	But thei of Troye so sore were beleyn	*assailed*
5195	On every half thorugh the Grekis pride	*each side*
	That thei ne myght aforn hem nat abide:	
	For newe and newe the hardy Achilles	
	Assailled hem with his Mirmidones	
	That thei compelled of necessité,	
5200	In meschef, wern maked for to fle	*distress*
	Home to the walles and gates of the toun,	
	To gret damage and confusioun	
	Of her party that abak so goon.	
	The whiche thing, whan Margariton	
5205	Behilde and sawe how the game goth,	
	In his herte he gan to wexe wroth	*grow angry*
	And passingly for to have disdeyn;	
	And as the story recordeth in certeyn,	
	That he was bothe hardy and famus	
5210	And sone also unto Kyng Priamus,	
	A noble knyght and of gret worthines.	
	And whan he saw the meschef and distresse	*distress*
	Of hem of Troye and how thei gan to fle,	
	He caste anoon avengid for to be	*thought immediately*
5215	Upon Achilles for al his grete myght,	*despite*
	And ran to hym ful like a manly knyght,	
	On horsebak for the townys sake,	
	And hym enforseth Achilles to take	*strives*
	Amyd the feld amonge his knyghtes alle.	
5220	But Achilles — allas, it shulde falle —	
	That day hym slowe by cruel aventure,	
	Wherthorugh Troyens myghte not endure	
	The felde to hold, but home gan hem hiye,	*hasten*
	And mortally to make noise and crie:	
5225	Firste, for the deth of Margaritoun,	
	And for the pursut that Kyng Thelamon	
	Made on the chaas thorugh his cruelté	*pursuit*
	Home to the gatis of Troye the cité,	

	That slow and kylled alweie as he rood,	*slew*
5230	Albe that Paris manly hym withstood	*Although*
	With his brethre that in baste wer born.	*brothers; illegitimate*
	But for al that, her ground thei have lorn,	*lost*
	Lefte and forsake outterly the felde;	
	And home thei went and broughten on a shelde	
5235	The dede cors of Margariton;	
	And after that her gatis shette anon.	*shut*
	The whiche meschef, as Hector gan behold,	*harm*
	Of verray ire his herte gan to colde,	*to grow cold*
	And seide platly withoute more delay	*plainly*
5240	He wolde avenge his deth the same day,	
	And made in haste his stede to be fet,	*horse; brought*
	And up he stirte, and on his basenet —	*headpiece*
	Unwist the kyng, or who be lefe or loth	*Unbeknownst to; glad*
	(Ther was no geyn) — forthe anon he goth,	*avail*
5245	Til he was passid the gatis of the toun,	
	More furious than tigre or lyoun;	
	At whos comynge, thikke as swarm of ben,	*bees*
	Toforn his swerd Grekis gonne flen —	
	Thai thought it was tyme to withdrawe.	
5250	And first, I fynde how that he hath slawe	
	Two worthi dukes, as he with hem mette,	
	That besy wern his weie for to lette:	*intent; obstruct*
	The ton ycalled was Eurypalus,	*The one was called*
	And the tother highte Hascydyus.	*The other was called*
5255	And so Troyens the feld ageyn han wonne,	
	And of newe manfully begonne	
	Grekis to sue, and folwen on the chaas.	*pursue; chase*
	And yit at meschef Daungh Pollydamas	*distress; Lord*
	The same tyme was of Grekis take;	*by; taken*
5260	But Hector hath so born him for his sake,	
	Where as he sorest was beleyn,	*set upon*
	And thorugh his knyghthod reskued him ageyn,	
	And put the Grekis in so gret distresse	
	Thorugh his manhod and his worthines,	
5265	That whersoevere thilke day he rood,	*that*
	His sharpe swerd he bathed in her blood —	
	He was so cruel and so mercyles.	

But than a knyght called Leothydes
Shope him anon with Hector for to mete,   *contrived*
5270 While he was moste irous in his hete,   *angry in his rage*
And sette on hym ful presumptuously;
But Hector tho, devoyde of al mercy,
Anoon hym slow and threw hym in the feld:
The whiche thing whan Achilles behelde,
5275 The grete slaughter and the woundis wyde
That Hector made uppon every syde,
He gan anon compassen in his herte,   *devise*
And up and doun casten and adverte   *think; consider*
How the Grekis never mow be sure   *might*
5280 Ageyn her foon to fighten or endure
Nor kepe a felde with hem for to stryve,
Al the while that Hector were alyve.
Wherfore, he shope and caste many weie
Be what engyne Hector myghte deye,   *stratagem; die*
5285 At avauntage yif he myght hym fynde;
And therto eke Polycenes of Ynde,
A worthi duke, was also of assent —
Only for he of herte and hool entent   *because*
In hope stood his suster for to wyve,   *wed*
5290 For love of whom he felt his herte ryve.   *split*
And in hir grace better for to stonde,
He caste fully for to take on honde   *decided*
This highe emprise, as I have yow tolde.
But while that he was on him most bold,
5295 Hector hym slow — ther was non other geyn;   *remedy*
The whiche anoon as Achilles hath seyn,   *seen*
For ire he wexe in his herte as wood   *mad*
As boor or tigre in her cruel mood
Upon Hector avenged for to be
5300 And furiously on hym he gan fle.   *fly*
But Hector kaught a darte sharpe grounde,
And threw at hym, and yaf him swiche a wounde
Thorughoute the theighe, upon outher side,   *thigh*
That in the feld he myghte nat abide,
5305 But hym withdrow, and anoon is went
With his men home unto his tent,

And made anoon a surgeyn to bynde
His mortal wounde; and after, as I fynde, *deadly*
Whan he was staunche and cesseth for to blede,
5310 In al haste ageyn he toke his stede:
And liste he were of that wounde ded *lest*
Afterward, as it was grete drede, *fear*
He thoughte first avengid for to be
Upon Hector, yif he myght hym se, *if*
5315 Of hap or sort, yif it wolde falle: *chance*
For hym thoughte, to his peynes alle
It were to hym the beste remedye
Of his honde yif he myghte dye;
For of his lyf he roughte nat a myte, *set no value*
5320 Be so that he Hector myghte quyte *If; repay*
Deth for deth in conclusioun;
For that was hooly his entencioun,
Of his desire fully suffisaunce
By deth unwarly to yeven hym meschaunce. *without warning to give*
5325 But al this tyme, Hector up and doun,
As he was wont, pleieth the lyoun
Amonge Grekis in many sondri place
And with his swerd gan hem so to enchase *pursue*
That as the deth, where thei myght hym sen,
5330 Thei fledde aforn hym like a swarm of ben: *bees*
For noon so hardy was hym to withsette. *confront*
And in this while, a Grekysh kyng he mette,
Were it of hap or of aventure, *chance*
The whiche in soth on his cotearmure *surcoat worn over armor*
5335 Enbroudrid had ful many riche stoon *Embroidered*
That yaf a light, whan the sonne shoon, *gave*
Ful bright and clere, that joie was to sene:
For perlis white and emeraudis grene,
Ful many oon, were thereinne set
5340 And on the cercle of his basenet *headpiece*
And rounde enviroun of his aventaille *face and neck covering*
In velwet fret, al above the maille, *velvet adorned; mail*
Safirs ynde and other stonys rede, *blue*
Of whos array, whan Hector taketh hede, *dress; heed*
5345 Towardis hym faste gan hym drawe. *approach*

206

	And firste, I fynd how he hath him slawe;	
	And after that, by force of his manhede	
	He rent hym up aforn him on his stede	*dragged*
	And faste gan with hym for to ride	
5350	From the wardis a litel oute aside,	*divisions*
	At good leiser pleynly, yif he may,	*if*
	To spoillen hym of his riche array,	*plunder*
	Ful glad and light of his newe emprise.	
	But out, allas, on fals covetyse,	
5355	Whos gredy fret — the whiche is gret pité —	*gnawing*
	In hertis may nat lightly staunchid be;	*extinguished*
	The etyk gnaweth be so gret distresse	*stimulus*
	That it diffaceth the highe worthines	*disfigures*
	Ful ofte sythe of thies conquerours	*times*
5360	And of her fame rent aweie the flours.	
	Desyre of havynge in a gredy thought	
	To highe noblesse sothly longeth nought;	*truly; belongs*
	No swiche pelfre, spoillynge, nor robberie	*pilfering*
	Apartene not to worthi chivalrye:	
5365	For covetyse and knyghthod, as I lere,	*learn*
	In o cheyne may nat be knet yfere;	*chain; knitted together*
	For kouthe it is that ofte swiche ravyne	*known; greed*
	Hath cause ben and rote of the ruyne	*root*
	Of many worthi — whoso liste take hede —	*wishes*
5370	Like as ye may now of Hector rede	
	That sodeinly was brought to his endynge	
	Only for spoillynge of this riche kyng.	*despoiling*
	For of desire to hym that he hadde,	
	On horsebake oute whan he hym ladde,	
5375	Reklesly, the story maketh mynde,	
	He cast his shelde at his bak behynde,	
	To welde hymsilf at more liberté,	*move*
	And for to han opportunyté	
	To spoillen hym, and for no wyght spare,	
5380	So that his brest disarmyd was and bare:	
	Except his platis ther was no diffence	*armor*
	Ageyn the strok to make resistence.	
	Allas, why was he tho so rekeles,	*then*
	This flour of knyghthod, of manhod pereles,	*unequalled*

5385	Whan that his fo al that ilke day	*same*
	For hym allone in awayte lay,	
	Yif in meschef, of hate and of envie,	*If; harm*
	In the feld he myght hym oute espie,	
	This Achilles, cruel and venemous,	
5390	Of hertly hate most malencolyous,	
	Whiche covertly havynge hym beside,	
	Whan that he saw Hector disarmyd ride,	
	He hent a spere, sharpe grounde and kene,	*grabbed*
	And of ire in his hateful tene	*rage*
5395	Al unwarly, or Hector myght adverte,	*unforeseen before; notice*
	(Allas the whyle) he smote hym to the herte,	
	Thorughoute the brest, that ded he fil doun	
	Unto the erthe, this Troyan champioun,	
	Thorugh necligence only of his shelde.	*carelessness*
5400	The deth of whom, whan Odemon behelde,	
	The worthi kyng myght hym nat restreyne,	
	But to Achilles rood with al his peyne,	
	And hit hym so myd of al the pres,	*troops*
	Maugre the myght of his Mirmidones,	*Despite*
5405	That for ded, Guydo seith certeyn,	
	Of that wounde he fil gruf on the pleyn,	*prone*
	But his knyghtes on a sheld alofte	*Except that*
	Thei leiden hym and caried hym ful softe	
	Unto his tent in al the haste thei can;	
5410	And there I leve this dedly wounded man,	*leave; mortally*
	Ful sore seke, til he may releve.	*rise again*
	And after that, whan it drowe to eve,	
	Thei of Troye with gret reverence	
	Dide her labour and her dilligence	
5415	The dede cors to carien into toun	*corpse*
	Of worthi Hector, whan Titan wente doun.	*the sun*
	And to the temple dolfully thei wende;	*turn*
	And of that day this was the woful ende —	
	I can no more — but thus the longe nyght	
5420	In hevynes, as it was skil and right,	*proper*
	I wil hem leve and ageyn returne	
	To my mater to help hem for to morne.	
	But now, allas, how shal I procede,	

In the story, that for wo and drede
5425 Fele myn hond bothe tremble and quake,
O worthi Hector, only for thi sake,
Of thi deth I am so loth to write.
O who shal now help me to endyte, *compose*
Or unto whom shal I clepe or calle? *call*
5430 Certis to noon of the Musis alle *Muses*
That by accorde singen ever in on
Upon Pernaso, besiden Elycon, *Parnassus; Helicon*
So angelik in her armonye
That tonge is noon that may specefie *describe*
5435 The grete swetnes of her goodly song;
For no discorde is founden hem among,
In her musik thei bene entunyd so. *brought into harmony*
It syt hem nought for to help in wo *is not fitting for them*
Nor with maters that be with mournynge shent, *impaired*
5440 As tragedies al totore and rent,
In compleynynge pitously in rage
In the theatre with a ded visage;
To hem, allas, I clepe dar nor crye *call*
My troubled penne of grace for to guye, *guide*
5445 Nouther to Clyo nor Callyope,
But to Allecto and Thesyphone
And Megera that evere doth compleine,
As thei that lyve evere in wo and peyne
Eternally and in turment dwelle
5450 With Cerberus depe doun in helle,
Whom I mote praie to be gracious *must*
To my mater, whiche is so furious. *frenzied*
For to a whight that is compleynynge *person; lamenting*
A drery fere is right wel sittynge, *sad companion; appropriate*
5455 And to a mater meynt with hevynes *mingled*
Acordeth wel a chere of drerynes *face; sadness*
To ben allyed, as by unyté. *joined*
Wherefore, helpe now, thou woful Nyobe,
Som drery ter in al thi pitous peyne
5460 Into my penne dolfully to reyne;
And helpe also thou cruel Yxioun
And Belydes, that doth the boget gon; *Danaids; bucket*

And with thi stoon helpe thou, Zeziphus;   *Sisyphus*
And in thi river helpe eke Tantalus,
5465   That for hunger haste so huge pyne,
This woful pleint helpe me for to fyne,   *conclude*
Me to forthre doth youre besynes.
For now the stok and rote of worthines,
Of knyghthod grounde, of manhod sours and wel,
5470   That toforn alle bare aweie the belle   *prize*
Of dorynge do, this flour of highe prowes —   *desperate courage*
And was exaumple also of gentilnes,
That nevere koude don amys nor seie,
Allas, Hector, allas, why shuldestou deie?
5475   O cruel Parchas, why toke ye noon hede,
So cruelly to twyne his fatal threde?   *cut*
Ye were to hasty! Allas, why were ye so,
And namely the threde to breke atwo,
Thou Antropos, thorugh thi grete envie!
5480   O Troye, allas, wel maist thou wepe and crie
And make a woful lamentacioun,
Whiche hast of newe to thi confusioun   *destruction*
Loste thi diffence and thi stronge wal,
Thi berer up, thi sureté royal,
5485   Be whom thin honour chefly was begonne.
Allas, allas, for now thi brighte sonne
Eclipsed is, and thou stanst desolat
Of al comfort and discounsolat;
Thi light is lost, and thou in dirkenes
5490   Iploungid art: for in sothfastnes,
Of alle worthi thou hast the worthiest
This day yloste and the knyghtlyest
That is, or was, or shal, I the ensure,   *assure*
Bene evere born, while the world may dure.   *last*
5495   No wonder is thaugh thou wepe sore
And day be day compleyne hym evermore   *lament*
That was thi sheld, bothe in joie and wo,
Whom thou were wont for to love so,
So tendirly with al thin hole herte
5500   That it may nat lyghtly the asterte   *escape*
To have hym evere in thi remembraunce,

Whiche was in soth thi ful suffisaunce.
For, as Guydo maketh mencioun,
Ther was no man dwellyng in the toun
5505 That he ne had of verray kyndenes,
For love of hym, as he writ expresse,
His child more lef to have died in this cas   *gladly*
Outher his eyr — so wel beloved he was —   *heir*
Yif the goddis, Fate, or destyné   *If*
5510 Disposid had that it myght have be.   *Arranged*
Wommen also of every maner age
Bene for his deth falle in swiche a rage,   *so crazed*
Thorugh the cyté, aboute in every strete
That with sobbyng and salt teris wete
5515 And here torent for her dedly wo,   *hair torn out; their*
Furiously ronne to and fro —
So mortal was her adversité   *deadly*
That to beholde, allas, it was pité.
Yonge maydenes and matrones olde
5520 Sobbe and sighe, and her festis folde,   *clasp their hands*
And loude crie, and seide fynally:
"Allas, now shal oure fadris cruelly
In oure sight be slayen day be day!
Allas the whyle, and no man shal seie nay!
5525 Farwel oure helpe, now Hector is goon,
In whom the surnes of us everychon   *security*
Was wont to reste: now is he ded, allas."
Of whom the body whan it caried was
Into presence of Priamus the Kyng,
5530 Anoon he lost the offys of spekyng,   *capacity*
And gan hymsilfe in salte teris drowne,
And pitously therwith fil aswowne   *fainted*
Upon the cors, cold as any stoon,
Inly desyrous for to deie anoon
5535 Withoute tariynge, on hym as he lay,   *delay*
But that he was by force rent awey.   *pulled*
His bretheren eke, whan thei token hed,
Trist and pale, for sorwe wer nyghe ded   *Sad*
And han hemsilfe with rage al totorn,
5540 That never was, I trowe, seyn aforn

Of brethere yit swiche another care:

For eche of hem with hymsilf gan fare · *act*

As thei wolde have died on the cors; · *corpse*

For of their lif platly thei yaf no fors, · *plainly; did not care*

5545 But at the grounde with many swoghes sore, · *sighs*

Liche wylde boris thei gan crye and rore, · *boars*

That routhe was her dedly wo to sene —

An herte of stele myght it not sustene.

What schal I seyn of Eccuba the Quene, · *Hecuba*

5550 Or his suster, yonge Pollycene, · *Polyxena*

Or Cassandra, the prudent and the wyse,

Or of his wyf, the sorwe to devise, · *describe*

Whiche rent hemsilf in torment and in wo

As finally thei wolde hemsilfe fordo

5555 By cruel deth, so thei wepe and waille —

That yif I shulde make rehersaille · *if*

To wryte her sorwes and her compleynynges,

Her pitous sobbynge, throwes, and wepynges, · *throes*

The woful cries, and the pitous sowns,

5560 Her drery pleyntis and lamentaciouns,

And al her wo for to specifie, · *list*

A large boke it wolde occupie,

Yiffe eche thinge I shulde in order telle — · *If*

I trowe it were to longe for to dwelle, · *think*

5565 For any man and tedius to here.

For many day after, as I lere, · *learn*

The wommen wepte afore the cors liynge,

Hemsilfe diffacynge in her compleynynge; · *disfiguring*

That wonder was how thei myght endure

5570 But that thei han it sothly of nature · *Except; are inclined; truly*

And of kynde for to wepe and pleyne;

Thei sighe sore and into teris reyne, · *dissolve into tears*

Til the tempeste of her woful rage

May be processe lyte and lyte aswage.

5575 And thus I leve hem sighe and sorwe make,

This cely wommen in her clothes blake, · *hapless*

Shroude her facis, and wympled mourne in veyn,

While I turne to my mater ageyn,

To telle pleynly how Kyng Priamus

212

5580	In herte was inly desyrous	
	To caste a weie in his entencioun	*devise*
	The cors to kepe from corrupcioun,	
	Whiche naturelly, but men take hede,	*unless*
	Corrupte muste right of verray nede:	
5585	For of kyndely disposicioun	
	Ther may be made noon opposicioun,	
	Above the grounde yif the body lie,	*if*
	That of resoun it mut putrefie;	*must*
	But yif crafte be above nature,	*Unless art overcomes*
5590	Uncorrupte it myghte nat endure.	
	Wherefore, the kyng shope him to ordeyne	*prepared*
	To preserve it hool fro thinges tweyne —	
	From odour and abomynacioun —	
	And therwith eke by crafty operacioun	
5595	That in sight it be not founde horrible,	
	But that it be lifly and visible	
	To the eye, as be apparence,	
	Like as it were quyk in existence.	*living*
	What it cost the kyng wil spare nought	
5600	But made anoon aforn hym to be brought	
	The craftiest maisteres of the toun,	*most skillful*
	Swiche as hadde moste discrecioun	
	To parforme his axeynge coriously.	*wishes ingeniously*
	And thei obeie his byddynge feithfully	
5605	With al her wille and enter dillygence	*complete*
	In the temple, moste of reverence	
	Of al the toun, whilom dedicat	
	And of ful yore also consecrat	*long ago*
	To Appollo of olde fundacioun,	
5610	Beside a gate stondynge of the toun,	
	Callyd Tymbria in her Troyan tonge,	
	As the story is bothe red and songe.	
	And in this phane that I spake of here,	*temple*
	Thei made firste be the highe auter,	*by; altar*
5615	By gret devis, a litel oratorie	*art*
	Perpetuelly to be in memorie,	
	Where was set a riche receptacle	
	Made in maner of a tabernacle,	

      Egal of sight, for a large ymage

5620 That reised was on a riche stage,

      That was born up at eche of his corneris

      Of purid golde upon foure pilers;

      And on everych ful craftily ydight   *made*

      An angel stood of golde burned bright,   *burnished*

5625 Coriously the werke to sustene   *artfully*

      With crafty archis, reised wonder clene,

      Enbowed over al the werke to cure —   *Bent; roof*

      So merveilous was the celature   *embossing*

      That al the rofe and closure enviroun

5630 Was of fyn gold platid up and doun,

      With knottis grave wonder corious,   *knobs carved*

      Fret ful of stonys riche and precious,   *Adorned*

      Of every kynde that man can devyse,   *describe*

      So rially and in so thrifty wyse,

5635 That the dirknes of the blake nyght

      With the bemys of her clere light

      Enchacid was where thei dide shyne.   *Driven away*

      And from the grounde upright as a lyne

      Ther wer degres, men by to ascende,   *stairs*

5640 Made so wel that no man koude amende   *improve*

      The werkemanship; and thei were everychon

      Parformyd up al of cristal stoon,   *Made of*

      Attenyng up fro the table bas   *Extending upwards; low*

      Where the stondyng and the resting was

5645 Of this riche crafty tabernacle,

      Havynge above upon eche pynacle

      A riche ruby; and reised highe on heighte

      Stood an ymage, huge and large of weighte,   *figure*

      Of massyf gold, havynge the liknes

5650 Of worthi Hector that gan his face dresse   *turn*

      Toward Grekis where he dide stonde,

      Ay thretynge hem with his swerd on honde.

      And amyddes al the grete richesse

      Thei han yset by good avisenesse   *consideration*

5655 The dede cors of this worthi knyght,   *corpse*

      To sight of man stondynge as upright

      By sotil crafte as he were lyvynge,

	Of face and chere, and of quyk lokynge,	*living appearance*
	And of colour sothly, and of hewe	
5660	Beinge as freshe as any rose newe	
	And like in al, as be supposaille,	*supposition*
	As he lyvede in his apparaille:	*apparel*
	For on his hede, like as it is tolde,	
	Thorugh smale pipes wrought and made of gold	
5665	That be mesour wern enbowed doun	*bent*
	To an entré makyd in his crown	
	Be grete avys and subtylité	
	To eche party and extremyté	
	Of his body lyneally porrect,	*extended in a straight line*
5670	Thorugh nerfe and synwe driven and direct,	*nerve; sinew*
	Be secré poris craftely to extende,	*hidden tubes*
	Wherby the licour myghte doun discende	*liquid*
	To kepe hym hool fro corrupcioun,	
	Withouten any transmutacioun	
5675	Of hyde or hewe in any part to tourne.	
	And at his hede of gold was an ourne	*urn*
	That was filde with bawme natural	*balm*
	That ran thorugh pipes artificial	
	Thorugh nekke and hed into many place,	
5680	Penytrable by veynes of the face,	
	That thorugh vertu and force of the lycour	*properties*
	He was conserved lifly of colour,	
	Fresche of hewe, quyke, and no thinge pale,	*alive; not at all*
	So myghtely the bawme dide avale —	*have effect*
5685	Comparysownyd, as it were semblable,	*Comparable; similar*
	To a sowle that were vegetable,	
	The whiche withoute sensibilité	*power of sensation*
	Mynystreth lyf in herbe, flour, and tre,	
	And semblably into every veyne	*similarly*
5690	Of the cors the vertu dide atteyne,	*corpse*
	By brest and arme spredynge enviroun:	
	For the moisture by descencioun	
	To hand and foot sothly, as I rede,	
	Thorugh bon and joynt gan his vertu shede	
5695	And distillynge myghtely to flete.	*flow*
	And at his feet, ful of gommys swete,	*plant resins*

	A viol stood, temprid with bawme and meynt,	*vial; balm; mixed*
	That be processe may nat wexe feynt	*be diluted*
	But day be day encresen and amende,	*grow stronger*
5700	Of whiche the vapour upward gan ascende,	
	Causynge the eyr enviroun be delys	*delight*
	To resemble a verray paradys:	
	For the flavour more holsom was and soote	*sweet*
	Than the odour of spice, gomme, or rote.	
5705	And of pure gold were foure lampis light,	
	Tofore the cors brennynge day and nyght	*burning*
	With oyle in soth, yif it be credible,	
	That was be crafte made inextinguyble;	
	For it ne myght, myn auctor seyth certeyn,	
5710	Nouther be queint with tempest, winde, nor reyn,	*extinguished*
	Nor be processe wasten of no yeris —	
	Whiche in the eyr be bright borned weris	*wires*
	Ful craftely reised werne alofte,	
	Of whos swetnes men rejoysseden ofte,	
5715	In her corage it likede hem so wel.	*hearts*
	And whan this werke was complete everydel	
	Rounde enviroun, ful riche and freshe to se,	
	Thei made a parclos al of Eban tre	*railing; ebony*
	That so longe laste may and dure;	
5720	The whiche tre only of nature,	
	Whan it is kut, smelleth wonder swete	
	And may nat waste ne brenne with noon hete,	
	Though it be leide amonge the colis rede,	*coals*
	Mid the flawme of many firy glede:	*live coal*
5725	It nat consumeth, though men assaien ofte;	*try*
	And in water it hoveth eke alofte,	*hovers*
	And kyndely to the grounde it goth,	*naturally*
	To swymme on heighte in soth it is so loth.	
	And like also as techeth Pluvius,	*Pliny*
5730	This tre whilom was passingly famus,	*once*
	Of so hyghe pris and reputacioun	*value*
	That in the large myghti regioun	
	And worthi lond of Ethiope and Ynde	
	Of yore agon the folkis, as I fynde,	*time passed*
5735	Hadden this tre in so gret honour	*Held*

	That thei yaf tribut to the emperour,	*gave*
	As is remembrid of antyquyté,	
	Of gold and yvor and this riche tre,	
	With these giftes famous and royal	
5740	To quyte her dette to hym in special.	*pay*
	And whan Priam in ful thrifty wyse	*proper*
	Parformed hath, as ye han herde devyse,	*described*
	This riche werke, noble and excellent,	
	Of hertly love in al his beste entent	
5745	Ordeyned eke, as Guydo can yow telle,	
	A certeyn noumbre of prestis for to dwelle	
	In the temple in her devociouns	
	Contynuelly with devout orisouns	*prayers*
	For the soule of Hector for to preie,	
5750	That the goddis his spirit list conveie	*might wish*
	Eternally with hem to dwelle yfere	*together*
	In joie and blisse above the sterris clere.	
	To whiche prestis the kyng yaf mansiouns,	*gave houses*
	Ther to abide, and possessiouns,	
5755	The whiche he hath to hem amortised	*deeded*
	Perpetuelly, as ye han herd devysed.	
	And whiles thei knele, preie, and wake,	
	I caste fully an ende for to make	*plan*
	Finally of my thridde boke,	
5760	On my rude maner as I undirtoke;	
	And whiles thei of Troye wepe and mourne,	
	Unto the Grekis I wil ageyn retourne	
	And with dul stile on the story trace,	*stylus; move along*
	Only born up with support of your grace.	

Book 4

Hector thus ded, as ye han herd me seid,
And Achilles in his tent ileied
With his woundis mortal, freshe, and grene,
Upon a morwe, whan the sonne shene
5   Enchasid had away the dirke nyght,
Agamenoun, the wyse worthi knyght,
In his werkis passingly prudent,
Hath in al haste for his lordis sent.

[*Agamemnon is convinced that Fortune has sealed Troy's doom. He advises that the Greeks wait for Achilles's wounds to heal and seek a two months' truce from Priam to burn the dead and forestall the threat of pestilence. During the truce, Palamedes renews his dispute over Agamemnon's governance. Agamemnon chooses his moment and then confronts Palamedes in open audience with the Greek leaders (lines 9–152).*]

"Sothly," quod he, "yif ye taken hede,   *if*
Me semeth pleinly it were no nede,
155   Avisely yif ye list adverte,   *Wisely; wish to consider*
To muse so nor grucchen in youre herte   *be discontented*
Of al this hoste that I have governance,
Wisly considered every circumstaunce,
How I th'estat (whiche no man may denye)   *position*
160   Wolde in no maner never occupie
By other title than fre elleccioun,
Nat interrupt by mediacioun   *hindered by means*
Of brocage, roted upon mede,   *bribery; gifts*
Ay undermeynt with favour or falshede,   *mingled*
165   Depict with colour of trewe entencioun
To support swiche false ambicioun;   *such*
Of whiche thing here I wil me quyte   *prove myself innocent*
Tofore yow alle that I am not to wyte   *to be blamed*
In any wyse of so highe offence
170   But stonde clere in my conscience

	Withoute spot of any swiche veynglorie	
	Touchinge th'estat, whiche is transitorie.	
	Yet nevertheles I have do my cure	*exerted myself*
	With al my wit to helpen and procure	
175	That everything touching the commounté	*community*
	Persevere myght in prosperité,	
	Havyng the eye of myn inward sight	
	Unto the estat of every maner wyght	*person*
	That were committed to my governance,	*Who was*
180	With gret labour and besy attendaunce,	
	Indifferent unto highe and lowe,	
	To helpe and fostre wher I coude knowe	
	That any stood in meschef or in nede,	*distress*
	Day and nyght for to taken hede,	
185	As I best koude, by avisenesse,	*prudence*
	Ay dillygent that nat felle in distresse.	
	For sothfastly, whoso loke aright,	
	Mi daies thinkyng and my wache anight	
	And of myn hert th'inly advertence	*inner*
190	Withoute fraude, slouth, or necligence	
	Was feithfully with al my fulle myght	
	Me to aquyte to every maner wight,	*behave*
	Liche his estat withoute excepcioun;	*According to*
	So that no man justly of resoun,	
195	Greke nor other that is now alyve,	
	Unto my gilt dewly may ascrive	
	Any falsehed, engyn, or trecherie	*stratagem*
	Of love or hate, favour or flaterie	
	In any cause named in special,	
200	But that I have ben eliche egal	*alike*
	To oon and alle with al my besy peyne,	
	That no man hath mater to compleyne	
	For his party, of highe nor lowe estat.	*Of his part*
	And to devoide al rancour and debat	*remove*
205	Amongis yow, I have do my dever	*duty*
	In general thing and particuler,	
	That hertoward nothing hath mescheved.	*So that; miscarried*
	And God wot wel, it shuld nat agrevid	*knows; cause grief*
	To my herte t'aset at any prys,	*to take lightly*

210	Yow t'achose by youre discret avis	*Your choosing*
	Som other to this domynacioun	*lordship*
	And I to have ben in subjeccioun	
	With ese of herte and tranquillité	
	Liche other lordis here of my degré	
215	And in my wil fully han obeied —	
	Like on of yow outterly to have deyed	
	In the quarel that we han undirtake,	
	Yif destiné had it so yshape:	*If; determined*
	I seie in soth, me is ful loth to feyne.	*I am reluctant*
220	And overmore also, wher ye compleyne	
	That I was chose withoute your assent,	*chosen*
	Merveileth nat, sith ye ne were present;	
	Nor longe after, yif ye remembre aright,	*if*
	Toward Troye your weie was nat dight.	*prepared*
225	Yif ye considre, it was after ner	*If; nearly*
	Or that ye cam passed ful two yer;	*Before*
	And so longe t'abide youre commynge	
	It hadde ben to Grekis gret hyndrynge,	*would have been; hinderance*
	Passynge harme, and ful gret damage,	*Surpassing*
230	And huge lettynge unto oure viage.	*hinderance*
	For yif we had withouten any wene	*doubt*
	On your comynge taried at Athene,	
	It likly is — ye can nat wel seie nay —	
	To have be there yit into this day.	
235	And whereas ye, though it be nat credible,	
	Affermen eke for an impossible	
	That Grekis shuld in any maner wyse	
	Dor take on hem any gret emprise	*Dare*
	In youre abscence manly to achewe,	*accomplish*
240	It is but wynde, nothinge for to leve.	*believe*
	For so it be to you noon offence,	
	The Grekis han withoute youre presence	
	Thorugh her force on water and on lond	
	Ful many thing parformed with her hond	
245	And acheved thorugh her worthines.	
	And of o thing that in me ye gesse	
	(This to seyne, that of my degré	
	I shulde in herte so rejoisshe me	

Of this lordshipe and this grete estat,
250 The more to be pompos and elat   *proud*
In chere or port that I it occupie)   *appearance; behavior*
But me to aquite trewly and nat lye   *act*
And to devoide al suspecioun,
I wil make a resignacioun
255 Tofore yow alle, for to excuse me.
Now beth avised discretly for to se   *be prepared*
Whom ye list han ageyn tomorwe prime   *wish; tomorrow at the first hour*
Withoute settynge of any lenger tyme,
Prolonging forthe, or any more delay."
260 And thus thei made an ende of that day
And went her weye only for that nyght
Til on the morwe that Titan shadde his light,   *when*
At whiche tyme a conseil general
The Grekis hilde; but moste in special   *held*
265 Of lordis was ther congregacioun,
As I have tolde, for the eleccioun.
And whan thei were alle met ifere,   *together*
Agamenoun anoon, as ye shal here,
Seide evene thus, with sadde countenaunce.
270 "Lo, sirs," quod he, "touchynge governaunce
That I have had and domynacioun,   *lordship*
I have herto with hool affeccioun
And clene entent do my besynes
That everything might in welfulnes
275 To youre encres perseveren and contune.
Recorde I take of God and Fortune,   *Call to witness*
Whiche han conservid and the cause be
You for to floure in felicité,
That youre honour and highe noblesse
280 Stant hool and sounde yit in sikirnes.   *security*
And while your fame is most in flouringe,
As semeth me, it is right wel sittinge   *it is appropriate*
Myne estat fully to resygne,
Specially while Fortune is benygne;
285 For of so many that be now present
I am allone insufficient
Withoute helpe for to bere a charge: *burden*

Men with to moche may overlade a barge   *overload a ship*
And namely in tempest and in rage.   *especially*
290 And sith ye bene so discret and sage,
Of my berthene late me be releved
So that no man therwith be agrevid;
But late us alle of oon entencioun,
Withoute strife or dissencioun,
295 Chesen swiche oon that be most acceptable   *Choose*
To yow echon and most covenable,   *appropriate*
Yow to governe by discressioun."
And thei echon with hool affeccioun
Assentid ben. To speke in general,
300 Here men may se how it is natural
Men to delite in thinge that is newe:
The trust of peple is feint and untrewe,
Ay undiscrete and ful of doubilnes
And variable of hir sikernesse,
305 Ay awaitynge in her oppinioun   *looking for*
After chaunge and transmutacioun,
Selde or never stondyng hool in oon   *Seldom; steadfast*
(Today thei love, tomorwe it is gon),
In whom ful selde is any sikernes.
310 For only now of newfongilnes
That hath enbracid her affeccioun   *feeling*
Thei have in stede of Agamenoun
Of newe chose, only of favour,
Pallamydes to ben her governour,
315 And of Grece, liche as thei desyre,
To have the septre of the hool empire,   *sceptre*
And to be called in every cost
Emperour of the Grekis host,
Right as toforn was Agamenoun.   *before*
320 And this was fyn and conclusioun
For thilke day of her parlement.   *that same*
And after that, every man is went
To his loggynge, home the righte wey.

[*After the truce expires, Priam takes the field with one hundred and fifty thousand troops. His old hatred for the Greeks now doubled by Hector's death, he slays many foes. The King of Persia is killed in the fighting, and the next day Priam seeks a truce in order to embalm his body. Meanwhile, the funeral rites for Hector begin, and warriors from the two sides exchange visits. Achilles is taken by a desire to visit Troy (lines 324–550).]*

	And forthe he went on a certein day	
	Toward Troye in al the hast he may,	
	Unarmyd sothly, as myn auctor seith,	
	Withoute assurance or any other feith	
555	Excepte the trew, whoso be lefe or loth.	*truce; liked it or not*
	And first of al unto the temple he goth	
	Of Appollo. Halwed was the feste	*Observed*
	Thorughoute the toun doun unto the lest,	*people in lowest social position*
	That clepid was the anyversarie,	*called*
560	As ye han herde — what shuld I lenger tarie —	
	And many worthi present wer therat	
	Amyd the temple, of highe and lowe estat,	
	Lordis and ladyes of affeccioun	
	From every part gadered of the toun.	
565	Now was the cors of this worthi knyght	*corpse*
	As freshe of colour kepte unto the sight,	
	As lifly eke and as quik of hewe	*alive*
	To beholde as any rose newe	
	Thorugh vertu only of the gommys swete	*plant resins*
570	And the bawme that gan aboute flete	*balm; flow*
	To every joynt and eche extremyté.	
	And at this feste and solempnyté	
	Was Eccuba and yonge Polycene,	*Hecuba; Polyxena*
	So wommanly and goodly on to sene,	
575	With many other of highe estat and lowe	
	Tofore the cors sittynge on a rowe	
	With heer untressid, clad in wedis blake,	*black clothes*
	That evere in on swich a sorwe make	*in unison*
	That routhe was and pité for to sene	
580	How thei pleyne and the deth bemene	*bemoan*
	Of worthi Hector, of knyghthod grounde and welle.	
	But trowe ye (as Guydo list to telle)	*know*
	That Polycene in al hir woful rage	
	Ichaungid hath upon hir visage	*face*
585	Hir natif colour, as fresche to the sight	

223

As is the rose or the lillye whight, *white*
Outher the freshenes of hir lippes rede, *Or*
For al the terys that she gan to shede
On hir chekis, as any cristal clere?
590 Hir heer also resemblyng to gold wyre, *wire*
Whiche lay abrood like unto the sight
Of Phebus bemys in his spere bright *sphere*
When he to us doth his light avale. *send downward*
And ay she rent with hir fyngeris smale
595 Hir golden here on hir blake wede, *clothes*
Of whiche thing Achilles toke good hede
And gan merveille gretly in his thought
How God or Kynde ever myght have wrought *Nature*
In her werkis so fair a creature: *their*
600 For he thought he myghte nat endure
To beholde the brightnes of hir face,
For he felt thorugh his herte pace *pass*
The percyng stremys of hir eyen two; *eyes*
Cupides brond hath hym markid so *brand*
605 For love of hir that in his desire
He brent as hoote in soth as any fire,
And after sone with sodeyn colde he quoke,
And alweye fix on hir he hadde his loke,
So that the arwe of the god Cupide
610 Percid hym evene thorugh the syde
To the herte and yaf hym swiche a wounde *gave*
That nevere was lyke for to sounde. *likely; heal*
And ay in oon his loke on hir he caste, *the same*
As he durste, and gan to presse faste
615 Toward hir, namly, with his eye,
That hym thought he most nedis deye
But yif that he founde in hir some grace. *Unless*
Ther was no geyn, for pleinly in that place *remedy*
Of newe he was kaught in lovis snare,
620 That of helth and of al welfare
He was dispeired in his herte so
That he ne knew what was best to do.
Eche other thing, I do yow wel assure,
He set at nought and toke of hit no cure;

224

625	His thought was hool on hir and on no mo.	*wholly*
	The longe day thus went he to and fro,	
	Til Phebus char lowe gan declyne	*chariot*
	His golden axtre that so cler doth shine	*axis*
	(This to seyne, the sonne wente doun)	
630	Whan Eccuba, Quene of Troye toun,	
	And hir daughter Pollycene also	
	Oute of the temple to the paleis go;	
	And ay Achilles on hir hadde a sight	
	While he myght, til for lak of light	
635	He may no more have leyser oportune	
	To loke on hir, cursed be Fortune.	
	For whiche in haste he makid hathe his went	*has taken his way*
	With his knyghtes home unto his tent,	
	Wher he anon withoute more tariyng	*immediately*
640	To bedde goth, ful trist in compleyning,	*sad*
	Ay in hymsilf casting up and doun	
	In his mynde and eke in his resoun	*also*
	From hed to foot hir bewté everydel.	*every detail of her beauty*
	And in his hert he felt and knewe ful wel	
645	That final cause of his languysshinge	*reason*
	Was Polycene, of bewté most passinge:	
	For love of whom so moche peine he felte	
	That with the hete he thought his herte melte,	
	Ay on his bedde walwyng to and fro	*tossing*
650	For the constreint of his hidde wo,	
	For whiche almost him thoughte that he deide;	
	And to himsilfe even thus he seide.	
	"Allas," quod he, "how me is wo begoon,	
	That of my sorwe knowe ende noon,	*Who*
655	For I suppose, sith the world began	*since*
	Ne was ther nevere a wofuller man:	
	For I that whilom was of so gret myght,	
	So renomed of every maner wyght	*type of person*
	Thorughoute the world, bothe of highe and lowe,	
660	For ther was noon in sothe that koude knowe	*truth; might*
	A man in armys that was more famus	
	Nor iholde more victorius,	*held*
	Tofore this tyme remembrid be no stile	*stylus*

Into this day — allas, the harde while —
665 Nouther Hector pleinly nor noon other,
Of Polycene that was the worthi brother,
That power had whan thei with me mette,
For al her myght, me to oversette, *vanquish*
Nor in the felde my force for to daunte, *subdue*
670 Here prively as I me dar avaunte. *boast*
But now, allas, a mayde of tender age
Hath sodeinly me brought in swiche a rage *passion*
That with the stremys of hir eyen tweyne
She percid hath and corve every veyne *pierced*
675 Of myn hert, that I may nat asterte *escape*
For to be ded thorugh constreint of my smerte. *pain*
For who shal now wissen me or teche, *advise*
Or who, allas, shal now be my leche, *physician*
Or who shal now helpe me or save?
680 Ther is but deth and after that my grave,
For other hope pleinly is ther noon,
Save in hir mercy, allas, and that is goon.
For nouther prayer, tresour, nor richesse,
Force nor myght, nouther highe prowesse,
685 Highnes of blood, birthe, nor kynrede *family*
May availlen or helpen in this nede
To meven hir, nor my sadde trouthe, *sincere promise*
Upon my wo evere to have routhe.
What newe furie or importune rage *grievous*
690 Hath brought myn herte into swyche outrage *extremity*
Ageynes whiche I can not debate: *contend*
To love hir best that dedly doth me hate.
And in good feith, who wisly list adverte, *consider*
Litel wonder though she me hate of herte,
695 Sith I am come hyder fro so ferre *Since*
On hir kynrede for to make werre,
In the whiche to my confusioun *distress*
Hir knyghtly brother, most worthi of renoun,
Have fatally with myn hondis slawe, *slain*
700 Whiche in this worlde hadde no felawe *equal*
Of worthinesse nor of manlyhede.
Allas, allas, now may I quake and drede

226

	And of my lyf fallen in dispeire,	
	For how shuld I be bold to have repeire	*return*
705	Or dorn, allas, comen in hir sight,	*dare*
	I woful wreche, I unhappy wyght?	*person*
	Or how shal I ben hardy to appere	
	In the presence of hir eyen clere?	*eyes*
	Certys, I se non other mene weye	
710	But finally that I muste deye,	
	So dispeired I stonde on every syde,	
	Of other helpe I can me nat provyde."	
	And right anoon with profounde sighes depe	
	This Achilles brast oute for to wepe	
715	With dedly chere, pale and funeral,	
	And with his face turned to the wal,	
	That routhe was and pité for to sene	
	The hertly furie of his peynes kene.	
	For so oppressed he was in his thought	
720	Of lyf nor deth that he roughte nought,	*paid attention to nothing*
	And this contuneth til it drow to nyght,	
	That Titan hath withdrawe his clere light.	
	And evere in oon lith this woful man	*continually*
	Iliche sike, of colour pale and wan,	*Constantly*
725	Withoute slepe, so fretyng was his sorwe,	*consuming*
	Til Lucifer on the nexte morwe,	*the morning star*
	Tofore the sonne, with his bemys clere	
	Ful lustely gan for to appere	
	In the orient, whan this Achilles,	
730	Unpacient, withoute reste or pes,	*Impatient*
	Quakynge evere in his fevere newe	
	(As it was sene pleinly in his hewe),	
	Til he abreide of anguysshe sodeynly	*started*
	And called oon that was with hym prevy	*intimate*
735	And of counseil whom he tristeth wel;	
	And unto hym he telleth everydel	
	From point to point with him how it stood	
	And sent him forthe because he koude his god	*knew what was good for him*
	On his message streight to Troye toun	
740	With ful avis and informacioun	*knowledge*
	Of this mater to Eccuba the Quene	

Thorugh his wisdam for to ben a mene,   *intermediary*
Yif he myght by his discrecioun   *If*
Fynde any waye of savacioun
745   Unto his lord that he lovyd so.
And to the quene anon he is go
And his mater wysly gan conveie
Toforn or he of grace wolde preie   *Before*
That she enjoieth to yeve hym audience,   *give*
750   For in his tale ther was noon offence: *message*
He was no fool or newe for to lere.   *inexperienced man*
Wherfore the quene goodly gan hym here   *hear*
Of al that evere hym liketh for to seyn;
Ther was no worde ylost nor spoke in veyn,
755   For his tale no man koude amende.
And craftely he gan to discende   *carefully*
To the substaunce and tolde clerly out,
With premisses ful wel brought about,
That finally in conclusioun
760   The chefe, he seide, of his entencioun   *aim*
Effectuously, yif it wolde be,   *In effect, if*
Was for to make pes and unité
Atwene Grekis and the folke of Troye.
To whiche thing he knew no better woye   *means*
765   Than of the werre, for her alder ese,   *for both of their advantages*
By his wit prudently t'apese
The mortal strife and the bitter rage
By allyaunce only of mariage,
Yif that hir liste, this wyse, worthi quene,   *If; she wished*
770   That hir doughter, faire Pollycene,
May weddid be unto Achilles.
Wherthorugh ther myght be a final pes,
Yif Eccuba thorugh hir discresioun,
Thorugh hir wit and mediacioun
775   And hir prudence myght aboute brynge
That Priamus were fully assentynge
That Achilles myght his doughter wyve,
So that it myght performyd ben as blyve   *quickly*
(Lyke as I have made mencioun)
780   By covenaunt only and condicioun

228

	That the Grekis shal her werre lete	*their war abandon*
	And suffre him to lyven in quyete,	
	Yif the mariage of this ilke tweyne	
	Parformed be and knyt up in a cheyne.	
785	And whan the quene hath knowen his entent,	
	Ful sobirly, by good avysement,	*consideration*
	Toforn or that any word asterte,	*Before; might escape*
	Ful pitously she syghed in hir herte,	
	And at the laste with a sobir chere	
790	She seide thus to the messager.	
	"My frend," quod she, "touching thi request,	
	I can no more make the beheste,	*grant; bidding*
	But at the leste I wil condiscende	*agree*
	What lyth in me to bringe to an ende	
795	Thi lordis wil with al myn herte entere.	
	But hereupon I muste firste requere	*ask*
	The kynges wil, yif he wil yeve assent	*give*
	To the purpos for whiche thou art sent.	
	And overmore I muste wyte also	*know*
800	Yif that Parys be willyng eke therto,	*If*
	Of whiche thing with every circumstaunce	
	I wil mysilfe maken enqueraunce	
	Ful feithfully of Priam and Parys	
	The menewhyle, what is her avys,	*counsel*
805	Withoute more withinne dayes thre,	
	At whiche tyme come ageyn to me	
	From Achilles, yif he wil the sende,	*send you*
	And finally thou shalt knowe an ende	
	Of this mater and an answere pleyn."	
810	And home he goth to Achilles ageyn	
	With ful glad chere, his lord the mor to plese;	
	And for to sette his herte bet at ese,	
	Avisely of highe discrecioun,	
	He hath so made his relacioun	
815	And told his tale in so thrifti wyse,	*proper*
	As he that koude his wordis so devyse	*construct*
	To bringe in hope to his lordis herte	
	With ful reles of his peynes smert,	*injury*
	Wherby he made his sorwe to withdrawe.	

820	And thus while hope gan for to adawe	*rise*
	Amyd his brest, Eccuba the Quene	
	To Priam spak of this Polycene,	
	Touchinge the sonde of this Achilles	*message*
	And of his profre for to make a pes;	
825	She tolde hym al and forgat nothinge.	
	Wherof astonyd, Priamus the Kyng	*astonished*
	Spak nat a word half an oures space	
	But in hymsilfe gan for to compasse	*ponder*
	Ful prudently what it myghte mene	
830	That Achilles wolde have Polycene	
	Unto his wyf, ay wondring mor and more;	
	And at the last, sighynge wonder sore,	
	He discloseth the conceit of his herte	*thought*
	And seide, "Allas, how sore it doth me smerte	*injury*
835	To remembre how I may have no pes —	
	The grete offence of this Achilles	
	Towardis me pleinly whan that he	
	Slowe worthi Hector thoru his cruelté,	*Slew*
	That hooly was upon every side	
840	Th'assuraunce, governour, and guyde	
	Of me and myn platly for to seyne	
	And therwithal of myn eyen tweyne	
	He was allone the verray sothfast lyght,	
	Shelde, and protectour thorugh his grete myght	
845	And his manhod ageyn the mortal rage	
	Of Grekis werre in my croked age.	*bent*
	But now, allas, to my confusioun	*distress*
	He slawen is, so worthi of renoun,	
	Be Achilles, whiche may not out of mynde,	*By*
850	That in myn hert I can nevere fynde	
	To ben allyed with my mortal foo,	
	Rote and grounde of al my sorwe and wo.	*foundation*
	It were ful harde myn herte to apese	*induce*
	To loven hym that causeth myn unese	
855	On every half, wherthorugh my cruel foon,	*foes*
	The proude Grekis, hertid ben echon	*encouraged*
	Ageynes me, now Fortune is contrarie,	
	Torned of newe my quarel to apaire,	*cause damage*

230

	That causeth Grekis, wood and furious,	
860	On me, allas, to be presumptuous	
	Only for Hector is me berafte away.	*Only because*
	But sithen I noon other chese may,	*since*
	Ageynes herte, though it for anger ryve,	*split*
	In this mater assay I shal to strive,	*try*
865	Though me be loth and sitteth me ful sore;	
	Yit to eschewe harmys that ben more,	
	Whiche likly ben hereafter for to falle,	
	And for to save myn other sonys alle,	
	I wil concent that this Achilles,	
870	So that he make a trewe final pes	*Provided; truly lasting peace*
	Atwene Grekis and also this cité	
	Withoute more pleinly, how that he	
	Have unto wyfe my doughter Polycene.	
	But list that he any tresoun mene,	*lest*
875	My wil is, first, howso that it wende,	*turn out*
	Of his beheste that he make an ende	
	Withoute fraude — this is myn avis."	
	To whiche conseil assenteth eke Parys	
	And more rathe in conclusioun,	*readily*
880	For ther was made noon excepcioun	
	In the treté of the Quene Eleyne,	
	That Menelaye evere shulde atteyne	
	Hir to recure ageyn unto his wyf,	*return*
	For whiche Paris withoute noise or strife	
885	Or grucchinge outher unto this entent	
	Withinne hymsilf was fully of assent,	
	Therby hopynge withoute fere or drede	
	Perpetuelly Eleyne to possede	*possess*
	Right at his lust and no man shal seie nay.	
890	And after this uppon the thridde day	
	Achilles hath, to wyte of this mater,	*know*
	To Eccuba sent his messanger;	
	And she tolde hym the answere of the kyng,	
	Ceriously gynnynge and endynge,	*In due order*
895	And how that he assenteth wel therto	
	And Paris eke and she hirsilfe also,	
	Yif it so were pleynly, she hym tolde,	*If*

231

Touchinge the pes that the purpos holde

And firste that he his heste bring aboute — *promise (pledge)*

900 That thei be sure; thanne him dar not doute

That he shal have his purpos everydel,

Yif that he wirke prudently and wel.

And hereupon with informacioun

This messanger oute of Troye toun

905 Withoute abood, in al the haste he may, — *delay*

To Achilles helde the righte way

And tolde him hool th'effect of this mater.

And he alweie fervent and entere

In herte brent hoot as any glede — *coal*

910 And saw ther was no waye for to spede — *prosper*

But only pes, as ye han herd me telle;

And ay his brest with sighes gan to swelle

For the love of this Polycene

And cast alway amonge his peines kene — *[he] considered always*

915 To his purpos a weie for to fynde.

And whiles he was besy in his mynde

How he shuld his purpos bringe aboute

And in hymsilf cast many a doute,

Anoon Dispeir in a rage upsterte — *At once; arose*

920 And cruellé caughte hym by the herte,

Whiche hath hym throwe into swiche a were — *uncertainty*

That hym thoughte it nas in his power — *was not*

His beheste to fulfille in dede,

Excepte he hadde wel the lasse drede — *apprehension*

925 Everything to putten in certeyn, — *make certain*

Wenyng no Greke wolde his lust withseyn, — *Thinking; wish reject*

From his desire to be variable.

And to hymsilf thus was he favourable

For to parforme and no thing denye — *in no way renounce*

930 Al that was lusty to his fantasye, — *desirable*

As is the maner of lovers everychon,

That thei suppose to acheve anon

What thing it be that thei take on honde,

In what disjoint that the mater stonde, — *extreme condition*

935 Altheigh it be a verray impossible:

In her foly thei ben so credible. — *willing to believe*

	And so Achilles trusteth finally	
	To fulfille his hestes outterly,	*promises entirely*
	Supposyng ay for his worthines,	
940	For his manhod and his highe prowes,	
	In whiche he dide hymsilfe glorifie	
	Somwhat of pride and of surquedie,	*arrogance*
	How the Grekis shulde be dispeired,	
	Bothe of her trust and her myght apeired	*weakened*
945	Upon Troyens to wynnen any londe,	
	Yif it so were he withdrowe his honde	*If it happened*
	To helpen hem, and therwithal also	
	Home into Grece that thei wolde go	
	From the sege only for his sake	
950	And her quarel outterly forsake,	
	But it so were this hardy, ferse Achille	
	With hem abood the cité for to spille.	*overthrow*
	For whiche thing the lordis by assent	
	Assemblid wern to heren the entent	
955	Amonge hem alle of this Achilles,	
	By the biddynge of Pallamydes.	
	And whan thei wern gadrid alle ifere,	*together*
	Toforn hem alle, like as ye shal here,	
	This Achilles hath his tale gonne	*begun*
960	And seide: "Sirs, that so moche konne	*know*
	Bothe of wisdam and of highe prudence,	
	So renomed eke of sapience	*wisdom*
	Thorughoute the worlde and of discrecioun,	
	And ben so worthi also of renoun,	
965	Kynges, dukis, of whom the rial name	
	From est to west flouring yit in fame,	
	Bothe of knyghthod and of manlihede,	
	To that I seie I praye you taketh hede:	
	This to seyne, yif that ye considere	*if*
970	The pleyn entent of oure comynge hider	*intention*
	By good avis and discrecioun	
	Had no grounde founded on resoun	
	Nor cause roted on no titel of right,	*claim*
	Yif it so be, that ye liften up youre sight	
975	And adverten clerly in youre mynde,	*reflect*

233

Ful fer abak wit was sette behynde,
Prudent lokynge and avisenesse.
For first whan we of foly hastynesse
Toke upon us to come fro so ferre   *far*
980   Ageynes Troyens for to gynne a werre
And to juparde oure lyves everychon   *risk*
For the love of o man allone —
Ye weten alle, I trowe, whom I mene,   *think*
Kynge Menelay, defrauded of his quene,
985   To telle trouthe (me list nat for to feyne) —   *I do not wish*
For ye wel wite only that Eleyne   *Helen*
Was grounde and gynnynge of al this debate,   *strife*
For whom so many worthi of estate,
Recurles of any remedye,   *Without hope*
990   Life and good han putte in jupartie,
Oure londis left and oure regiouns,
Oure cités eke and oure riche tounes,
Whiche by oure absence stonde desolat.
Wives and childer eke disconsolat
995   In wo abide, mournynge, and distresse,
Whiles that we, the sothe to expresse,   *truth*
Fro day to day beset on every syde,
Lyn in the felde and oure deth abide
In sorwe and care, in labour and in wo.
1000   And with al this ye wete wel also,   *know*
Sithen tyme that the werre began,   *Since*
Of oure Grekis how many worthi man
Hath loste his lyf thorugh dethis fatal wounde,
That myght herto have lyved and be sounde   *otherwise*
1005   At home in Grece assured wel in joye,
Yif thei ne hadde comen unto Troye —   *If*
That to remembre it is ful gret pité.
And over this I seie also for me:
Amonge Troyens in her cruel mood
1010   I have ylost so moche of my blood
That hath ful ofte made me pale of hewe.
This other day also, grene and newe,
I hadde of Hector swiche a mortal wounde
With a quarel sharpe whet and grounde   *bolt sharply whetted*

1015	Above the thighe — so kene was the hed —	
	The same day aforn that he was ded,	*before*
	Of verray hap as it was yshape,	*chance*
	That fro the deth unnethe I myghte eskape.	*scarcely*
	Whiche yit al freshe is uppon me sene	
1020	Large and wyde and as yit but grene,	
	The smert of whiche sore yit I pleyne.	*injury; lament*
	And in good feith, me semeth that Eleyne,	
	Yif ye adverte wysly in your thought,	*consider*
	With swiche a pris shulde nat be bought,	
1025	Wherthorugh oure lyf and oure good yfere	*possessions*
	And oure honour arn yput in were	*doubt*
	And dredfully hangen in ballaunce.	
	For yif that ye in youre remembraunce	
	Conceyve aright and casten up and doun	
1030	The sodeyn chaunge and revolucioun	
	That fallen hath sith the werre gan,	*since*
	The slaughter and deth of many worthi man	
	That for hir sake hath here lost his lyf,	
	Yet the werst of this mortal strif	
1035	Doth most rebounde into oure damage	
	To disencres and eke disavauntage	*detriment*
	And likly is to encrese more,	
	Yif ordynaunce be nat made therfore	
	And remedie shape on outher side,	
1040	By fyn only that Eleyne abide	
	With hem of Troye, stille here in the toun.	
	And late us cast by good inspeccioun	
	For oure ese som other mene way	*means*
	So that the kyng called Menelay	
1045	Chese hym a wyf in som other lond	
	Lyk his estat be suraunce or be bonde,	*Appropriate to; pledge*
	Under wedlock confermed up of newe,	
	That unto hym wole be founde trewe,	
	Sithen that he withoute gilt or synne	*Since*
1050	May be the law from Eleyne twynne;	*separate*
	For of dyvos causis ben ynowe	*divorce; enough*
	Thorughoute the worlde of every wight knowe	*person*
	Of avoutri for the foule vice.	*adultery*

For to lawe is no prejudice,
1055 Though Menelay justly hir forsake
Whan so hym list and another take — *Whenever he wishes*
That shal him bet bothe queme and plese. — *gratify*
And so to us it shal be ful gret ese,
Whan the werre is brought to an ende,
1060 Whiche likly is many man to shende, — *destroy*
Yif it so be that it forthe contune. — *continue*
The grete labour is so inportune — *severe*
That we ne shal no while mowe sustene; — *be able to*
For this is soth withouten any wene: — *true; doubt*
1065 Troyens yit ben flourynge in her myght
And with hem han ful many worthi knyght
To helpen hem, of highe and lowe degré;
And therwithal so stronge is her cyté
On every parte withouten and withinne
1070 That we ar nat likly for to wynne
In oure purpos, though we evere abide.
Wherfore be wisdam lete us voide pride — *do away with*
And wilfulnes, only of prudence
To han the eye of oure advertence — *foresight*
1075 To oure profyt more than to veynglorie;
And while oure honour shyneth by victorie,
A wysdam is to withdrawe oure hond,
Sith we may nat constreyne by no bond — *Since*
Fortunys whele for to abide stable.
1080 Wherfor I rede, or she be mutable, — *advise before she changes*
This gery goddes with hir double cher, — *fickle goddess*
Let us yeve up swiche thing as lithe in wer — *give; adheres to war*
Whiles that we mow oure worship save: — *honor*
For of the werre the laude yit we have, — *praise*
1085 Considered wel how by oure manlyhede
Oure moste fo, Hector, is now dede. — *greatest*
And while that we in oure honour floure,
My counseil is, or Fortune loure, — *before; frown*
As I seide er, to chaunge hir brighte face, — *before*
1090 While that best we stonde in hir grace,
By on assent and oon oppinioun
Withouten any contradiccioun

236

Of hert and wil, bothe of on and alle,

Or oure honour on any party palle, *Before; lessen*

1095 Into Grece home that we retourne.

For yif that we lenger here sojourne

On the quarel that we have longe swed, *pursued*

Douteles — it may nat bene eschewed —

Ful gret damage — this withoute faile —

1100 Or we have don shal folwen at the taile: *in the end*

Wherfore best is oure foly up resigne.

And while oure hap is welful and benygne, *fortune*

Most blaundisshinge and of face faire,

The tyme is best to maken oure repeire, *return*

1105 While that we stonde in party and in al *part*

With oure enemyes in honour perigal *equal*

And fer above pleinly, yif that we *if*

Koude han an eye to oure felicité,

Whiche that is in his ascenceoun.

1110 But list som man wil make objeccioun *lest*

That we may nat so oure honour save,

To repeire pleynly but we have *return; unless*

Eleyne ageyn that is cause of al,

To whiche thing anoon answer I shal:

1115 Yif any man in his fantasie *If*

To dishonour or to vyllenye

Arrette wolde in any maner kynde *Ascribe*

We to gon hom and leven hir behynde,

Shortly to seyn, I holde it be no shame,

1120 Sith that we han on as gret of name *Since; have one*

As is Eleyne and of berthe as good,

Amongis us ycome of kynges blood,

Suster to Priam, lord of Troye toun,

Exyona, whom that Thelamoun *Hesione*

1125 In kepyng hath, yif I shal nat feyne,

In Troye toun as Paris hath Eleyne.

And sithe now it may bene noon other,

Lete the ton be sette ageyn the tother *the one; the other*

And the surplus of olde enmyté

1130 Betwyxen us and Troye the cité.

My conseil is, for oure bothen ese, *ease of both of us*

By on assent wysly to appese,   *pacify enmity*
This al and som, and that we hennes wende.   *hence depart*
I can no more; my tale is at an ende."
1135 To whom anoon Kyng Menelaus,
For verray ire wood and furious,   *mad*
And Kyng Thoas, the duke eke of Athene,
As thei that myght no lenger hym sustene   *tolerate*
(To suffren hym thei were so rekeles),
1140 Spak alle attonis unto Achilles.   *at once*
Nat only thei but thorugh inpacience
The court, perturbid, withoute providence,
With tumult gonne to repreve
This Achilles and proudly hem commeve   *roused*
1145 Ageynes hym and hys oppinioun,
And seide shortly in conclusioun
Unto his reed thei nold nevere assent   *advice*
Nor condescende to nothing that he ment,
To be governed by hym in this cas.
1150 For whiche thing anoon Achilles was
So full of ire and rancour in his hert
That sodeinly from his se he sterte,   *seat*
And went his way, as he were in a rage,
Triste and pale, and a wood visage,
1155 And shortly seide, for hym list nat feyne,   *dissimulate*
That he ne wolde lenger don his peyne
To helpen hem, howso that thei spede,   *whatever happened to them*
Ageynes Troyens for no maner nede,
And bad anon, this hardy Achilles,
1160 To his knyghtes called Mirmidones
That thei no more with spere nor with shelde
To helpe Grekis entren into the felde
But kepe hem clos at home withinne her tent.
Thus in his ire he yaf commaundement   *gave*
1165 To alle his men, as ye han herd devise,   *described*
Hem to withdrawe at every hyghe emprise,
Whansoevere thei goon into bataille.   *they (the Greeks)*
And in this while skarsenes of vitaille   *food*
Fil in the hoste of fleshe, bred, and wyn,
1170 That many Greke brought unto the fyn,

For thei ne myght endure for distresse,
Constreint of hunger dide hem so oppresse,
Til at the last Kyng Pallamydes,
As he that was in no thing rekeles,   *in no way*
1175 Hath therupon maked purviaunce,
Remedie, and redy ordinaunce.
And by assent and counseil of echon
He hath ysent wyse Agamenoun,   *dispatched*
The worthi kyng, to Messa there beside,
1180 A litel ile, only to provide   *island*
For the Grekis, yif he myghte spede,   *if; have success*
Hem to releve in this grete nede.
And Thelephus, kyng of thilke lond,   *that same*
Of gentilnes hath put to his hond,
1185 As he that was large and wonder fre   *generous*
And renomyd of humanité,
To socour hem, commaundinge anoon
His purvyours in al haste to goon
From every party abouten enviroun
1190 Thorugh alle the boundis of his regioun
And feithfully to cerchyn every coste   *explore*
To take up vitaille for the Grekis host.   *army*
And after that ful hastely he made
To stuffe her shippes pleinly, and to lade
1195 With everything that was necessarie
To the Grekis, and be water carie
At the request of Agamenoun,
Withoute tariynge or dilacioun.   *delay*
And so the kyng with plenté of vitaille
1200 Fraught and ylade gan anon to saille   *laden*
Toward the sege, he and his meyné,   *troops*
Ay costeiynge by the Grekysshe se.   *sailing along the coast*
The wynde was good, and the kyng as blyve   *quickly*
With his navie at Troye dide aryve
1205 In fewe dayes, and Grekis anon right
Of his repeire were ful glad and lyght,   *return*
Of his expleit and his gode speed,
That he so wel hath born hym in this nede.   *acquitted*
And after this Pallamydes anoon,

239

1210	As seith Guydo, is to his shippes goon	
	For to considre and loken al aboute	
	Wher nede was withinne and withoute,	
	Any of hem to mendyn or repeire,	
	As he that list for no cost to spare	*wished*
1215	In everything, withoute necligence,	
	Touching his charge to don his dilligence,	
	Til the trews fully wern oute ronne	*was*
	And the werris new ageyn begonne,	
	Whiche many man sothly dere abought.	
1220	And ceriously to write how thei wrought	*in due order*
	My purpos is pleinly in sentence,	
	Under support of youre pacience.	

[*When the war resumes, Deiphebus, one of Priam's sons, is mortally wounded by Palamedes. He calls on Paris to avenge him, and Paris kills Palamedes with a poisoned arrow, as the Greeks are routed. Only the valor of Ajax Telamon saves them from complete destruction. The Greeks appeal to Achilles for help, but he does nothing, fearing to offend Polyxena. With Palamedes dead, Agamemnon reassumes his role as the Greek leader. Troilus inflicts heavy losses on the Greeks, and they seek a two-month truce from Priam, during which Agamemnon sends Ulysses and others to prevail on Achilles to return to battle. Achilles refuses, and the Greek lords, meeting in council with Agamemnon, are at the point of abandoning the war, until Calchas tells them that they are destined to conquer Troy (lines 1223–2028).*]

	The trewes passid of the monthes tweyne,	*truce*
2030	Into the feld the Grekis hem ordeyne,	*draw into battle formation*
	And thei of Troye ageyn hem issen oute.	*against them*
	And worthi Troylus with an huge route	*company*
	The Grekis gan alderfirst assaille,	*first of all*
	And with his swerd he made first to raile	*flow*
2035	The rede blod thorugh her harnes bright,	*their armor*
	That as the deth thei fledde fro his sight;	
	For he that day thorugh his cruelté	
	Cast hym fully avenged for to be	*Proposed*
	Upon the deth of Hector, outterly.	*utterly*
2040	And as Dares reherseth specially,	*describes*
	A thousand knyghtes this Troyan champioun	
	That day hath slayn, ridyng up and doun,	

As myn auctor, Guydo, list endite,   *wishes to write*
Save after hym I can no ferther write —
2045   In his boke he yeveth him swiche a name —   *gives*
That by his manhod and his knyghtly fame
The Grekis alle wer put unto the flight
Al thilke day, til it drowe to nyght.   *that same*
And on the morwe in the dawenynge,
2050   The Grekis han at Phebus uprysynge
Iarmed hem with gret dilligence,   *Armed themselves*
Ageyn Troyens to stonden at diffence.
Amonges whom that day, as I rede,
So wel hym bar worthi Diomede
2055   That many Troyan thorugh his cruelté
Hath loste his lyf, til Troilus gan to se
This Diomede in the feld ridyng,
To whom anoon withoute more tariyng,   *immediately*
With his spere throwe into the reste,   *thrust*
2060   This Troilus rod and hit hym oon the breste
So myghtely that of verray nede
Doun of his hors he smet Dyomede,   *off; smote*
Albe of wounde he hadde no damage.   *Although*
And furiously Troilus in his rage
2065   Of envie gan hym to abreide,   *upbraid*
Whan he was doun, the love of Cryseide,
Of his deceit and his trecherie.
And Grekis than faste gan hem hye   *hasten*
Amonge the hors in meschef where he lay,
2070   To drawe him oute in al the hast thei may;
And on a sheld, brosed and affraied,   *bruised*
Thei bare him hom, so he was dismaied
Of the stroke, home unto his tent.
And Menelay the same while hath hent
2075   A myghty spere t'avenge Dyomede
And to Troilus faste gan hym spede,
Fully avysed to unhorsen hym anon.   *intending*
But Troylus first made his stede goon
So swyfte a course toward Menelay
2080   That he anoon at the erthe lay,   *at once on*
So myghtely he hit hym with his spere

	That shelde and plate myghte hym nat were	*protect*
	To saven hym from a mortal wounde.	
	But his knyghtes, anon as thei him founde,	
2085	Oute of the pres whan thei han hym rent,	*troop; taken*
	Thei bar hym hom to his owne tent,	
	The Grekis ay stondyng in distresse	
	Thorugh the knyghthod and the highe prowes	
	Of this Troylus, whiche hath hem so beleyn	*set upon*
2090	On every part, where he rod on the pleyn,	
	Til unto tyme that Agamenoun	
	Into the felde is avaled doun	*descended*
	With many worthi abouten his baner	
	That shon ful shene ageyn the sonne cler.	*bright*
2095	And with his knyghtes ridyng enviroun,	*around*
	He sore enchased hem of Troye toun,	*drove away*
	Woundeth and sleth and put hem to the flight,	
	Hymsilfe aquytynge lik a manly knyght;	
	But for al that, withoute more abood	*delay*
2100	Amongis Troyens fersely as he rood,	
	This worthi kyng, grete Agamenoun,	
	With a spere Troylus smet hym doun	
	Maugre his Grekis — ther geineth no socour.	*Despite*
	And whan thei sawe her lord, her governour,	
2105	In swyche meschef at the grounde lyende,	*distress*
	Thei hent hym up and made hym to ascende	*took*
	Thorugh her manhod on his stronge stede.	
	And he of wyt gan to taken hede	
	And consider wysly in his thought	
2110	In what disjoynt Troylus had hym brought	*peril*
	And how the Grekis, for al her grete pride,	
	Toforn his swerde myghte nat abide.	
	He prudently of highe discrecioun,	
	This noble knyght, Kyng Agamenoun,	
2115	As he that hadde ay his advertence	*thought*
	On governaunce thorugh his providence	
	Whanne he sawe his Grekis gonne faille	*begin to*
	And wexe feble to stonden in bataille	*grow*
	For lak of stuf that shulde hem recounforte,	*inspire*
2120	Ful prudently he made hem to resorte,	*retire*

Everyche of hem, to his owne tent.
And after that he hath to Priam sent
For a trew, to Troye the cité,   *truce*
For sixe monthes, yif it myghte be.   *if*
2125   And by his conseil Priamus the Kyng
Withoute abood granted his axyng,   *delay*
Albe that somme, as Guydo list endite,   *Although; wishes to write*
Were evel apaied so longe to respite   *displeased; grant a respite to*
Her mortal fon in any maner wyse;   *foes*
2130   But yit his graunt, as ye han herd devise,
Stood in his strengthe fully, as I rede.
In whiche tyme, of verray womanhede,
Cryseyde list no lenger for to tarie,
Though hir fader wer therto contrarie,
2135   For to visite and to han a sight
Of Diomede, that was become hir knyght,
Whiche had of Troylus late kought a wounde.
And in his tent, whanne she hath hym founde,
Benignely upon his beddis syde
2140   She set hir doun in the silve tyde,   *same time*
And platly cast in hir owne thought,   *plainly*
Touchinge Troylus, that it was for nought   *Concerning*
To lyve in hope of any more recure,   *recovery*
And thought she wolde for no thing be unsure   *in no way*
2145   Of purvyaunce nor withoute stoor: *sufficient supply*
She yaf anoon, withouten any mor,   *gave at once; further delay*
Hooly hir herte unto Diomede.
Loo, what pité is in wommanhede,
What mercy eke and benygne routhe
2150   That newly can al her olde trouthe,
Of nature, late slyppe asyde
Rather thanne thei shulde se abide
Any man in meschef for hir sake!   *distress*
The change is nat so redy for to make
2155   In Lombard Strete of crowne nor doket: *ducat*
Al paie is good, be so the prente be set.   *money; impression [on a coin]*
Her lettre of change doth no man abide.   *exchange; wait for*
So that the wynde be redy and the tyde,
Passage is ay, whoso list to passe.   *wishes*

2160	No man is lost that list to seke grace;	
	Daunger is noon but counterfet disdeyn;	*Resistance; pretended*
	The se is calme and fro rokkis pleyn:	*unobstructed*
	For mercyles never man ne deide	
	That soughte grace. Recorde of Cryseyde,	*Think*
2165	Whiche finally hath yoven al hir herte	*given*
	To Diomede in reles of his smerte,	*remedy; injury*
	And praide hym to be right glad and light,	
	And called hym hir owne man, hir knyght,	
	And hym behight, rather than he deie,	*promised*
2170	In everything how she wolde obeye	
	That were honest, hym to do plesaunce:	
	For levere she had chaunge and variaunce	*she would prefer*
	Were founde in hir thanne lak of pité,	
	As sittyng is to femynyté,	*fitting*
2175	Of nature nat to be vengable,	*vengeful*
	For feith nor othe but rather mercyable	*merciful*
	Of mannys lyf stondyng in distresse.	

[*Agamemnon goes himself to prevail on Achilles to return to the war. Achilles refuses but allows his Myrmidons to fight. In the ensuing battle, many of Achilles's men are slain, and he is caught between his love for Polyxena and his grief for his men. After another truce, Troilus attacks the Myrmidons so furiously that their cries and the threat of a Trojan victory finally move Achilles to take the field in anger. He and Troilus meet and wound one another. When his wound heals, Achilles calls his men together and plots Troilus's death (lines 2178–2646).*]

	. . . This felle envious Achilles	*cruel*
	To his knyghtes, called Mirmidones,	
	Upon Troylus gan hym to compleyne,	
2650	Besechynge hem for to done her peyne	
	Ageyn this Troylus in the feld that day	
	To cachen hym at meschef yif thei may,	*disadvantage if*
	And besely to done her dilligence	
	On hym to han her ful advertence,	*give heed*
2655	By oon assent, wherso that he ride —	
	Al other thing for to sette asyde	
	And of nought ellis for to taken hede,	
	Sauf finally ageyn hym to procede	

	Yif thei myght cacche hym in a trappe	
2660	And withinne hemsilf Troilus for to clap,	*shut up inside with a bang*
	To enclose and sette hym rounde aboute	
	In al wyse that he go nat oute.	
	And whan he were beset amonge hem alle,	*surrounded*
	Nat to slen hym, whatsoevere falle,	*whatever might happen*
2665	But thorugh her myght manly hym conserve,	*keep*
	Til he hymsilfe come and make hym sterve	*die*
	With his swerd, he and noon other wyght.	*person*
	Lo, here a manhod for to preise aright!	
	Vengaunce of deth, of rancour, and of pride,	
2670	Compassid tresoun, knyghthod leyde aside!	*Devised*
	Worthines be envie slawe,	*by; slain*
	Falshed alofte, trouthe abak ydrawe!	*suppressed*
	Allas, in armys that it shulde falle,	
	Of trecherie that the bitter galle	
2675	Shuld in this world in any knyght be founde,	
	That be to trouthe of her order bounde.	
	Allas, allas, for now this Achilles	
	Conspired hath with his Mirmidones	
	The deth of oon the worthiest wyght	
2680	That evere was and the beste knyght.	
	Allas, for wo I fele myn herte blede	
	For his sake, this story whan I rede.	
	But whan Fortune hath a thing ordeyned,	
	Though it be evere wailled and compleined,	
2685	Ther is no geyn nor no remedie	*avail*
	Though men on it galen ay and crye,	*exclaim against it*
	I can no more touchinge this matere	
	But write forthe, lik as ye shal here,	
	How Mirmidones han her lord behight	*promised*
2690	With al her power and her fulle myght	
	To fulfillen his comaundement;	
	And into feld with Grekis thei be went.	
	But Troylus first, in the opposit,	*on the opposite side*
	Of verray knyghthood hath so grete delit	
2695	Withoute abood manly hem to mete;	*delay*
	He was ybrent with so fervent hete	
	Of hardines and of highe corage,	

Of worthines and of vasselage

That hym ne list no lenger to abide   *he did not wish*

2700 But with his folk in began to ride

Amonge Grekis, this stok of highe renoun.   *stock (source)*

And with his swerd he woundeth and bereth doun,

Sleth and kylleth upon every halfe   *side*

So mortally that ther may no salve

2705 Her sores sounde; for ther was but deth,   *heal*

Wherso he rood, and yelding up the breth,

So furiously he gan hem enchase   *drive away*

And made hem lese in a litel space   *lose*

Her lond echon and aforn hym fle:

2710 In Troylus swerd ther was swiche cruelté

That maugre hem he the feld hath wonne.   *despite*

The same tyme whan the brighte sonne

Highe in the south at mydday marke shon,

Evene at the hour whan it drowe to noon,

2715 Whan Mirmidones, gadred alle in oon,

In compasse wyse rounde aboute hym gon   *Encircled*

And furiously of oon entencioun,

Thei made a cercle aboute hym enviroun,

Whan thei sawe him of helpe desolaat.

2720 But he of hert nat disconsolat

Upon no side, thorugh his manlyhede,

Lik a lyoun toke of hem noon hede,

But thorugh his famus knyghtly excellence

As a tigre stondeth at diffence,

2725 And manfully gan hem to encombre,   *press on*

And to lasse and to discres her noumbre.   *lessen*

And somme he maymeth and woundeth to the deth,

And somme he made to yelden up the breth,

And somme he laide to the erthe lowe,

2730 And somme he made for to overthrowe

With his swerd of her blood al wet

At gret meschef at his horse fet;   *distress*

Upon his stede sturdy as a wal,

This worthy knyght, this man most marcial,

2735 Pleyeth his pley amonge Mirmidones,

Hymsilf, God wote, allone al helpeles.   *knows*

But tho, allas, what myght his force avail
Whan thre thousand knyghtes hym assail
On every part, bothe in lengthe and brede?
2740 And cowardly first thei slow his stede
With her speris, sharpe and square grounde;   *ground at a cutting angle*
For whiche, allas, he stont now on the grounde
Withoute reskus, refut, or socour,   *shelter*
That was that day of chivalrie flour.
2745 But, weillawey, thei han hym so beset   *set upon*
That from his hed thei smet his basenet,   *smote; headpiece*
And brak his harneis, as thei hym assaille,   *armor*
And severed of stele the myghti stronge maille.
He was disarmyd bothe nekke and hed,
2750 Allas the whyle, and no man toke noon hede
Of alle his knyghtes longynge to the toun;
And yit alweye this Troyan champioun
In knyghtly wyse, naked as he was,   *unprotected*
Hymsilfe diffendeth, til Achilles, allas,
2755 Cam ridynge in, furious and wood.
And whan he sawe how Troilus nakid stod,
Of longe fightyng awaped and amaat   *stunned and wearied (check-mated)*
And from his folke allone disolat,
Sool by hymsilf at meschef pitously,   *Alone; peril*
2760 This Achilles wonder cruelly,
Behynde unwarly, or that he toke hed,   *without warning before*
With his swerd smyteth of his hed
And cast it forthe of cruel cursed herte;
And thought pleynly, it shuld him nat asterte   *fail*
2765 To shewe his malys, this wolfe unmerciable.
Ful unknyghtly to be more vengable
Upon the body that lay ded and colde —
Allas, that ever it shuld of knyght be tolde,
Wryte, or rehersed, to do so foule a dede,   *Written*
2770 Or in a boke, allas, that men shuld rede
Of any knyght a story so horrible,
Unto the eris passingly odible —   *ears exceedingly hateful*
For this Achille of cruelté, allas,
The dede cors toke oute of the taas,   *corpse; heap*
2775 And vengably bond it, as I fynde,

247

	At the taille of his hors behynde,	
	And hatfully, that every wyght behilde,	
	Drowe it hymsilf endelonge the feld	*the length of*
	Thorugh the rengis and the wardis alle.	*ranks; divisions*
2780	But, O allas, that evere it shulde falle	
	A knyght to bene in herte so cruel	
	Or of hatred so dispitous fel	*pitiless cruelly*
	To drawe a man after that he were ded.	
	O thou, Omer, for shame be now red	*Homer*
2785	And be astonyd, that haldest thisilfe so wyse,	*astonished*
	On Achilles to setten swiche a pris.	*value*
	In thi bokes for his chivalrie	
	Above echon dost hym magnyfye,	*celebrate*
	That was so sleighty and so ful of fraude —	*wily*
2790	Whi yevest thou hym so highe a pris and laude?	*worth*
	Certis, Omer, for al thin excellence	*Certainly*
	Of rethoryk and of eloquence,	
	Thi lusty songes and thi dites swete,	*verses*
	Thin hony mouthe that doth with sugre flete,	*flow*
2795	Yet in o thing thou gretly art to blame:	
	Causeles to yeve hym swiche a name,	*give*
	With a title of triumphe and glorie	
	So passingly putte hym in memorie,	
	In thi bokes to seyn and write so,	
2800	Thorugh his knyghthod he slowe Hectoris two —	
	First hym that was lik unto noon other,	
	And Troilus after, that was his owne brother.	
	Yif thou arte meved of affeccioun,	*If*
	Whiche that thou hast to Grekis nacioun,	
2805	To preise hym so, for thou canst endite,	*compose*
	Thou shuldest ay for any favour write	
	The trouthe pleinly, and ben indifferent,	
	And seie the sothe clerly of entent.	*truth*
	For whan he slowe Hector in the felde,	
2810	He was aforn disarmyd of his shelde	*in front*
	And besy eke in spoylyng of a kyng:	*pillaging*
	For yif he had be war of his comyng,	*if*
	He had hym quytte thorugh his chivalrie	*He would have repaid him (Achilles)*
	His fals deceit and his trecherie,	

2815	That he ne had so lightly from hym gon.	
	Troilus also was naked and allone,	
	Amyd foure thousand closed and beshet	*hemmed in*
	Whan Achilles hath his hed of smet,	*off*
	At his bak of ful cruel herte,	
2820	Whan he no thing his tresoun dide adverte.	*in no way; foresee*
	Was that a dede of a manly knyght,	
	To slen a man forweried in fight,	
	Feynt of travail, al the longe day	*Tired out by his effort*
	Amonge so many stondyng at abay,	
2825	A kynges sone and so highe born,	
	Naked the hed, his armure al totorn,	
	Evene at the deth on the silfe point,	*very*
	At disavauntage, and pleinly oute of joynt,	*in peril*
	Of his lyf stondyng on the wrak,	*near destruction*
2830	Whan Achilles cam falsly at the bak,	
	Assaillynge hym whan he was half ded,	
	And lyk a coward smot of thanne his hed,	
	That was toforn hurte and wounded sore?	
	Wherfor, Omer, preise hym now no more.	
2835	Lat nat his pris thi rial boke difface	*renown*
	But in al haste his renoun oute arace:	*erase*
	For his name whan I here nevene,	*uttered*
	Verrailly up unto the hevene	
	(As semeth me) infect is the eyr,	*air*
2840	The sown therof so foule is and unfair.	*sound*
	For yif that he had hadde his advertence,	*if; paid heed*
	Outher the eye of his providence	
	Unto knyghthod or to worthines,	
	Outher to manhod or to gentilnes,	
2845	Or to the renoun of his owne name,	
	Or to the report of his knyghtly fame,	
	In any wyse to have taken hede,	
	He hadde never don so foule a dede:	
	So vengably for to have ydrawe	*drawn*
2850	A kynges sone after he was slawe —	
	And namly hym, that was so gode a knyght,	
	Whiche in his tyme, whoso loke aright,	
	Passed Achille, I dar it wel expresse,	

Bothe of manhod and of gentilnes.
2855 But for al that, he is now ded, allas.

[*King Menon reproves Achilles for the treachery of Troilus's death. He wounds Achilles, who is rescued by the Myrmidons. Achilles then plots Menon's death in the same way he earlier contrived to surround and kill Hector and Troilus. All Homer's rhetoric cannot disguise Achilles's fraud and treachery. The Greeks drive the Trojans into the city. Their sorrow at Troilus's death is beyond the power of Boethius, Statius, or Ovid to describe. Priam asks for a truce and builds tombs for Troilus and Menon (lines 2856–3097).*]

	But I purpose ceriously to telle	*in due order*
	How Eccuba, as I can endyte,	*Hecuba; compose*
3100	Hir caste fully Achilles to quyte	*planned; repay*
	His tyranny, sothly, yif she may.	*if*
	And unto hir she calleth on a day	
	Alysaundre in ful secré wyse	*Alexander (Paris)*
	And unto hym, as I shal devyse,	*describe*
3105	With wepynge eyen and with hevy chere	
	Seide evene thus, lyk as ye shal here.	
	"Parys," quod she, "allas, sauf Goddis wille,	
	Thou knowest wel how the ferse Achille	*fierce*
	My sonys hath slayen nyghe echon;	*sons*
3110	Ther is non lefte but thisilf allone:	
	He hath me made (allas, ther is no geyn),	*remedy*
	Ful cowardly, of children now bareyn,	
	Bothe of Hector and of Troylus eke therto	
	Whiche were to me in every trouble and wo	
3115	Fully counfort, plesaunce, and solace.	
	Wherfore, I caste pleynly to compasse	*intend; devise*
	By som engyn his deth to ordeyne;	*stratagem*
	And lyke as he by tresoun dide his peyne,	
	Traytourly with his swerd to smyte,	
3120	Right so, I think, with tresoun hym to quyte,	*repay*
	As sittyng is of right and equyté.	
	And sith thou wost pleynly how that he	*know*
	Hath sette his herte and his love clene	
	On my doughter, yonge Polycene,	*Polyxena*
3125	To fyn only to haven hir to wyve;	
	For whiche I caste to hym sende blyve	*plan; at once*

For to come and trete of that mater
In the temple of Appollo here,
In the temple most chef of this cité.
3130 Whiche tyme my wil is that thou be
Thisilven armyd ther ful prively,   *secretly*
With certeyn knyghtes in thi company
Armyd also ageyn the same day,
That in no wyse he skape nat away   *escape*
3135 From your hondis but that he be ded,
As I have seid; and therfor take good hed
Unto this thing, with al myn herte, I praie,
Fro point to point my biddyng to abeie."   *follow*
And he assenteth with al his hoole herte,
3140 Behotyng hir he shulde nat asterte.   *Promising; escape*
And with hym toke twenty and no mo
Of manly men that wel durste do;
And in the temple by ful good avys
Thei wern yhyd by byddyng of Paris,   *hidden*
3145 While Eccuba, covert in hir entent,   *secret*
Hir messager to Achilles hathe sent,
As ye han herde, in conclusioun,
To come in haste unto Troye toun
After th'effect was of hir message,
3150 Only to trete for a mariage.   *negotiate*
And he in haste cometh at hir sonde,   *message*
As he that koude no thing undirstonde   *in no way*
Hir tresoun hid nor pleinly it adverte: *foresee*
He was so hote marked in his herte
3155 With lovys brond and his firé glede,   *brand; coal*
Of lyf nor deth that he toke noon hede
But sette aside wit and al resoun,   *intelligence*
To caste aforn by gode discrecioun
What was to do, with lokyng ful prudent.
3160 But he in soth was with love blent,   *blinded*
Into Troye whan he shulde goon,
Lyke as it fareth of lovers everychon:
Whanne thei have kaught in herte a fantasie,   *desire*
For no pereil, though thei shulde deye,
3165 Thei have no myght nor power to be ware,

Til thei unwarly be trapped in the snare:
Her maladie is so furious.
And thus Achilles and Anthilogus,
Nestoris sone, han the weye nome   *taken*
3170 Toward the toun and ben togidre come
Into temple, as ye han herd me telle.
And Paris tho list no lenger duelle   *delay*
But, unwarly, with his knyghtes alle
On Achilles is at meschef falle,
3175 Everyche of hem with a swerd ful bright.
And somme bokis seyn it was by nyght,
Whan his deth, longe aforn desired,
By Eccuba and Paris was conspired.
But Achilles in this mortal caas,
3180 Amonge hem alle naked as he was,   *unarmed*
Hent oute a swerde in the silve stevene;   *at the very moment*
And like a knyght he slow of hem sevene
Of verray force, maugre al her myght.   *despite*
But whan Paris therof hadde a sight,
3185 Thre dartes raught that were kene and square,   *arrows; seized*
And sodeinly, or that he was ware,   *before*
Ful secrely hid under the shade,
Markyng at hym and no noyse made,
Caste at hym evene as evere he can,   *Shot*
3190 That hed and shafte thorugh the body ran;
And therwithal knyghtes nat a fewe
With sharpe swerdis gan upon him hewe   *cut*
And left hym nat til he lay at grounde
Ful pale ded, with many mortal wounde.
3195 And rightfully, of resoun as it sit,
Thus was the fraude and the falshede quit   *repaid*
Of Achilles, for his highe tresoun:
As deth for deth is skilfully guerdoun   *proper recompense*
And egal mede, withouten any fable,   *equal payment*
3200 To hem that be merciles vengable.
For thilke day, Guydo writeth thus,   *that same*
That Achilles and Anthilogus
Of Paris wern in the temple slawe;   *slain*
And afterward the body was out drawe

3205	Of Achille fro the holy boundis	*precincts*
	And cruelly throwen unto houndis	
	To be devourid in the brode strete,	*wide*
	The canel rennynge with his wawes wete	*gutter; waves (of blood)*
	Withoute pité or any maner routhe.	
3210	Loo, here the ende of falshed and untrouthe,	
	Loo, here the fyn of swiche trecherie,	
	Of fals deceit compassid by envie.	*devised; hatred*
	Loo, here the knot and conclusioun,	*main point (see note)*
	How God quyt ay slaughter by tresoun.	*requites*
3215	Loo, here the guerdoun and the final mede	*prize; reward*
	Of hem that so deliten in falsehede:	
	For everything, platly for to seyne,	
	Like as it is, his guerdoun doth atteyne,	*reward*
	As ye may se of this Achilles,	
3220	Whiche on a nyght in the temple les	*lost*
	His lyf; for he was ay customable	*accustomed*
	By fraude and tresoun for to be vengable.	
	But it befel at request of Eleyne	*happened*
	That the bodies of this ilke tweyne	
3225	Conservid wern from the hungri rage	
	Of best and foule, gredy and ramage.	*wild*
	And yit thei laie amyddes the cité	
	Ful openly, that men myght hem se,	
	To grete gladnes to hem of the toun,	
3230	Into tyme that Agamenoun	
	To Kyng Priam sent his massageris	
	To have licence to fet hem hom on beris;	*permission; biers*
	By graunt of whom thei han the corsis take.	*corpses*
	For whom Grekis swiche a sorwe make	
3235	That pité was and routhe for to here.	

[*After Achilles's death, Agamemnon challenges the Greeks to exact vengeance. Ajax Telamon urges them to send for Achilles's son, Pyrrhus, whom prophets say will bring the downfall of the city. Menelaus is dispatched to bring him to Troy. In June, the Greeks take the field. Ajax Telamon rides without armor, carrying only a sword. He has survived many battles, but Fortune now turns against him. Paris shoots him with a poisoned arrow. Ajax, mortally wounded, splits Paris's skull in two. Troy is thrown into shock by the death of the last of Priam's sons, and Helen cannot contain her grief. Priam closes the gates of the city and will not give battle to the Greeks, despite Agamemnon's challenge (lines 3236–3757).]*

	And yit in soth cause of his tariynge	*truth; delay*
	Was for the hardy Quene of Femynye	
3760	Toward Troye faste gan hir hiye	*hasten*
	Oute of hir lond, a litel regioun,	
	The whiche, as bokis make mencioun,	
	After the syyt of the firmament	*position; sphere of the fixed stars*
	Is in the plage of the orient,	*region*
3765	And called is the regne of Amazonys,	
	Of whiche the custom and the wone ys	*habit*
	That only wommen therin shal abide:	
	And thei ar wont armyd for to ryde	
	And han in armys gret experience;	
3770	For her labour and her dilligence	
	Is finally to haven excersyce	
	Fro day to day in Martis highe servyse.	
	And overmore her custom and usaunce,	
	As to this day is maked remembraunce,	
3775	Is that no man shal hem nyghe ner,	*come near them*
	But yif it be thre monthes in the yer:	*Except for*
	This to seyn, in June, April, and May;	
	And than the wommen han in custom ay	
	Unto an yle a litel therbesyde,	*island*
3780	Wher as the men by hemsilfe abide	*remain*
	Fro yere to yere togidre everychon,	
	Unto the men oute of her lond to gon,	
	And there abide in that regioun	
	Til tyme cometh of concepcioun,	
3785	Withoute tariynge any lenger while;	
	For thanne anoon home unto her ile	
	Thei repeire oute of that contré	
	Unto tyme that thei delyvered be.	
	And as faste as the childe is born,	
3790	For lak of kepynge that it be nat lorn,	*lost*
	He fostrid is til thre yere be agoon	*past*
	Amonge the wommen; and thanne right anon	

	To the ile besiden adjacent	
	Unto the men the childe in haste is sent,	
3795	Yif that it be of kynde masculyn.	*If; nature*
	And yif it falle that it be femynyn,	
	With the wommen abide stille it shal	
	Til that it be in actis marcial	
	Ful wel experte and that she can eke knowe	*also*
3800	To handle a spere or to drawe a bowe,	
	Lyke the statutis of that regioun,	*laws*
	The whiche, as bokes make mencioun,	
	Is set betwene Ewrope and Asya.	
	And of this lond was Pantysyllya	*Penthesilea*
3805	Whilom lady and governeresse,	
	Ful renomed of strengthe and hardynes	
	Thorughoute the world, bothe in lengthe and brede;	
	And yit in soth to speke of wommanhede,	*truth*
	For al her myght she had an huge pris,	*worth*
3810	For bothe she was vertuous and wys,	
	Wonder discret, and had an honest name,	
	Natwithstondynge the excelle of fame	
	Of hir renoun in armys and the glorie:	
	For of conquest and of highe victorie	
3815	She was most surmountyng out of drede	
	Of any womman that I can of rede;	
	And sothly yit bokes bere witnesse,	
	Of wommanhede and of gentilnesse	
	She kepte hir so that nothinge hir asterte.	*she was never indiscreet*
3820	The whiche loved with al hir hoole herte	
	Worthi Hector and with al her myght,	
	Only for he was so noble a knyght	
	That hir joye and worldly plesaunce,	
	Hir hertly ese and sovereyne soffisaunce,	*contentment*
3825	In verray soth, where she wake or winke,	*sleep*
	Was evere in oon upon hym to thinke,	*the same*
	Of verray feith, withouten any slouthe.	
	And unto hym she was be bond of trouthe	
	Confederat of olde affeccioun,	
3830	That whan she herd how that Troye toun	
	Besegid was of the Grekis felle,	*cruel*

This hardy quene liste no lenger dwelle   *wishes*
But hasteth hir as fast as evere she may
Toward Troye in ful good array
3835 With alle the worthi wommen of hir londe,
Ful wel expert and preved of her honde,
Wel horsed eke and armed richely.
And as I fynde, in her company,
A thousand maidenes ridinge by her side,
3840 This worthi quene, that durste wel abide, *stand firm*
She with hir brought in steel armyd bright
For love of Hector, hir owne trewe knyght.
And on hir weie fast she gan to spede
To helpen hym yif she seie nede: *if; saw*
3845 For in nothinge she koude hir more delite
Thanne towarde hym feithfully hir quyte, *act*
For that was al hir lust and hertis joye.
But whan that she comen was to Troye
And herde telle by relacioun
3850 That he was ded, most worthi of renoun,
To whom she was so lovinge and so trewe,
Anoon she gan to chaungen cher and hewe,
And pitously for to wepe and crye,
And ferd in soth as she wolde deye
3855 For verray wo and hertly hevynes,
And thought she wold thorugh hir worthines
Avenge his deth platly, yif she may, *openly*
On the Grekis; and so uppon a day
She preieth Priam with gret affeccioun
3860 For to oppene the gatis of the toun,
And to gon oute with Grekis for to fight,
That thei may knowe and be expert aright *trained by experience*
Of this womman the grete worthines,
And of this quene the famous hardines;
3865 And so the kyng, hopynge for the beste,
Withoute abood grauntet hir requeste *delay*
The nexte morwe, whan Phebus shon ful shene;
And al toforn out goth Phylymene, *Philomene*
The noble kyng, with hem of Paffaganye;
3870 And after hym other knyghtes manye

Folwed after with worthi Eneas,
The Troyan eke, Daungh Pallydamas.   *Lord*
And thanne the Quene Pantasyllya
By the gate called Dardanyca
3875 Toward Grekis proudly issed oute,
With hir wommen ridyng hir aboute.
The whiche anoon whan Grekis dide espie,
Into the felde gan hem faste hiye: *hasten*
And first of alle worthi Meneste,
3880 Pantasillia whanne he dide se,
With his sporis made his stede gon,
And with a spere rood to hir anoon,   *at once*
Of whom the quene astonyd neveradel,   *dismayed*
Caught eke a spere that was squarid wel,   *cut at the proper angle*
3885 Rounde the shafte, and the hed wel grounde,
Whiche as thei coupe smet him doun to grounde   *met in tilting*
And maugre hym reved him his stede.   *despite; deprived*
And thanne in haste in cam Diomede
And cruelly to the quene gan ride;
3890 And she as faste on the tother side   *the other*
Rood eke to hym in platis bright and shene;
And as thei mette with her speris kene,
She hitte so this felle Diomede,   *cruel*
For al his myght and his manlyhede,
3895 That she hym made his sadel for to lese.   *lose*
Ther is no more — he myght tho nat chese.   *he had no choice*
And in dispite of his men echon,
She hath his sheld hym beraft anoon   *dispossessed*
And it delyvereth, proudly as she rood,
3900 To a maide that uppon hir abood.   *waited*
And like a tigre in his gredinesse
Or like, in soth, to a lyounesse,
That day she ferde, ridynge up and doun   *acted*
Amonge the Grekis, til that Thelamoun   *Telamon (son of Ajax and Hesione)*
3905 Gan beholde the slaughter that she made,
Of highe dispit and rancour overlade,   *overflowing*
As he that myght for ire not sustene,   *bear it*
Gan ren his hors to falle uppon the quene.   *turned*
But whan that she his comynge dide espie,

257

3910	She fil on hym in hir malencolye	*fury*
	So mortally, maugre his knyghtes alle,	*despite*
	That to the grounde she made him for to falle	
	And Grekis put in so grete disaray,	
	Wherevere she rood al that ilke day;	
3915	For thei myght aforn hir nat sustene.	*hold out*
	And thorugh the helpe of Kyng Philymene,	
	As myn auctor recordeth in his boke,	
	Amyd the feld Thelamoun she toke	
	And sent hym forthe thorugh her highe renoun	
3920	As prisoner toward Troye toun,	
	Til unto rescus cam cruel Diomede,	
	And cruelly on hem that gan him lede	
	He fil unwarly with an huge route	*without warning; troop*
	Of his knyghtes ridynge hym aboute,	
3925	And from her hondis, maugre al her myght,	*despite*
	He hym delivereth like a manly knyght.	
	At whiche tyme, this hardy quene anon,	
	With hir wommen aboute hir everychon,	
	The Grekis hath aforn hir on the pleyn	
3930	(As writ Guydo) so mortally beleyn	*set upon*
	That she hem made of necessité	
	Oute of the feld with her swerd to fle,	
	That verrayly it was incredible	
	And to leve a maner impossible	*believe*
3935	To sene the wommen Grekis so enchase,	*drive away*
	Whiche myghte nat abide aforn her face	
	Nor in the feld in any wyse stonde:	
	For thei hem dryve to the silfe stronde,	*shore itself*
	Doun to the clyf of the salte se	
3940	And slowe of hem so huge gret plenté	*slew*
	That finally thei had be distroyed	
	For everemore and outterly accloied,	*annihilated*
	Nadde Diomede stonden at diffence	*Had not*
	And of knyghthod maked resistence:	
3945	For he that day in parti and in al	
	For Grekis stood as a sturdy wal	
	And was allone her helpe and chef socour.	
	But for al that, with worship and honour	

258

Pantasillya, as made is memorie,
3950 Repeired is with conquest and victorie,   *Returned*
    With alle hir wommen into Troye toun
    Upon the hour of Phebus goynge doun.
    And by the side of this hardy quene
    Armyd in stel rood Kyng Phylymene,
3955 Whom Priamus hath with gret reverence
    Knyghtly reseved and dide his dilligence   *received*
    Hem to refreshe with every maner thing
    That myghte be unto her likyng,
    As her hertis koude best devyse.   *imagine*
3960 And after this, in ful goodly wyse,
    He thanked hath the noble hardy quene
    Of hir goodnes that hir lyste to sene   *wished; attend*
    To helpyn hym in his grete nede
    And offrid hir (in Guydo as I rede)
3965 Al that he hath, tresour and richesse,
    Hopynge fully thorugh hir worthines
    Upon Grekis avengid for to be
    And for to kepe hym and his cité
    Maugre Grekis, whiche of hem seye nay.   *Despite*
3970 For as I rede, after day be day
    She stinte nat proudly hem t'assaile,   *stopped*
    Ageyn whos swerd thei myghte nat availe,
    So mortally she made her sides blede.

[*Meanwhile, Menelaus arrives at Troy with Pyrrhus. Agamemnon knights him, and the Myrmidons pledge him their fealty. Pyrrhus carries his father's arms into battle, and he is ashamed when Penthesilea drives the Myrmidons back and reproaches him for Achilles's cowardly murder of Hector. She unhorses Pyrrhus, and the Myrmidons have to rescue him from her. Fighting continues daily for a month, during which a hundred Amazons are slain. Fortune, never stable, begins to turn her favor from Penthesilea (lines 3974–4280).*]

    The fatal hour, harde for to remewe,   *escape*
    Of cruel deth, which no man may eschewe
    Nor in this lyfe finally eskape,
    Specially whan Parchas han it shape,   *determined*
4285 Aproche gan — it may noon other bene,
    Allas the while — of this hardy quene,

Whiche on a day, furious and wroth,
Into the feld oute of Troye goth
And gan on Grekis proudly for to sette.
4290   And alderfirst Pirrus with hir mette   *first of all*
Of mortal hate and indignacioun;
And she in haste by the rengis doun   *ranks*
Rood unto hym swiftly on hir stede,
Whos sporis sharpe made his sides blede.
4295   And as thei mette, her speris in the rest,   *support for a lance*
Thei bare so evene, markyng at the brest,   *came straight aiming*
That her shaftis, sothly this no tale,   *truly*
Gan to shyvere alle on pecis smale   *splinter*
Withoute bowynge outher bak or chyne:
4300   For nouther made other to enclyne,   *bend*
Save the hed forged harde of steel
Of Pantasillya, that was grounde wel,
In Pirrus brest percid hath so depe
That plate in soth nor maille myght hym kepe,   *protect*
4305   But the sharpnes of the speris hede
Was of his blod in party died rede.   *dyed*
The whiche strok whan Grekis gan espie,
Forastonyd loude gan to crye
And alle attonys for the noise and soun   *at once; sound*
4310   Upon this quene in the feld cam doun,
In compas wyse goynge enviroun.   *encircling*
But thorugh hir prowesse and hir highe renoun
She hir diffendeth, that it was mervaille;
But thei, allas, so sore hir gan assaille
4315   That al tohewe thei han hir basenet;   *cut apart; head armor*
Amyd Grekis so thikke she was beset   *surrounded*
That with axes and her swerdis square   *sharpened*
Hir hed in soth maked was al bare
And hir shuldris were nakid eke, allas,   *exposed also*
4320   The maille hewe of and the rerebras.   *armor to protect upper arm and shoulder*
And Pirrus than, lyke as it is founde,
For anguyshe only of his grene wounde,
In doute pleynly wher he shulde eskape,   *whether*
Toward this quene faste gan hym rape   *ride hastily*
4325   To be avengid, whatsoevere falle,   *whatever might happen*

Amyd the feld amonge the Grekis alle.
And whan she sawe that he cam so faste,
Of force only to mete him yit she cast *prepared*
And with hir swerd first gan hym assaille;
4330 But of hir strok it happed hir to faille,
Amonge the pres so narwe she was beset. *closely; surrounded*
And Pirrus swerd was so sharpe whet
That sodeinly of hir arme he smette. *off*
Allas, ther was non armour hym to lette *stop*
4335 But raceth thorugh al the shulder bon, *cut through*
So that this quene fil doun ded anon.
And of malys for to venge hym more, *spite*
At his hert the ire frat so sore *consumed*
That with a chere of verray angir pale *expression*
4340 He hath hir hewe al on pecis smale, *cut; into*
The whiche was so foule a cruel dede.
But evere in on Pirrus so gan blede, *continually*
Nighe to the deth of his mortal wounde,
For lak of blod that he fil to grounde.
4345 In a trawnce ful longe gruf he lay, *prone*
Til his knyghtes in al the haste thei may
Han take hym up and leide him on a sheld;
And doolfully home oute of the feld
Thei han hym born, wounded as he was.
4350 And the wommen of the quene, allas,
For verray sorwe and inward dedly wo,
Whan thei sawe her lady was ago,
For to be ded thei were so desirous
That in al haste, wood and furious, *mad*
4355 In a rage, withoute governaile, *discipline*
Grekis thei gan of newe for to assaille —
T'avenge her quene thei wer so hertly kynde — *disposed*
That thei slowe, sothly as I fynde, *slew*
Two thousand Grekes — on hem thei wer so wod.
4360 But, O allas, in gret disjoint thei stood, *peril*
Only for lak thei have no governour; *commander*
For she was goon that was her chef socour,
Whiche was also, to speke of hardynes,
Of wommen alle lady and maistresse,

4365	As of hir hond that I can of rede.	
	O ye Troyens, ye stonden in gret drede,	
	Amyd the feld al oute of governaunce.	
	The day is come of youre unhappi chaunce,	*misfortune*
	For now have ye leder noon nor gyde:	
4370	Farwel youre trust now on every side.	
	And Grekes ben upon you so stronge	
	That ye the feld may nat kepe longe;	
	For thei cast hem fully you to quyte	*planned; avenge*
	This same day, as Dares list endite;	*chose to write*
4375	For as he writ, homward as thei drawe,	
	Ten thousand Troiens wern of Grekis slawe.	*slain*
	For alle her wardis cam attonys doun	*divisions*
	And mortally, withoute excepcioun,	
	Thei kille and sle al that hem withstood;	*stood against them*
4380	And moste thei wern on the wommen wood	*insane*
	To be avenged, pleinly as I rede,	
	On every halfe and her blood to shede	*side*
	Withoute mercy or remyssioun,	
	Chasyng Troiens home into the toun	
4385	Oute of the felde; for ther was noon abod,	*delay*
	So pitously tho with hem it stood	
	That thei ne can noon other recure caste	*remedy think of*
	But kepe her toun and shet her gatis faste,	*their*
	For al her hope clene was agoon	
4390	Anymore to fighte with her foon.	
	For now her trust of knyghthod was away,	
	Her worthi men slayen, weillaway.	
	Refut was noon but in her cyté	*Protection*
	To kepe hem clos — it may noon other be.	*shut up*
4395	For hem thought thei myght it kepe longe,	
	Her walles wern so myghti and so stronge,	
	Yif thei had plenté of vitaille;	*If*
	Though al the world attonis hem assaille,	*at once*
	Thei may be sure while thei kepe hem in	
4400	Foreveremore that no man shall hem wynne.	*conquer*
	Yet nevertheles erly and eke late	
	The Grekes made toforn every gate	
	Ful myghti wache and await ful stronge,	*guard*

262

	With pryvy spies goynge in amonge,	*secret*
4405	That of her foon noon eskape away	*foes*
	By noon engyn, as ferforthe as thei may.	*cunning*
	And in this while, withinne Troie toun,	
	More than I can make descripcioun,	
	For the quene ther was so gret a sorwe	
4410	Of every whight bothe at eve and morwe,	*person*
	That she, allas, was slayen for her mede,	*efforts (reward)*
	Whiche cam so fer to helpe hem in her nede;	
	And aldermost for thei ne myghte have	*most of all*
	The dede cors to burie and to grave	*inter*
4415	With reverence and with honour dwe,	
	For whiche thei gan to the Grekis swe	*entreat*
	With gret praier and grete besynes.	
	But al in veyn and in ydelnesse	
	Was her requeste — the Grekis wer so wrothe.	*their*
4420	And finally, with many sondry othe,	
	Only of malys and of hoot envie,	
	The dede cors to hem thei denye	
	And shortly seide of mortal enmyté	
	That of houndis it shal devoured be —	
4425	Ther was no geyn — her rancour to compesse.	*avail; restrain*
	But Pirrus thanne of verray gentilnesse	
	Nolde assent to so foule a dede;	*Would not*
	But wood and wrothe, cruel Diomede	*mad*
	Seide openly that it was fittynge	
4430	That she faile of hir buriynge,	
	That slayen hadde so many worthi man.	
	And thus the strif amonge the Grekis gan,	
	With grete rumour and altercacioun,	
	Til at the laste under Troye toun	
4435	Of hir thei han the dede cors ytake,	
	And cruelly in a profounde lake	*deep*
	Thei han it cast, where I lete hir lye,	
	And unto Troie ageyn I wil me hye	*hasten*
	To telle forthe howe thei lyve in pyne.	*grief*

[*Lydgate reproves Mars for his delight in murder, death, and dissension. Mars has brought treason and discord to Troy in the conspiracy of Anchises, Aeneas, Antenor, and Polydamas to betray the city. They urge Priam to return Helen and sue for peace, even though they know the Greeks will never accept anything less than the end of Priam's lineage and dynasty. Priam holds a council to discuss the peace proposal. Antenor's loyalty and integrity are publicly disputed, but Aeneas uses his skill at verbal subterfuge to argue for peace. Priam reminds both of them of their own complicity in the events that have led to the war. They leave in rage, while Priam can scarcely contain his grief and sense of doom. He conspires with his son Amphimachus to kill them at a council, but word of the plot escapes, and Aeneas, Antenor, and the others swear their determination to destroy Troy, if the Greeks will spare them and their possessions. When Priam convenes the council again, the conspirators show up in force. Aeneas seizes the initiative to persuade the Trojans to seek peace. Priam must concede and allows Antenor to be the Trojan emissary to the Greeks (lines 4440–5098).]*

	And in this while that Anthenor was oute	
5100	For to trete with the Grekis stoute,	*negotiate*
	As ye han herde, for a pes final,	*peace*
	In the toun aboute on every wal	
	Thei of Troie gan ascende blyve	*quickly*
	With the braunchis of many freshe olive	
5105	In tokne of pes; and Grekes eke ageyn	
	Amyd the feld endelonge the pleyn	*along the length of*
	Shewed hem, that alle myghte sene,	
	Eke of olyve lusti bowes grene.	*beautiful*
	And to conferme this fro point to point	
5110	And that nothing stood in no disjoint,	*uncertainty*
	The worthi kyng, grete Agamenoun,	
	Committed hath of highe discrecioun	
	Fully power and auctorité	
	For the Grekis pleinly unto thre	
5115	First of al for a pes to trete:	*negotiate*
	Unto the wyse worthi Kyng of Crete,	
	To Ulixes, and to Diomede.	
	To chese mo hem thought it was no nede,	*choose*
	For what thei do thei wil holde stable	*remain steadfast*
5120	And finally nat be variable	
	From the ende platly that thei make.	*plainly*
	And hereuppon was assurance take	
	Of outher part by bonde of sacrament.	*oath*
	And so thei be with Anthenor ywent	*went*
5125	Oute aside, these worthi lordes thre.	

	And whanne thei wern at her liberté,	
	From al tumulte allone prively,	
	This Anthenor, ful of trecchery,	
	Replet of falsehod and of doubilnesse,	
5130	Gan his purpos unto hem expresse,	*intention*
	Byhotynge hem to traisshe the cité,	*Promising; betray*
	So thei wolde make hym sureté	*On condition that*
	That first hymsilfe and with hym Eneas	
	Shal fredam han in every maner caas	
5135	With her allies and goodis everychon,	*possessions*
	Wher that hem list at large for to goon	*wish; freely*
	At her chois or dwellen in the toun	
	With her richesse and posessioun	
	Withouten harme or any more damage,	
5140	Liche as thei se it be to avauntage	
	Of her personys to voiden or abide.	*leave*
	And thei wer sworn on the Grekis side	
	Covenaunt to holde in parti and in al,	*part*
	As was rehersid aforn in special,	
5145	And as thei werne by her othes bounde,	*were bound by their oaths*
	So that ther be no variaunce founde	
	On outher parti platly nor no strif,	
	And thei behighte up pereil of her lyf.	*promised*
	And whan he had assuraunce of hem thre,	
5150	He charged hem to kepen in secré	
	Al that was seid, that nothing be discured	*revealed*
	Unto tyme that thei ben assured	
	Of the ende, grocid up in dede:	*put into effect*
	For it were good that thei toke hede,	
5155	List her purpos perturbed were or shent	*Lest; ruined*
	By communynge, withoute avisement,	*conversation*
	Of this tongis that be so longe and large.	
	Wherfore he gan conjuren hem and charge	*beseech; instruct*
	In alle wyse for to bene prevé,	*secretive*
5160	So that no wyght but he and thei thre,	
	Of noon estat, nowther highe nor lowe,	*neither*
	Fully the fyn of her entent ne knowe.	*aim*
	"And covertly oure purpos for to hide,"	*secretly*
	Quod Anthenor, "upon every side	

5165	To voide aweie al suspecioun,	*drive*
	This myn avys: that to Troye toun	*counsel*
	The wyse kyng called Taltibyus	
	Shal go with me to Kyng Priamus,	
	For he is hoor and yronne in age,	*grey-haired; advanced*
5170	Coy of his port, sleighti and right sage,	*Retiring in manner, crafty; wise*
	And therwithal sadde, demwr, and stille.	*serious, gentle in disposition*
	Of whom Troyens nothing shal mysille,	*suspect*
	But that he come to tretyn for a pes,	*negotiate*
	To ben assured and witen douteles	*know*
5175	Wher the Troiens agreen wil therto	
	In everything finally to do	
	As Anthenor the Grekis hath behight.	*promised*
	Thus shal thei ben devoided anoon right	*made free*
	Thorugh his comynge from al suspecioun,	
5180	Til that we han oure conclusioun,	
	As ye han herde, parformed everydel."	*achieved*
	Of whiche thing the Grekis like wel	
	And ben apointed upon everything	*agreed*
	What thei wil do and how this olde kyng	
5185	With Anthenor shal to Troye goo.	
	And after this, he axede eke also	
	Of Pantasile the body for to have,	*Penthesilea*
	In the cité that men myght it grave	*inter*
	With due honour longynge to hir estat,	
5190	To voide aweie suspecioun and debat.	*drive*
	And Anthenor (for it drowe to eve)	
	Of the Grekis taken hath his leve	
	And with the kyng repeireth into toun.	*returns*
	Whereof was made anoon relacioun	
5195	To Kyng Priam withoute more delay.	
	And he in hast upon the nexte day	
	Made assemble alle his citezeyns,	
	Secrely devoidyng alle foreyns,	*getting rid of all outsiders*
	Where Anthenor in open audience,	
5200	Thorugh the halle whan maked was silence,	
	His tale gan with sugred wordis swete,	*speech*
	Makyng the bawme outward for to flete	*soothing influence; flow*
	Of rethorik and of elloquence,	

	Of cher nor word that ther was noon offence;	
5205	In shewynge oute so circumspect he was	*appearance*
	That no man koude in no maner cas,	
	Be signe outward nor by countenaunce,	*By*
	Parceive in hym any variance	
	(So harde it was his tresoun to espie),	
5210	Th'effect declaringe of his embassatrie	*embassy*
	With cler report of his answer ageyn,	
	In his menyng though he wer nat pleyn.	
	For undernethe he was with fraude fraught,	*laden*
	This sleighti wolfe, til he his pray hath kaught:	*crafty; prey*
5215	For he was clos and covert in his speche	*hidden; secret*
	As a serpent, til he may do wreche,	*take vengeance*
	Hydinge his venym under floures longe;	
	And as a be that stingeth with the tonge	*bee*
	Whan he hath shad oute his hony sote —	*poured out its sweet honey*
5220	Sugre in the crop, venym in the rote —	*head (of a flower)*
	Right so in soth with tonge of scorpioun	
	This Anthenor, rote of al tresoun,	
	His tale tolde with a face pleyn,	
	Liche the sonne that shyneth in the reyn,	
5225	That faire sheweth though the weder be	
	Wonder divers and troubly for to se.	
	So this tigre, ful of doubilnesse,	*duplicity*
	So covertly his tresoun dide expresse,	
	As he nat ment but trouthe to the toun,	
5230	Fully affermyng in conclusioun	
	How the Grekis myghti were and stronge,	
	And likly eke to abide longe	
	Day be day redy hem t'assaille,	
	And hadde also plenté of vitaille,	
5235	Concludynge ay ther was no remedie	
	Ageynes hem to holde champartie	*contend successfully (see note)*
	Nor with hem anymore to stryve.	
	For (he seide) thei had yet alyve	
	Her worthi knyghtes, hardy as lyouns,	
5240	Her manly men and her champiouns,	
	Whiche here lyves platly to juparte,	*risk*
	From the cité caste hem nat departe	*plan*

Til her purpos acheved be in al.   *Until*
"For finally nouther tour nor wal

5245   Nor youre gatis of iren though ye shette,
The Grekis shal on no side lette,   *obstruct*
But that thei wiln us wynne at the laste.   *conquer*
Wherfor, it nedeth a mene weie to caste,   *middle*
Sithen of myght nor favour of Fortune   *Since*

5250   We may nat longe ageynes hem contwne.   *continue*
Wherfore," quod he, "so ye condescende,   *agree*
I can right wel al this thing amende,
Remedien, so that ye nat varie
To that I seie for to be contrarie —

5255   This to mene, shortly out of doute,
Embassatour whan that I was oute
With the Grekis last whan ye me sent,
Thei seide goodly how thei wold assent
Unto a pes with this condicioun:

5260   That ye wil make restitucioun
Of the harmys and the violencis,
The wrongis done, and also the offencis
By Paris wrought in Grece at Citheroun,
As it is right, me semeth, of resoun.

5265   For her request is meint with equité,   *joined*
And we be driven of necessité
Unto her lust justly to enclyne,   *their wish; bow*
Maugre oure wil the werre for to fyn: *Despite our intention*
For al is now in her elleccioun;

5270   We may nat make no rebellioun;
Now the mater is so fer ybrought,
To strive ageyn, in soth, it helpith nought;
It may apeire but nothing availle.   *cause damage*
Wherfore the beste that I can consaille,

5275   As in proverbe it hath be seied of yore,
That yif a man be constreyned sore
And may nat fle to fallen in a treyne,   *trap*
Lete hym chese the lasse harme of tweyne
And the gretter prudently eschewe.

5280   And lete oure gold that is kepte in mewe,   *concealment*
To save oure lif make redempcioun:

	For better it is, demeth of resoun,	
	Spoiled to ben only of richesse	*Plundered*
	Than wilfully deyen in distresse.	
5285	The lyf is bet than gold or any good —	
	Set al at nought in saving of your blood,	
	For foly is a man for his welfare	
	Thorugh covetyse any gold to spare.	
	And now oure lyf dependeth in balaunce,	*hangs*
5290	Late gold fare wel and goon with meschaunce;	*bad fortune*
	We may hereafter by sort or aventure	*chance*
	Gold by grace and good ynowgh recure.	*recover*
	And sithen we, as I have yow tolde,	*since*
	May byen pes finally with golde	*purchase peace*
5295	And with oure tresour stinten eke the werre,	*stop also the war*
	It were foly pleinly to differre	*delay*
	With the Grekis outterly t'acorde:	
	For yif so be I to hem recorde	*report*
	That ye assent withouten variaunce,	
5300	Ther may of pes be no parturbaunce —	
	It is so lyght now to be recured.	*easy; regained*
	For as sone as thei ben assured	
	By just report of youre entenciouns,	
	Thei wil do write obligaciouns	*promises*
5305	Of covenauntis, that nat be byhynde;	*be lagging*
	And that ye shal in hem no faute fynde,	*fault*
	Whan assuraunce from outher parte is hadde,	
	Theruppon endenturis shal be made,	*deeds (agreements)*
	So that of feith ye mow hem nat repreve.	*might; reject*
5310	And for that thei fully trust and leve	*believe*
	Withoute fraude my relacioun,	
	I wil now make no dilacioun	
	To signefie to hem in certeyn	
	Hooly th'effect of that ye wil seien."	

[*The Trojans accept Antenor's proposal and appoint Antenor, Aeneas, and old King Talthybus to make a final peace. Helen asks Antenor to act as an intermediary and help reconcile her with Menelaus. Antenor goes to talk with the Greeks, while a funeral is prepared for Penthesilea and her corpse is embalmed for the journey to her homeland and final burial. Ulysses, Diomede, and the King of Crete return to Troy with Aeneas. Ulysses asks for a huge quantity of gold as compensation and for the banishment of Amphimachus, the latter at Antenor's suggestion. During the discussion of these terms, a great tumult breaks out. Ulysses and Diomede are frightened, but Antenor hides them. Ulysses suspects treachery on Antenor's part. Antenor then explains one complication in their plan to betray Troy (lines 5315–5551).]*

	"Iwys," quod he, "I take unto witnesse	*Indeed*
	The highe goddes, that everything may se,	
	Withoute feynynge that I have besy be	
5555	Fro point to point your purpos to acheve;	
	But finally, so it yow nat greve	*wish*
	And paciently that ye list to here,	
	There is o thing perturbeth this mater,	
	Whiche that I shal, so it be noon offence,	
5560	Pleinly remembre here in youre presence:	*mention*
	This to seyn, of olde antiquité,	
	First at the bildyng of Troye the cité,	
	That whilom was ycalled Yllyoun —	
	For cause only at his fundacioun	
5565	Kyng Ylyus, sithen go ful longe,	*Ilius, a long time ago*
	The founder was of the walles stronge,	
	After whom, as made is mencioun,	
	It called was and named Ylyoun —	
	In the whiche with grete and besy charge	*effort*
5570	In Pallas name he made a temple large,	
	That passyngly was hadde in reverence.	
	And whan this phane of most excellence	*temple*
	Parformed was by masounri ful wel	*built*
	And, save the rofe, complet everydel,	
5575	Of myghti stoon the bildynge wel assured —	*[was] made certain*
	But or it was with led and tymber cured	*before; covered*
	Ageynes tempest for to bene obstacle,	
	Ther fil a wounder only by myracle	
	That I dar wel afferme it in certeyn,	
5580	Swiche another was there nevere seyn —	
	Whoso list se and considren al —	
	This merveil was so celestial.	
	For ther cam doun from the highe hevene,	
	By Pliades and the sterris sevene	

5585	And thorugh the eyr holdyng his passage,
	Like a fairy a merveillous ymage
	That in this world, though men hadde sought,
	Ne was ther noon halfe so wel ywrought.
	For, as it is trewly to suppose,

5585   And thorugh the eyr holdyng his passage,
      Like a fairy a merveillous ymage
      That in this world, though men hadde sought,
      Ne was ther noon halfe so wel ywrought.
      For, as it is trewly to suppose,
5590   Pigmalyon, remembrid in the *Rose*,   *mentioned*
      In his tyme hadde no konnyng   *craft*
      To grave or peint so corious a thing: *beautifully wrought*
      For it was wrought with dilligent labour
      By hond of aungil in the hevenly tour,   *angel*
5595   Thorugh Goddes myght and devyn ordinaunce,
      And hider sent thorugh his purvyaunce
      For a relik, only of his grace,   *As*
      And provided to the same place,
      Ther t'abide for a proteccioun,
5600   For a diffence and salvacioun,
      Perpetuelly whil the world may dure,
      Ageyn al meschef and mysaventure,   *peril*
      Every trouble and tribulacioun,
      In sustenynge and revelacioun
5605   And sovereyn helpe eke of this cité.
      The whiche never may distroyed be
      By noon engyn that men may purchase: *device*
      The goddes han graunted swiche a grace
      And swiche vertu annexed eke therto,   *power*
5610   That Troye in soth may never be fordo   *truth; destroyed*
      Til this relik stole be away.
      And yit in soth ther is no man that may
      From the place stere it nor remewe,   *stir nor remove*
      But the prest to whom it is dwe   *proper*
5615   Only of offys to touche it with his hond.
      So myghtely conservyd is the bond
      That who attempteth in conclusioun
      It to remewe of presumpcioun,
      At the fyn platly he shal fayle: *In the end utterly*
5620   For force noon may him nat availle;
      For it in soth wil nat remeved be
      Excepte of hym to whom of dueté
      It aparteneth, as ye han herde toforn.

And overmore ther is no man yit born
5625 That rede can nor telle in no degré   *make out*
Verraily wher it be stoon or tre,
Nor how it was devysed nor ywrought —
Ther is no wyght so sotil in his thought
Ceriously to tellen the manere.   *In due order*
5630 For Minerva that is so freshe and clere,
The sterne goddesse, thorugh hir grete myght,
That is so dredful bothe of loke and sight,
Whiche on hir brest haveth of cristal
Hir shilde Egys, this goddesse immortal,   *shield Aegis*
5635 Igraunted hath, in bokes as I lerne,
Thorugh hir power whiche that is eterne
This holy relik for a memorial
To hir temple of bildyng most royal,
It to conserve from al assaut and drede
5640 And to socour in every maner nede
Ageyn her foon unto Troye toun,   *their foes*
While it is kept with devocioun:
So that alweye by successioun,
From kyng to kyng in the lyne doun,
5645 By just title lyneally succede,
Hereto annexed that thei taken hede,
Prudently avoidynge necligence,
It to conserve with due reverence,
As thei are bounde and yholde of right.
5650 Thanne shal noon enmy power have nor myght
To do damage in hyndrynge of the toun.   *harming*
And whi it is called Palladyoun,
Like as clerkis write of it and seyn,
Is for Pallas to make hir toun certeyn,
5655 This relyke sent fro the hevene doun;
And to conclude shortly my resoun,   *explanation*
This is the cause oure purpos is so let."   *obstructed*
"Than," quod Ulixes, "sith it may be no bet,   *since*
Oure labour is in ydel and in veyn,
5660 Withoute recure, yif it be certeyn,   *remedy; if*
As thou hast seyd, this toun in no degré
Thorugh this relyk may not distroied be:

272

	It was foly the to undirtake	
	Unto Grekis beheste for to make	*promise*
5665	Withoute this — thou haddest be ful sure."	
	Quod Anthenor, "Yit ther is recure:	*remedy*
	As I have hight, ye shal have the toun,	*promised*
	Altheigh ther be a dilacioun;	*delay*
	And the maner anoon I shal telle,	*at once*
5670	Yif it so be ye list a whyle dwelle	*wish*
	Withoute noyse outher perturbaunce.	
	The prest, the whiche hath the governaunce	
	Of this relyk, shal be spoke unto	
	By good avys and ytreted so	*entreated*
5675	That he shal be ful of oure assent;	
	For he with gold and tresour shal be blent,	*blinded*
	That he accorde shal to oure purpos,	
	To bringe the relike, whiche is kept so clos,	*guarded*
	To what place that ye list assigne.	*you wish to designate*
5680	Beth stille of port, goodly, and benigne	*quiet of bearing*
	In youre werkis, til I have brought aboute	
	Fully this thing; and beth no thing in doute,	*not at all*
	I dar mysilfe take it wel on honde."	*undertake*
	And whan thei had his menyng undirstonde,	
5685	Thei toke leve and wente oute of the toun.	
	But first to voide al suspecioun,	*allay*
	At her goynge Anthenor hath hight	*promised*
	How that he wold goon the same nyght	
	To Priamus, "to maken ordinaunce	
5690	How the bondis and the assuraunce	
	Of the pes shulde ymaked be	
	And for to knowe eke the quantité	
	Of the gold that ye shal receyve:	
	Thus shal I best the purpos aparceyve	*observe*
5695	Of the kyng and knowe it everydel."	
	And thei concent and like wonder wel	
	Everything that Anthenor hath seide;	
	And so thei parte, glad and wel apaide,	*pleased*
	And wente her way and made no tariyng.	
5700	And Anthenor goth unto the kyng,	
	Hym counseillynge he make no delay	

	To calle his lordis ageyn the nexte day	*on*
	And his liges to assemble yfere,	*together*
	Finally t'engrosse this matere,	*arrange*
5705	As it was sittinge and expedient.	
	And whanne the kyng in open parlement	
	Crowned sat in his regalie,	*kingship*
	This Anthenor gan to specefie	*state explicitly*
	In audience, that men myghte knowe,	
5710	To eche estat, bothe highe and lowe,	
	The Grekis wille, yif thei agré therto,	
	And what the some was of gold also	
	Whiche thei axe, yif the pes shal stonde:	
	Twenti thousand marke to have in honde	
5715	Of pured gold, whiche most anon be paid;	*immediately*
	And of silver, that may nat be delaied,	
	Thei most eke han the same quantité;	
	And over this, as thei accorded be,	
	Certeyn mesours be covenaunt also have	*quantities*
5720	Of whete and flour, her lyves for to save	
	In her repeire by the large se,	*return*
	Whan thei saille home to her contré,	
	And that the collect maked be anoon	*collection*
	By good avis of hem everychoon,	*intention*
5725	That al be redy be a certeyn day.	
	Ther was no man that durst tho seie nay	
	Nor contrarie that Anthenor hath seide,	
	Wherso thei wer wel or evele apaide,	*Whether; pleased; displeased*
	But ful assent in conclusioun.	
5730	And in al haste thorughoute al the toun	
	The colytours gadrid up the gold,	*collectors*
	Like the somme as I have you told —	
	Of pore and riche ther wer spared noon.	
	The whiche tyme Anthenor is goon	
5735	Unto the prest that called was Thonaunte,	
	Yif he myght in any wyse hym daunte:	*control (suborn)*
	To make his herte fully to enclyne,	
	Ful craftely he leyde oute hoke and lyne,	
	With lusty bait of false covetyse,	
5740	Excitynge hym in ful secré wyse,	

274

That he wolde ben of his assent

And condescende unto his entent,   *agree*

To putten hym in pocessioun

Of the relik called Palladioun,

5745 Withoute abood it may delyvered be;   *delay*

And yaf hym gold an huge quantité;

And hym to blende moche more him behyght — *deceive; promised*

And this was don ful prevely by nyght —

Shortly concludynge, yif he condescende,   *agree*

5750 That he wolde his estat amende   *status; change*

So passyngly that forevermore

He and his heires shulde have gold in store,

Plenté ynowe, that noon indigence

Shulde have power him to done offence.

5755 "For unto the, this avow I make,"

Quod Anthenor, "and pleinly undirtake:

Of gold and good thou shalt have suffisance

And of tresour passinge habundaunce,

That thou shalt in verray sikernesse   *true security*

5760 Al thi kyn excellen in richesse,

Yif thou delyvere like to myn axynge

Palladioun, whiche is in thi kepynge.

And I behote — thou maist treste me —   *promise*

By bond of feith it shal be secré,

5765 List it were hindringe to thi name: *Lest; slander*

For yif so be, that thou drede shame

To be ensclaundrid of so foule a dede,

I shal shape that the thar nat drede   *devise; need not worry*

Nor ben agast in no maner wyse;

5770 For swiche a way in soth I shal devise

That no man shal be suspecious   *suspicious*

To thi persone nor engynyous

To deme amys, how this mater goth.

For be wel ware, that me were as loth

5775 To be diffamed with so false a thing,

To knowe therof, or be assentynge

In any maner, that thei of the toun

Sholde to me have suspecioun.

Lat be, lat be — levere I hadde deie.   *rather*

5780	We shal therfor cast another weie,	*plan*
	Oure honour save, so that thou and I	
	Shal goon al quyte. I seie the outterly,	*Shall get off unblamed*
	That nouther shal be holde partener	*neither of us; accomplice*
	Of this thefte but stonde hool and cler	
5785	Whatevere falle, withouten any shame:	
	For Ulixes shal beren al the blame	
	Of this dede and this thefte also.	
	For men shal sein, whan that it is go,	
	By his engyn and his sleighti wyle,	*craft*
5790	Thorugh his treynes and his false gyle,	*tricks*
	That he hath stole aweye Palladioun	
	From the temple in lesyng of the toun,	*overthrowing*
	That finally duringe al his lyve	
	Men shal to hym this falshed ascryve,	
5795	And al the gilt arretten his offence,	*impute to*
	That thou and I, only of innocence,	
	Thorughoute the world of this iniquité	
	Shal be excused platly and go fre.	
	It nedeth not tarie in this matere.	
5800	Come of attonys! Lo, thi gold is here!	*Come away at once*
	For thou ne shalt lenger delaied be.	
	And sith thou seste that no difficulté	*since; see*
	Is on no part, pereil nor repref,	
	Shame nor drede, sclaunder nor meschef,	*danger*
5805	Delaie nat to take this thing on honde."	
	And first this prest gan hym to withstonde	
	Ful myghtely and seide, for nothinge,	
	Nouther for praier nor for manacinge,	*threats*
	For gold nor good, ne no maner mede	*bribery*
5810	He nolde assent to so foule a dede.	*would not*
	Thus he answered at the prime face.	*at once*
	But ofte sithe it happeth men purchase	*often*
	By gifte of good, to speke in wordis pleyn,	
	That trouthe in povert myght never atteyne:	*poverty*
5815	For mede more by falshede may conquere	*bribery*
	Than title of right, that men in trouthe lere;	*learn*
	And giftes grete hertis can encline;	*gifts; bend*
	And gold, that may no stele and marbil myne,	*penetrate*

276

	This prestis hert hath so depe grave	*dug into*
5820	That Anthenor shal his purpos have,	
	For to possede the Palladioun	*possess*
	Thorugh false engyn and conspiracioun	
	Of this prest that called was Tonaunt,	
	Whiche of falshede myght hym best avaunte,	*speak boastfully*
5825	That this relik fro the temple rent.	*stole*
	And to Ulixes Anthenor it sent	
	Oute of the toun, in al the haste he myght,	
	By a servaunt secrely by nyght:	
	Wherof Troyens mortally dismaied	
5830	And thorugh tresoun finally outtraied,	*overcome*
	Wrought by this prest with covetise blent,	*blinded*
	False Anthenor beynge of assent.	

[*Lydgate complains against the duplicity of Thonant and the covetousness of priests. When the Trojans try to sacrifice to Apollo, the fire will not burn and the entrails of the animals are carried off by an eagle who drops them over the Greek ships. Cassandra explains to them that the first sign means they must purge Apollo's temple of the pollution caused by Achilles's murder there. The second sign, she says, is a token of treason, for Troy and Ilium will surely fall. The Greeks also seek an explanation; Calchas assures them of a good end to the war and advises them to prepare offerings to Pallas (lines 5833–6022).*]

	Bysshop Calchas with his lokkes hore,	*grey*
	Traitour forsworn sithen go ful yore,	*since long ago*
6025	That falsid hath trouthe and his lygaunce,	*betrayed*
	Whom clerkis han putte in remembraunce	
	In her bokis with lettris olde and newe,	
	To exemplifie no man be untrewe —	*to illustrate by example*
	For though yeris passe faste aweye,	
6030	Ruste of sclaundir lightly wil nat deye;	*be slain*
	The fret therof is so corosif	*anger*
	That it lasteth many mannys lyf	
	And is ful hard to arrace away;	*wipe out*
	Of whos venym ful selde is made alay;	*poison; abatement*
6035	Reporte therof blowen is so wyde	*Rumor*
	Perpetuelly that it wil abide,	
	Remembrid new and freshly had in mynde —	
	Recorde of hym that koude a weye fynde.	*Remember*

	Olde Calchas (evele mote he sterve)	*die*
6040	Under colour of offringe to Mynerve,	
	To make Grekes entren into toun,	
	This sleighti serpent, fader and patroun	*deceitful*
	And fynder-up of tresoun and of gyle,	
	Compassid hath and yfounde a wyle	*Contrived*
6045	How Grekis shal the cité wynne and take,	
	Pretendynge hem sacrifise to make	
	Unto Pallas, as I shal yow expresse:	*set forth*
	For this traitour, merour of falsnesse,	*mirror (paradigm)*
	The Grekis bad for to do her peyne	*ordered; endeavor*
6050	To Minerva an offeringe to feyne	*pretend*
	And in al haste that thei shuld hem spede.	
	And of assent thei dide make a stede	*horse*
	Large and wyde, of coper and of bras,	
	By crafte of Synoun, that contrived was	
6055	That it myght resseive large and wel	*contain*
	A thousand knyghtes armed bright in stel,	
	Thorugh the sleighte and the compassynge,	*artfulness*
	The sotil wit and merveillous werchinge	*workmanship*
	Of this wyse and crafty Greke Synoun,	
6060	Whiche thorugh his castynge and discrecioun,	
	Parformed hath this riche stede of bras,	*Produced*
	As ye han herd, be biddinge of Calchas	*at the*
	And by th'avys of Appius the wyse,	
	That halpe also the stede to devyse,	
6065	To fyn only that of devocioun	
	Grekis myght requeren of the toun,	*ask*
	Whan it were made, to graunte hem licence	*permission*
	It to present in the reverence	
	Of myghti Pallas, in stele armyd bright,	
6070	Amyd hir temple, large and ful of light —	
	By the offringe to fynde occasioun	
	To have entré frely into toun,	
	By pilgrimage her vowes to fulfille:	
	In whiche stede daren shal ful stille	*horse lurk*
6075	A thousand knyghtes, as Calchas be devis	
	Ordeyned hath, that was so slighe and wys.	
	By crafte of Synoun and of Appius,	

	This large stede of makynge merveillous,	*construction*
	Under pretence of oblacioun,	*offering*
6080	Was complet ful to his perfeccioun	
	Of werkemanshipe, as I tolde afore,	
	The same yere that Troye was forlore,	*brought to ruin*
	Whan the sege sothly gan to fyne,	*end*
	And the cité was brought to ruyne	
6085	Thorugh Grekis myght, and the walles stronge	
	Were bete doun — large, thikke, and longe —	*beaten*
	The whiche yere, as made is mencioun,	
	A lite aforn takynge of the toun,	
	Kynges echon that come fro so ferre	*each one*
6090	Alyve lefte after the mortal werre,	
	Whan thei saw how Priam be covenaunte	
	Unto Grekis hath outterly made graunte	
	Al hast possible to paien his ransoun:	
	Thei toke leve and went oute of the toun.	
6095	And first I fynde how Kyng Philymene	
	With hym ladde the body of the Quene	
	Pantasillya home to hir contré,	*Penthesilea*
	Ful richely ther to buried be;	
	And of two thousand knyghtes that this kyng	
6100	Brought unto Troye first at his comyng,	
	No mo than fifty home with hym he ladde.	
	And of the wommen that the quene eke hadde,	
	Of a thousand, the story seith certeyn,	
	But foure hundrid repeired hom ageyn.	*returned*
6105	And thus whan alle were fro Troie gon,	
	The morwe next Priamus anon	*at once*
	With his lordis rood oute of the toun,	
	As was th'acord for confirmacioun	*agreement*
	Of pes final upon outher syde.	
6110	And in the feld Grekis hym abide;	
	And on relikes openly yborn,	
	Ther thei wern on outher parti sworn	
	On the forme to yow afore recorded,	*In the way*
	As Anthenor with Grekis was accorded.	
6115	And for Grekis firste swore Diomede,	
	Thei of Troie takynge lytel hede	

How the othe was in condicioun,

Cured above under false tresoun, — *Covered*

Sithen Grekis tho in her sweryng — *Since*

6120 Ne bounde hemsilfe to no manere thing

To stonde to, as in special,

But for to holde and kepe in general

The poyntes hool engrosid and no mor, — *written down*

In thilke treté that Daungh Anthenor — *negotiations; Lord*

6125 With Grekis helde, this traytour fraudelent.

In whiche thei werne ful double of entent —

Meint with tresoun, as ye han herd toforn — — *Mixed*

Whiche to observe only thei wer sworn

By fraude of othe and nat by wordis pleyne,

6130 Her adversaries to taken in a treyne, — *trick*

Excludyng hem fro her menyng ferre, — *their intention by a long way*

Pes in the face but in the herte werre,

Al openly confermyd with her hond,

Inly to tresoun, by assurance of bond. — *Inwardly; promise*

6135 But though the venym be closid with a wal,

It was nat hid from him that knoweth al:

For certeynly, so as clerkes teche,

Who that swereth falsly in his speche,

Florisshinge outward by a fair colour — *Adorning with rhetoric*

6140 For to desseive his trewe neghebour, — *deceive*

He is forsworn, whatsoevere he be.

The tresoun hid though men may nat se,

Howso the word be away yborn, — *apprehended*

Who swereth by craft is by craft forsworn;

6145 Ther may be made noon excusacioun.

For God, that knoweth the entencioun,

Demeth the herte and the word right nought; — *Judges*

For he the wil knoweth and the thought

Of every man, nyghe and eke afere: — *afar*

6150 Therfore be war, no man him forswere,

As Grekis dide Troiens to deceyve,

That the fraude koude nat conceyve, — *perceive*

Supposinge that the Grekis hadde be

Feithful and trewe of her sureté —

6155 But nothing oon thei in herte thought —

	Whiche in the ende thei ful dere abought,	*paid for*
	Whan thei founde fully the revers	
	And to her speche the dede so divers.	*deed*
	It were but veyn by and by to write	
6160	Her feyned othes, nor her wordis whyte,	
	Nor the cheris that thei koude feyne.	*facial expressions*
	But to conclude with, the Quene Eleyne	
	Duringe the treté, upon the same day,	*conference*
	Delyvered was to Kyng Menelay;	
6165	And after that was payed the raunsoun,	
	Grauntid toforn and gadrid in the toun,	
	Gold and silver, whete and also flour;	*wheat*
	And to her shippes with dilligent labour,	
	In ful gret hast everything was brought,	
6170	Wherthorugh the cité after cam to nought.	
	And Grekis thanne by symulacioun,	
	Makyng a colour of devocioun,	*appearance*
	Thorugh holynes, under ypocrosye,	
	Falsly feyned by fraude and flaterie,	*pretended*
6175	The kyng han preied to han liberté	
	Frely to entre into the cité,	
	To make aseth by oblacioun	*amends*
	For the thefte of Palladioun	
	And offren up the riche stede of bras	
6180	To the goddes that called is Pallas —	*goddess*
	Whan Kyng Priam liketh to assigne —	*to designate [a place]*
	That she to hem be willy and benygne	*favorable*
	In her repeire, seilynge be the se	*return*
	Home into Grece toward her contré,	
6185	Whan she is quemed with the large stede.	*conciliated*
	Of whiche, allas, Priam toke noon hede:	
	The tresoun hidde he koude nat adverte	*hidden; foresee*
	But graunted hem with al his hole herte,	
	Whan that hem list to bringe it into toun,	
6190	By false entising and suggestioun	
	Of Anthenor and also of Enee,	
	Havynge no drede nor ambyguyté	
	In his entent, nor suspecioun	
	Nouther of feynyng nor of fals tresoun,	

6195	But right frendly, liche to his beheste,	*according to his promise*
	Condescendeth unto her requeste,	*Agreed*
	Her avowes that thei myght observe,	
	To offren up this hors unto Minerve.	
	And Grekis tho, with grete dilligence,	
6200	Ful gret honour and huge reverence	
	Han shapen hem with processioun	*undertaken*
	To bringe the stede into Troie toun,	
	The men of armys being ay therinne,	
	By whom thei cast Troie for to wynne	*planned*
6205	In short tyme, for it stood on the date.	*Without further delay; it was time*
	And whan this hors brought was to the gate,	
	It was so narwe that ther was no space	
	For the stede into the toun to passe,	
	Albe that thei assaied overal.	*Although; tried*
6210	Wherfore Priam bete adoun the wal	*broke*
	To make it large, right at her devys,	*just as they had planned*
	In whiche thing, allas, he was unwis;	
	For cause chef of his confusioun	*destruction*
	Was that this hors cam into the toun.	

[*The Greeks make offerings at Pallas's temple. The Trojans are comforted and hopeful, but all too often adversity and misadventure come after gladness. The Greeks leave the horse in the custody of Sinon and tell Priam they wish to go toward Tenedos and thence sail homeward. To save Helen from danger, they advise sending her secretly to Tenedos (lines 6215–75).*]

	And whanne thei had at leiser and good ese	
	Fro Troye seiled unto Tenedoun	
	With her navie, the false Greke Synoun	*fleet*
	In Troie waker gan to take kepe	*vigilantly; heed*
6280	The hour whan men wern in her first slepe;	
	And in al haste, with his sleighty gyn	*subtle craft*
	Many vys and many sotyl pyn	*clasp*
	In the stede he made aboute goon,	
	The crafty lokkes undoynge everychon;	*locks*
6285	And oute he goth and gan anoon to calle	
	Withinne the hors the worthi knyghtes alle,	
	So secrely no man myght espie;	

	And traitourly he gan hym for to hiye	*hasten*
	Upon the walles the silfe same nyght	
6290	And toward Grekis gan to shewe a lyght,	
	Where as thei leye tofore Tenedoun,	*before*
	Redy armyd to falle uppon the toun.	
	And whan thei hadde the sodein light espied,	
	On horsebak anoon thei han hem hyghed	*hurried*
6295	Toward Troye, armed clene at al;	*properly*
	And in thei went by the same wal	
	Whiche for the hors was but late broke;	*recently; broken down*
	And mortally, for to ben awroke,	*avenged*
	The knyghtes eke in the stede of bras	
6300	Han with hem mette, a ful sterne pas,	*joined, a ferocious maneuver*
	And gan anoon thorughoute the cité	*at once*
	On every half for to kylle and slee	
	With blody swerd upon every side,	
	And made her wondes brode, large, and wyde,	
6305	While thei, allas, nothing advertinge,	*anticipating*
	At mydnyght hour abedde laie slepynge	
	Ful innocent and thoughte nought but good,	
	Al forbathed in her owne blood,	*awash*
	Bothe man and childe withoute excepcioun,	
6310	The Grekis sparinge no condicioun	*circumstance*
	Of old nor yong, womman, wif, nor maide —	
	That with the cry Priamus abraide	*started*
	Oute of his slepe and sodeynly awoke,	
	Whiche laye al nyght and noon hede toke	
6315	Of the slaughter and mordre in the toun.	
	But tho he wist that ther was tresoun	*knew*
	Falsly compassid unto his cité	*contrived*
	By Anthenor and also by Enee,	
	Of whos malis he was no mor in doute;	*ill will*
6320	For the venym was now broken oute,	
	And now the galle of conspiracioun,	*conspiracy*
	That under sugre of symulacioun	*dissimulation*
	Hath so longe closid ben and hidde,	*covered*
	In dede is now execut and kyd.	*revealed*
6325	And now the fraude fully of tresoun,	
	The cast also of false collusioun	*purpose*

283

	Be raked oute and abrood yblowe,	*disclosed; blown*
	And the autours openly yknowe.	*originators*
	Now hath envie and contrived hate	*artfully devised*
6330	Of her engyn set abrood the gate;	*cunning*
	Now hath deceit and olde conspiracie	
	And feyned othes, alle of oon allie,	*akin by nature*
	Openly shewed her falsnesse	
	And disclosid al hir doubilnesse	*duplicity*
6335	So fer abrod that now is ther no geyn.	*avail*
	For now, allas, the wilde fire is seyn	*seen*
	In touris highe with the wynde yblasid,	*blown*
	Wherof Priam, astonyd and amasid,	*astonished; terrified*
	Al awaped sterte oute of his bedde	*bewildered*
6340	And counfortles to the temple is fledde	
	Of Appollo, to save hym yif he myght.	
	And ay the flawme of the fires bright	
	Brent in the toun and conswmeth al	*Burned*
	The riche bildinge, whilom so royal,	*once*
6345	That the walles with her roves huge,	*roofs*
	Covered with leed for a chef refuge,	*protection*
	Were now, allas, bareyn and bare ymaked.	
	The Grekis ay with her swerdes naked	
	Mordre and sle whereso that thei go,	
6350	That twenti thousand thilke nyght and mo	*that same*
	Thei kylled han, longe or it was day;	*before*
	And in this slaughter and this grete affray	*disturbance*
	Spoile and robbe and take what thei fynde,	
	Tresour and good, and lefte nat bihinde,	*nothing*
6355	Be myghti hond and sturdi violence.	
	And the temples withoute reverence	
	Thei han dispoilled thorughoute al the toun	*pillaged*
	And gredely rent and racid doun	*torn; cut*
	Of golde and silver the ornementes alle	
6360	Tofore the goddes — foule mote hem falle —	*let evil befall them*
	Kyng Priam ay with a dedly chere	
	To Appollo makyng his praiere	
	Furiously, this hertly woful man,	
	As he in soth that no red ne can	*truth who knows no help*
6365	But waite his deth in his fatal ewre.	*destiny*

284

	And Cassandra, the holy creature,	
	Of inward wo desirous to sterve,	*die*
	Compleynynge ran unto Minerve,	
	Makynge to hir a lamentacioun	
6370	With other gentilwommen of the toun.	
	And ther, allas, as thei wolde dye,	
	Ful pitously thei sobbe, wepe, and crie.	
	And in her dool ther Y lete hem dwelle;	*sorrow; I*
	For alle her sorwes yif I shulde telle	
6375	In this story and her wo descrive,	
	Mi penne shuld of verray routhe rive,	*split*
	Rehersinge eke how in every strete,	*Describing*
	Her clothes blake, rodi, moiste, and wete,	
	As thei, allas, bothen oon and alle,	
6380	On her lordes doun aswone falle,	*swooning*
	With her blod bedewed and yspreint,	*sprinkled*
	Wher men may seen the cristal teris meynt	*mixed*
	Of her wepinge in ther woundes grene,	*fresh*
	That lay and bledde ageyn the sonne shene,	*against*
6385	With dedly eyen casting up the whyte:	
	It were but veyne al her wo to write	
	Nor the maner of her mortal sorwe.	
	But Guydo writ that on the same morwe	
	How Anthenor and with hym fals Enee	
6390	Conveied han thorughoute the cité	
	The myghti Grekis unto Ylyoun,	
	The royal tour and riche mancioun	*palace*
	That whilom was of most excellence;	*once*
	In the whiche thei founde no diffense	
6395	Of highe nor lowe nor of noon estat,	
	For it was left allone dissolat,	
	With al the gold and richesse of the toun	
	Shet and closed in the chefe dongoun.	*Locked up; tower*
	But for ther was no man that withstood,	
6400	Thei brake the lokkes and raught the good	*plundered*
	And the tresour that was shet withinne,	
	Eche for his party that he myghte wynne:	
	Thei yaf no fors who was lef nor loth.	*gave no care*
	And Pirrus after to the temple goth	

6405	Of Appollo by gret cruelté,	
	And fil on Priam knelynge on his kne,	
	And with his swerd, furious and wood,	*mad*
	Tofore the autere shadde there his blood,	*altar*
	That the stremys of his woundys rede	
6410	So highe raught, bothe in lengthe and brede,	*high reached*
	That the statue of gold bornyd bright	*burnished*
	Of this Appollo, for al his grete myght,	
	For al his power and his sterne face,	
	Defouled was and pollut al the place —	
6415	Only by deth of this worthi kynge	
	By Pirrus slayn while he lay knelynge,	
	Of olde hatrede and envious pride,	*For*
	While Anthenor and Enee stod aside,	
	That routhe was and pité to beholde	
6420	To sen hym lyn on the stonys colde,	*lying upon*
	So pitously toforn the auter blede.	*altar*
	Whereof, allas, whan Eccuba toke hede	*Hecuba*
	And hir doughter, faire Polycene,	*Polyxena*
	With here torent as any gold wyr shene,	*hair torn; wire bright*
6425	Inly supprised with sorwe to her herte,	*overcome*
	Whan thei began considren and adverte	*notice*
	The noble kyng, with blody stremys rede	
	Al fordrowned, with his eyen dirke and dede,	
	With Pirrus swerd girt thorugh outher side,	*pierced*
6430	For mortal fere thei durste nat abide;	
	But inwardly thorughdarted with the sight,	*pierced through*
	Al in a rage toke hem to the flight.	*fury*
	And yit in soth thorughoute the cité	
	Thei wiste never whiderward to fle,	*knew*
6435	Reskus was noon nor no remedie	*Deliverance*
	Of kyn nor frend nor of noon allie;	
	With Grekis swerd the toun was so beset.	*set upon*
	And in her flight this woful quen hath met	
	Eneas, causer of al this wrak,	*destruction*
6440	Unto whom, rebukynge, thus she spak:	
	"O thou traitour, most malicious!	
	Thou false serpent, adder envious!	*spiteful*
	Crop and rote, fynder of falsnesse,	*Branch and root, deviser*

Sours and welle of unkyndenesse,   *unnaturalness*
6445 How myghtestow in thin herte fynde
Unto thi kyng to be so unkynde?   *unnatural*
Gynner and ground, exaumple of tresoun,   *Beginner*
And final cause of oure destruccioun,
How myghtestow, devoide of al pité,
6450 Behold, allas, thorugh thi cruelté
Of thi kyng to shede so the blood,
That evere hath ben so gentil and so good,
So gracious lord, specialy to the,
And overmore thorugh his highe bounté   *beneficence*
6455 The honoured and ymagnified   *Thee; praised*
Al his lyve — it may nat be denyed —
That lith now ded in the temple, allas?   *lies*
Thou wer nat only traitour in this cas
But to his deth conspiryng and unkynde,
6460 Pirrus conveiyng where he shuld him finde,
Toforn Appollo myd of this cité,
Where thou sholdest of verray dueté
Rather have ben his protectioun,
His myghti sheld and savacioun,
6465 That hast this cité and this toun ylorn   *destroyed*
In whiche thou were fostrid and yborn,
On the gretest of reputacioun   *One of*
Of alle the lordis dwellyng in this toun,
In whiche thou haddest whilom most plesaunce.   *once*
6470 But al is now oute of remembraunce.
Yit in thin herte yif any drope be   *if*
Of gentilnesse, merci, or pité,
In this dedly rage ful of tene,   *anger*
Rewe on my doughter, yonge Polycene,   *Take pity*
6475 From Grekis swerd hir youthe for to save.
Yif thin herte may eny routhe have,   *If*
Of manly pité on hir maydenhede
Diffende hir now and kepe hir oute of drede,   *danger*
Yif thou canst fynde any weye
6480 In any wyse that she may nat deye,
That herafter, whan men sen and rede
The false tresoun and the foule dede

That thou hast don unto Troye toun,
It may in parti be proteccioun
6485 To thi fame, the venym to allaye   *reputation; diminish*
Of this tresoun. Whan men wiln assaie   *try*
By just report thi name to accuse,
This dede may the helpen to excuse   *you*
Ageyns tonges that speken of Enee;
6490 Than wiln thei seyn thou haddist yit pité
On Polycene only of gentilnes,
Therwith to sugre al the bitternesse
Of thi decert, blowe forthe by fame,   *punishment, proclaimed; report*
By rehersaille of the foule blame
6495 That shal of the thorugh the world be born,
With sclaunder infect whan thou art al totorn,   *diseased*
That thou ne shalt the shame mowe sustene.   *be able to bear*
Than shal my doughter faire Polycene
Be thi defence ageyns swiche famus strif,   *rumored discord*
6500 Yif it be so now thou save hir lyf.
Of me no fors, though thou make as blive   *no matter; quickly*
The swerde of Grekis thorugh myn herte rive."   *cleave*
And so by praier of this woful quene,
This Eneas toke to hym Polycene,
6505 Whos traitour hert, for al his cruelté,
On hir youthe was mevid of pité,
Only of routhe that in his brest aros,
And secrely putte hir up in clos,   *confinement*
List that Grekis founde occasioun   *Lest*
6510 Ageynes hym. And Ajax Thelamoun
Toke to his warde Andronemecha,   *division Andromache*
Ectoris wyf and wyse Cassandra   *Hector's*
Oute of the temple longinge to Minerve,   *belonging*
From Grekis swerd her lyves to conserve.
6515 And Menelay toke the Quene Eleyne
Into his garde, for whom so grete a peyne   *custody*
Bood in his hert many day toforn,
By whom, allas, the cité is now lorn.
And Grekes ay were besy in her ire
6520 To sleen and kylle and cruelly to fire   *burn*
On every side and to bete doun

	Palais and house and walles of the toun:	
	Thei spare nought, for al goth to the fire.	
	So fervent hate brent in her desire	
6525	Of olde envie avenged for to be	
	That thei ne lefte withinne the cité	
	Nothing unbrent, and also Ylyoun	*Ilium*
	Was in this rage turned upsodoun.	*fury*
	Ther maked wern noon excepciouns,	
6530	Only outake the possessiouns	*except*
	Of Anthenor (evele mote he fare)	*let evil befall him*
	And Eneas, whom the Grekis spare,	
	As thei to hem were bounde by her othe.	
	And thus the Grekis, furious and wrothe,	
6535	Han al that day robbed and ybrent,	
	Til that the Kyng Agamenoun hath sent	
	For his lordis to assemble ifere	*together*
	In Pallas temple, only for to here	
	Her wyse avis uppon thinges tweyne:	*counsel*
6540	First, yif thei wolde holde and nat feyne	*if*
	Holy her feith, withoute excepcioun,	
	To hem by whom thei wan first the toun?	
	And overmore he axed hem also,	
	Touching the goodis, what thei wolde do	
6545	With gold, tresour, and possessioun	
	That thei have wonne thorugh her highe renoun?	
	And thei answerid, withoute more tariyng,	
	Thei wolde her feith kepe in everything	
	As thei wer sworn and her hestis holde;	
6550	And over this thei seide how thei wold	
	That gold, tresour, and good of the cité,	
	As right requereth and also equyté,	
	Be justly partid by divisioun,	
	To every wyght made distribucioun	
6555	Liche his merit, of highe and lowe degré;	*According to*
	And that the kyng eke of resoun se	
	Eche to rewarde after his labour,	
	So as it longeth to a conquerour,	*As it is appropriate*
	That no man have mater to compleyne.	

[Ajax Telamon insists that Helen deserves death, while Ulysses tries to save her. Agamemnon asks for Cassandra as his prize; Aeneas and Antenor plead that Helenus be spared for saving Achilles's body from defilement. Helenus, in turn, asks Agamemnon to save the lives of Hector's sons and Hecuba, which he grants. The Greeks prepare to sail, but a storm detains them for a month. Asked by the Greeks to explain the cause of the storm, Calchas falsely says that the gods and furies are still unappeased for Achilles's death. Only the sacrifice of Polyxena, he tells them, will satisfy the deities, since her beauty was the root cause of Achilles's death. Enraged, Pyrrhus searches for her, and Antenor at length betrays her hiding place. Pyrrhus drags her into the presence of Agamemnon, who assigns her to Pyrrhus. Polyxena is led to the place of her execution, Achilles's grave. The Greeks weep in pity and compassion for her, but they are convinced, at Calchas's suggestion, that they will never return home unless she dies. She kneels down and offers her lament to the gods (lines 6560–6730).]

	"O ye almyghti that this world governe	
	And everything considren and discerne,	
	By whom this world, so huge, large, and rounde,	
	Bothe eyr and see, hevene and eke the grounde	
6735	At youre devis with a word was wrought,	*pleasure*
	And sothfastly knowen every thought,	
	Right as it is, of every maner wyght,	
	Withoute lettinge, so percynge is youre sight,	*Without delay*
	That nothing is conselit nor ywrye	*concealed; hidden*
6740	From the beholdyng of youre eternal eye,	
	And everything may attonis se,	*at once*
	Upon my soule hath merci and pité.	
	And of youre grace and benigne cure,	*concern*
	Upon my wo and pitous aventure	
6745	Haveth som routhe, now that I shal dye,	
	My woful spirit to leden and conveye	
	Whereas yow list, now that I shal pace.	*wish*
	For unto you in this silfe place,	
	I me confesse with al humylyté,	
6750	That hedertowarde I have in chastité	
	Lad al my lyf and kept my maydenhede	
	In youre servyse, bothe in thought and dede,	
	In port and chere, and in countenaunce,	*behavior; appearance*
	Or forfeture of any dalyaunce,	*wrongdoing; speech*
6755	With o mysloke I never yit abreide,	*sinful mislooking; raised [my eyes]*

So that in soth I deye shal a mayde,
As ye wel knowe, of synne al innocent,
Though I be now dempte by jugement   *condemned*
For to be ded, withoute gilt at al:
6760   Witnesse of you that ben inmortal,
Clene of entent of that I am accused.
And yit, allas, I may nat be excused
But that the swerd of vengaunce mote byte   *must*
Routheles, whiche am no thing to wyte   *Pitiless; not at all to blame*
6765   But stonde clere and pure of al offence,
And dischargid in my conscience,
I dar afferme, and fully gilteles
Touchinge the mordre of worthi Achilles,
Whiche slowe my brother, and after loved me,   *Who slew*
6770   And is now cause of myn adversité:
And yit in wil, dede, word, nor thought,
Unto his deth assentid was right nought   *not at all*
But therof was right sory in myn herte,
Albe that I may nat now asterte   *Although; escape*
6775   For to be ded, only for his sake.
On me allone vengaunce shal be take   *taken*
Withoute merci, in ful cruel wyse,
With my blood to make sacrifice
To the goddis, her wrathe for to queme.   *appease*
6780   O peple blinde, in soth, amys ye deme;   *judge*
Ageynes me youre herte is to cruel,   *too*
To merciles, to irous, and to fel,   *savage*
Withoute routhe, to mykel indurat,   *much callous*
To sleen a maide, allone disolat.
6785   Oute of youre herte, allas, pité is gon —
Harder in trouthe than outher stok or stoon   *tree*
And more cruel in youre oppinioun,
For lak of pité, than tigre or lyoun.
Certis, ye ben gretly for to blame
6790   And oughte herof for to have gret shame
To assent to so foule a dede,
To slen a maide, quakyng in her drede,
And graunte hir noon oportunyté
For to bewepe hir virginité: *lament*

6795	That of this cruel and pitous wreche	*vengeance*
	My blood youre gilt herafter shal apeche	*inform on*
	And accuse also youre grete envie	
	To the goddes, that shal justefie	*judge*
	Every unright, bothe of highe and lowe,	
6800	Ful egally, and make to be knowe	*equally*
	The trouthe plein, and spare no degré	*social rank*
	But maken open that is nowe secré.	*expose*
	I seie nat this nor mysilfe compleyne	
	To have redres of my fatal peyne,	*relief*
6805	For deth is now more welcom unto me	
	Than is my lyf and more itake at gré,	*goodwill*
	Sithen my brethere, most worthi of renoun,	*Since*
	Be slayen alle and buried in this toun:	
	My fader ded in his unweldy age,	*feeble*
6810	And I allone lefte in al this rage,	
	And have abide pitously to se	
	Fynal ruyne now of this cité,	
	Whiche at myn herte sitteth now so sore	*is so distressed*
	That levere I have thanne to wepe more	*rather*
6815	Deye attonis in reles of my wo,	*I would die*
	Sith al my kyn is passed and ago —	*Since*
	Lenger to lyve were to me a deth.	
	For bet is me to yelden up the breth	
	Than to be ladde oute of this cité,	
6820	Amonge straungeris to live in poverté.	
	O deth, welcome, and no lenger lette	*hold off*
	Thi dredful dart to filen and to whette,	*sharpen; grind*
	My tendre hert therwithal to ryve;	*split*
	Ageyn thi myght I shal never strive.	*Against*
6825	Now is tyme to kythe thi power	*make known*
	On me that am of wil and herte entere	*entirely*
	A clene maide, so as I began,	*pure*
	Withoute touche of eny maner man	
	In al my lyf to this same day.	
6830	This lite avaunte make yit I may,	*small boast*
	In myn ende, to the goddes alle,	
	After whos helpe now I clepe and calle.	*appeal*
	And to her merci mekely I commende	

	My woful spirit and praie hem that thei sende	
6835	To every maide better happe and grace	*chance*
	Than I have now and a lenger space	
	In hertly joie and honour to contune,	
	Withoute assaut of any infortwne	
	To lede her lyf in prosperité.	*their lives*
6840	And alle maidenes, remembreth upon me	
	To take exaumple how ye shal yow kepe	
	And that ye wolde a fewe teris wepe	
	Whan that ye thinke uppon Polycene,	
	That was of age and of yeris grene	
6845	Whan she was slayn by cruel aventure.	
	And to the goddes, for to han in cure,	*charge*
	My dredful goost hooly I betake	*fearful spirit; entrust*
	Eternally; and thus an ende I make."	
	And with that word hir hed she gan enclyne	*bow*
6850	Ful humblely, whan she shulde fyne,	*die*
	And of hir eyen helde the lydes down.	
	And Pirrus thanne, woder than lyoun,	
	Dismembrid hath with his sharpe swerd	*Beheaded*
	This maide yonge, dredful and aferd;	
6855	And overmore, his cruelté to shewe,	
	On pecis smale he hath hir al tohewe	*small bits; cut*
	Endelong his fadris sepulture.	*All along*
	Allas, how myght his cruel herte endure,	
	Merciles to done so foule a dede?	
6860	I am astonid sothly whan I rede,	*amazed*
	After hir deth, how it dide hym good,	
	Like a tiraunte to cast abrood hir blood	
	Or a tigre, that can no routhe have,	
	Rounde enviroun aboute his fadris grave	
6865	He spreint of hate and of cruelté.	*sprinkled*
	O thou Pirrus, thou maist ful wel ybe	
	Achilles sone by lyneal discent;	
	For like to hym of herte and of entent	
	Thou wer in soth devoide of al pité	
6870	And wers than he yit in o degré:	*measure*
	For of thi fader in al his lyvynge	
	Ne redde I nevere yit so foule a thing —	

293

Though I wold of hatrede hym abraide — *accuse*
For no rancour that evere he slow a maide.
6875 I fynde wel that he hadde his part
Whilom in love of Cupides dart,
That made hym sore in his lyve smerte, *pain*
Whan that he was wounded to the hert
With the castyng only of an eye,
6880 Wenynge therby wisly for to deye — *Thinking; surely*
He myghte nat the sodeyn stroke eskape.
And afterward, as his fate hath shape, *determined*
He mordrid was for love of Polycene,
Whom thou hast sleyn in thi cruel tene *rage*
6885 Furiously, withoute routhe or shame:
For whiche thing the foule hatful fame *rumor*
Thorugh al the world herafter shal be sprad,
Whan the story rehersid is and rad; *recited*
Than shal be seide how Pirrus routheles
6890 Slowe in his ire a maide gilteles
And warie shal thi name most odible *cursed*
For this dede passingly horrible,
For love only of faire Polycene.
The deth of whom when Eccuba the Quene
6895 Hath seyn, allas, as she beside stood,
For verray wo gan to wexe wood, *go insane*
And for sorwe oute of hir wit she went, *mind*
And hir clothes and hir heer she rent *hair; tore*
Al in a rage, and wot nat what she doth, *knew*
6900 But gan anoon with hondis and with tothe
In her furie cracchen and eke byte, *strike*
Stonys caste, and with fistes smyte
Whom she mette; til Grekis made her binde, *had her bound*
And sent hir forthe, also, as I fynde,
6905 Into an ile to Troye pertenent, *belonging to*
Wher she was slayn only by jugement
Of the Grekis and stonyd to the deth.
And whan she had yolden up the breth, *yielded*
This woful quene, by cruel aventure,
6910 The Grekis dide make a sepulture
Coriously of metal and of stoon; *Artfully*

	And toke the cors and buried it anoon	*corpse*
	With gret honour and solempnité,	
	That longe after ther men myghte se	
6915	The riche toumbe, costful and royal,	
	There set and made for a memorial	
	Of Eccuba, whilom of grete fame;	*once*
	And after yaf to that place a name	*gave*
	And called it, to be long in mynde,	
6920	*Locus infestus*, in Guydo as I fynde.	
	And thus the quene only for sorwe wood,	*mad*
	Whan hir doughter hadde shad hir blood,	
	Of Grekis stonyd dide hir ende make,	
	As ye han herde, pleinly for the sake	
6925	Of Polycene, whilom by Calchas	*once*
	Unto Appollo falsly offrid was,	
	By Pirrus swerd Achilles avengynge,	
	To make the se calm and blawndisshinge,	*inviting*
	That the goddes take no vengaunce	
6930	Upon Grekis. That an evele chaunce	*Let misfortune befall*
	Come to theis false goddes everychoon	
	And her statues of stokkes and of stoon,	*wood*
	In whiche the serpent and the olde snake,	
	Sathan hymsilf, gan his dwellinge make,	
6935	And fraudently folkes to illude,	*trick*
	Ful sotilly kan hymsilfe include	
	In ymagis for to make his hold,	*dwelling*
	That forget bene of silver and of gold —	*forged*
	That by errour of false illusioun,	
6940	He hath ybrought to confusioun	*destruction*
	Thorugh myscreaunce the worthi kynde of man,	*misbelief*
	Sithen tyme that aldirfirst began	*Since; first of all*
	The false honour of ydolatrie	
	And the worship unto mawmetrie	*idolatry*
6945	By sacrifice of bestis and of blood,	
	T'apesen hem whan that thei are wood	
	And to queme, bothe at eve and morwe.	*pacify*
	I praie to God, yeve hem alle sorwe,	*give*
	Wherso thei ben, withinne or withoute.	
6950	I noon excepte of the false route —	*crowd*

295

Satorn nor Mars, Pallas nor Juno,
Jubiter, Mercurius, nor Pluto,
Nouther Flora that doth the floures sprede,
Nouther Bachus with grapis whyte and rede,
6955   Nor Cupido with his eyen blinde,
Nouther Daphne closed under rinde,   *tree bark*
Thorugh Tellus myght, of the laurer tre,
Nor thou Diane with thi chastité,
Mighti Venus, nor Cytherea
6960   With thi dartis, nor Proserpyna
That lady art depe doun in helle,
Nor Belides that draweth at the welle,
Ixyoun, nor thou Zeziphus,   *Sisyphus*
Nor with thin appil, thou cruel Tantalus,
6965   Nor the Furies that bene infernal,
Nor ye that spynne the lives threde fatal
Upon the rokke of every maner man,   *distaff*
Nor the Muses that so singen can
Atwen the coppis of Nysus and Cirra,   *summits*
6970   Upon the hil beside Cirrea,
Nor the, Cibeles, nor Ceres with thi corn,   *you, Sybil*
Nor Eolus of whom the dredful horn
Is herde so fer, whan thou list to blowe,   *wish*
Nor Janus Bifrons with bak corbed lowe,   *bent*
6975   Nor Priapis, nor Genyus the prest
That curseth ay, with candel in his fist,
Hem tho echon that froward be to Kynde,   *each one; perverse; Nature*
Nor Imeneus whos power is to bynde
Hertis that ben conjunct in mariage,   *joined*
6980   Til the goddesse of discorde and rage
Discevereth hem by divisioun,   *Separated*
Nouther Manes that han her mansioun   *The spirits of the dead; place*
Mid the erthe in derknesse and in wo,
Nor theis elves that are wont to go
6985   In undermeles whan Phebus is most shene,   *early afternoons; bright*
Nouther fawny in tender grevis grene,   *fauns; thickets*
Water-nymphes, nor this nayades,   *Naiads*
Satiry, nouther driades   *Satyrs*
That goddesse bene of wode and wildernes,

6990	Nor other goddes — nouther more ne lesse —	
	As Morpheus that is the god of slepe.	
	I holde hym wood that taketh any kepe	*pays any attention*
	To done to hem any observaunce:	
	He may nat faille for to have meschaunce	*misfortune*
6995	At the ende pleinly for his mede.	*reward*
	For al swiche feined falsnes, oute of drede,	
	Roos of the devel and first by his engyn	*cunning*
	And of his sleighti treynes serpentyn,	*tricks*
	Only mankynde whane he made loute	*bow*
7000	To false ydoles, the whiche, oute of doute,	
	Are but develis. David bereth witnesse	
	In the Sauter, where he writ expresse	*Psalter; positively*
	And confermeth ther as he endites	*writes*
	How the goddes of paganysme rytes,	
7005	On and alle (he excepteth noon),	
	Be made of gold, of silver, and of stoon,	
	Forged of bras, of metal, and of tre,	*wood*
	And eyen han and yit thei maye nat se,	
	And alle are fendes, so as David seith:	
7010	That who in hem haveth any feith,	
	Hope, credence, or in hem delite,	
	It is no drede that thei wil hym quyte	*doubt; repay*
	With swiche guerdoun as the soule sleth	*reward*
	Perpetuelly, so that the fyn is deth	*end*
7015	Of her servise whan men hennes passe	
	And in her lyf unhap and evele grace,	*misfortune*
	Meschef and wo, and confusioun,	*destruction*
	As men may sene exanple be this toun,	
	That wende wel assured for ta be	*thought [itself]*
7020	And to have stonde in longe prosperité	
	Ageyn her fon thorugh helpe of Appollo,	*foes*
	Of Venus eke, and favour of Juno,	
	Thorugh Pallas myght, Diane and Minerve,	
	Whom thei wer wont to honour and to serve	
7025	With cerymonyes and with sacrifise,	
	As ye toforn han herde me devise,	*recount*
	That hem have brought now unto ruyne,	
	By cruel deth maked hem to fyne.	*die*

297

Here may ye sen how the venym bites
7030 At the ende of swiche olde rytes,
By evidence of this noble toun.
What may availle now Palladioun?
May now ought helpe her frauded fantasie   *anything; baseless fancy*
Of al her olde false ydolatrie?
7035 Allas, allas, thei bought it al to sore.
Now farewel, Troye, farwel for everemore.
Farwel, allas. To cruel was thi fal.
Of the no more now I write shal.
For thi sake in sothe, whan I take hede,   *truly*
7040 Of inward wo myn herte I fele blede,
And whan that I remembre in my thought,
By ruyne how thou art brought to nought,
That whilom were so noble and so riche,   *once*
That in this world I trowe noon was liche   *like*
7045 Nor perigal, to speken of fairnesse,   *equal; beauty*
To speke of knyghthod and of worthinesse,
As clerkis seien that thi bildyng knewe,
That al the world oughte for to rewe
On thi pitous waste walles wylde,   *devastated*
7050 Whilom so rial whan men gan to bilde
Thin touris highe and Kyng Priamus
The first began, most riche and glorious,   *You*
And sette his se in noble Ylyoun.   *throne*
O, who can write a lamentacioun
7055 Convenient, O Troye, for thi sake?   *Fitting*
Or who can now wepe or sorwe make,
Thi gret meschef to compleyne and crie?   *misfortune*
Certis, I trowe nat olde Jeremye,   *Jeremiah*
That so bewepte the captivité
7060 Of thilke noble rial chefe cité
Jerusalem and his destruccioun,
With al the hole transmygracioun
Of the Jewes; nor thou Ezechiel,
That were that tyme that the meschef fel
7065 Unto the kyng ycalled Sedechie
In Babilon and for thi prophesie
With stonys were cruelly yslawe;   *slain*

298

Nor he that was departed with a sawe —
Ye bothe two, that koude so compleyne —
7070   Nor Danyel that felt so grete peyne
For the kynges transmutacioun
Into a beste, til thorugh the orisoun
Of Daniel he restored was
To mynde ageyn and ete no more no gras.
7075   Yet verrailly, though ye alle thre
With youre weping had alive be
And present eke at the destruccioun
Of this noble worthi royal toun,
To have beweiled the meschef and the wo   *misfortune*
7080   And the slaughter at the sege do   *done*
On outher party in ful cruel wyse,
Alle youre teris myghte nat suffise
To have bewepte her sorwes everychon,   *lamented*
Be tresoun wrought, as wel as be her foon.   *By; foes*
7085   Hereof no more, for it may nat availle.
But like as he that gynneth for to saille
Ageyn the wynde, whan the mast doth rive,   *Against; break*
Right so it were but in veyn to strive
Ageyn the fate, bitterer thanne galle,
7090   By highe vengaunce upon Troye falle
Nor to presume her furies, sharpe whette,
Ceriously in this boke to sette: *In due order*
So gret a thing I dar nat undirtake
But evene here a pitous ende I make
7095   Of the sege, after my sympelnesse.
And though my stile, blottid with rudenes   *writing instrument; faulty*
As of metre, be rusty and unfiled,
This ferthe boke, that I have compiled
With humble hond, of fer that doth me quake,   *makes*
7100   Unto youre grace holy I betake,   *commit*
Of youre merci no thing in dispeir,   *not at all*
So as I can, makyng my repeir   *returning*
To the Grekis and no lenger dwelle,
Her aventures of the se to telle
7105   In ther resort home to her contré   *return*
And how that thei there received be,

Only of support, so ye not dispise,   *if; disdain*
The fifthe boke shortly shal devise.   *set forth*

Book 5

	Whan Eolus, which doth the windes rore,	*causes the winds to roar*
	Apesid was, that he blewe no more,	*Appeased*
	Which is of stormys governour and lord,	
	And was also fully of accord	
5	With myghti Juno, lady of the eyr,	
	To make the skye and the wedir fair,	
	That cloude noon in hevene dide appere,	
	And Neptunus, blaundisshing of chere,	*inviting*
	Was of assent, the stori seith forsothe,	*truly*
10	To make the se fro tempest calm and smothe,	
	Withoute boilyng or trouble of any wawe,	*wave*
	The myghti Grekis to shipward gan hem drawe	
	For to repeire home to her contré,	
	After thei had wonnen the cité	
15	And put her fomen fully at the worse.	*foes; defeat*
	But Fortune, ay froward and perverse,	*ever obstinate and contrary*
	Hath with her myrthe meynt adversité;	*mixed*
	For whan thei wende ful assurid be	*thought*
	And have stonde stedefast in quiete,	
20	This blinde lady falsly made flete	*flow*
	Into her sugre galle of discordance,	
	Amonge hemsilf to bring in variaunce	
	And her hertis, of rancour and of pride,	
	Contagiously to severyn and devyde,	
25	Whan thei sat hiest in her glorie	
	With the palme of conquest and victorie,	
	Fully rejoyssinge, thorugh her highe renoun,	*strength*
	The crowne of laurer in possessioun,	*laurel*
	And had also at her lust al wonne.	*pleasure*
30	Whan brightest shon the lusti freshe sonne	
	From est to west of her worthines,	
	A cloudy sky unwarly with dirknesse	*without warning*
	Eclipsed hath a parti of her light	

	And diffacid the holsom bemys bright	*blotted out*
35	Of her welfare and prosperité	
	By th'envious fals contagiousté	*corrupting influence*
	Of the serpent, pompos and elat,	*arrogant and exultant*
	Amonge hemsilfe to make hem at debat,	*set them at odds*
	Inducinge in rancour and discord.	*Bringing*
40	For or thei entre withinne shippes bord,	*before*
	Ageyn Ulixes worthi Thelamoun,	
	In presence of Kyng Agamenoun,	
	Purposed hath pleinly his matere	*Put forth; case*
	Tofore Grekis, anoon as ye shal here.	*forthwith*

[*Ajax objects to awarding the Palladium to Ulysses, but Menelaus and Agamemnon decide in favor of Ulysses. When Ajax threatens vengeance, he is murdered; Menelaus, Agamemnon, and Ulysses fall under suspicion. Antenor invites the Greek leaders to a feast, where they discuss Aeneas's hiding Polyxena. Aeneas is banished, and he advises the Trojans to elect Antenor as their king, so that he might kill Antenor when he returns to accept the office. Antenor leaves Troy for the island of Corbodya, where he is welcomed. Cassandra prophesies the death of Agamemnon.*

Meanwhile, King Naulus plans to exact revenge on the Greeks because he believes the false story that his son Palamedes, who replaced Agamemnon as the Greek leader, was murdered by Ulysses and Diomede, though he was actually killed by Paris. With his son Oetes, Naulus builds signal fires to lure the Greek ships onto the rocks, where two hundred ships are lost. Oetes also writes Clytemnestra that Agamemnon has wed a Trojan princess. Aegisthus, Clytemnestra's lover, murders Agamemnon on his return; and Orestes, Agamemnon's son, is secretly sent to Crete. Oetes seeks to destroy Diomede as well by telling his wife, Egra, that Diomede killed her brother Assandrus on the voyage to Troy and has taken another wife. Egra banishes Diomede from his kingdom; he wanders forsaken until Aeneas calls him to Troy to help him. Diomede becomes the chief protector of Troy. As his reputation spreads, his wife, fearing his might, convokes her parliament, rescinds his banishment, and welcomes him back to his kingdom, where he lives happily. Aeneas then leaves Troy with his men and reaches Carthage with his father, Anchises. The Aeneid *records his losing Creusa, betraying Dido, and conquering Italy, but* Troy Book *says no more about him.*

Orestes undertakes vengeance for the murder of Agamemnon, with the aid of several kings. He captures the city of Methene and imprisons Clytemnestra, while his men kill Aegisthus. The next morning Orestes kills Clytemnestra, hacks her body into small pieces, and carries them outside the city boundaries to be fed to the beasts and dogs. Menelaus tries to deprive Orestes of his crown because of matricide, but Nestor supports Orestes. Orestes and Menelaus are reconciled, and Orestes marries Hermione, the daughter of Menelaus and

Book 5

Helen, while Erigona, the daughter of Aegisthus and Clytemnestra hangs herself. The story next moves to the adventures of Ulysses (lines 45–1780).]

	O Ulixes, by ordre in my writyng	
	Thin aventures commen on the ring,	*arrive in time*
	Ful wonderful bothe on lond and se,	
	Entermedlid with grete adversité!	*Mixed*
1785	For Guydo, first discrivinge thi repeire,	*describing; return*
	Seith how thou founde weder foule and faire,	*weather*
	Now agreable, now the thounder sowne,	*sounds*
	Now stille and smothe, now with clowdis frowne;	
	And seith also that thou dedist ordeyne	*command*
1790	To thi passage myghty shippes tweyne	
	Apparailled al for marchaundise,	*goods*
	That thou myghtest in most secré wyse	
	Every meschef of the se eskape.	
	But for al that thou haddist a fel jape:	*serious misfortune*
1795	For as this auctor thi resort doth wryte,	*return*
	He seith Ulixes, for al his wordis white,	*flattering speech*
	Irobbed was of riches and of good;	
	Contrarious wynde so ageyn him stood	
	That he was drive, to his confusioun,	*driven*
1800	Into the myghty stronge regioun	
	Where Thelamoun regned by his lyve;	*Ajax; when he was alive*
	And there he was hent and take blyve,	*seized; eagerly taken*
	Be myghti hond sesid by the brest,	
	And merciles put under arest;	
1805	For thei him had suspect in werkyng,	*suspected him of treachery*
	Touching the mordre of the same kyng.	
	But he so wrought by his sleighti wyle	*contrived; cunning*
	And his tale sette in swiche a stile	
	That hem alle he pleinly hath bejaped,	*deceived*
1810	And fro her hond frely is eskaped,	
	Except that he, for al his queynte fare,	*cleverness*
	Of his tresour was ymade ful bare.	
	And for his passage was to him unkouthe,	*because; unknown*
	He fil ageyn into the wolves mouthe;	
1815	For verraily, as it is specified,	*mentioned*
	Kyng Naulus men han hym eft espied,	*afterwards*

303

Take and bounde and cheyned mercyles
For the mordre of Kyng Pallamydes.
But the story reherseth in certeyn   *relates*
1820   By his prudence he eskaped is ageyn —
For he was bothe expert, wys, and olde —
Althei the maner be not fully tolde
Of his eskape, thorugh his besy peyne,   *diligence*
Out of daunger of these kynges tweyne —
1825   Til thorugh fortune he cam fro meschef fre
To the presence of Kyng Ydumee   *Idomeneus (see note)*
In symple array and torne apparaile.
Wherof the kyng gretly gan mervaile
To sen his povert in so lowe maner;   *poverty*
1830   But for al that he maked him good cher;   *nonetheless*
Though thilke tyme he were infortunat,   *same*
He hym resseiveth liche to his estat.   *according to*
And whan thei wern bothe tweyne allone,
In compleynyng Ulixes made his mone   *lament*
1835   Unto the kyng, as he that was ful sage,
Ceriously the sort of his passage,   *Point by point; fortune*
With face sad and a sobre chere,   *serious*
Fro point to point, anon as ye shal here.
"My lord," quod he, "shortly to expresse,   *said*
1840   Of trust I have in youre gentilnes,   *Because of*
I shal to yow myn aventures alle
Rehersyn her, right as it is falle.   *Relate here*
First, whan that I Troye lond forsook
And the water with my shippes took,
1845   I was anoon with wynde pesible blowe   *immediately; gentle*
To an yle whiche was to me unknowe,
Callid Mirma, of gret haboundance;
And alle thing that was to my plesaunce,
That may for silver or for gold be bought,
1850   I redy fonde, and wantid right nought,   *lacked nothing*
And ther abood ful longe while in joie   *remained*
With the tresour that I gat at Troye.
My shippes stuffed, my men hool and sounde,
And for commodité of that ilke grounde,   *suitability; region*
1855   We lyked so the contré enviroun   *surrounding*

That for disport and recreacioun   *diversion*
Oure tariyng ther we thought not longe,
For no man dide unto us no wronge.
Til on a day that the eyr was stille,
1860 The wynde also fully at oure wille,
We seyled forthe in quiete and in pes
Unto a port called Clanstafages,
Wher with my meyné long and many day   *followers*
I fond al thing according to my pay —   *satisfaction*
1865 The wedir lusty, agreable, and feir.   *pleasant*
But who may trust outher in wynde or eyr?
For upon feith of the smothe skye
Ageyn to ship fast I gan me hye,   *hasten*
Taried nought, but tok anoon the see,   *immediately*
1870 Smothe and calm enduring daies thre,
That in the wedir founde was no lak.
But sodeynly the hevene turned blak;
The hydous tempest and the wawes grene   *waves*
Oute of hope han me dispeired clene,   *drove me into despair*
1875 Troublid my spirit and made me pensif,   *melancholy*
Withoute refut t'eskape with the lyf,   *means*
Possid and drive by many sondri yle,   *Tossed; driven past; isle*
Til at the last, cast up at Cecyle,   *Sicily*
Recuryng lond with gret annoy and peyne,   *Reaching*
1880 Wher thilke tyme regned kynges tweyne.   *same*
And as I can remembre douteles,
The ton of hem called Sorigenes,   *one*
Whiche unto me ful contrarious was,   *hostile*
And the tother named Coclopas —   *other*
1885 Brethren of birthe and in conclusioun
Ilyche cruel of condicioun: *Equally; by temperament*
For though my sort had shape for the nonys,   *fortune; seemed set for the moment*
Bothe tweyne fil on me attonys,   *at the same time*
Oppressing me in ful gret distresse,   *Bearing heavily on me*
1890 Spoiled my shipes of tresour and richesse,   *Robbed*
And for no pité liked not to spare,
Til I was left destitut and bare
Of al my good. Allas, my mortal chaunce!
And most of al was to me grevaunce,

1895	Whan of my gold thei myght no more restreyne,	*seize*
	Thei sent doun her myghti sonys tweyne —	*their*
	Alipham, that was ful large and long,	
	And Polipheme the myghti geaunt strong —	
	Whiche on my men t'avenge hem wer so fayn	*eager*
1900	That thei of hem han an hundred slayn,	*them*
	Disaraied to stonden at diffence.	*Too disordered*
	And of malys, with sodeyn violence	
	Thei token me, for meschef almost lorn,	*distress; lost*
	And Alphenor, myn owne brother sworn,	
1905	And hatfully, as thei han us founde,	
	In cheynes cast and in stokkys bounde,	
	And after that ylokked in presoun.	
	And for to make platly mencioun,	*plainly*
	This myghti man, this grete Polypheme,	
1910	A suster had, shortly for to deme,	*judge*
	Oon the fairest that ever yit was born;	
	She myght in bewté so be set aforn —	
	Nature hir gaf swiche a prerogatyf —	*preeminence*
	A clene mayde, sothly, and no wyf,	
1915	Flouryng bothe in fairnes and bounté.	
	Whom Alphenor whan he dide se,	
	Albe he was fetrid in prisoun,	*Although*
	For love he lost wit and eke resoun,	
	And wex al mad — so narwe she dide him binde —	*grew*
1920	Save upon hir alwey was his mynde	
	And closid alwey was his perlous wounde.	
	And sixe monthes thus we leie bounde,	
	Bothe he and I, to seyn the platte trouthe,	*plain*
	Til Polypheme had upon us routhe;	*pity*
1925	And thorugh his grace and mediacioun,	
	He quyt us fre out of that prisoun	*released*
	And shewed us, of mercy and pité,	
	After oure sorwe gret humanité.	
	But Alphenor, yliche of oon entent,	*always*
1930	Was with the brond of Cupide brent	*brand; burned*
	And felt his part with many mortal fyt,	*was in love; severe attack*
	Til he so wrought by his sotil wyt	*caused; cunning*
	That on a nyght, who was lef or lothe,	*no matter who liked it or not*

	He stale this mayde, and his weye he gothe	
1935	Thorugh help of men with him at that tyme.	
	But on the morwe at the hour of pryme	*hour of sunrise*
	Poliphemus gan us for to sewe,	*follow*
	Whos myghti hond we myght nat eschewe;	*escape*
	And swiche asaut on us thei gan make	
1940	That of force thei han the mayde take	
	From Alphenor, maugre al his rage.	*despite*
	And Polypheme unto my damage	*harm*
	With his knyghtes so sore upon me lay	
	That I myght unnethe eskape away	*scarcely*
1945	To save my lyf, compassid enviroun,	*surrounded*
	To deth purswyd of that champioun.	
	But whan I sawe ther was non other geyn,	*remedy*
	To fle the deth, shortly for to seyn,	
	While this geaunt most fersly on me sette,	
1950	With my swerd oute his eye I smette;	*struck*
	And unto ship with my companye	
	I fledde in haste, that no man myght espie	
	Where I becam nor Alphenor my fere.	*companion*
	And whan the wawes gonne for to clere,	*subside*
1955	And gracious wynd gan to us awake,	*rouse*
	Thilk contré we han anoon forsake:	*immediately*
	It was nat holsom for us to abide."	
	But of this man, like as writ Ovide,	
	Poliphemus the geaunt, out of drede,	*without a doubt*
1960	Had an eye mydde of his forhede,	*in the middle of*
	Whiche Ulixes smot out at a stroke;	
	And like the bowes of a braunchid oke	*boughs; branched*
	Was al his heer and his longe berde —	
	On whom to loke childer were aferd.	*children*
1965	And whan that he hadde lost his sight,	
	Amonge the hilles he renneth day and nyght	
	In a rage to fynde hym som refuge,	
	Caste roches and grete stones huge	
	On every part enviroun the contré,	
1970	On Ulixes avenged for to be.	
	Thus seith Ovide in conclusioun;	
	In his boke of transformacioun,	

Methamorphoseos, ther ye may it se,
Whansoevere that your leyser be   *leisure*
1975 Ceriously the story for to rede.   *Point by point*
And in writinge forthe I wil procede,
How Ulixes, with face ded and pale,
To Ydumee tolde forthe his tale,
Rehersyng thus, supprised and awapid.   *amazed*
1980 "Fro Polipheme whan we wern eskaped,
Thorugh oure unhap and infelicyté   *misfortune*
Into an yle myddes of the see
We were dryve, whan it gan to nyghte;
And Elodium that litel kyngdam hyghte,
1985 Wher that Circes, the gret enchaunteresse,
Thilke tyme was lady and goddesse,   *At that time*
That koude hir craft so wondirfully performe,
Al sodeynly a man for to transforme
To have the liknes (and lesen his resoun)   *lose*
1990 Of hors or bere, tigre or lyoun,
Wolf or fox, or what hir list devise.   *what she pleased to imagine*
Hir dredful craft was shapen in swiche wise: *of such a nature*
So myghti wern hir straunge pociouns,
Her letuaryes and confecciouns.   *medicines*
1995 And she also so fair upon to se
That fro hir power no man myghte fle.
For be the werke of this sorceresse,
I was so fonned uppon hir fairnesse   *infatuated with*
That finally thus with me it stood:
2000 That al a yere I with hir abood   *remained*
And pleynly had power noon ne myght
For to depart, nouther day ne nyght,
So lusti was the lyf that I ladde.   *pleasant*
In whiche tyme by me a child she hadde,
2005 Right inly fair and goodly to the sight."   *Extremely*
And Thelagonius in sothnes he hight,   *truth; was named*
Whiche afterward, I reherse can,   *relate*
By processe wex a manly man.   *grew to be*
"And be my sotil secré providence,
2010 Of hir craft I hadde experience,
That maugre hir enchauntementes olde,

	I stale away — she myght me nat holde.	
	And finally my fate to conclude,	
	With my konnyng hir craft I gan delude,	*skill*
2015	That with my men I skaped fro her hond	*escaped*
	And went at large fre out of hir lond.	*without restraint*
	But al this thing me litel dide availe.	
	For on my way as I gan to saile,	
	For al my sleight, in a litel while	
2020	I blowe was up into an yle	
	Wher Calypha, suster to Circes,	*Calypso*
	Was crowned quene and held her scepter in pes;	
	Whos craftis wern so myghty and so strong,	
	Maugre my wil she held me ther ful long.	*Despite*
2025	But she in sothe, to speke of wommanhed,	*truth*
	Of bounté, fredam, and of goodlyhed,	
	Surly had so sovereyn excellence	
	That myn abood to me was noon offence.	*delay*
	But whosoevere therat crye or clappe,	*talk noisily*
2030	At the last I skaped fro hir trappe	
	And cam to an yle, right as any lyne,	*immediately*
	Whiche specialy thorugh high power devyne	
	Ordeyned is of yore be myracle —	
	As it were, a spiritual oracle —	
2035	A man to have in a temple there	
	Sodeyn answere of what him list enquere,	*Prompt*
	Of questiouns and demaundes alle,	
	And of soules what shal eke befalle,	
	Whan men ar dede and graven under stoon.	*buried*
2040	And I gan axe in the temple anoon	*ask about; immediately*
	Myn aventures that shuld after swe	*follow*
	And wher a man myght his fate eschewe;	*avoid*
	And of al this, lyk to myn entent,	
	I had answere ful convenient —	*fitting*
2045	Save what befalleth whan a soule is goon,	
	Diffynycioun unto me was noon.	*Precise statement*
	Swiche thing t'asoile acordeth nat to right:	*solve*
	It is reserved unto Goddes myght	
	And excedeth resoun and wit of man.	
2050	And fro thens forthe to seile I gan,	

Dreven with wynde and no part socoured,
Wher I was lyk to have be devourid
Of Caribdis with his profounde welle,
Where Sirenes — Meremaydnes — dwelle,
2055 That fro the brest with skalis silver shene   *scales; bright*
Ben of her shap fysches freshe and clene,
And uppermore, Kynde doth compasse   *Nature; devise*
Hem to apere femynyn of face,
Lyk virgines that were of nature
2060 Withoute spot, undefouled pure.
And of custom, in wawis as thei flete,   *waves; float*
The song of hem is so hevenly swete,
So angelik and ful of armonye
That verrailly the sugred melodie
2065 Ravisshe wolde any man alyve,   *Entrance*
Of inly joie almost his herte ryve,   *internal; break*
Make a man, of sodeyn highe plesaunce,
Foryete hymsilf and lese his remembraunce,
Devoide hym clene from his owne thought,   *Withdraw*
2070 Til unwarly he be to meschef brought.   *unexpectedly*
And with her song, or he take kepe,   *before he is aware*
He shal be brought in a mortal slepe;
And thei anoon, it may not be withdrawe,   *revoked*
Wil drenche his ship lowe under the wawe.   *sink*
2075 Thus the swetnes of her hevenly soun
Bringeth a man to confusioun,   *ruin*
Whosoevere by her boundis pace.   *boundaries sail*
But with the lif I eskaped by grace;
For myn erys with wex and gommys clere   *ears; gums (from plants)*
2080 Were stoppid so that I ne myghte here
Touche nor werble of her instrumentis,   *note; melody*
Wherby the resoun of man yblent is.   *blinded*
And finally, thorugh my sotilté,   *cunning*
I and my men ben eskapid fre,
2085 Seiling forthe, al mat of werynesse,   *exhausted*
Til we cam up with ful gret distresse
At Phenyce, and toke anoon the lond,   *Phoenicia; reached*
Cast anker, and oure shippes bond.   *tied up*
But sothly ther it fil us ful unfaire;   *truly; bad luck befell us*

2090	For the peple, cruel and contraire,	*hostile*
	Only of malis fil on me anoon	*at once*
	And slowe my men almost everychon;	*slew; everyone*
	Tresour and good, litel that I hadde,	
	Was me byraft; and al with hem thei ladde;	*despoiled; carried off*
2095	And fewe of hem that wer left alive	
	Thei token hem and put in prisoun blyve.	*quickly*
	Thus hath Fortune lad me on her daunce	
	With litel joie and plenté of meschaunce,	
	Of whos daunger lerned and expert,	
2100	I am falle in meschef and povert;	*poverty*
	And with gret dool and sorwe ful my brest,	*sadness*
	On se and londe, by southe and nat by est	
	I am com unto youre presence	
	And have declared pleinly in sentence	*substance*
2105	Myn aventures to youre worthinesse,	
	Of trust only and of feithfulnesse	*Out of*
	That I have to yow in special.	
	And now I have rehersid and told al	*narrated*
	To youre highnesse in my beste wyse,	
2110	Withoute more — it doth to me suffise."	
	And thaugh in hert he was constreyned sore,	*distressed*
	Thilke tyme Ulixes spak no more	*At that time*
	But held his pes, ful hevy in lokyng.	
	And Ydumeus lik a gentil kyng	
2115	Counforted hym al that evere he myght,	
	And besy was his herte for to light,	*comfort*
	And hym besought his hevynesse lete;	*entreated; abandon*
	And as long as hym list in Crete	*he wished*
	With hym abide, he made hym sureté	
2120	He shulde faren also wel as he	
	And nat want of what may do him ese.	
	And whan his sorwe somwhat gan apese,	*moderate*
	That his rage drow unto an ende,	*reached*
	Leve he toke and seide he wolde wende	*go*
2125	Oute of that londe home to his contré.	
	But first the kyng, of fredam and bounté,	*liberality*
	Yaf unto hym gret riches and array	*Gave*
	And whatsoevere was unto his pay —	*satisfaction*

Gold, tresour, and many other thinges;
2130 And at the partynge of these tweyne kynges,
There wer shippes whan him list to saile,
Redy stuffid with meyné and vitaile.   *provided; followers*
And thus Ulixes gan hym redy make;
And whan he hathe his leve fully take,
2135 He hasted hym, and toke anoon the se,   *hastened*
And gan saile toward his contré.
But first he went to Kyng Alphenoun,
Whiche passingly hadde affeccioun   *greatly; desire*
To sen Ulixes at his homecomyng
2140 And desirous over alle thing
To han of hym newly aqueyntaunce:
For unto hym was inly gret plesaunce   *extremely*
To here hym talke, for his elloquence,
For his wysdam and his highe prudence.
2145 And ther he was, after al his smert,
Receyved pleinly with as glad an hert   *fully*
As evere yit was any maner man
Sithen tyme that the world began;   *Since*
And to encres of his felicité,
2150 Ther herd he first of Penolope,
His trewe wyf, withoute spot or blame,
Of whom yit grene is the noble fame,   *alive*
Whiche from hir lord, for al his long absence,
In thought nor dede nevir dide offence
2155 But sothly was, bothe in chere and dede,   *truly; appearance; deed*
Thorughoute Grece example of wommanhede.
And yit was she, as bokes list expresse,   *wish*
Thorughoute the world merour of fairnes,   *mirror (example)*
And among Grekis born of highest blood,
2160 Called of auctours bothe fair and good;   *by authors (see note)*
And yit seyn bokes of hir, douteles,
Was never noon that had so gret pres   *crowd [of lovers]*
But she hir kepte, chaunging for no newe,   *kept herself*
Unto hir lord evere iliche trewe,
2165 Of hert ay oon, nat partid into tweyne,
That she is called quene and sovereyne
Of wyfly trouthe in this bokis olde.

	And oft, I fynde, hir herte wolde colde;	*become cold*
	She turne pale for hir lord so ferre,	
2170	In hir closet to heren of the werre,	*private room*
	Of drede she had, and for fere eke quake,	
	Of fantasies for hir lordes sake;	*imaginings*
	For his absence, bothe eve and morwe,	
	Was deth to hir and inportable sorwe.	*unbearable*
2175	And ay in sothe for joie or any game,	*truth in all circumstances*
	Whan it fel she herd Hectoris name,	*happened*
	In any place anoon she fil aswowne	*at once; in a faint*
	And gan hirsilf al in teris drowne;	
	Of wommanhed so she was aferde	
2180	To here the slaughter of his mortal swerde,	
	List hir lord, of knyghtly surquedie,	*Lest; pride*
	Hadde of fortune falle in jupartye,	
	Of hap or sort tamet that worthi knyght,	*By chance or fate pierced*
	That selde or never she felt hir herte light.	*rarely*
2185	And many dremes anyghtes dide hir gaste,	*at night; frighten*
	Al the while that the sege laste;	*siege*
	And every play was venym in hir sight,	
	Whan that she was from hir owne knyght:	
	For in this world she had joie noon	
2190	Of highe nor lowe, pleinly, but of oon,	
	For whos sake al myrthe she refuseth.	
	And whoso be that in his herte museth	*think*
	Of any womman anything but good,	
	Of malencolye mevid in his blood,	
2195	Lat hym adverte of wisdam and se,	*consider*
	And remembre on Penolope,	
	For his decert list that he be blamyd.	*just punishment lest*
	And, O Guydo, thou shuldest ben ashamed	
	To seyn of wyves anything but wele;	*good*
2200	For in good feith, as fer as I can fele,	
	Though oon or two do among offence,	
	She that is good thorugh hir providence	
	Is therof no thing for to wyte.	*not at all; blame*
	And though Guydo in his boke endite	*describe*
2205	The variaunce of Eleyne or Cryseyde	
	Or Medea, that for sorwe deyde,	

313

Lete ther ageyn, of right and equité,   *Let him be aware of*
The wyfly trowthe of Penolope,
The maydenhed of yonge Policene,
2210   And the goodnes of Eccuba the quene,
Of Cassandra eke the stedfastnes;
And with al this, take the kyndenes
Of Pantasile, withoute variaunce;
And put al this togidre in balaunce,
2215   And ye shal fynde, yif ye list acounte,   *wish to take into account*
Maugre who grucchith, trouthe shal surmounte —   *No matter who complains*
I dar aferme — and bere aweye the pris:
Ther wil no man replie that is wys —
He were to feble in his oppinioun!
2220   And while Ulixes was with Alphenoun,
It was to hym made relacioun   *described*
Of an hatful conspiracioun,   *conspiracy*
That certeyn lordis enviroun his contré   *around*
Ravisshe wolde his quene Penolope,   *Carry off*
2225   Maugre alle tho that were ther ageyn,   *Despite*
Albe that she was evere ilike pleyn,   *always honest*
In hir trouthe stidefast as a wal.
Yet thei have cast pleynly that she shal
Be take of force, it may nat be eschewed,   *by; avoided*
2230   But it so be in haste she be reskewed.   *Unless*
For thei hem cast the tyme nat ajourne,   *planned; deferred*
For day and nyght with hir thei sojourne,
Inly in herte for love disamaied.
But of wisdam she hathe hem so delaied
2235   That ther was noon so manly nor so sage
That koude on hir geten avauntage,   *get the better of her*
So avise she was in hir wirkyng.   *cautious*
And whan Ulixes conceyved al this thing,   *learned*
And fully knewe by open evidence,
2240   And also had in special credence   *secret message*
Sent unto hym fro Penolope,
The mater hool declaringe in secré,
His owne sone Thelamoneus,
He wexe in herte wood and furious,   *grew; mad*
2245   And wolde make no delacioun,   *delay*

314

But in al haste besoughte Alphenoun,
The myghti kyng, of his high bounté
To releve hym in his adversité,   *assist*
And that he wold thorugh his myghti hond
2250 Of gentilnes conveye hym to his lond.
He graunteth hym and seith nat onys nay;   *once*
And bothe two in ful gret array
Taken the se whan the wynd was good;
Wel fortuned, for nothing hem withstood,   *stood against*
2255 Thei be arived and hadde no lettyng,   *obstacle*
Wher Ulixes, as ye han herd, was kyng.
And secrely anyght thei wer conveied   *at night*
To hem that han his ligaunce disobeied;   *authority over his vassals*
And merciles, or thei myght awake,
2260 In her beddes thei han hem alle take,
Makyng noon prolongyng til on the morwe,
But in al hast, for no wyght durst hem borwe,   *stand surety for*
Smet of her hedes by jugement final,   *Smote*
And set hem up on the castel wal,
2265 Everyche by other endelong the rowe,   *all along*
Upon the hour whan the cok gan crowe.
And thus al nyght thei kept hemsilfe cloos,   *were on guard*
Til that Phebus meryly aroos
In the orient, whan the larke song;
2270 And tho this kynges with her meyné strong,   *these; followers*
Freshely beseyn, entre the cité.   *brightly clothed*
Who was tho glad but Penolope?
Who made joie but this goodly quene,
Ful desirous hir owne lorde to sene?
2275 But yif I shulde al in ordre sette   *if*
The grete myrthe thei made whan thei mette,
Make rehersaile of compleintes olde
And how thei gan her hertes to unfolde   *open*
Eche to other and list nothing concele,   *wish*
2280 And the gladnes that thei inly fele;   *inwardly*
Yif I shulde put al in memorie —   *If*
The rejoisshinge and the hertly glorie
That his liges made at his comynge,   *vassals*
The costis eke thei hadde at his metynge,   *expenses; meeting him*

315

2285	The giftes grete and presentis riche	*gifts*
	(In al this world, I trowe, noon ilyche) —	
	It were to long tariyng for my boke —	
	And how that he newe assuraunce toke	
	Of his lordis and his liges alle,	*vassals*
2290	And how that thei to his grace falle,	*came to his favor*
	The chere he made eke to Alphenoun	
	Of gentilnes thorugh his highe renoun,	
	And how the doughter, inly debonaire,	*gracious*
	Of Alphenoun, Nausia the faire,	
2295	By Ulixes mediacioun	
	Iwedded was unto Thelamoun,	
	Born by discent (ther may no man say nay)	
	To rejoisshe his crowne after his day —	*have possession of*
	And thus cam in by his purviaunce	
2300	Of two regnes the myghti alliaunce —	
	And how al this brought was to the knotte,	*conclusion*
	Men wolde deme me pleinly to sotte	*foolish*
	To presume of oppinioun	
	For to delate a descripcioun,	*expand*
2305	Sithen Guydo, touching but the chef	*main points*
	In this mater, of stile was but bref,	*writing*
	Shortly rehersing how Kyng Alphenoun	
	Repeired is hom to his regioun	*Returned*
	And Ulixes in his chefe cité	
2310	Abood stille with Penolope,	
	Where I hym leve in joie and in solace	
	Til Antropos liketh to purchace	*arrange*
	For to ficche finally the date,	*determine*
	The thred untwyne of his lyves fate.	*cut*

[*Lydgate now turns to the story of Pyrrhus and follows his author in describing the descent of Pyrrhus's line. Pyrrhus tries to restore his grandparents Peleus and Thetis, whom Atastus has banished from their realm. He lands in the region where they are exiled. Dressed as a pauper, he kills Atastus's two sons and then, dressing in purple, he tells Atastus he is one of Priam's sons, imprisoned by Pyrrhus. Atastus asks where Pyrrhus is, and Pyrrhus shows him the cave where Peleus is hiding. As Pyrrhus prepares to slay Atastus, Peleus and Thetis intervene to stop him. Pyrrhus and Atastus agree to divide the kingdom of Thessaly, and then Atastus resigns the kingdom to Pyrrhus. Afterwards, Pyrrhus falls in love with Orestes's wife,*

Book 5

*Hermione, though Andromache, Hector's widow, is now his wife and he has a son,
Achilleidos, by her. He carries off Hermione, and the two women are soon at odds. After
Hermione writes to Menelaus, complaining that Pyrrhus cherishes Andromache more than
her, Menelaus tries to kill Andromache but fails. Afterwards, Orestes slays Pyrrhus at Delos,
where he has gone to pray for Achilles. The kingship of Thessaly passes to Achilleidos. When
he comes of age, Achilleidos resigns the kingdom to his half-brother, Lamedonte, Hector's
son, who frees all the Trojan captives. At this point, Guido adds the story of King Menon,
whom Achilles slew when he tried to rescue Troilus. After Menon's queen dies, she appears
at his tomb next to Troilus, takes his bones out of the tomb, puts them in a chest made of
gold and precious stones, and then disappears. Some say she was an angel or a goddess or
the soul of the king, but these matters surpass my knowledge. Lydgate turns at this point to
his final chapter, the fate of Ulysses (lines 2315–2936).]*

Lowe on my knees, now I muste loute	*bow*
To thilke god that maketh men to route	*snore*
And causeth folke to have glad swevenes,	*dreams*

2940 Bothe at morwe and on lusti evenes,
      Whan Morpheus, with his slepi wond,   *wand*
      Whiche that he holdeth alweie in his hond,   *ever*
      Hath marked hem ageyn the dirke nyght,
      To maken men bothe mery and lyght,
2945 And somwhile for to han gladnes,
      And sodeynly to falle in hevynes,
      Lyk as to hem he yeveth evydence
      By sondry signes in his apparence.
      Unto that lord now moste I mekely preie
2950 At this tyme my stile to conveye,   *pen*
      Of Ulixes the dreme to discrive,
      The laste of alle he hadde be his lyve,
      Declaryng hym be tokenes ful notable
      And by signes verray demonstrable,
2955 As he slepte ageyn the pale mone,   *moon*
      His fatal day that shulde folwe sone.
      For it fel thus: as he abedde lay   *happened*
      After mydnyght, tofore the morwe gray,
      Hym thought he sawe appere a creature
2960 To his sight celestial of figure —
      Noon erthely thing but verraily devyne,   *truly*
      Of port, of chere wonder femynyne,

	And as hym sempte in his fantasye,	*imagining*
	Like a thing sent oute of fairie;	*land of supernatural creatures*
2965	For the bewté of hir goodly face	
	Recounforted pleynly al the place,	
	Moste surmountynge and most sovereyne;	*surpassing*
	And the clernes of hir eyne tweyne	
	Al sodeynli, or men myght adverte,	*notice*
2970	Perce wolde evene to the herte —	
	Diffence noon myghte be devysed.	
	And Ulixes, with hir loke supprysed,	
	Gan hir beholde alweie more and more	*continually*
	And in his slep for to sighe sore,	
2975	Presyng ay with ful besy peyne	*Striving; urgently*
	Hir t'enbracen in his armys tweyne;	
	But ay the more he presed hir to se,	
	Ay the more from hym she gan to fle;	
	And ay the more he gan to purswe,	
2980	She ageynwarde gan hym to eschwe,	*escape*
	So contrarie to hym was Fortune.	
	And whan she sawe he was importune,	*persistent*
	She axed hym shortly what he wolde;	*wanted*
	And he to hir the platte trouthe tolde.	*plain*
2985	"Certis," quod he, "my lyves emperesse,	
	Wher that ye ben woman or goddes	
	I can not deme nor jugen half aright,	
	I am so dirked and blendid in my sight;	*clouded*
	But I dar wel affermyn in this place,	
2990	My lyf, my deth stant hooly in your grace,	*power*
	More of merci requiryng thanne of right	
	To rewe on me, whiche am your owne knyght,	*feel pity*
	And of pité and compassioun	
	Goodly to sen to my savacioun:	
2995	For my desire but I may fulfille,	*unless*
	This silfe nyght to have of yow my wille,	
	To my recure I can no remedie,	*recovery*
	For lak of routhe but I moste dye.	*pity*
	Now have I al atwexe hope and drede	*between*
3000	Mysilf declared to youre wommanhede."	
	And after that she kepte hir clos a while,	*guarded*

	And ful sadly gan on hym to smyle,	*gravely*
	And, as it is put in remembraunce,	
	Seyde unto hym, with sobre countenaunce.	
3005	"Sothly," quod she, "thin affeccioun	*Truly; desire*
	Wolde fully turne to confusioun	*destruction*
	Of us bothe; it is so perillous,	
	So inly mortal and contagious	*pernicious*
	That outterly ther geyne may no red,	*altogether; be no remedy*
3010	But oon of us moste anoon be ded:	*at once*
	This is the fyn of the hatful chaunce	*end; fortune*
	That shulde folwe after oure plesaunce."	
	And as Ulixes gan to neyghe nere,	*approach*
	Beholdyng ay on hir hevenly cher,	*face*
3015	Whereas she stood upright on the grounde,	
	He sawe hir holde a spere longe and rounde,	
	The hed therof al of burned stele,	*burnished*
	Forged new and grounde wonder wele;	
	And theruppon in his avisioun	
3020	He sawe a baner blased up and doun,	*adorned with heraldic devices*
	The felde therof al of colour ynde,	*blue*
	Ful of fysshes betyn, as I fynde,	*shaped by hammering into a thin sheet (see note)*
	And in som bokys like as it is tolde,	
	In the myddes a large crowne of golde.	*middle*
3025	And or that she turne gan hir face,	*before*
	Likly anoon to parte oute of the place,	*directly*
	She spak to hym and seyde in wordes pleyn:	
	"This ful tokene of partyng of us tweyn	
	Foreveremore, nowther for sour nor swete,	
3030	After this day never ageyn to mete."	
	And disapering, anoon hir leve she toke.	
	And after that he sodeynly awoke	
	And gan to muse in his fantasie	*imagination (see note)*
	What thing this dreme myghte sygnyfie;	
3035	But wher it ment owther evel or good,	
	The secrenes he nat undirstood,	
	For it surmountid sothly his resoun.	*exceeded*
	Therfore he sent thorugh his regioun	
	For swiche as wern sotil expositours	*such; skillful*
3040	Of fate or sort, or crafti devinours,	

For alle the clerkis soget to his crowne,   *subject*
T'assemble in oon his swevene to expowne.   *together; expound*
And whan thei knewe be informacioun
The maner hool of his avisioun,
3045   Thei conclude, accordynge into oon,   *agreement*
The tyme aprocheth and shal come anoon
That oon that is nexte of his kynrede
With a spere shulde make hym blede.
Lat se wher he his fate can remewe   *escape*
3050   Sith it is hard destyné to eschewe,   *Since; avoid*
As seyn tho folke in ther oppinioun
That werke and truste on constellacioun.   *astrology*
And Ulixes, musyng on this tale,   *pondering*
Chaungeth colour and gan wexe pale,
3055   Wonder dredful and ful of fantasies,   *fears*
Gan in hymsilf seke remedyes
To voide aweie thing that wil nat be: *avoid*
He stareth brode, but he may nat se;   *looks with open eyes*
His inward loke was with a cloude shent.   *judgment; clouded*
3060   But wenyng he to have be prudent   *thinking (see note)*
Made calle his sone Thelamoun,   *Caused to be summoned*
And to be take and shette up in presoun,
He supposyng fully in his wit   *mind*
Fro alle meschef therby to go quyte.   *free*
3065   He nat adverteth nor ne toke noon hede   *consider*
To the sharpnes of the speris hed,
Nor to the fysshes in the baner bete,   *hammered into shape*
Nor to the se, wher thei swymme and flete,   *float*
Nor of the quene that called is Circes,
3070   That signes brought of werre and nat of pes,
Nor of the crowne, tokene of dignité
Of oon that shal holde his royal se
Mid the wawes, bothe fel and wood,   *cruel; mad*
Amonge the fysshes in the large flood.
3075   And he shal make the devisioun,   *he (Telegonus)*
Toforne remembrid in th'avisioun,   *As foretold*
Ageyn his wil, of verray ignoraunce,   *true*
And execute the fatal purveiaunce   *foresight*
Up of the dreme with his spere of stele,

320

3080	Whiche Ulixes considereth nevereadele,	*not at all*
	Nor to no wyght hath suspecioun	*person*
	But to his sone called Thelamoun,	
	That is closed and shet up in a tour.	
	And Ulixes with coste and gret labour	
3085	Fro day to day doth his besynes	
	For hymsilf to make a forterresse,	
	Bilt on a roche, of lym and square stonys,	*lime*
	Depe diched aboute for the nonys,	*occasion*
	That no man may entre on no side,	
3090	Where he casteth al his lyve t'abide	*plans*
	With certeyn men chose in special,	
	Night and day to wache on the wal	
	That no wyght shulde have noon entré,	
	But it so falle that he be secré,	*Unless; happen; discreet*
3095	Knowe of olde, and to counceil sworne.	*sworn to secrecy*
	Now as the story rehersed hath toforne,	*before*
	The olde fool, this dotard Ulixes,	
	A sone hadde begeten on Circes —	
	Freshe and lusti, yonge and coraious —	
3100	And he was called Thelagonyus,	
	Born in the se amonge the flodis rage,	
	That was also, for to rekne his age,	
	Fyve and twenti yere or thereaboute.	
	But of his fader he was ay in doute	
3105	What man he was or who it myghte be,	
	Beinge thereof in noon sureté,	
	Til on a day he, desirous to knowe,	
	To his moder fil on knees lowe,	
	Beseching hir goodly (and nat spare)	*incessantly*
3110	Of his fader the trouthe to declare;	
	What he was and where he shulde dwelle,	
	He besought that she wolde telle.	
	But sothly she long and many daies	
	Of prudence put hym in delayes,	
3115	Til that she sawe she myght have no reste,	
	So inportune he was in his requeste;	*persistent*
	And whanne she knewe ther was non other bote,	*remedy*
	Fro point to point she tolde hym crop and rote	*the whole*

Of Ulixes and where that he was kyng.

3120 And he anoon made no lettyng,   *delay*

But toke leve — it may no better be —

And seide pleinly he wolde his fader se,

Wherof the quene gan in herte colde.   *became cold*

But whan she sawe she myght him nat withholde,

3125 She hym besought with chere debonaire   *face kindly*

That he wolde sone ageyn repeire.   *return*

And forthe he seileth onward on his wey

Withoute abood the silfe same day

By many port and many fer contré,

3130 Til he was brought there he wolde be —

To Achaia, a lond of gret renoun.

And he gan cerche thorugh the regioun

After the place and paleis principal

Whereas the kyng helde his se royal;   *royal seat*

3135 And he so long in the contré rood,

Til he was taught where the kyng abood,

Ther Ulixes was shet up in mewe,   *hiding*

To whiche place in haste he gan purswe,

A gret party releved of his sorwe.

3140 And on a Monday, erly be the morwe,

Unto the brigge the righte weie he toke   *drawbridge*

And fond a porter deynous of his loke;   *gatekeeper haughty*

And lowly first he gan hym to preie

That he wold goodly hym conveie

3145 Into the courte and make no tariyng,

For a message he hadde to the kyng.

But proudly he denyed hym the gate,

And shortly seide that he cam to late

To entre there in any maner wyse,

3150 And ungoodly gan hym to dispise,   *treat with contempt*

Frowarde of speche and malicious.   *Threatening*

But in al haste Thelagonyus,

As he that was in herte nat afferde,

The proude porter hente be the berde   *seized*

3155 And with his fyste roof his chawle boon,   *broke his jaw bone*

That he fil ded, muet as a stoon;   *silent*

And other eke that hym tho withstood

	He made proudly to lepen into flood;	*water*
	And whan mo cam to make resistence,	
3160	He hent a swerde be manly violence,	*seized*
	And furiously in his irous tene	*rage*
	(The story seith) he slowe of hem fiftene,	
	Hymsilfe almoste wounded to the deth,	
	And gan, forwery, sothly faile breth.	*extremely weary, truly*
3165	And Ulixes, what for noise and soun,	
	To the brigge is descendid doun,	*drawbridge*
	Findinge his men at entré of the gate	
	Ded and slayn be ful mortal hate;	
	And he ful irous hent anoon a darte,	*seized immediately*
3170	Of aventure stonding tho aparte,	*By chance*
	And cruelly caste at Thelagoun.	
	But the stroke, as in conclusioun,	
	Damageth nat, for it glood aside;	*slipped*
	And he for haste no lenger wolde abide,	
3175	Hent up the darte withoute more areste,	*Snatched; delay*
	And smot the kyng lowe under the breste	
	Thorugh the ribbes, shortly for to seie,	
	That of the wounde he moste nedis deie,	
	Having tho noon oppinioun	*no idea*
3180	That he was kyng, nor suspecioun,	
	Nor that he had his owne fader slawe.	*slain*
	Whiche faste gan to his ende drawe;	
	His wounde was so dedly and so kene	
	That he myght himsilve nat sustene,	
3185	But pale and wan to the grounde gan glide,	*fall*
	His men aboute upon every side,	
	That besy wern to help hym and releve.	*assist*
	But his sore gan so ake and greve	*wound; ache; cause pain*
	That he wel felte that he muste be ded;	
3190	But abrayding, as he lifte up his hed,	*gaining consciousness*
	Havyng as yit mynde and good resoun,	
	Remembre gan on his avisioun	
	And how it was tolde him oute of drede	*certainly*
	That oon that was nexte of hys kynrede,	
3195	Descendid doun from his owne lyne,	
	His swevene shal parforme to the fyne	*realize fully*

And acomplisshe it with a darte of stele.

And for he coude nat conceyve wele   *because*

What that he was nor who it shulde be,

3200 He bad anoon unto his meyné,   *immediately; followers*

Withoute harme or any violence,

Fette anoon unto his presence   *Fetch*

The yonge man whiche at the gate stood,

That hath that day shad so moche blood.   *shed*

3205 And whan he was aforn Ulixes brought,   *before*

Of hym he hath enquered oute and sought   *inquired into*

Firste of his kyn and nexte of his contré.

"Certis," quod he, "I was born in the se,

Amonge fysshes myd the wawes grene,"   *waves*

3210 And seide also his moder was a quene

Called Circes, of whom the name is kouthe   *known*

Bothe est and west and right fer be southe,

And tolde also his fader was a kyng,

That hym begat at his homecomyng   *homeward voyage*

3215 Fro Troye toun toward his contré.

"And as my moder Circes tolde me

Secrely that he Ulixes highte,   *was named*

Of wham desirous for to han a sighte,

I entred am this myghti regioun,

3220 And have pursuyd unto this dongoun   *castle keep*

Only in hope my fader to have seyn;

But I se wel my labour is in veyn.

And sith in soth loste is my traveyl   *truth; effort*

And that it may on no side aveyle,

3225 It were foly lenger here to dwelle.

Lo, here is al that I can you telle

Of my kynred; axeth me no more."   *ask*

With that Ulixes gan to syghe sore   *greatly*

For lak of blood, as he that was ful pale,

3230 And seide anoon, whan he herde his tale: *immediately*

"Now wote I wel my woful destiné   *know*

Fulfilled is — it may noon other be!

Now wote I wel that it is to late

To grucche or strive ageyn my pitous fate;   *complain*

3235 For my sone, as clerkes whylom tolde,   *once*

	Hath made an ende of my daies olde,	
	Theron expectant, with peynes ful grevous!"	*waiting*
	And with that word Thelagonyus,	
	Whan he wist ageyn Natures lawe	*knew*
3240	That he, allas, hadde his fader slawe,	
	Whiche in that lond longe bar his crowne,	
	Withoute abood he fil anoon aswowne,	*delay; immediately fainted*
	His clothes rent, his yolwe here totorn.	*yellow hair tore at*
	"Allas," quod he, "that evere was I born!	
3245	For cursid is my woful destiné	
	And my fortune, whiche I may nat fle!	
	Cursid my sort, cursid myn aventure,	*fate; luck*
	And I, refus of every creature,	*rejected by*
	Forwaried eke my disposicioun!	*Cursed also my temperament*
3250	And cursid is my constellacioun,	*stars under which I was born*
	Cursed also and infortunat	
	The hour in whiche my fader me begat!	
	So wolde God withoute lenger red,	*delay*
	T'aquiten hym anoon, that I were ded,	*To repay; forthwith*
3255	To leie my lif for his deth to borwe!"	*pledge; as surety*
	And whan the kyng sawe his grete sorwe	
	And wist he was his sone of Circes born,	*knew*
	By many signe rehersed heretoforn,	*described herebefore*
	He unto hym anoon forgaf his deth,	*forthwith forgave*
3260	As he myght for want and lak of breth,	
	So inportable was his passioun.	*grievous; suffering*
	And his sone ycalled Thelamoun,	*named*
	Whiche hath in presoun so many day be shet,	
	To his presence in al haste was fet,	*brought*
3265	Whiche, whan he saw his fader in swiche point,	*in such a plight*
	Upon the deth stondyng in disjoint,	*at the extremity*
	And knewe also and the trouthe founde	
	By whom he had his laste dedly wounde,	
	A swerd he hent and mortally irous	*seized*
3270	And wolde have ronne on Thelagonius,	
	Of highe dispit avenged for to be.	*hatred*
	But Ulixes of faderly pité	
	Made his men hold hym and restreyne;	
	And amyd of al his grevous peyne,	

3275	By his prudence — and that was don anoon —	
	He made his sones for to be al oon	*reconciled*
	And gaf in charge unto Thelamoun,	*gave*
	Of enternes and affeccioun	*close friendship*
	And of hool herte, feyned neveradel,	*not at all*
3280	Al his lyve to love his brother wel,	
	To parte with hym tresour, gold, and good,	*To share*
	As to the nexte born of al his blood.	
	And tho in soth was no lenger taried	*then truly without delay*
	That Ulixes rially was caried	
3285	Of Achaya to the chefe cité,	
	And after that lyved daies thre,	
	Withoute more, and tho gaf up the gost.	*Without delay; then gave*
	I can nat seyn pleynly to what cost	*abode*
	After this lyf that his soule is goon,	
3290	But in a towmbe of metal and of stoon	
	The body was closed and yshet;	
	And after that maked was no let	*delay*
	That Thelamoun with gret sollennité	
	Icrowned was in his fadres see,	*Crowned; throne*
3295	Swerd and septer delivered to his hond	
	Of Achaya, a ful worthi lond,	
	Right abundaunt of tresour and of good.	
	And Thelagoun with hym ther abood	
	A yere complet, wel cherisshed in his sight,	
3300	And of his brother toke the ordre of knyght;	*from*
	And for hym list no lenger ther abide,	*because (when)*
	The kyng for hym wysly gan provide,	
	That he with gold, gret tresour, and plenté	
	Repeired is home to his contré;	*Returned*
3305	And his moder, of age wexe sad,	*grown*
	Of his repeire passingly was glad,	*return*
	As she that sawe be hir sorserie	
	He skaped was many jupartie,	*escaped*
	Many pereil, and many gret distresse.	
3310	And after that she fil into seknesse	
	And hir dette yalde unto nature,	*debt yielded*
	Whiche eskape may no creature	
	In al this world that is here lyvyng.	

	After whos deth hir sone was made Kyng	
3315	Of Aulydos, the merveillous contré,	*Aulis*
	As I have tolde, enclosed with a see,	*surrounded*
	Amonge rokkes, wher many shippes drowne;	
	And sixti yere ther he bar his crowne,	
	This manly man, Thelagonyus.	
3320	And his brother, Thelamonyus,	
	Regned also in his regioun	
	Seventi wynter, as made is mencioun.	
	And after that thei made a royal ende,	
	And bothe two to Iubiter thei wende,	*Jupiter*
3325	To regne there among the sterris bright.	

	But now the lanter and the clere light	*lantern; bright*
	Is wastid oute of Frigius Darete,	*Darius*
	Whilom of Troye wryter and poete.	*Once*
	Guyde have I noon, forthe for to passe:	*to continue on to a new topic*
3330	For evene here in the silfe place	
	He ficched hath the boundis of his stile,	*set the limit of his writing*
	At the sege he present al the while;	
	And ay in oon with hem dide abide	*always; agreement*
	Dites the Greke on the tother side;	*Dictys; other*
3335	And bothe two as in her writyng	
	Ne varie nat but in litel thing	
	Touching mater, as in special,	
	That is notable or historial.	
	I do no fors of incidentes smale,	*pay no heed*
3340	Of whiche in soth it is but litel tale,	*truth; account*
	Save this Dites maketh mencioun	
	Of the noumbre slayen at the toun	
	Lastinge the sege, affermyng out of drede	*During; certainly*
	Eyghte hundrid thousand and sixe wer ther dede	
3345	On Grekis side, upright in the felde;	
	And as Dares also there behelde,	
	On Troye party in the werre kene	
	Six hundrid thousand seventi and sixtene	
	Were slayen there — in Guydo ye may se —	
3350	With hem that cam to helpe the cité	
	Fro many coost and many regioun	*country*

In diffence and reskus of the toun.

And ful ten yere, so as I can caste,   *estimate*

And sixe monthes the myghti sege laste

3355   Or it was gete — Dares writ hymsilve —   *Before victory was achieved*

And overmore complet dayes twelve

Or Grekis hadde ful pocessioun,   *Before*

By fals engyn of the Greke Synoun,   *cunning*

Like as toforn rehersid was but late.   *before; recently*

3360   I have no more Latyn to translate

After Dites, Dares, nor Guydo;

And me to adden any more therto

Than myn auctours specefie and seyn,   *relate*

The occupacioun sothly wer but veyn,   *labor*

3365   Lik a maner of presumpcioun.

And tyme complet of this translacioun   *time for finishing*

By just rekenyng and accountis clere

Was a thousand and foure hundrid yere,

And twenti ner — I knowe it out of drede —   *surely*

3370   After that Crist resseyved oure manhede

Of hir that was Emperesse and Quene

Of hevene and helle and maide clene —

The eyghte yere by computacioun

Suynge after the coronacioun   *Following*

3375   Of hym that is most gracious in werkyng,   *deeds*

Herry the Fyfthe, the noble worthi kyng

And protector of Brutis Albyoun,

And called is thorugh his highe renoun,

Thorugh his prowes and his chivalrie,

3380   Also fer as passeth clowde or skye,

Of Normaundie the myghti conquerour.

For thorugh his knyghthod and diligent labour,

Maugre alle tho that list hym to withseyn,   *Despite; wish; resist*

He hath conquered his herytage ageyn

3385   And by his myghti prudent governaunce

Recured eke his trewe title of Fraunce,   *Recovered also*

That whoso liste loken and unfolde

The pedegrew of cronycles olde   *pedigree (genealogical tables)*

And cerchen bokes ywrite longe aforn,   *search; written; before*

3390   He shal fynde that he is justly born

To regne in Fraunce by lyneal discent.

And onward now he is made regent   *from now on*

Of thilke lond durynge his fader lyf,   *that same*

Of his goodnes to voide werre and stryf,   *do away with*

3395 He to rejoisshe withoute more delay   *have possession of*

Septer and crowne after the kynges day,

As it is clerly in conclusioun

Enrolled up in the convencioun;   *treaty*

And thanne I hope the tyme fortunat

3400 Of the olde worlde called aureat   *golden*

Resorte shal, by influence of grace,   *Restored*

That cruel Mars shal no more manace

With his lokis furious and wood,

By false aspectus for to shede blood   *astral inflences*

3405 Atwene the folkes of this rewmys tweyne,   *realms*

Whiche every wyght oughte to compleyne.

But as I trust in myn oppinioun,

This worthi kyng of wisdam and resoun

And of knyghthod shal so doon his peyne   *endeavor*

3410 To maken oon that longe hath be tweyne.

I mene thus: that Yngelond and Fraunce

May be al oon withoute variaunce,   *disharmony*

Oute of hertis old rancour to enchase   *banish*

By influence of his myghti grace,

3415 That called is of clerkis douteles

The sovereyn lord and the prince of pes.

And I hope his grace shal now reyne

To sette reste atwene this rewmys tweyne;

For in his power sothly stondeth al,   *truly*

3420 And alliaunce of the blod royal,

That is knet up by bonde of mariage,

Of werre shal voide aweie the rage,   *drive*

To make pes with brighte bemys shyne.

And on that is called Kateryne   *one*

3425 And namyd is right good and faire also

Shal be mene atwixe bothe two,   *intermediary*

Of grace enprentid in hir wommanhede,   *strongly marked*

That to compleyne we shal have no nede.

And I hope hir gracious arryvaille

3430	Into this lond shal so moche availle	
	That joie, honour, and prosperité	
	Withoute trouble of al adversité	
	Repeire shal and al hertly plesaunce,	*Return*
	Plenté, welfare, and fulsom abundaunce,	*great*
3435	Pes and quiete, bothe nyghe and ferre,	*near and far*
	Withoute strife, debat, or any werre,	*conflict*
	Meschef, povert, nede, or indygence,	
	With ful ceessyng of deth and pestilence —	
	Sothly, al this I hope ye shal sen	*Truly*
3440	Come into lond with this noble quene,	
	That we shal seyn of hert and feyne nought:	
	Blessed be she that al this hath us brought!	
	And he that hath thorugh myght of his werkyng,	*deeds*
	Of his knyghthod concluded al this thing,	*brought about*
3445	And swiche mervailles in armis don and wrought,	
	And his purpos fully aboute brought	
	Of highe wisdam set in his inward sight,	*faculty of judgment*
	Rejoisshynge al that longeth to his right,	*Taking possession*
	And highest sit of worthinesse in glorie	
3450	With the scepter of conquest and victorie —	
	I praie to God only for his beste,	
	Whan he hath al set in pes and reste	
	And is ful put in clere pocessioun	
	Of al that longeth to his subjeccioun,	*belongs; power of authority*
3455	To sende hym home with as gret honour	
	As evere yit hadde any conquerour,	*yet*
	Longe after in joie and in quyete	
	For to regnen in his royal sete.	
	Thus shal I ay — ther is no more to seye —	
3460	Day and nyght for his expleit ypreye	*success pray*
	Of feythful herte and of hool entent,	
	That whylom gaf me in commaundement	*once gave*
	Nat yore ago, in his faderes tyme,	*long*
	The sege of Troye on my maner to ryme,	
3465	Moste for his sake, to speke in special.	
	Although that I be boistous and rual,	*untaught; unrefined*
	He gaf me charge this story to translate,	*gave*
	Rude of konnynge, called John Lydgate,	*learning*

	Monke of Burie be professioun,	
3470	Usynge an habite of perfeccioun,	*Wearing; holiness*
	Albe my lyf acorde nat therto.	*Although*
	I feyne nat; I wote wel it is so —	*know*
	It nedeth nat witnesse for to calle;	
	Record I take of my brethren alle,	*Call to witness*
3475	That wil nat faille at so gret a nede.	
	And al that shal this noble story rede	
	I beseche of support and of grace	
	Ther I offende in any maner place	*Where*
	Or whersoevere that thei fynde errour,	
3480	Of gentilnesse to shewe this favour:	
	Benygnely for to done her peyne	*Kindly; endeavor*
	To correcte rather than disdeyne.	
	For wel wot I moche thing is wrong,	*know*
	Falsly metrid, bothe of short and long;	
3485	And yif thei shuld han of al disdeyn,	*if*
	It is no drede, my labour wer in veyn.	*Undoubtedly; would be*
	Late ignoraunce and rudnesse me excuse:	*Let*
	For yif that ye platly al refuse,	*if; plainly; reject*
	For certeyn fautes whiche ye shal fynde,	
3490	I doute nat, my thank is set behynde;	*given up (see note)*
	For in metring though ther be ignoraunce,	
	Yet in the story ye may fynde plesaunce	
	Touching substaunce of that myn auctour wryt.	
	And thoughe so be that any word myssit,	*be unsuitable*
3495	Amendeth it with chere debonaire;	*mood kindly*
	For an errour to hyndren and appaire	*disparage; speak badly of*
	That is nat seide of purpos nor malys	
	It is no worshippe to hym that is wys;	*honor*
	And no wyght gladly so sone yeveth lak	*person; censure*
3500	(Specialy behynden at the bake)	
	As he in sothe that can no skyl at al.	*truly; knows no craft*
	He goth ful hool that never hadde fal,	*safely*
	And I nat fynde, of newe nor of olde,	
	For to deme ther is noon so bolde	
3505	As he that is blent with unkonnyng —	*blinded by ignorance*
	For blind Baiard cast pereil of nothing,	*perceived*
	Til he stumble myddes of the lake —	*in the middle; pool*

	And noon so redy for to undirtake	*criticize*
	Than he in soth nor bolder to seie wers	*truly*
3510	That kan no skyl on prose nor on vers;	*knows; craft*
	Of alle swiche that can nat be stille,	
	Litel forse wher thei seie good or ille.	*It matters little*
	For unto hem my boke is nat direct	
	But to swiche as haven in effect	*such*
3515	On symple folke ful compassioun,	
	That goodly can by correccioun	
	Amende a thing and hindre nevereadel,	*disparage not at all*
	Of custom ay redy to seie wel.	
	For he that was gronde of wel-seying	
3520	In al hys lyf hyndred no makyng,	*disparaged no poetic composition*
	My maister Chaucer, that founde ful many spot;	*very many blemishes*
	Hym liste nat pinche nor gruche at every blot,	*carp; complain*
	Nor meve hymsilf to parturbe his reste	
	(I have herde telle), but seide alweie the best,	*always*
3525	Suffring goodly of his gentilnes	
	Ful many thing enbracid with rudnes.	*compositions enclosed by*
	And yif I shal shortly hym discryve,	*if*
	Was never noon to this day alyve,	
	To rekne alle, bothe yonge and olde,	*take account of*
3530	That worthi was his ynkhorn for to holde.	
	And in this lond yif ther any be	*if*
	In borwe or toun, village or cité	
	That konnyng hath his tracis for to swe,	*skill; written practices to follow*
	Wher he go brood or be shet in mwe,	*Whether; is free; confined*
3535	To hym I make a direccioun	
	Of this boke to han inspeccioun,	
	Besechyng hem with her prudent loke	
	To race and skrape thorughoute al my boke,	*erase; scrape off (text)*
	Voide and adde wher hem semeth nede;	*Delete*
3540	And though so be that thei nat ne rede	
	In al this boke no rethorikes newe,	*elegant expressions*
	Yit I hope thei shal fynde trewe	*Nevertheless*
	The story pleyn, chefly in substaunce.	
	And whoso liste to se variaunce	*wishes; inconstancy*
3545	Or worldly thing wrought be daies olde,	
	In this boke he may ful wel beholde	

Chaunge of Fortune, in hir cours mutable,

Selde or nat feithful outher stable —   *Seldom*

Lordes, princes from her royalté

3550   Sodeinly brought in adversité,

And kynges eke plounget in povert,   *also overwhelmed by poverty*

And for drede darynge in desert;   *lurking in wild regions*

Unwar slaughter compassed of envie,   *Unforeseen; devised*

Mordre execut by conspirasie,

3555   Awaite liggyng, falshede, and tresoun,   *Lying in ambush*

And of kyngdammys sodeyn eversioun;   *kingdoms; overthrow*

Ravysshyng of wommen for delyt,   *Carrying off*

Rote of the werre and of mortal despit,   *Cause; hatred*

Fals mayntenaunce of avouterye,   *adultery*

3560   Many worthi causyng for to dye,

Synne ay concludynge, whoso taketh hede,   *Sin; resulting in*

Vengaunce unwar for his final mede: *unforeseen; reward*

To declare, that in al worldly lust,   *desire*

Who loke aright, is but litel trust,

3565   As in this boke exaumple ye shal fynde,

Yif that ye list enprente it in your mynde —   *If; wish; imprint*

How al passeth and halt here no sojour,   *holds*

Wastyng away as doth a somer flour,

Riche and pore, of every maner age.

3570   For oure lyf here is but a pilgrymage,

Meynt with labour and with moche wo,   *mixed*

That yif men wolde taken hede therto   *if*

And toforn prudently adverte,   *before; consider*

Litel joie thei shuld han in her herte   *their*

3575   To sette her trust in any worldly thing;   *their*

For ther is nouther prince, lord, nor kyng,

Be exaumple of Troye, like as ye may se,

That in this lif may have ful sureté.

Therfore, to Hym that starf uppon the Rode,   *died; Cross*

3580   Suffringe deth for oure alder goode,   *good of us all*

Lyfte up youre hertis and thinke on Him among:

For be ye nevere so myghti nor so strong,

Withoute Hym al may nat availle;

For He can yif victorie in bataille   *give*

3585   And holde a felde, shortly to conclude,

With a fewe ageyn gret multitude.
And be grace He maketh princes stronge,
And worthi kynges for to regne longe,
And tirauntis sodeynly oppresse — *be put down*
3590 (Throwe hem doun for al her gret richesse); — *despite*
And in His hond power He reserveth — *retains*
Eche man t'aquite liche as he disserveth. — *repay*
To whom I preie with devocioun,
With al myn herte and hool affeccioun
3595 That He list graunt longe contenuaunce, — *wish*
Prosperité, and good perseveraunce,
Helthe, welfare, victorie, and honour
Unto that noble myghti conquerour,
Herry the Fyfthe, toforn yspecefied, — *before mentioned*
3600 So that his name may be magnified — *glorified*
Here in this lyf up to the sterres clere — *stars bright*
And after that above the nynthe spere,
Whan he is ded, for to han a place.
This praie I God for to send hym grace,
3605 At whos biddynge, as I tolde late, — *just now*
First I began the *Sege* to translate; — *Siege [of Troy]*
And now I have hooly in his honour
Executed the fyn of my labour. — *end*
Unto alle that shal this story se,
3610 With humble herte and al humylité
This litel boke lowly I betake, — *commit*
It to supporte, and thus an ende I make.

Envoy

	Most worthi prince, of knyghthod sours and welle,	*fountainhead*
	Whos highe renoun thorugh the world doth shine,	
	And alle other in manhood dost excelle,	
	Of merit egal to the worthi nyne,	*Nine Worthy*
5	And born also by discent of lyne	*lineal descent*
	As rightful eyr by title to atteyne,	
	To bere a crowne of worthi rewmys tweyne,	
	And also fer as Phebus in his spere	*sphere*
	From est to west shedeth his bemys bright	
10	And Lucyna, with a shrowdid chere,	
	Goth compas rounde with hir pale light,	
	Thou art rekned for the beste knyght,	*considered (see note)*
	To be registred worthi as of name	
	In the highest place of the hous of fame,	
15	To holde a palme of knyghthod in thin hond	*hand*
	For worthines and for highe victorie,	
	As thou that art drad on se and lond,	*revered*
	And evermore with laude, honour, and glorie,	*praise*
	For just conquest to be put in memorie,	
20	With a crowne made of laurer grene	*laurel*
	Upon thin hed, tofore that famus quene —	*before*
	Whilom ordeyned only for conquerours,	*Long ago*
	Stable of herte, with longe perseveraunce,	
	And gaf nat up til thei wer victours,	*gave*
25	Emprises take for no sodeyn chaunce,	*Undertakings*
	Whos name ay floureth with newe remembraunce	*prospers*
	And fadeth nat of yeris yore agoon,	*long past*
	Amonge whiche thou maist be set for oon.	*you may be reckoned*

For thorugh the world in every regioun
30 Reportid is with fame that fleth wyde · · · · · · · · · · · · · · · *travels swiftly*
That naturelly thi condicioun
On thing begonne is knyghtly to abide
And for the tyme manly sette aside
Reste and ese, what cost theron be spent, · · · · · · · · · · · · · · · *whatever*
35 Til thou have cheved the fyn of thin entent. · · · · · · · *realized; purpose*

Most circumspect and passinge avysee, · · · · · · · · · · · · · · · *well contained*
Al thi werkes conveied with prudence, · · · · · · · · · · · · · · · · · *governed*
Saad and demure, like to Josue · · · · · · · · · · · · · *Serious; sober; Joshua*
Ageyn whos swerd is no resistence, · · · · · · · · · · · · · · · · · · · *Against*
40 And hast also hevenly influence, · · · · · · · · · · · · · · · · · · · *you have*
With Salomon wysly to discerne,
Only be grace thi peple to governe;

Mercy eke meynt with thi magnificence, · · · *also mixed; greatness of nature*
On alle oppressed for to have pité,
45 And of rebelles be manly violence · *by*
Abate canst the grete cruelté; · *Put down*
And so with David thou hast kyngly pité
And highe prowes with Sesar Julius, · · · · · · · · · · · · · · · · · · · *Caesar*
In his tyme most victorius.

50 And manly holdest in thin hondes two,
Who can beholde by clere inspeccioun,
The swerd of knyghthod and the scepter also:
The ton to bring to subjeccioun · *one*
Hertes made proude by fals rebellioun,
55 And with the scepter to rewle at the beste
Thi pore liges, that wolde live at reste. · · · · · · · · · · · · · · · · · *vassals*

Now, thou that haste manhod, vertu, and grace, · · · · · · · · · · · *power*
Attemperaunce, fredam, and bounté,
Lowly I praie, with a dredful face, · · · · · · · · · · · · · *terrified expression*
60 Disdeyne nat benyngely to se · · · · · · · · · · · · · · · · · · · *kindly; look*
Upon this boke rudely made by me,
To fyn only to agreen thin highnesse, · · · · · · · · · *For the purpose; please*
And rewe of merci upon my sympilnesse, · · · · · · · · · · · · · · *have pity*

Envoy

	And eke in thi knyghtly advertence	*also; reflection*
65	Considre and se, my sovereyn lord most dere,	
	Of thi innat famous sapience	*wisdom*
	That Crist Jesus received with good chere	
	The twey mynutes yove of herte entere	*two mites given freely*
	By the wydowe, whiche of wille and thought	
70	Gaf al hir good and kepte hirsilf right nought.	*Gave; possessions*

	By whiche ensample, so that it nat offende	
	Thorugh myn unkonnynge to thin highe noblesse,	*ignorance*
	Late good wil my litel gift amende,	*make amends for*
	And of thi mercy and renomed goodnesse	*renowned*
75	Have no disdeyn of my bareyn rudnesse,	*bare [of art and interest]*
	And, in makyng though I have no Muse,	*poetic composition*
	Late trewe menyng the surplus al excuse.	*sincerity what remains*

	More than good hert hath no maner wyght	*person*
	To presente nouther to God nor man,	
80	And for my part to the, as it is right,	
	That gyf I hool as ferforthe as I can,	*give; completely to the extent*
	Ay to persevere fro tyme that I gan,	*began*
	With wil and thought for thin estate to preie,	
	Whiche to conserve thus finally I seie:	*preserve*

85	First of al, Almyghti God to queme	*please*
	With al that may be to His plesaunce,	
	And to thi crowne and thi diademe	
	Grace and good eure with long continuaunce,	*luck*
	Of thi liges feithful obeisaunce,	
90	And eche vertu that man may specefie,	
	I praye God graunte unto thi regalye!	*kingship*

	Go, litel bok, and put the in the grace	*yourself*
	Of hym that is most of excellence;	
	And be nat hardy to apperen in no place	*presumptuous*
95	Withoute support of his magnificence;	*glory*
	And whosoevere in the fynde offence,	*you*
	Be nat to bold for no presumpcioun:	

Thisilfe enarme ay in pacience   *arm always*
And the submitte to her correccioun.   *yourself*

100   And for thou art enlumined with no floures   *adorned*
      Of rethorik but with white and blak,
      Therfore thou most abide alle showres
      Of hem that list sette on the a lak;   *wish; find fault with you*
      And whan thou art most likly go to wrak,   *come to ruin*
105   Ageynes hem thin errour nat diffende   *them*
      But humblely withdrawe and go abak,
      Requerynge hem al that is mys to amende.   *Asking them; amiss*

Notes

Prologue

8–10   The allusions here are to the humors, of which there are four: phlegm, sanguine (blood), choler, and melancholy. Each humor is marked by specific conditions of temperature and moisture, which contribute to its influence on human behavior. Phlegm is cold and moist and seated in the liver; it has a clammy, inhibiting effect upon behavior that leads to equanimity or sluggishness and dullness. Sanguine is hot and moist and is seated in the heart; its character is usually cheerful, passionate, or aggressive. Choler is hot and dry, and is gathered in the gall; it helps natural heat and the senses, but also leads to anger. Melancholy is cold and dry; situated in the spleen, it makes one reflective and morose, but is a curb to the two hot humors. Although Mars is choleric — hot and dry and filled with anger and rage — his melancholic humor restrains him somewhat.

11   *fyré*. Bergen emends to *fyry*; see 2.3748 and 4.3155.

19–20   The planets are more at home in some houses (mansions) of the zodiac than others. Lydgate indicates that Mars is most influential when residing in the tenth mansion, Capricorn, but he is weak and troublesome when in Taurus, the second mansion. It was on his visit to Taurus that he made love to Venus and was weakened and exposed by Vulcan to ridicule amongst the gods. See note to line 23.

22   *Vulcanus*. MS: *Wlcanus*.

23   *meschef*. The mischievous bedding of Mars and Venus is told in Ovid's *Ars Amatoria* 2.561–92 and became a favorite literary topic throughout the Middle Ages. See Chaucer's elaborate dramatization of the "visit" in his "Complaint of Mars" and "The Complaint of Venus." Gower tells the story in his discussion of the jealousy of lovers, *Confessio Amantis*, 5.635–725. Both draw upon Jean de Meun's *Roman de la Rose*, lines 13847–14186.

38   Othea is a goddess of wisdom and instructor to Hector; see Christine de Pisan's *Epistle of Othea*.

40, 46   *Clio* and *Calliope*. Lydgate invokes the same Muses that Chaucer did in his telling of Book 2 (Clio) and Book 3 (Calliope) of *Troilus and Criseyde*, as if to gain the support of history (Clio) and eloquence (Calliope) in the unfolding of his great Troy story.

41   *Pernaso*. MS: *Pernasa*. A mountain near Delphi, sacred to Apollo and the Muses. Pegasus broke open the spring of the muses, whose waters sustain the arts. See note to line 44.

42   *Elicon*. Mount Helicon, a favorite haunt of the Muses which rivalled Parnassus for that honor. Lydgate follows Chaucer in making Helicon a well on Parnassus.

43   *stremys*. MS: *stemys*.

44   *Caballyn*. Lydgate's source is the Prologue to Persius's *Satires*: "Nec fonte labra prolui caballino / nec in bicipiti somniasse Parnaso / memini, ut repente sic poeta prodirem" (lines 1–3). Chaucer uses the same source for his various references to Parnassus (Franklin's Tale, V.720; *Troilus and Criseyde* 3.1810; *The House of Fame*, line 521; *Anelida and Arcite*, line 16). Persius is alluding to the Hippocrene — the well, as Lydgate says in the next line, "[t]hat sprang by touche of the Pegasee." Persius is ironic in treating the tradition of poetic inspiration associated with Helicon and Parnassus. His phrase "labra prolui" is a consciously exaggerated way of saying "drink." "Caballino" is a term taken from popular speech and applied sarcastically to Pegasus (hence "the nag's well"). Lydgate evidently missed the intended irony and took *fons caballinus* as a conventional epithet.

51   *Parchas and Furies*. The Parcae are the Roman goddesses of Fate — Clotho, Lachesis, and Atropos — derived from the Greek Moirai. The Furies (Erines) — Tisiphone, Allecto, and Megaera — are chthonian powers who inflict retribution for wrongs and blood-guilt, especially in the family.

52   *Cerberus*. The watchdog of Hades, born of Typhon and Echidna, along with the Hydra and Chimaera. Hesiod gives him fifty heads, but most medieval versions designate three heads. Orpheus charmed him with his music, thereby succeeding in passing by him without harm.

53   In a number of instances I have followed Bergen, who adds a final -*e* to regularize the meter of Lydgate's verse. For example, here the MS reads: *best*, which I print as *beste*. See also the following instances: **Prologue**: *trouthe* (116), *myghte* (130), *dirke* (143), *nere* (159), *grete* (174), *Withoute* (178), *pleyne* (194), *Withoute* (204), *grete* (240), *trouthe* (259), *trouthe* (288), *veyne* (290); **Book 1**: *grete* (66), *rekeles* (82), *herte* (151), *moste* (157), *londe* (726), *syghte* (785), *scharpe* (798), *Troye* (811), *hadde* (931), Withoute (990), *alle* (1058), *myghte* (1059), *helpe* (1077), *grete* (1103), *truste* (1106), *grete* (1111), *mente* (1121), *schippe* (1149), *graunte* (1157), *myghte* (1189), *oughte* (1844), *yeve* (1847), *grete* (1935), *myghte* (2002), *caste* (2006), *herte* (2011), *herte* (2027), *faire* (2093), *herte* (2107), *shulde* (2122), *hole* (2134), *goode* (2885), *beste* (2971), *oughte* (3230), *hoole* (3244), *nekke* (3279), *raughte* (3306), *moste* (3352), *brighte* (3391), *scharpe* (3401), *doute* (4054), *herde* (4063), *horse* (4086), *felte* (4090), *Nadde* (4106), *rede* (4157), *horse* (4160), *scharpe* (4162), *herte* (4167), *scharpe* (4183), *horse* (4197), *grete* (4256), *myghte* (4290), *scharpe* (4300), *scharpe* (4306), *newe* (4379), *broughte* (4382), *goode* (4401), *firste* (4426); **Book 2**: *wante* (144), *weye* (192), *heyghte* (519), *longe* (685), *highte* (736), *alofte* (907), *schulde* (933), *stronge* (949), *myghte* (959), *righte* (1818), *herte* (1826), *newe* (1838), *herte* (2327), *trouthe* (2367), *hire* (2400), *game* (2412), *brighte* (2418), *myghte* (2430), *brighte* (2459), *righte* (2509), *grete* (2591), *moste*, (2597), *faste* (2659), *herke* (2711), *righte* (2791), *herte* (2798), *feste* (3440), *feste* (3462), *joye* (3479), *stronge* (3502), *newe* (3531), *herte* (3546), *herte* (3566), *hoote* (3583), *oughte* (3626), *weye* (3633), *hadde* (3639), *hadde* (3642), *brighte* (3664), *herte* (3721), *righte* (3749), *moste* (4702), *myghte* (4739), *hymsilfe* (4752), *myghte* (4757), *moste* (4876), *myghte* (4877), *myghte* (6579), *faste* (6586), *consumpte* (6621), *hadde* (6649), *grete* (6658), *hadde* (6660), *juste* (6694), *stonde* (6707), *alle* (6716); **Book 3**: *dirke* (4), *durste* (7), *myghte* (556), *herte* (571), *silfe* (593), *scharpe* (764), *myghte* (775), *myghte* (790), *laste* (792), *horse* (808), *truste* (827) *scharpe* (831), *grete* (841), *myghte* (877), *herte* (881), *lefte* (986), *highte* (996), *horse* (1022), *worthinesse* (1045), *herte* (1053), *wolde* (1061), *firste* (1062), *myghte* (1064), *stronge* (1075), *scharpe* (1091), *truste* (1896), *herte* (1921), *durste* (1943), *nadde* (1967), *yonge* (2043), *wylde* (2136), *faste* (2294), *brighte* (2667), *dirke* (2676), *brighte* (2681), *stronge* (2697), *gayne* (2736), *sente* (3109), *righte*

(3118), *myghte* (3134), *myghte* (3197), *myghte* (3204), *fulle* (3207), *Thilke* (3235), *herte* (3737), *goode* (3741), *myghte* (3839), *fulle* (3877), *herte* (3919), *holde* (3966), *happe* (4032), *myghte* (4066), *hidde* (4101), *gonne* (4111), *helpe* (4145), *shulde* (4183), *myghte* (4211), *hoole* (4234), *gilte* (4237), *laughe* (4292), *secte* (4356), *fulle* (4406), *myghte* (4902), *thoughte* (4918), *nexte* (4918), *felle* (4925), *herte* (4967), *routhe* (4989), *assente* (4997), *herte* (5045), *myghte* (5089), *myghte* (5112), *myghte* (5158), *myghte* (5222), *sharpe* (5266), *caste* (5283), *myghte* (5284), *myghte* (5304), *grete* (5312), *thoughte* (5313), *thoughte* (5316), *beste* (5317), *myghte* (5318), *roughte* (5319), *myghte* (5320), *awayte* (5386), *wente* (5416), *brighte* (5486), *salte* (5531), *myghte* (5590), *myghte* (5672), *brenne* (5722); **Book 4**: *fulle* (191), *alle* (267), *thinge* (301), *righte* (323), *routhe* (579), *myghte* (600), *wente* (629), herte (648), *thoughte* (651), *knowe* (654), *hadde* (700), *muste* (710), *roughte* (720), *herte* (812), *myghte* (829), *grete* (844), *herte* (853), *Eleyne* (888), *thridde* (890), *righte* (906), *trowe* (983), *stonde* (993), *shulde* (1024), *Eleyne* (1050), *moste* (1086), *brighte* (1089), *myghte* (1181), *fledde* (2036), *hadde* (2063), *faste* (2068), *faste* (2076), *myghte* (2082), *grete* (2111), *myghte* (2112), *myghte* (2124), *soughte* (2164), *fulle* (2690), *brighte* (2712), *helpe* (2719), *stronge* (2748), *hoole* (3139), *shulde* (3164), *sharpe* (3192), *grete* (3229), *hoole* (3820), *durste* (3840), *wolde* (3854), *myghte* (3936), *salte* (3939), *myghte* (3958), *stinte* (3971), *myghte* (3972), *maille* (4304), *sharpe* (4332), *myghte* (4413), *grete* (4417), *myghte* (5107), *alle* (5159), *faire* (5225), *hadde* (5587), *grete* (5631), *nexte* (5702), *myghte* (5709), *false* (5739), *wolde* (5741), *treste* (5763), *holde* (5783), *stonde* (5784), *graunte* (6067), *grete* (6199), *thoughte* (6307), *lefte* (6354), *myghte* (6402), *shadde* (6408), *durste* (6430), *wiste* (6434), *yonge* (6474), *herte* (6502), *wolde* (6544), *fynde* (6875), *myghte* (6881), *myghte* (6914), *grete* (6917), *hadde* (6922), *oughte* (7048), *grete* (7070), *myghte* (7082); **Book 5**: *queynte* (1811), *alle* (1848), *longe* (1851), *ilke* (1854), *grete* (1909), *platte* (1923), *gonne* (1954), *hadde* (1965), *Caste* (1968), *tolde* (1978), *myghte* (1996), *herte* (2066), *myghte* (2080), *beste* (2109), *Thilke* (2112), *herte* (2116), *hevynesse* (2117), *shulde* (2120), *alle* (2140), *herte* (2168), *wolde* (2168), *herte* (2184), *herte* (2192), *yonge* (2209), *trouthe* (2216), *hemsilfe* (2267), *trowe* (2286), *thilke* (2938), *myghte* (2971), *platte* (2984), *silfe* (2996), *moste* (2998), *geyne* (3009), *myghte* (3034), *shulde* (3048), *myghte* (3105), *silfe* (3128), *righte* (3141), *hente* (3154), *longe* (3241), *grete* (3256), *wexe* (3305), *silfe* (3330), *helpe* (3350), *oughte* (3406), *brighte* (3423), *hadde* (3502), *Awaite* (3555); **Envoy**: *beste* (12).

54–68   In his invocation, Lydgate describes his task as "making" (fashioning verse in a technical sense) rather than original poetic composition and as

342

rhetorical amplification (see below Pro.324–52). He subsequently (Pro.245–323) seeks to distinguish the truth of chronicle histories from the deceitful, invented fables of the poets, along the lines sketched out by Benoît (lines 45–70 and 110–16) and Guido (4.204 and 276).

63–75　　An extended modesty trope of the poet apologetically standing to correction. See also Pro.379–84.

74　　*My lordes bydding.* That is, at the pleasure of Henry V, Lydgate's patron. See Introduction, pp. 7–9.

81　　*fyn.* MS: *fynde.*

84　　*vertuous besynesse.* See Chaucer's Second Nun's Prologue: "leveful bisynesse" (VIII.5) and "feithful bisynesse" (VIII.24).

89　　*Vygecius.* Flavius Vegetius Renatus, whose military manual *Epitoma rei militaris* (written between 383 and 450) remained an authority into the eighteenth century on Roman military practices.

95　　*eldest sone.* Henry, Prince of Wales, later Henry V; Shakespeare's Prince Hal.

104　　*Brutus Albyoun.* The phrase echoes "The Complaint of Chaucer To His Purse," a supplication to King Henry IV, where the poet addresses the king as "conquerour of Brutes Albyon" (line 22). In Geoffrey of Monmouth's *History of the Kings of England*, Brutus, a descendant of Aeneas, conquers Albion to establish his rule on the island, hence the name Britain.

109　　*Guido.* Guido delle Colonne, whose *Historia destructionis Troiae* is Lydgate's source.

115　　*in Latyn and in Frensche.* Bergen questions whether Lydgate knew any French version of Guido first hand (4:211).

124　　*Fourtene complete.* Lydgate began the poem in 1412, during the reign of Henry IV, and completed it in 1420.

126   Lydgate's astronomical reference recalls the calculations mentioned in the *Canterbury Tales* in the introduction to The Man of Law's Tale (II.1–14), The Nun's Priest's Tale (VII.3187–97), and The Parson's Prologue (X.1–9).

133   *cold*. MS: *coldyng*.

141   *upryst*. MS: *upright*.

146   *Sagittarie*. The mansion of Sagittarius, the ninth house in the astrological scheme of time. Lydgate names it as if it were an inn where Apollo might spend the night.

149   *auctours*. MS: *auntours*.

150   *Of the dede the verreie trewe corn*. MS: *Of the dede of the verreie trewe corn*. In medieval scriptural and literary exegesis, wheat and chaff commonly distinguish verbal ornament from the interior meaning of a text; see Chaucer's The Nun's Priest's Tale: "Taketh the fruyt, and lat the chaf be stille" (VII.3443).

168–70   Torti, p. 174, observes that these lines echo *Troilus and Criseyde* 1.365–69, where Troilus recalls seeing Criseyde in the temple.

172   *slayen*. MS: *slayn*. In a number of instances I have supplied a medial vowel or ending inflection where the meter and syntax require it. See also *dirked* for *dirk* (175); **Book 1**: *Ageynes* for *Ageyn* (182), *sythen* for *syth* (241), *growen* for *growe* (783), *Ageynes* for *Ageyns* (862), *hastily* for *hastly* (959), *bryngen* for *bryng* (1097), *dawenyng* for *dawnyng* (1155), *femynynyté* for *femynyte* (1860), *Kyndely* for *Kyndly* (1877), *restreynen* for *restreyn* (1879), *freelté* for *frelte* (1923), *schewen* for *schew* (2023), *trewely* for *trewly* (2063), *Ageynes* for *Ageyns* (2099), *hooly* for *hool* (2862), *douteles* for *doutles* (2930), *trewely* for *trewly* (2946), *hennes* for *hens* (2976), *slayen* for *slayn* (4113), *Ageynes* for *Ageyns* (4150), *douteles* for *doutles* (4203), *pereles* for *perles* (4282), *amonges* for *among* (4413), *rudenesse* for *rudnesse* (4331); **Book 2**: *douteles* for *doutles* (554), *dayes* for *day* (572), *citezeyns* for *citzeyns* (782), *pleies* for *pleis* (792), *conquerouris* for *conquerous* (857), *chaunteplure* for *chauntplure* (914), *lasten* for *last* (989), *nounsureté* for *nounsurte* (1892), *douteles* for *doutles* (2298), *loveres* for *lovers* (2519), *Amonges* for *Among* (3481), *seyen* for *seyn* (3564), *Ageynes* for *Ageyns* (3578), *wisten* for *wist* (3720), *douteles* for *doutles* (4709),

pereles for *perles* (4710), *joyneden* for *joynden* (4748), *gruccheth* for *grucche* (6529), *seyth* for *sey* (6529), *whiles* for *whils* (6606), *hennes* for *hens* (6629); **Book 3**: *trewely* for *trewly* (2078), *kyndely* for *kyndly* (2087), *Ageynes* for *Ageyns* (2668), *genterye* for *gentrye* (3214), *rekeles* for *rekles* (3873), *hennes* for *hens* (3923), *Ageynes* for *Ageyns* (3953), *ageynes* for *ageyns* (4157), *Ageynes* for *Ageyns* (5018), *sureté* for *surté* (5088), *broughten* for *brought* (5234), *rekeles* for *rekles* (5383), *pereles* for *perles* (5384), *namely* for *namly* (5478), *slayen* for *slayn* (5523); **Book 4**: *namely* for *namly* (289), *Ageynes* for *Ageyns* (691), *Ageynes* for *Ageyns* (857), *Ageynes* for *Ageyns* (863), *putten* for *putte* (925), *Ageynes* for *Ageyns* (980), *casten* for *cast* (1029), *Douteles* for *Doutles* (1098), *hennes* for *hens* (1133), *rekeles* for *rekles* (1139), *Ageynes* for *Ageyns* (1145), *Ageynes* for *Ageyns* (1158), *rekeles* for *rekles* (1174), *trewes* for *trews* (2029), *dawenynge* for *dawynge* (2049), *helpeles* for *helples* (2736), *endelonge* for *enlonge* (2778), *slayen* for *slayn* (3109), *disaray* for *disray* (3913), *stonden* for *stonde* (3943), *slayen* for *slayn* (4392), *slayen* for *slayn* (4411), *slayen* for *slayn* (4431), *douteles* for *doutles* (5174), *Ageynes* for *Ageyns* (5236), *ageynes* for *ageyns* (5250), *sithen* for *sith* (5565), *Ageynes* for *Ageyn* (5577), *haddest* for *hast* (5665), *behyght* for *hyght* (5747), *offeringe* for *offringe* (6050), *neghebour* for *neghbour* (6140), *yborn* for *born* (6143), *conspiracioun* for *conspiracoun* (6321), *myghtestow* for *myghtstow* (6449), *Ageynes* for *Ageyns* (6510), *gilteles* for *giltles* (6767), *Ageynes* for *Ageyns* (6781), *slayen* for *slayn* (6808), *Endelong* for *Endlong* (6857), *gilteles* for *giltles* (6890), *nayades* for *naydes* (6987), *hennes* for *hens* (7015); **Book 5**: *ymade* for *made* (1812), *letuaryes* for *letuarye* (1994), *soules* for *soule* (2038), *yblent* for *blent* (2082), *hevynesse* for *hevynes* (2117), *slayen* for *slayn* (3342), *slayen* for *slayn* (3349), *douteles* for *doutles* (3415), *avouterye* for *avoutrye* (3559); **Envoy**: *benyngely* for *benyngly* (60), *Ageynes* for *Ageyns* (105).

220 *trouth*. Bergen reads *trouthe*.

224 *the keye of remembraunce*. See Chaucer, *The Legend of Good Women* F 26.

227 *and*. MS: *of*.

229 *Crop and rote*. See *Troilus and Criseyde* 2.348 and 5.1245. Pearsall (1970, p. 99) remarks that Lydgate uses this phrase as well as "sours and welle" to indicate the full realization of a virtue, quality, or vice; see 3.4935 and Env.1.

230   *Stace*. Publius Papinius Statius (45–96 A.D.), author of the *Thebaid*, which tells the story of Oedipus and his sons. Chaucer's Criseyde reads such a romance of Thebes to pass the time at the beginning of Book 2 of *Troilus and Criseyde*. After *Troy Book*, Lydgate wrote *The Siege of Thebes* under the fiction that he joins the Canterbury pilgrims on their return journey and is asked to tell the first tale.

246   *cronycleris*. Bergen emends to *cronyculeris*.

263   *veyn*. Bergen emends to *veyne*.

286   *is*. Accepting Bergen's addition.

290   *Reyseth*. MS: *Rysed*.

293   *fame blowe*. Lydgate's phrase recalls Chaucer's description of the rock of ice on which the palace of Fame stands (*The House of Fame*, line 1139) and the satirical and skeptical treatment of fame and renown later in *The House of Fame*, lines 1567–1867.

298   *many worthi knyght*. Bergen emends the phrase to *many a worthi knyght*.

303   *it*. MS: *he*. I follow Bergen's emendation so that the obscure speech rather than Ovid ensnares the readers who see it. *entriketh*. Lydgate describes Ovid's writing in the same way as the fountain of Narcissus in the *Roman de la Rose*; see *Romaunt of the Rose*, line 1642.

309   Here and in Chaucer's *The House of Fame* (line 1468) and *Troilus and Criseyde* (1.394), Lollius is presented as an authority on the Trojan War. Modern scholars believe that medieval poets knew Lollius as an author because of an error in the manuscript tradition and subsequent references to Horace, *Epistulae* 1.2.1–2, which make it seem as if Lollius were the greatest of the authors on the Trojan War instead of Maximus Lollius, whom Horace addresses in his poem.

316   Lydgate makes the same claim for the essential agreement of the chronicles that is commonly adduced for the unity of the Bible.

319   *Cornelius*. Cornelius Nepos (c. 99–c. 24 B.C.) was one of the first writers of biography. His *De viris illustribus* deals with famous people, both Roman and foreign.

320   *Salustius*. Gaius Sallustius (c. 85–35 B.C.). Sallust was a Roman Tribune forced out of office by Caesar, who in retirement became an historian and dealer in moral commonplace. Lydgate alludes, perhaps, to his *Historiae* or possibly to his *Bellum Catilinae* or his *Bellum Iugurthinum*.

324–52 Lydgate here gives a list of topics that can be used for rhetorical amplification.

324   *al*. Accepting Bergen's addition.

333   *Or*. MS: *Of*.

344   *lengest dide*. MS: *dide lengest*.

348   *strif*. MS: *stif*.

366   *hathe*. Bergen reads *hath*.

373   *excellest*. MS: *excellent*.

377   *whom*. Lydgate uses this syntactic device again at 2.1038, 3.3829, and 5.1916.

Book 1

3   *Pelleus*. Lydgate conflates Pelias, the devious uncle of Jason, with Peleus, King of Phthia, who married the sea nymph Thetis, upon whom he fathered Achilles. Griffin (p. 289) notes that Guido and Benoît conflate Dares's Pelias with Dares's Peleus, who participated in the destruction of Lamedon's Troy.

8   *the*. Accepting Bergen's addition.

9   *Myrmidones*. Bergen reads *Myrundones*; see 1.67 and 3.579.

10   *Ovyde.* Publius Ovidius Naso (43 B.C.–A.D. 17). Author of more works popular with medieval literati than any other classical writer. His *Amores, Heroides, Ars Amatoria, Remedia Amoris, Metamorphoses,* and *Fasti* were frequently drawn upon and alluded to by English writers.

31   *roomyng.* Bergen reads *rooming.*

38   *Where.* Bergen reads *Wher.*

49   *Confortles.* Bergen reads *Comfortles.*

56   *for to schyne.* MS: *so for to schyne.*

68–69   *lyfe . . . Of Seynt Mathewe.* The tradition that Matthew preached in the land of the Myrmidons originates in the apocryphal *Acts of Andrew and Matthias* (second–third century A.D.). According to the story, Matthew is assigned to preach in the city of Myrmidonia, whose inhabitants are cannibals. He is imprisoned, but a miracle brings the other apostles to rescue him. The story was popularized by Gregory of Tours's *Liber de miraculis Beati Andreae Apostoli* (c. 593). Several Old English translations exist. In his *De situ terrae sanctae,* Theodosius (sixth century) writes that Sinope, which was then called "Myrmidona," is the place where Andrew freed Matthew from prison.

74   *suppose.* MS: *schal suppose.*

92   *Whiche.* MS: *Wiche.*

96   Line misplaced in MS.

98   *be.* Bergen normalizes to *by.*

104   *wrought.* MS: *wrout.*

105–06   *lere/here.* MS reverses the rhyme.

126   *resygnacioun.* MS: *resygnacoun.* Bergen reads *resygnacion.*

131   *Medee.* Medea, daughter of Aeëtes, king of Colchis (Oetes in Benoît, Guido, and Gower; Cethes in Lydgate). Lydgate removes her healing of Eson from

the story that he subsequently tells in order to introduce Jason. In Gower, after Medea has saved Jason she retores old Eson to youth at the expense of her own beauty, whereafter the scoundrel Jason abandons her for Creusa.

133   *pociouns.* MS: *porciouns.*

134   *wyrchyng.* Bergen emends to *wyrchynges.*

135   *quentyse.* Bergen emends to *queintyse.*

136   *hir enchauntementys.* Bergen emends to *enchauntementys.*

137   *as is.* MS: *as it is.*

139   *she it.* MS: *it is.*

144   Sentence must be read with Eson or "he" understood as the grammatical subject of *was.*

160–61   Lydgate employs the humility topos that Chaucer exploits throughout his work.

161   *discreye.* Bergen emends to *discryve.*

164   *his.* MS: *the.*

197   *for.* MS: *for for.*

214   *sought.* Bergen emends to *thoughte.*

224   *can.* Bergen emends to *ther can.*

225   *secré.* MS: *secrete.*

229   *unto.* Accepting Bergen's addition.

234   *he wer.* Bergen emends to *he ne wer.*

237   *as.* Bergen emends to *so as.*

724 *hir.* Bergen reads *her.*

729 *Symeonte.* Dares, Benoît, and Guido make the river Simois, a tributary of Scamander (chief river of the Trojan plain), into the harbor of Troy.

731 Lydgate continues in this passage with a series of subordinate clauses, but the main clause logically begins here; if the conjunction *And* is silently dropped, the rest of the passage follows clearly.

737 *or.* Bergen emends to *nor.*

741 *on.* Bergen emends to *upon.*

763 *deth.* Bergen emends to *myschief.*

768 *wer.* Bergen reads *were.*

769 *many man and many worthi.* Bergen emends to *many a man and many a worthi.*

791 *Is.* Accepting Bergen's addition.

793 *it is.* Bergen emends to *it was.*

801–04 Lydgate's explanation of the causes (and later the consequences) of Troy's fall draws on Boethius's idea of Fortune. Benson contends that Lydgate has three distinct but often confused views of Fortune — a sense of determinism and pessimism derived from Guido, a rejection of transitory, secular things derived from Boethius, and a belief that Fortune is a means for divine punishment for evildoers and material rewards for the good (1980, pp. 120–24); see Lois Ebin (1985), pp. 43–44. Lydgate refers directly to Boethius's view of Fortune at 4.3008–12.

802 *passyng.* Bergen emends to *passyngly.*

811–75 Lydgate uses the medieval commonplace of *translatio imperii*, the idea that Troy is the authorizing origin of later cities and nations.

Notes – Book 1

855   Lydgate, following Guido (Book 2), has Aeneas founding Naples in Sicily.

860   *cast*. Bergen emends to *caste*.

868   *went*. Bergen emends to *wente*.

870   *ther*. Accepting Bergen's addition.

871   *him*. MS: *hem*.

875   *Ysidre*. Isidore of Seville (c. 560–636). His *Etymologiae* was an enormously popular encyclopedia (preserved in over a thousand manuscripts) on diverse topics, particularly those pertaining to natural phenomena, word origins, and classical lore. It is regularly cited as the authority behind ideas in medieval lapidaries, bestiaries, and discussions of all things natural.

891   *wher that he is grave*. Bergen emends to *wher as he is grave*.

922   *thei*. Bergen emends to *he*, but *ches* can take a plural subject and the sense of the passage is that Jason and Hercules are acting together (see earlier 1.723–40).

932   *for*. Accepting Bergen's addition.

944   *Swyche*. Bergen reads *Swiche*.

946   *wer seie*. Bergen reads *were seie*.

950–53   See the representation of rumor as sound in *The House of Fame*, lines 711–24, and as gossip in *The House of Fame*, lines 1914–76 and 2060–2111, where *rounen* is used as a verb for private conversation made public.

958   *Without*. Bergen emends to *Withoute*.

982   *this*. Bergen emends to *his*.

984   *for yow to schewe*. Bergen emends to *with yow for to schewe*.

1001   *perturbaunce*. Bergen reads *parturbaunce*.

1064   *payed*. Bergen emends to *apayed*.

1067   *sort*. Lydgate's usage of the term, derived from Latin *sors, sortis*, moves among the meanings of *chance, fate*, and *fortune*; see 2.1802, 3.2725, 3.5315, 4.5291, 5.1836, 5.1887, 5.2183, 5.3040, 5.3247.

1069   *honestly*. MS: *honestlyche*.

1076–77   The meaning of the sentence is "Everyone of us shall help to carry out what Lamedon has foolishly chosen to begin."

1079   *This to seyne*. Bergen emends to *This is to seyne*.

1080   *on hymsilfe schal*. Bergen emends to *schal on hym silfe*.

1088   *this*. Bergen emends to *his*.

1093   *unto hym was*. Bergen emends to *was unto hym*.

1109   *gret*. Bergen emends to *grete*.

1110   *the Kyng*. Bergen emends to *thi king*; see 1.1156, 1172 for similar readings.

1112   *And the*. Bergen emends to *And*.

1113   *unto*. MS: *to*.

1156   *the*. Bergen emends to *thi*.

1166   *to*. Bergen emends to *unto*.

1170   *that*. Accepting Bergen's addition.

1172   *the*. Bergen emends to *thi*.

1178   *be ye*. MS: *ye be*.

1183   *swyche*. Bergen reads *swiche*.

1187   *Is.* MS: *Iis. for to.* Bergen emends to *to.*

1823 ff.   The story of Jason and Medea was popular with the generation of English writers prior to Lydgate, who served as his mentors. See Chaucer's *The Legend of Good Women*, lines 1580–1679, based on Ovid's *Heroides* 6 and 12, Ovid's *Metamorphoses* 7, and Guido, who is Lydgate's source; and, especially, see Gower's retelling of the story in *Confessio Amantis* 5.3247–4222, which is based on Benoît, lines 703–3926, rather than Guido. Gower's version is more sympathetic to Medea and her plight than Lydgate's is. Gower's Medea is shy, reflective, and modest; she demonstrates constancy in women rather than inconstancy, as in Lydgate.

1826   *yeres.* Bergen reads *yeris.*

1834   *Considered.* Must be taken as parallel with *Comaunded* (1.1829).

1844   *man.* Bergen emends to *wise man.*

1845   *ever.* MS: *every.*

1847   *yeve.* MS: *yif.*

1850   *and.* MS: *and so.*

1870   *That.* Must be taken syntactically as "so that."

1876–80   These lines ironically evoke Chaucer's description of Jason in *The Legend of Good Women*, lines 1580–88.

1878   *performe.* Bergen reads *parforme.*

1882   *wolde God.* Syntax requires the subjunctive to take the noun clause beginning "That" (1887) as the complement; see 1.2038–40.

1883   *him.* MS: *hem.*

1887   *ensample.* MS: *ensaple.*

        wommen. MS: *wommei.*

1901   *mewe*. See Chaucer's description of Troilus after he falls in love with Criseyde: "he wolde werken pryvely, / First to hiden his desir in muwe" (*Troilus and Criseyde* 1.380–81); see 2.3600.

1915–18 Bergen indicates a full stop after "sool" (line 1917), but the complete sense of the sentence requires the main clause provided in line 1918.

1925   *his*. Accepting Bergen's addition. *doth*. Bergen reads *dothe*.

1935   *worth*. MS: *worthi*.

1964–84 The description of Medea's contemplating the figure that Jason creates in her mind recalls Criseyde's musing on Troilus in *Troilus and Criseyde* 2.656–67. In both poets, the object of the lover's desire is presented not as he is but as he is seen.

1968   *began*. Bergen emends to *gan*.

1974   *enprenteth*. MS: *enprenteh*.

1977   *sonnelyche*. Bergen emends to *sonnysshe*.

1982   *sufficiaunce*. Bergen emends to *suffisaunce*. See *The Book of the Duchess*, line 1037: "My suffisaunce, my lust, my lyf."

1994   *yolde body, herte, and al*. The phrase has a distinctly Chaucerian ring to it. See *The Book of the Duchess*, lines 116 and 768, where Alcyone and then the Black Knight yield themselves to love "With good wille, body, hert, and al."

2018   *no*. MS: *to*.

2019   *No*. MS: *Nor*.

2029   *schewen*. MS: *schewem*.

2033   *scheweth*. MS: *schewey*.

2042   *schyning*. MS: *schying*.

2049 *hevene.* See *Troilus and Criseyde* 3.1251: "Thus in this hevene he gan hym to delite" and Criseyde's earlier response to Troilus's entrance: "It was an heven upon hym for to see" (2.637).

2057 *not me.* Bergen emends to *me not.*

2074 *thei thinke.* MS: *the think.*

2078 *the.* Accepting Bergen's addition.

2079 *though.* MS: *thorugh.*

2081 *pretende.* MS: *pretente.*

2083 *And.* Taking *flaterie* as grammatically parallel with *florissyng.*

2084 *dowbilnes.* MS: *dowmbilnes.*

2085 *is.* MS: *it.*

2090 *blewe is lightly died into grene.* Blue is fidelity; green is inconstancy. See Chaucer's "Against Women Unconstant" with its refrain "In stede of blew, thus may ye were al grene," where the poet objects to women's "newfangelnesse" (line 1) and "unstedfastnesse" (line 3), objections which resonate in Lydgate's critique in lines 2091–92.

2105 *and parfyte.* MS: *and so parfyte.*

2112 *hem.* MS: *here.*

2117 *my.* MS: *the.*

2141 *halle.* MS: *the halle.*

2813 *the cok, comoun astrologer.* A direct echo of the scene of the *aubaude* in Chaucer's *Troilus and Criseyde* 3.1415 after the lovers' consummation.

2818 *weren.* MS: *ben.*

2820   *wayten*. Bergen emends to *to awayte*.

2830–32   The image is a set of three hounds on a leash turned into a pair by the old woman's leaving the lovers alone.

2834   *hath*. Accepting Bergen's addition.

2844   *rich*. MS: *rial*. See Benoît, lines 1622–23. In Book 4 of Boccaccio's *Filocolo*, Florio and Biancifiore are married before a statue standing for all the gods; some scholars believe that this served in turn as a source for the pledges exchanged in *Troilus and Criseyde* 3.1254–60.

2851   *take*. MS: *to take*.

2852   *lothe*. MS: *for lothe*.

2864   *his*. MS: *his his* (canceled to *his*).

2868–80   See Jason's perfidy and duplicity in both the Hypsipyle and Medea episodes in *The Legend of Good Women*, lines 1368–1679, where Hercules is fully involved in the conscious plot to deceive Hypsipyle.

2878   *nothing*. Bergen glosses MS *no thing* as "not," but the sense of the passage is that nothing contrived and false was revealed under Jason's false appearance.

2895   *schuldest*. MS: *schulde*.

2905   *comprehende*. Takes *bounté* as its complement.

2919   See *The Legend of Good Women*, lines 2559–61: "Be war, ye wemen, of youre subtyl fo, / Syn yit this day men may ensaumple se; / And trusteth, as in love, no man but me."

2923   *oute*. Bergen reads *out*.

2924   *hir*. Bergen reads *her*.

2936   *maner*. MS: *the maner*.

2949-50   Echoes portrait of Jason at start of Chaucer's story of Medea: "For to desyren thourgh his apetit / To don with gentil women his delyt, / This is his lust and his felicite" (*The Legend of Good Women*, lines 1586–88).

2951   *contrerie*. Bergen reads *contrarie*.

2953   See Hypsipyle's "usaunce / To fortheren every wight, and don plesaunce / Of verrey bounte and of curteysye" (*The Legend of Good Women*, lines 1476–78).

2957   *routhe*. MS: *roughte*.

2963   *ful*. Bergen emends to *fulle*.

2967-86   Jason's speech here uses the conventions of the *aubade* but turns them not to the poignancy of the lovers' parting so much as to the mechanics of his gaining the Fleece.

2968   *pryme*. Prime marks the first division of the day, from 6:00 a.m. to 9:00 a.m. It likewise designates a canonical hour of prayer. Here the sense seems to be "daybreak."

3020-21   The text reads: *a riche ring . . . al venym distroye*. Bergen's note (4:101) suggests that the stone is agate. That makes sense in that agate, according to the Peterborough Lapidary, which also cites "Isidore" as its source, indicates that agate can sometimes be green and that it "ben good aȝens venymm & aȝens biȝting of serpentes & he kepeth a man fro euell thinges" (*English Medieval Lapidaries*, ed. Joan Evans and Mary S. Serjeantson, EETS o.s. 190 [Oxford: Oxford University Press, 1933; rpt. 1960], pp. 64–65). The Sloane Lapidary, in the same volume, notes the agate's virtue "against stinging edders," but does not identify any kind of agate as being green. See note to 1:3344, below.

3217   Lydgate breaks the syntax of this sentence by inserting *He* as the subject of *schope*.

3218   *forget*. Bergen emends to *forged*; but see 2.2508, 4.6938 as well as 1.4255 (*avenget*) and 3.4179 (*flickerit*).

3222   *what*. MS: *wat*.

3229   *syghe*. MS: *to syghe*.

3230   *rekeles*. MS: *rekles*.

3231   *sche bad*. MS: *sche him bad*.

3243   *schuld*. MS: *schul*.

3246   *the*. MS: *thi*.

3248   *fulli*. MS: *ffulli*.

3253   *certeyn*. Bergen emends to *certis*.

3255–56   Bergen transposes these lines, following other MSS.

3264   *the*. Accepting Bergen's addition.

3289   *kepe*. MS: *ke* (corrected to *kepe*).

3305   *wastid*. MS: *waftid*. Bergen's emendation.

3317   Sense requires "they were" as grammatical subject.

3320   *inhast*. Bergen emends to *enhaste*.

3333   *flaume*. Bergen reads *flawme*.

3334   *masid*. MS: *amasid*.

3338   *ther*. MS: *the*.

3340   *techith*. MS: *teched*.

            Ysydorus. There is no reference to Isidore or *bufo* (Latin "toad") in Benoît, lines 1677–1702 and 1929–32; see Guido, Book 3.

3341   *And*. MS: *And in*.

3344   *surmounteth every grene.* It is conceivable that Medea's wonderful, protective stone is emerald, rather than the agate mentioned earlier (not in this selection). According to the Peterborough Lapidary, emerald "ouerpasseth al the grennesse of grenhede" (*English Medieval Lapidaries*, ed. Joan Evans and Mary S. Serjeantson, EETS o.s. 190 [Oxford: Oxford University Press, 1933; rpt. 1960], p. 85). Lydgate, on the authority of "Isidyre," cites India as the provenance of Medea's stone (line 1342); the Sloane Lapidary designates Syria for emerald (*English Medieval Lapidaries*, p. 121). All sources indicate that this greenest of green stones is protection against lechery, which could be a factor in Medea's giving the ring to Jason. MED gives "desire, sexual passion" as a meaning n(2) for *grene.* Lydgate, perhaps, is punning in lines 3343–44, suggesting 1) that the stone must be kept pure and clean and that it surpasses all others in its greenness; and 2) that it must be kept chastely and cleanly, and with its color can overcome illicit passion ("grene"). The newlywed Jason draws upon its power and Medea's pure affection to overcome the dragon. The stone defends him from the "venym," but in doing so is turned into "pecis smale" (line 3356) so that it cannot protect Jason from the poison of Cupid's dart which, in the end, overwhelms him with desire for Creusa and which, in turn, proves a "dedly sorwe" for Medea (line 3712).

3346   *anoye.* MS: *noye.*

3360   *of malis.* Modifies *tame* rather than *men.*

3364   *the ston.* Bergen emends to *this ston.*

3369   *riche.* Bergen reads *rich* and emends to *riche.*

3383   *resistence.* MS: *of resistence.*

3384   *withstonde.* MS: *witstonde.*

3389   *many stroke.* Bergen emends to *many a stroke.*

3413   *upon.* MS: *on.*

3418   *as faste as.* Bergen emends to *in al the hast.*

4034   *to*. MS: *for to*.

4044   *of*. Bergen emends to *on*; see 3.3216 and 3.3857.

4046   *ward*. A military unit of fighting men, here rendered as "division."

4058   *ye gete of me no more*. See Chaucer's The Squire's Tale: "ye gete namoore of me" (V.343).

4061   *he riseth*. MS: *it ariseth*.

4065   *noble*. Accepting Bergen's addition.

4084   *sturdy as a wal*. See 3.4938 and 4.3946. The reference to Nestor ironically echoes against Chaucer's description of Hector as "the townes wal and Grekes yerde" (*Troilus and Criseyde* 2.154) and Criseyde's subsequent feeling that Troilus "was to hire a wal / Of stiel, and sheld from every displesaunce" (*Troilus and Criseyde* 3.479–80).

4094   *many wounde*. Bergen emends to *many a wounde*.

4095   *Ther*. Bergen emends to *Wher*.

4105   *discomfetid*. Bergen emends to *discomfeted*.

4115   *That*. MS: *Than*.

4118   *in*. Accepting Bergen's addition.

4121   *manly*. MS: *manfully*.

4122   *non*. MS: *on*.

4143   *he felt in hert*. Bergen emends to *in hert he felte*.

4155   *enbollid*. Bergen reads *embollid*.

4162   *whet*. Accepting Bergen's addition.

4170   *Cedar*. The young knight who rescues Lamedon by attacking Nestor appears in both Guido (Book 4) and Benoît (2507 ff.), who agree on the major details of the episode.

4176   *He*. Added for grammatical sense.

4184   *smyte*. MS: *to smyte*.

4185   *dispitous*. Bergen reads *despitous*.

4220   *the*. MS: *of his*.

4226   *have*. Accepting Bergen's addition.

4234   *that*. Accepting Bergen's addition.

4253   *a*. Bergen emends to *in*.

4254   *in al hast*. Bergen emends to *in al the hast*.

4255   *avenget*. Bergen emends to *avenged*.

4259   *have with hem*. Bergen emends to *with hem have*.

4262   *finaly that day*. MS: *that day finaly*.

4268   *he*. MS: *thei*. In the MS reading, the Greeks make woe — that is, cause grief — but the context indicates that it is Lamedon who expresses his grief and mourning.

4269   *pitus hert*. Lydgate refers obliquely to Chaucer's phrase "pitee renneth soone in gentil herte" (*Canterbury Tales* I.1761, IV.1986, V.479). See below 4.2148.

4285   *assaille*. Bergen reads *assaile*.

4286   *his*. Bergen indicates an emendation but *his* is the MS reading.

4289   *cam in*. MS: *in cam*.

4292   *severed*. Bergen reads *svered*, emended to *severed*.

4301   *til*. Bergen emends to *to*.

4303   *hast*. Bergen reads *haste*.

4304   *alyghte*. MS: *he lyghte*.

4315   *wer*. MS: *that wer*.

4317   *no*. MS: *nat. can no rede* is parallel with *wer forskatered*, and both are
          governed grammatically by *That* (who).

4326   *to*. MS: *into*.

4335   *the*. Bergen emends to *her*.

4340   *Her*. Bergen emends to *Hir*.

4366   *a*. Accepting Bergen's addition.

4367   *birthe*. Accepting Bergen's addition.

4371   *had*. Bergen emends to *hadde*.

4374   *vengaunce*. MS: *vengauce*.

4376   *thorugh*. MS: *thoghugh*.

4377   *liche*. Bergen emends to *light*.

4380   *to*. Accepting Bergen's addition.

4381   *the*. Bergen emends to *this*.

4386   Bergen's punctuation suggests that the syntax breaks at this point, but it is
          clear that the parenthetical interjection in lines 4385–86 divides the sub-
          ordinate clause from the main clause, much as in the opening of Chaucer's
          General Prologue to the *Canterbury Tales*.

4388   *plesyng*. Bergen emends to *pleysyng*.

4398   *fro*. Accepting Bergen's addition.

4412   *sufficiaunce*. Bergen reads *sufficaunce*.

4420–36   Lines addressed to Henry as Lydgate's patron.

4427   *now with quakyng hond*. MS: *with quakyng hond now*.

Book 2

1   *Fortunas*. MS: *fortunat*. Torti, p. 184n, remarks that the description of Fortune's mutability forecasts the attitude toward women in Guido and Lydgate. Finlayson, p. 150, sees the passage indebted to the description of Fortune in Chaucer's *The Book of the Duchess*.

3   *wil*. Bergen reads *will*.

134   *thei*. MS: *ye*.

141   *that*. Bergen emends to *the*.

142   *Antropos*. Atropos. One of the three daughters of Night, later identified as the three Fates. Atropos is the Fate who cuts the thread of a person's life; compare 2.880, 2.2290, 2.4695.

168   Echoes Chaucer's "The Complaint of Venus": "Syth rym in Englissh hath such skarsete" (line 80). Boffey, p. 31, notes that the line reappears in Lydgate's *Fall of Princes* (9.3312).

173   Accepting Bergen's emendation of a plausible, if less likely, reading in MS: *To schewe his stile in my transmutacioun*. MED cites no instances of *transmutacioun* used in a sense appropriate to the passage. Lydgate uses the term in the normal sense at 1.58; compare 4.7062.

178   *cam*. Bergen emends to *com*.

180 Lydgate follows the convention, defined by Cicero and St. Jerome, of translating meaning by meaning rather than word for word.

192–97 See the supposed rejection of rhetorical figures by Chaucer's Franklin (V.716–27). Lydgate repeats the allusion below at 3.551–56 and Env.100–01.

198 *in*. Accepting Bergen's addition for meter.

200 *anon I wil*. Accepting MS reading over Bergen's *I wil anon*.

288 *Hector the secounde*. Lydgate echoes Pandarus (*Troilus and Criseyde* 2.158).

481 *callyd*. Norton-Smith emends to *ycallyd* based on Digby 232 and Digby 230 to avoid a Lydgate line.

493 *Or*. MS: *Of*.

511 As Bergen notes, the phrase "with countenaunces glade" applies to the images and not the workmen; see 2.610.

515 *Appollo*. The reference should be to the craftsman Appelles who is mentioned in Walter of Chatillon's *Alexandreis* 7.383–84 (Norton-Smith, p. 133); Bergen suggests that Lydgate borrowed the passage from the Wife of Bath's recollection of her fourth husband's tomb (III.495–500).

523 *joignour*. Trisyllabic.

528 *Of*. MS: *Or*.

533 *wer*. Bergen emends to *were*.

534 *aboute*. Bergen emends to *abouten*.

542 *that*. Accepting Bergen's addition.

545 *defoulit*. Bergen emends to *defouled*.

552   Lydgate echoes the asseveration of Chaucer's Franklin in the *Canterbury Tales*: "I ne kan no termes of astrologye" (V.1266).

559   *in*. MS: *on*; see 4.2739.

560   *For*. Bergen amends to *But*.

564   *this*. Bergen emends to *his*.

569   *aforn*. Bergen emends to *toforn*, but see 2.3585 and 2.3703 for similar usage.

599   *peerles*. Trisyllabic. Bergen emends to *peereles*.

602   *Tymbria*. The second gate of Troy according to Guido (Book 5), the fifth in Benoît (line 3152). It is mentioned again at 3.5611.

614   *tour*. MS: *tourn*.

616   *on*. MS: *up on*.

618   *serpentys*. Bergen reads *serpentis*.

628   *And*. MS: *A*.

629   *non*. Bergen emends to *noon*. The sense of the clause is that anyone contemplating an attack would be dissuaded by the iron grating that hangs down over the gates.

634   *barrerys*. MS: *barreys*.

639   *paleys*. MS: *hous*.

640   *thorughout*. MS: *thorugh*.

654   *babewynes*. MS: *bakewynes*.

655   *koynyng*. MS: *kaxenyng*. Norton-Smith emends to *copurnyng* from Digby 232 (*kopurnynge*) and Digby 230 (*copurnynges*), but the emendation is hypermetric.

656   *Vynettis*. Bergen reads *Vynnettis*.

668   *the*. Bergen emends to *this*.

672   *morwe*. MS: *the morwe*.

681–82   Here and elsewhere (e.g., 2.669) Lydgate uses the language applied earlier to the conduct of statecraft to suggest the resemblance between practical wisdom in political affairs and the rational construction of New Troy according to an informing plan. At the end of Book 2, Agamemnon's care in arranging his camp will furnish a small echo of Priam's design. Guido emphasizes the skill of the mechanical arts in Troy, while Lydgate stresses the intellectual power of design. Geoffrey of Vinsauf's *Poetria Nova*, in a passage that Chaucer parodies in *Troilus and Criseyde* (1.1065–69), compared the invention of a poem to the architect's plan for his building.

689   *reclinatories*. Bergen speculates that these may be couches with canopies over them. Norton-Smith glosses it as "a covered place provided with a half-seat" and treats it as Lydgate's coinage.

695   *cured was*. The grammatical construction is parallel with *raught* (line 698) and *paved* (line 701).

710   *hymsilfe*. MS: *hem silfe*.

720   *square grounde*. Bergen emends to *ygrounde*, but see 2.2561. MED defines *square* (adj. 2a) as "ground or whet at a cutting angle or to a point."

722   *Bowyers*. MS: *Bowers*.

    fast. Bergen emends to *faste*.

725   *also*. Bergen indicates MS reading is his emendation.

737   *that*. Bergen emends to *this*.

769   *enabite*. Bergen emends to *enhabite*.

777   *many*. Bergen emends to *any*.

784   *to*. Accepting Bergen's addition.

788–926   The account of Priam's steps to "magnyfye" his new city and increase its renown provides a good example of the poet's skill at *amplificatio*. Lydgate describes the civil activites of Priam's reinvention of a healthy society after the fall of Lamedon's Troy. He adds tournaments, jousts, and tilting to the "diuersa genera" of games that Guido mentions vaguely (Book 5), and he significantly expands the discussion of chess. His greatest addition is in the description of theatre. He not only defines genre but gives details of production, such as staging and sets (a "theatre schrowdid in a tent," line 900); masks ("viseris") used for disguise (lines 901–02); the signs and formulaic expressions used to convey joy, heaviness, trust, gladness, and mixtures of emotions, always "from point to point" (line 910), answering to the requirements of the play; the place of music and rhetoric in the plays; and the controlling themes (e.g. the fall-of-prince topos, or the Boethian themes of fate and fortune). Priam's "fantasye" provides a glimpse of the idealized social and ideological geography of fifteenth-century urban life. Meek (p. 286n) suggests that Guido misread Benoît's claim that Troy's inhabitants could find all these pleasures in the city (*trovassent*, line 3182).

790   *observaunce*. MS: *observaunces*.

802   *other*. MS: *ther*.

806–23   Persian, Indian, and Arabic texts refer to chess as early as the fifth century, but no unambiguous references appear before the seventh century. The game was popular by the tenth century, and entered the west by way of Spain in the tenth or eleventh century. European literary and documentary references date from around the year 1000. A short poem describing the game (*Versus de scachis*) survives in manuscripts from the 990s. In the eleventh and twelfth centuries the game was popular in both courtly and monastic milieux. Petrus Alfonsi's *Disciplina clericalis* (c. 1100) lists chess as one of the seven knightly accomplishments, and the game is frequently mentioned in chivalric romances. Lydgate champions Guido's claim that chess was first invented in Troy. He incorrectly ascribes a competing claim to Jacques de Vitry. Marquardt points out that Jacobus de Cessolis's *De ludo scaccorum* (c. 1280) is the source for claiming that Philometer is the inventor.

812   *juparties*. MS: *imparties*.

830   *be sodeyn variaunce*. Bergen emends to *with sodeyn variaunce*.

833   *plounged*. MS: *plaunged*.

835   Against Bergen, I punctuate with a full stop here because the line is the kind of summative statement that often ends Lydgate's longer sentences.

836–38   The passage needs to be taken in the sense that if one person succeeds in various games of chance, another person necessarily loses.

         A devaunte. Bergen suggests the possibility of separating *A* from *devaunt* (the name of a game of chance) and assigning it the value of the preposition *in*. *Hasord* and *passage* are, like *devaunt*, games played with dice.

837   *suffereth*. MS: *sufferey*.

842–59   The generic descriptions of comedy and tragedy are commonplaces. See, for example, Dante's Letter to Can Grande della Scala and the Prologue to Chaucer's The Monk's Tale (VII.1971–81).

861   Against Bergen, I punctuate with a full stop here because line 862 begins another independent clause.

864–69   In the medieval conception of classical drama, the poet recited his work while the action was mimed below him; see Isidore of Seville, *Etymologiae* 18.44 and 18.49.

867   *awncien*. MS: *awcien*.

875   *by old date*. Accepting Bergen's emendation for MS: *by date*.

876   See note to Prologue line 51.

878   *gan*. "The poet" is the understood subject of the sentence; see line 896. Lydgate speaks of a poet reciting but his image is of writing.

886   *highe*. Bergen emends to *in highe*. *distresse*. Bergen emends to *tristesse*.

887   *and*. Bergen emends to *or* for parallelism with the following two lines.

890   *that*. Accepting Bergen's addition.

902   *Disfigurid her facis*. The phrase is an absolute: the men's faces are disguised.

908   *or*. MS: *and*.

911   *now light*. Accepting Bergen's emendation for MS: *light*.

918   *hay*. MS: *bay*.

922   *the*. Bergen emends to *these*.

924   *ryht of tragedies olde*. The *of* is Bergen's addition.

927–1066   Lydgate's description of Priam's palace, like that of the city earlier (2.489–768), expands and changes the basic details in Guido (Book 5). These lines offer a *tour de force* in Utopian city planning, from the geometry of the layout, where the city itself becomes a kind of theater in the round (lines 941–57), down to the wood used for specific architectural functions; where equitable housing is provided for rich and poor, and where we are privileged to glimpse the decor of interiors of houses as well as religious practices. No poet in English before Lydgate has been so attentive to this kind of detail, as he depicts the aspirations and exuberance of early fifteenth-century expansion.

931   *werkes*. MS: *werkmen*.

940   *cast*. Sense requires the phrase to be understood as *was cast*, "was laid out by compasses." I have treated lines 939–40 as a subordinate clause modifying *Ilyoun*; Bergen punctuates them as an appositive beginning the next sentence.

943   *he most first*. Bergen emends to *first he moste*.

944–48   Lydgate follows the common practice of approximating *pi* by using its upper limit (3 1/7). The practice derived from the third proposition of Archimedes's *On the Measurement of the Circle*, which the Middle Ages knew in several translations. Plato of Tivoli produced an incomplete translation from the Arabic between 1134 and 1145. Gerard of Cremona completed a better translation, again from the Arabic, in the third quarter of the twelfth century. William of Moerbeke, Latin archbishop of Corinth, made a translation from the Greek in 1269. William's translation was incorporated into Johannes de Muris's *De arte mensurandi* around 1343.

949–50   *withinne the stronge wal . . . pleynly eke with al.* Bergen emends by transposing these phrases.

955   *reysed.* MS: *reysen.*

956   *unto.* Bergen emends to *to.*

961   *stond rounde.* MS: *stond rounde rounde.* Bergen emends to *stoode rounde.*

969   *fenestral.* Bergen emends to *eche fenestral.*

991   *his.* Bergen emends to *this.*

1006   *was set a dormont.* Bergen emends to *was a dormant.*

1012   *Right as any.* Bergen emends to *Right as.*

   opposyt. MS: *apposyt.*

1014   *riche.* Bergen reads *rich.*

1022   *With.* MS: *Withoute.*

1023   *of.* MS: *of of.*

1034   *and of.* Bergen emends to *of* but is willing to accept MS reading as equally good.

1037   *excellence.* MS: *excenlence.*

1050   *felicité.* MS: *ffelicite.*

1061   *his.* Bergen emends to *this.*

Notes – Book 2

1797–1902   Lydgate apostrophizes Priam as an imprudent ruler. He builds on Guido's suggestion (Book 6) that Boethian ideas about fortune and chance lead to Priam's renewing the war, but he relocates these ideas from the external world to the individual. His sentiment is akin to Gower's, who locates all disasters within the choices of individuals. See Ebin (1985), pp. 41–44.

1798   *new*. Bergen emends to *newe*.

1807   *savour*. MS: *more savour*.

1816   *to*. Accepting Bergen's addition.

1831   *chance*. Bergen reads *chaunce*.

1847   *Adverting*. MS: *Adverte*.

1851   *surly*. MS: *only*.

1853   *if*. MS: *it*.

1857   *rekles*. Bergen emends to *rekeles*.

1865   *royal*. MS: *rayal*.

1883   *this*. MS: *his*.

1892   *which in*. MS: *with*.

2184   *to*. Accepting Bergen's addition.

2197–2209   Hector argues for distributive rather than rectificatory justice. As Aristotle explains in Book 5 of the *Nicomachean Ethics*, distributive justice remedies discrepancies between persons of unequal worth by a geometrical progression, while rectificatory justice works among equals by an arithmetic progression. Thus an injury done a great person is greater in magnitude than one done a person of lesser social stature. Lydgate is expanding on a theme in Guido (Book 6).

2210   *gretly*. Accepting Bergen's addition.

2216   *instynt*. MS: *instymt*.

2246   *causeth*. MS: *caused*.

2264   *lak*. MS: *lat*.

2268   *many*. MS: *many other*.

2276   *at*. Bergen emends to *in*. The MS reading accords with Chaucer's usage in the *Canterbury Tales* (II.504, II.658, VII.1300) and *Troilus and Criseyde* (4.1106, 4.1532).

2292   *and sorow*. Bergen emends to *sorow*.

2297   *hold*. MS: *held*.

2298   *cowarddyse*. Bergen reads *cowardyse*.

2321   *Of*. MS: *To*.

2355   *unto*. Bergen emends to *to*.

2358   *Unto the whiche*. Bergen emends to *Unto whiche*.

2364   *yeve*. MS: *gif*.

            credence. MS: *credendence* (corrected to *credence*).

2365   *nat*. Bergen emends to *not*.

2373   *cherité*. MS: *cherte*.

2375   *upon*. MS: *on*.

2387   *Pirrous*. MS: *Pirous*.

2393   *Then out I roos*. MS: *Out I roos*. Bergen emends to *Up I roos out*.

2424   *severyd*. MS: *severy*.

2427	*thinne*. Bergen emends to *thorugh thinne*.
2434	*so fer*. MS: *fer*.
2435	*that I*. Accepting Bergen's addition to MS: *I*.
2440	*upon*. MS: *on*.
2448	*he*. Following the MS reading and taking the pronoun to refer to the horse that reaches a pleasant dell; Bergen emends to *I*, so that Paris is the grammatical subject.
2450	*yonge*. MS: *soft*.
2451	*alight*. MS: *light*.
2464	*aslepe*. Bergen emends to *asleped*.
2465	*wonder swevene*. Lydgate renders Guido's "mirabilem visionem" in a way that recalls the phrasing Chaucer gives to dreams in his dream visions; see "Me mette so ynly swete a sweven, / So wonderful" (*The Book of the Duchess*, lines 276–77).
2469	*first somdel*. Bergen emends to *somdel first*.
2482	*ravasched*. Bergen emends to *ravisched*.
2486–2516	*Fulgence*. The sixth-century mythographer Fabius Planciades Fulgentius, author of commentaries on the allegories supposedly contained in the pagan myths (*Mythologiae*) and in Vergil (*Vergiliana continentia*). Fulgentius is an important, though sometimes discredited, source for medieval and Renaissance writers, including Boccaccio (see *Genealogie deorum gentilium* 4.24 and 11.7). The mythological interpretations are largely Lydgate's addition. Fulgentius is sometimes confused with Saint Fulgentius, Bishop of Ruspe (d. 532 or 533). Lydgate's iconographical details for Mercury do not appear in the corresponding passages of Benoît and Guido. The details of the rod, the snakes, and the cock are in Fulgentius's *Mythologiae*; but Lydgate purges Fulgentius's association of Mercury with the mendacity of commerce, making him instead into an allegory of the more aristocratic virtues of good

governance and prudence. Vatican Mythographer 2 defines Mercury as "deus prudentie et rationis" (ch. 83) and "deus prudentie" (ch. 124). Lydgate also supplements the iconography of Fulgentius with the pipes of rhetoric and eloquence, and the sword. His likely source here is the story of the slaying of Argos told in Ovid's *Metamorphoses* 1.668–721, in which Mercury puts Argos to sleep with his pipes and then cuts off his head with a sword.

2490   *to take the moralité.* See the admonition at the end of The Nun's Priest's Tale: "Taketh the fruyt, and lat the chaf be stille" (VII.3443).

2508   *forget.* Bergen emends to *forged.*

              ymade. MS: *made. veyn.* Bergen reads *weyn.*

2519–20   *Cithera ... Juno, and Pallas.* The three goddesses (Venus, Juno, and Athena) whose beauty contest, judged by Paris, was one of the favorite stories in literature and art throughout the Middle Ages. The Judgment of Paris is often treated in art as the cause of the Trojan War.

2521   *this.* MS: *thus.*

2522   *dowes white.* Doves are a standard feature of Venus's iconography. They also figure prominently in the Song of Songs, which links them to innocence as well as passion. See *Roman de la Rose*, lines 15755–56 on the doves that accompany Venus. Morgan MS 132 fol. 117v has a drawing of Venus's chariot being drawn by six white doves as she sets out to assail chastity. The image is reprinted in Harry Robbins, trans., *The Romance of the Rose* (New York: E. P. Dutton & Co., 1962), p. 336.

2525   *schortly.* Bergen emends to *sothly.*

2526   *dowes verray innocence.* The innocence represented by the doves is identified with the turtle dove in Chaucer's *The Parliament of Fowls*, who blushes at the very thought of infidelity, or in the illusions of lecherous old lovers like January in Chaucer's The Merchant's Tale, or younger lechers like Absolon, in The Miller's Tale, who dramatize the innocence, piety, and purity of their lechery by quoting from the Song of Songs. In the *Roman de la Rose*, Guillaume de Lorris allegorizes this component of love as *Simpleice*, the second arrow to wound the lover's heart (lines 1734–45).

2531	*fairnes of the roses rede.* The rose is regularly affiliated with female desirablity, as in the lover's quest in the *Roman de la Rose.* It, more than any other, is the love flower. Bergen emends *fairnes* to *fresshnesse.*
2548	*ay with.* MS: *with many.*
2549 ff.	*Pallas I behelde.* Lydgate is meticulous in giving to Athena all her traditional iconography — the spear, the olive tree, and the owl.
2555	*his.* MS: *hir.*
2577	*chaunging.* MS: *chaungith.*
2578	*pley.* Bergen reads *play.*
2581	*Fulgense.* MS: *Fulgens.*
2596	*ther.* MS: *the.*
2598	*Fortune the fresche fetheris pulle.* Compare Chaucer's *Troilus and Criseyde* 5.1541–47.
2602	*oft.* Bergen emends to *ofte.*
2619	*attonys.* Bergen emends to *al attonys,* but see 2.4415: "And attonys done oure besynes."
2628	*an.* MS: *in.*
2642	*Discord.* Bergen observes that Discord is not mentioned by Guido.
2658	*deyvious.* Bergen reads *deynious,* which is equally plausible.
2670	*for.* Bergen emends to *of.*
2687	*onymentis.* Bergen emends to *oynementis.*
2692	*for.* Accepting Bergen's addition.

2695   *liche as bit Ovide.* Ovid's *Medicamina faciei*; see *Ars amatoria* 3.193–228.

2708   *fro.* MS: *therfro.*

2738   *unto.* MS: *to.*

2744   *stare.* MS: *to stare.*

2749   *fully.* MS: *ful.*

2760-65   Paris's inspection of the beauty of the goddesses' bodies emphasizes the elements of joining and order that appear in the earlier description of the building of New Troy, albeit now in an erotic vein.

2765   *jugen.* MS: *given.*

2769   *in.* Bergen emends to *of.*

2772   *Stremys* are "the rays sent out from the eye to the object seen" (MED).

2789   *without.* Bergen emends to *withoute.*

2793   *love and drede.* See Chaucer's description of the feelings that the people have for Walter — "Biloved and drad" — in The Clerk's Tale (IV.69).

2797   Bergen ends the sentence here, without a main clause. I punctuate it so that *Yif ye adverte* (line 2794) is completed by *I rede* (line 2798).

2800   *abood.* MS: *abote.*

3448   *As.* Bergen emends to *And.*

3470   *taketh.* Bergen emends to *took*, but see the combination of the preterite and historical present immediately below at 2.3476–77: "He spendeth ther, liche to his degré, / And quit hym manly in his oblaciouns."

             right. Bergen emends to *righte.*

3477   *oblaciouns.* MS: *oblacioun.*

3518–24   The report of Paris recalls the effect of rumor in the Piramus and Thisbe story; see Chaucer's *The Legend of Good Women*, lines 719–20: "The name of everych gan to other sprynge / By women that were neighebores aboute."

3527   *pylgrymage.* Bergen reads *pilgrymage.*

3531–51   For the possibilities of unlicensed behavior and erotic encounters, see the example of Chaucer's Wife of Bath who uses "pleyes of myracles" (III.558) as one occasion among many for entertainment and the company of "lusty folk." The signals described in the passage are Ovidian.

3545   *or.* MS: *of.*

3547   *stole.* Accepting Bergen's addition.

3575–3631   Lydgate significantly expands Guido's apostrophe in Book 7.

3594   *unto.* MS: *to.*

3600   *out of mwe.* See *Troilus and Criseyde* 1.381: "First to hiden his desir in muwe," where Chaucer describes Troilus's effort to hide his love. See also 2.3701–02.

3602   *as hare among houndis.* The proverb usually expresses fright rather than carelessness. It is so used by Chaucer in The Shipman's Tale (VII.103–05) and *Boece* (3m12.12) and by Gower (*Confessio Amantis* Pro.1061). Bergen emends to *the houndis.*

3624   *nadde.* MS: *nat.*

    wikke. MS: *wikked.*

3630   *on Troye.* MS: *Troye.*

3636   *Made.* "She" is the understood subject.

3646   *nist.* Bergen emends to *niste.*

3649   *wende.* Bergen emends to *ne wende.*

3654   *be.* MS: *have ben.*

3659   *considereth.* I take this verb as syntatically parallel with *thought*; Bergen begins a new sentence and requires "he" as the understood subject.

3672   Lydgate's phrasing recalls Chaucer's portrait of Criseyde in Book 5: "Paradis stood formed in hire yën" (*Troilus and Criseyde* 5.817).

3680   *want.* Bergen emends to *wante.*

3701–02   In adapting Guido, Lydgate ascribes to Helen the dissembling that Chaucer makes a feature of Troilus's response to first seeing Criseyde (*Troilus and Criseyde* 1.278–80).

3702   *no.* MS: *that no.*

3705   *plesance.* Bergen reads *plesaunce.*

3718   *eyen.* Bergen emends to *eye.*

3748   *fyré.* Bergen emends to *fyry*; see Pro.11 and 4.3155.

4344   *lightly.* Bergen emends to *slighly.*

          dissymble. MS: *dissymuble.* Lydgate returns to this problematic notion of prudence as dissembling when Priam later rebukes his men for attacking Diomede (2.7020) when Ulysses and Diomede come to Troy as ambassadors in the last diplomatic effort before the war begins.

4354   *kyndle.* MS: *kyndly.* Bergen emends the line to read *That he of vengaunce kyndle may the fer.*

4366   *good.* MS: *glad.*

          glad. MS: *good.*

          the. MS: *thou.* Accepting Bergen's transposition of *good* and *glad* for sense. Menelaus may be either good or glad in appearance, but he is advised to feign glad behavior in public.

4368   *woldest*. MS: *wost*.

4369   *grevaunce*. Bergen reads *grevance*.

4388   *of oure hevy*. Bergen emends to *oure hevy*.

4402   *undirstonde*. MS: *to undirstonde*.

4405   *happe*. MS: *hap*. Bergen emends to *or hap*, which then must be governed by *What that* and be taken as grammatically parallel to *befalle*; the phrase is, however, merely parenthetical: "come what may."

4427   *th'effect*. MS: *the theffect*.

4697   *Galfride*. Geoffrey of Vinsauf, whose *Poetria Nova* (c. 1210) became a standard school text for rhetoric even into the fifteenth century. Chaucer often cites Geoffrey, and quite playfully in The Nun's Priest's Tale, VII.3347, where the teller defers to his formulae as he attempts to explain the hubbub caused by Chaunticleer's ill-fate with the fox.

4704   The phrasing echoes Chaucer's mock deference to courtly lovers who compose ("make") as amateur poets: "[I] am ful glad yf I may fynde an ere / Of any goodly word that ye han left" (*The Legend of Good Women* F 76–77).

4711   *ethe to knowe*. Bergen emends to *ethe knowe* but notes MS reading.

4717   *Tempere*. Bergen reads *Tempre*.

        oure. Bergen reads *our*.

        vermyloun. Bergen proposes to read as four syllables — *vermilioun*.

4719   *folweth*. MS: *forweth*.

4731   *Baiard*. The proverbially proud horse; see Chaucer's *Troilus and Criseyde* 1.218 and The Canon's Yeoman's Tale (VIII.1413). Lydgate uses the figure again at 5.3506.

4732   *wey*. Bergen emends to *weye*.

4733   *on hede*. Bergen emends to *of hede*.

4736–62   Atwood (pp. 40–41) and Pearsall (1990), p. 41; (1970), pp. 55–58, note that Lydgate's portrait incorporates a number of details from Chaucer's portrait of Criseyde (*Troilus and Criseyde* 5.806–26).

4739   Bergen wrongly indicates that *be* must be added.

4740   *to lowe*. Bergen emends to *lowe*.

4747   *were*. MS: *where*.

4748   *And*. Accepting Bergen's addition.

4752   *ne*. Accepting Bergen's addition.

4761   *unstedfastnes*. MS: *unstefastnes*.

4861–95   The verbal portrait of Troilus derives from Chaucer's *Troilus and Criseyde* 5.827–40.

4863   *to*. MS: *for to*.

4864   *of*. Bergen emends to *on*. See *Troilus and Criseyde* 5.827 for description.

4865   See Chaucer's *Troilus and Criseyde* 5.830.

4887   *Grekis*. Bergen emends to *the Grekis*.

4888   *help*. Bergen emends to *shelde*.

6539   *is ther*. Bergen emends to *ther is*.

6553   *or*. Accepting Bergen's emendation of MS: *and*; see same phrase above at 2.6548.

6563   *eke in*. Bergen emends to *in*.

6600   *namly*. MS: *manly*.

6635   *broght*. Bergen reads *brought*.

6638   *decut*. Following Bergen who restores *decut* (from Latin *decoquo*), with the sense of "to ripen, digest in the mind by thinking over."

6640–61   Lydgate, amplifying Guido, introduces a Christian notion of choice into the evolving pattern of deterministic tragic action. Agamemnon concedes that the Greeks could have restored Hesione and so forestalled the events set in motion by Paris's sack of Cythera and his abduction of Helen. At the same time, however, he prepares to send the Trojans demands for recompense that they cannot accept.

6677   *to falle*. Bergen emends to *for to falle*.

6682   *for*. Accepting Bergen's addition.

8706   *boke*. Accepting Bergen's addition.

Book 3

11   *Flegonte*. Ovid (*Metamorphoses* 2.153–54) names four horses of Phoebus: Pyrois, Eous, Aethon, and Phlegon. Fulgentius (*Mythologiae* 1.12) points out that they correspond to the four periods of the day. Phlegon corresponds to sunset. Vatican Mythographer 2 derives his name from Greek for "loving the earth" because at the ninth hour of the day he follows the sunset to rest.

12   *oure*. MS: *her*.

24   *his manhod*. MS: *hie manhod*.

545   *wordis*. MS: *wardis*.

551–56   See above at 2.192–97 and later at Env.100–01.

569   *more, sothly*. MS: *sothly more*.

571   *Nor*. Bergen emends to *No. sade*. Bergen emends to *fade*.

572   *in*. Accepting Bergen's addition.

583   *his*. MS: *the. to*. MS: *of*. Accepting Bergen's emendations.

611   *lokkid in o cheyne*. Lydgate repeats the phrase at 3.3838, where Achilles describes his friendship with Patroclus to Hector as the two heroes prepare to settle the war by single combat between them. A version of the phrase — *lynke hym in a cheyne* (3.4859) — reappears in Lydgate's description of Criseyde's manipulation of Diomede.

618   *amonge hem*. Bergen emends to *anoon hym*.

745   *myght*. Bergen emends to *entent*.

746   *lik a doughty knyght*. Bergen emends to *ful inpacient*.

773   *Oute*. Bergen reads *Out*.

796   *lik a wode lyoun*. See Chaucer's description of Palamon in The Knight's Tale: "this Palamon / In his fightyng were a wood leon" (I.1655–56).

800   *ful*. Accepting Bergen's emendation.

834   *hem*. MS: *hym*.

836   *constreyned*. Bergen (4:221) takes this as an ablative absolute, but the grammar requires a passive sense for the verb ("he was compelled, forced").

840   *among*. Bergen emends to *maugre*, but the MS reading, in the sense of "in the presence of" is equally plausible.

843   *alle*. Bergen emends to *of*.

845   *avengid on hym*. Bergen emends to *on hym avengid*, but MS reading makes equal metrical sense if *avengid* is taken as two syllables (*aveng'd*), as it must be with either reading.

850   *callid*. Bergen emends to *called*.

870   *cam*. I have supplied the verb needed here, which repairs the meter and parallels *cam kyng Merioun* (line 876) in the later part of the clause.

           worthi. Bergen emends to *myghty* to avoid repetition.

880   *for*. Accepting Bergen's emendation.

896   *anon*. Accepting Bergen's emendation.

976   *the*. Accepting Bergen's emendation.

989   *hath*. Accepting Bergen's emendation.

994–1004 Lydgate uses anacoluthon here, but the main clause can be restored by dropping *And* (line 1000) and taking *he made* (line 1003) as the subject and verb. The overall sense is that while the three Trojans cut down the Greeks, Troilus is exceptionally deadly.

1006   *sawe*. Bergen reads *saw*.

1009   *Hent*. The subject (Menestheus) must be supplied.

1013   *the*. Accepting Bergen's emendation.

1038   *the*. MS: *your*.

1055   *enhasteth*. MS: *enhasteth hym*. *what*. MS: *wat*.

1087   *stronge*. MS: *so stronge*.

1096   *the light*. Bergen emends to *the ferful light*.

1097   Accepting the line Bergen supplies for the one missing in the MS.

1098   *And*. Accepting Bergen's addition.

1103   *hurtle*. MS: *hurkle*.

1897   *cast*. Bergen emends to *caste*.

           pleinly. Bergen emends to *platly*.

1898   *in haste*. Accepting Bergen's emendation.

1903   *distourbe*. MS: *distourble*.

1908   *with*. MS: *in. in*. Accepting Bergen's emendation.

1917   *ybonde*. MS: *bonde*.

1918   The line is an ablative absolute; the main verb, *Repeired is* (line 1920), requires "he" as the understood subject.

1945   *made also*. Bergen emends to *also made*.

1947   *in*. Bergen emends to *into*.

1964   *many other*. MS: *other many*.

1975–2035 Lydgate attributes Troy's fall to Fate, aided by Fortune; but he also insists that the proximate cause is Hector's lack of prudence. By connecting determinism to human choice, he offers a Christian view of pagan history. The thematic framework is in many respects the one that Boethius works out in the *Consolation of Philosophy* to accommodate divine foreknowledge and free will, but Lydgate complicates the explanation by insisting that other authentic human choices were possible. Tragic action is not the result of a discrepancy between necessity and limited human understanding; it stems from actual choices made from among real alternatives. At 3.2139–57 Lydgate reaffirms the possibility of a different outcome to the story.

1977   *welfulnes*. MS: *wilfulnes*.

1993   *wer set*. Bergen emends to *sete*.

2008   *unkyndnes*. Bergen emends to *unkyndenes*.

2024   *after*. MS: *asterte*.

2033–34   Lines transposed in MS.

2042   *that he was nyghe.* Bergen emends to *he was ful nyghe.*

2060   *of fortune.* Accepting Bergen's emendation for MS: *fortune.*

2097   *he of berthe.* MS: *of berth he.*

2128   *pleynly.* MS: *plynly.*

2137   *hir.* Bergen reads *her.*

2155   *lyk.* Accepting Bergen's addition.

    in. MS: *is*, followed by Bergen.

2245   *and the lamentacioun.* Bergen emends to *and lamentacioun.*

2248   *herte was.* MS: *hertes were.*

2264   *mercy, pité.* MS: *pity mercy.*

2278   *servytude.* MS: *servytute.*

2296   *troughth.* MS: *troughh.*

2308   *eye of his discreccioun.* By tradition, prudence has three eyes to survey past, present, and future. When she is in the Greek camp, Chaucer's Criseyde laments that she lacked one of prudence's three eyes (*Troilus and Criseyde* 5.744) — the capacity for foresight. Chaucer's reference may be to the famous image of three-eyed prudence on the chariot of the church in Dante's *Purgatorio* (29.130–32). As Charles Singleton notes, in the *Convivio* Dante equates prudence with wisdom (*The Divine Comedy*, trans. Charles S. Singleton, 6 vols. in 3 [Princeton: Princeton University Press, 1970–75], 2:723). Jerome Taylor points out that Hugh of St. Victor's *De sacramentis* identifies the three "eyes" of man before the fall as those of the flesh, reason, and contemplation (*The Didascalion of Hugh of St. Victor* [New York: Columbia University Press, 1961], p. 177n). These eyes see the world, man, and God respectively.

2311   *availeth*. Bergen emends to *vaileth*.

2680   *Or*. MS: *Of*.

2684   *anon echon*. Bergen emends to *echon anon*.

2687   *Thei*. MS: *The*.

2689   *on lyve*. Bergen emends to *alyve*.

2719   *Fro*. MS: *For*.

2726   *lif*. Accepting Bergen's emendation for MS: *silfe*; see *silfe* used immediately below (line 2728).

2741   *maked han*. MS: *maken*.

2744   *morwenynge*. MS: *morwnynge*.

3106–14   Priam's counselors comprise two groups — his sons and the men who will later conspire to betray Troy to the Greeks.

3108   *inwardly*. Accepting Bergen's emendation for MS: *inly*.

3110   *fame*. MS: *name*.

3113   *for*. Accepting Bergen's emendation for parallelism with line 3111.

3118   *The*. Bergen emends to *This*.

3137   *thereuppon*. MS: *hereuppon*.

3143   *caste*. Bergen reads *cast*.

3149   *pleinly*. Bergen emends to *now pleinly*.

3155   *as*. Accepting Bergen's emendation.

3163   *endynge*. Bergen emends to *ende*.

3168   *for.* Accepting Bergen's emendation.

3201–07 Aeneas unwittingly forecasts the exchange of Antenor for Thoas and Criseyde, and he ironically represents a situation in which right reason and prudence contribute to the overthrow of Troy.

3216   *of.* Bergen emends to *on.* Both forms appear in MS: see 1.4044: "venge him of his foon" and 3.3857: "How Achilles was vengid of his foo" (3.3857) but "To be vengid on youre grete pride" (3.2260). Chaucer's Melibee says "I shal nat venge me of myne enemys" (VII.1427); elsewhere in Melibee (VII.1280), Chaucer has forms of "venge on" and "venge upon."

3236   *maked.* "She" is the understood subject of the sentence.

3666   *and Thoas.* Bergen emends to *and of Thoas.*

3667   *delyvered shulde.* Bergen emends to *shulde delyvered.*

3671   *Oon.* MS: *And.*

3681   *hym.* Accepting Bergen's emendation.

3690   *Howe that.* Bergen emends to *Howe.*

3712   *sente.* MS: *wente.*

3719–51 Lydgate, following Guido, differs from Chaucer's version (*Troilus and Criseyde* 4.135–47) of the exchange. Lydgate and Guido also leave unexplained why Priam's hatred for Calchas (and so his resistance to granting Calchas's wish) is set aside so that the exchange may go forward.

3719   *hateful.* MS: *hathful.*

3729   *as.* MS: *a.*

3743   *the.* Bergen emends to *an.*

3749   *repellid.* Bergen emends to *repeled* to assure sense of "rescinded, revoked" rather than "repelled."

387

3761   *Blaundisshinge.* MS: *Blaundissinge.*

3764   *to vesite.* MS: *for to vesite.* Accepting Bergen's emendation to avoid repetition from preceding line, where meter requires the additional syllable.

3788   *whan.* MS: *wan.*

3794   *take.* MS: *taken.*

3810   *wolde.* MS: *wele.*

3830   *mysilf.* MS: *my lif.* The love of another as oneself is a fundamental value in the discussion of virtuous friendship in Aristotle and Cicero. Achilles's claim here is that his relation to Patroclus is the intimacy of such friendship rather than erotic desire. In Guido, he says that he did not love Patroclus less than himself (Book 19).

3837   *outterly.* Bergen emends to *enteerly. tweyne* must be read as a single syllable to rhyme with *cheyne.*

3838   *lokkid in o cheyne.* Lydgate echoes this phrase (3.5366) in the scene in which Hector tries to strip the armor off a dead Greek king and Achilles fatally wounds him.

3842   *darte.* Bergen emends to *doth darte.*

3843   *out of.* MS: *in.*

3844   *it shal.* Bergen emends to *shal* and suggests *trust* should be read as *trustë* to produce a pentameter line.

3852   *long.* Accepting Bergen's emendation.

3857   *of.* Bergen emends to *on.* See 3.3216 (above).

3887   *outher.* MS: *other.*

3889   *pursuweth.* MS: *pursuwet.*

3897	*right nor equité.* Hector employs the same formula that Priam uses earlier in arguing that King Thoas should be killed (3.3139).
3908	Torti, p. 181, notes that this line is echoed in a later reference to Troilus's love (3.4220).
3928	*shul.* MS: *shulen.*
3932	*al do.* Bergen emends to *ado.*
3981	*it quit in youre.* MS: *in quiete and in.*
3994	*seie.* MS: *seide.*
4009	*nat.* MS: *it nat.*
4018	*the whiche.* Bergen emends to *whiche.*
4029	Casting down the glove is Lydgate's addition. See Bergen 4:156.
4035	*dide yit.* Bergen emends to *yit dide.*
4053	*the.* Accepting Bergen's emendation.
4066–70	Priam's acceptance of the majority opinion recalls the earlier scene in which he accedes to his counselors and does not insist on killing Thoas (3.3219-21).
4070	*He.* Accepting Bergen's emendation.
4075–4448	Lydgate presents Troilus's story as if it were a *de casibus* tragedy, an example illustrating the general principle of Fortune's mutability as in the *Fall of Princes*, which he translated from Boccaccio's *De casibus virorum illustrium*, rather than the individualized, subjective experience that Chaucer emphasizes.
4078	*to be.* Bergen emends to *for to be.*
4079	*men.* Bergen emends to *folk.*

4085   *that*. Accepting Bergen's emendation.

4090   *felt*. Bergen emends to *felte*.

4090   *a peyne*. Bergen emends to *peyne*.

4093–94   Lydgate employs Chaucer's ominous rhyme *Criseyde / he deyde*. Later (3.4199–4200), he uses the rhyme to link Chaucer to the writing of *Troilus and Criseyde*.

4101   *which in*. MS: *that within*.

4104   *compleyninge*. MS: *compleynigne*.

4107   *behynde*. MS: *beside*.

4109   Lydgate echoes the line ending Arcite's speech when he sees Emily in The Knight's Tale: "I nam but deed; ther nis namoore to seye" (I.1122).

4119–20   The rhyme *Troye / joye* is pervasive in *Troilus and Criseyde*, beginning with the opening stanza.

4121   *the teris doun distille*. See Chaucer's Troilus as he speaks to Pandarus after the Trojan parliament has decided to trade Criseyde for Antenor: "This Troylus in teris gan distille, / As licour out of a lambyc ful faste" (4.519–20).

4122   *trille*. MS: *tille*.

4123   *hir blake wede*. In Chaucer, Criseyde is first seen "in hir blake wede" (1.177).

4133   *ascendyng*. MS: *ascendyn*.

4139   *whi shal we*. MS: *we shal*.

4159–85   Lydgate retells the events of Book 4 of Chaucer's *Troilus and Criseyde* but omits several parts, including Troilus's speech on predestination.

4177   *dowmb*. MS: *dowme*.

4179   *flikerit*. Bergen emends to *flikered*; see 4.6739, 5.3551.

4182   *ther*. MS: *the*.

4187   *Disconsolat*. Lydgate's use of the term here both echoes Chaucer and connects the lovers' loss of each other to the fall of the city; see below, 3.5488.

4189   *bother*. Bergen emends to *bothe*.

4192–95   Lydgate uses one of Chaucer's favorite rhetorical devices, *occupatio* (where you say what you say you are not going to say), as a means to praise him.

4197   *Chaucer*. MS: *Chauncer*.

4198   *so wel hath*. Bergen emends to *hath so wel*.

4202   *For*. Accepting Bergen's addition.

4203   *surquedie*. See *Troilus and Criseyde* 1.213.

4208   Lydgate rehearses the events in Book 1 of *Troilus and Criseyde*, where Troilus falls in love with Criseyde.

4214   *wise*. MS: *while*.

4216   *aftir*. MS: *first*.

4217   Lydgate describes Pandarus's role in the love affair by obliquely echoing Pandarus's own terms: "for the am I bicomen, / Bitwixen game and ernest, swich a meene / As maken wommen unto men to comen" (*Troilus and Criseyde* 3.253–55). See below, 4.742.

4218   *maked*. MS: *made*.

4224–28   Lydgate here echoes the ending of Chaucer's *Troilus and Criseyde* (5.1849–55).

4226   *fleshly*. Bergen emends to *fleshy*.

4227   *variacioun*. MS: *variaunce*. See Troilus's "double sorwe" (*Troilus and Criseyde* 1.1, 1.54).

4228   MS: *wordly*. Bergen amends to *worldly*, but MS form is an attested variant.

4233   *ever*. MS: *never*.

4234   *Chaucer*. MS: *Chauncer*.

4248   *as*. MS: *a*.

4251   Petrarch was crowned poet laureate by the Roman Senate on 8 April 1341. In 1330 he entered the service of Cardinal Giovanni Colonna and remained under the family's patronage until 1347–48.

4254–55   In *The House of Fame* (line 1469), Chaucer names Guido along with Homer, Dares and Dictys, "Lollius," and Geoffrey of Monmouth as writers on the iron pillar that bears up the fame of Troy.

4263   *joie*. Bergen reads *Ioy*.

4274   *fals*. Bergen emends to *false*.

4294   *is meynt ever*. Bergen emends to *ever is meynt*.

4296   *her sureté*. Accepting Bergen's addition of *her*.

4315–16   These lines are reversed in other MSS.

4323   *It shewed*. MS: *It is shewed*.

4327   *oblaciounes*. MS: *oblaciouns*. See 2.3531–51. The repetition of the allusion to the Wife of Bath links Criseyde to Helen; she is a second Helen, as Troilus is a second Hector.

4329   *seith*. MS: *seit*.

                 selle. See the Wife of Bath's remark about herself: "The flour is goon; ther is namoore to telle; / The bren, as I best kan, now moste I selle" (III.477–78).

4343–4448   In *The Legend of Good Women*, Chaucer portrays himself as woman's friend: "Be war, ye wemen, of youre subtyl fo, / Syn yit this day men may ensaumple se; / And trusteth, as in love, no man but me" (lines 2559–61). Lydgate offers a standard refutation of the misogynistic attack on women, arguing that there are a thousand virtuous women for each perfidious one; Chaucer incorporates the argument in The Merchant's Tale (IV.1362–74) and The Tale of Melibee (VII.1098–1102), with an accompanying list of Biblical heroines. But Lydgate also accepts the claim that female duplicity is part of women's nature. See Mieszkowski, pp. 117–26, for the contradictions in Lydgate's reproval of Guido. Torti, p. 177, proposes that Lydgate "puts still more subtle and ambiguous emphasis on Criseyde's inconstancy" than Guido. Watson, pp. 97–100, argues that Lydgate associates Chaucer with Criseyde as a way of rejecting *Troilus and Criseyde* and asserting the moral vision of *Troy Book*.

4356   *secte*. See the Clerk's reference to the Wife of Bath and "al hire secte" (IV.1171).

4359   *hym*. Bergen emends to *he*, which is an acceptable alternative.

4370   Jacobus de Voragine's *Legenda aurea* is the most popular late medieval source for the story of St. Ursula and the eleven thousand virgin martyrs of Cologne. According to legend, Ursula was the daughter of a British Christian king promised to a pagan, who managed to delay her marriage for three years, hoping to remain a virgin. During this period, she set out by ship with ten companions, each of them on an accompanying ship with a thousand companions of their own. The women traveled extensively and were eventually martyred by Huns at Cologne after Ursula refused to marry their chieftain. The citizens of Cologne buried them and built a church in their honor. The historical record of Ursula begins with an inscription dated around 400. The number of companions ascribed to Ursula is probably an error, reading an abbreviated text "XI MV" as 11,000 virgins ("undecim millia virgines") instead of eleven virgin martyrs ("undecim martyres virgines").

4382   *the nynthe spere*. In the Ptolemaic system, the planets and stars revolve around the earth in concentric spheres. The ninth sphere is the Primum Mobile, the First Mover who imparts movement to the other spheres, while God stands at a further remove, encompassing the universe. See below, 5.3602.

4417   *skippeth over wher ye list nat rede.* See Chaucer's admonition in The Miller's Prologue: "Turne over the leef and chese another tale" (I.3177).

4422   *the.* Bergen emends to *for.*

4426–27   See the scene of exchange in *Troilus and Criseyde* where Diomede is alert to the distress of Troilus and Criseyde when he takes the bridle of Criseyde's horse (5.85–91).

4428   *how that.* Bergen emends to *how.*

4435   *was.* MS: *wer.* Lydgate follows Guido's version of Criseyde's immediate acceptance of Diomede as a lover rather than Chaucer's consciously indeterminate account of her shift in affections: "Men seyn — I not — that she yaf hym hire herte" (5.1050).

4442   *Kyndes transmutacioun.* Chaucer describes Criseyde as "slydynge of corage" (5.825).

4446   *unto.* MS: *to.*

4820–69   The account here of Diomede's service as a courtly lover contrasts greatly with Chaucer's portrayal of Diomede as a calculating seducer. Criseyde, too, differs by carefully manipulating Diomede, whereas in Chaucer she is increasingly unable to exercise her will.

4827   *bothe megre and lene.* Diomede resembles Arcite in The Knight's Tale (I.1361–62) as he suffers *amor hereos*, the lover's melancholy; the phrasing in Lydgate, however, echoes the portrait of Avarice outside the garden in the *Roman de la Rose* (line 199); in Chaucer's *Romaunt*, "she was lene and megre" (line 218).

4829   *al.* Accepting Bergen's addition.

4849   *As wommen kan holde a man ful narwe.* See Chaucer's Boethian image (*Boece* 3.m.2.21–31) for Alisoun in The Miller's Tale (I.3224), the peregrine falcon's faithless lover in The Squire's Tale (V.610–20), and Phebus's wife in The Manciple's Tale (IX.163–74).

4853   *betwixe hope and drede*. Echoes Chaucer's description of Troilus (5.630, 5.1207; see also *Troilus and Criseyde* 3.1315).

4861   *him*. MS: *hem*.

4894   *shon*. Bergen emends to *roos* to avoid repetition, but Lydgate here seems to be using iteration both for stylistic elaboration and for contrast with the preceding night and Andromache's dream, whose clarity Hector fatally ignores.

4910–16   Lydgate invokes the vocabulary and dream categories of Macrobius's *Commentary on the Dream of Scipio Africanus*, the major literary source for medieval dreamlore, but he follows Chaucer's Prologue to *The House of Fame* (lines 7–11) in expanding Macrobius's five categories to six. See below 3.4969.

4935   *stok of worthines*. The image is not in Guido. Lydgate's phrase conflates the opening of Chaucer's moral balade *Gentilesse* ("The firste stok, fader of gentilesse") and Pandarus's description of Hector: "he, that is of worthynesse welle" (*Troilus and Criseyde* 2.178).

4936   *wont*. MS: *wonnt*.

4938   *This Troyan wal, Hector*. The image here is not in Guido but appears later in Hector's epitaph (Book 35); see *Troilus and Criseyde* 2.154 and below 4.3946. In the *Metamorphoses* 13.281, Ovid describes Achilles as "the Greeks' wall."

4942   *litel*. Bergen reads *litil*.

4950   *this*. Accepting Bergen's addition.

4959   *Seiyng*. Bergen emends to *Seying*.

4969–70   I have retained the MS readings for *oracle* and *myracle*, which Bergen reverses. Lydgate uses the Macrobian vocabulary inconsistently. The *oracle* (*oraculum*), for example, is a dream in which a figure of authority appears and then reveals what will occur. Andromache's dream best fits the general category of the prophetic *visio* (Macrobius, *Commentary* 1.3.9).

4972   *hem*. MS: *hym*.

4981   *and sovereinté*. Bergen emends to *and of sovereinté*.

5021   *in*. Accepting Bergen's addition.

5022   *Lyke*. Bergen reads *Lyk*.

5049   *on*. Accepting Bergen's addition.

5056   *to*. Bergen emends to *unto*.

5073   *Andronomecha*. MS: *Andronemaca*.

5093   *harded*. Bergen emends to *harde*. In Christian theology, the hard heart is a symbol of the lack of charity.

5096   *moren and renewe*. MS: *morne and remewe*.

5116   *the*. Accepting Bergen's addition.

5120   *is*. Bergen emends to *was*.

5129   *he*. MS: *hym*.

5138   *like a tigre or a lyoun wood*. In The Knight's Tale (I.1655–57), Chaucer compares Arcite and Palamon respectively to the tiger and the lion; see 3.5246, 3.796.

5139   *his*. Bergen emends to *hir*.

5150   *had anoon*. MS: *anoon had*.

5158   *ne myghte*. Bergen emends to *myghte*.

5164   *aboute*. Bergen emends to *upon*.

5165   *sese*. MS: *sesse*.

5183   *in.* Accepting Bergen's addition.

5185   *worthi.* Bergen emends to *myghty.*

5196   *ne.* Accepting Bergen's addition.

5215   *Achilles.* Bergen emends to *Achille,* though the addition of a syllable before the caesura is a common pattern in Lydgate.

5223   *home.* Bergen emends to *homeward.*

5225   *Margaritoun.* Bergen emends to *Margariton* to rhyme with *Thelamon.*

5226   *that.* MS: *of.*

5231   *in baste wer.* MS: *wer in baste.*

5247–48   Compare *Troilus and Criseyde* 2.193–94, as wondrous Troilus puts the Greeks to flight: "For nevere yet so thikke a swarm of been / Ne fleigh, as Grekes for hym gonne fleen." See also *Troy Book* 3.5330.

5249   *Thai.* Bergen reads *Thei.*

5275   *grete.* MS: *grete.* Bergen reads *gret* but emends to *grete.*

5277   *compassen.* MS: *compassed.*

5279   *mow.* Bergen emends to *may.*

5280   *or.* Bergen emends to *nor.*

5282   *that.* Accepting Bergen's addition.

5283–84   Lydgate undercuts Achilles's heroic stature by showing in him a mixture of epic furor and calculation; as used elsewhere in the poem (1.1945, 3.5284, 4.197, 4.3117, 4.4406, 4.5789, 4.5822, 4.6330, 4.6997, 5.3358), *engyne* is a term for deviousness.

5289   Guido (Book 21) follows Benoît (lines 16166–68) in including the detail that Polycenes hopes to marry Achilles's sister.

5291   The line ironically echoes the description of Chaucer's Squire in the General Prologue to the *Canterbury Tales*: "In hope to stonden in his lady grace" (I.88).

5301   *darte*. Bergen emends to *quarel*, a bolt from a crossbow.

            grounde. Bergen emends to *ygrounde* for meter.

5303   *the*. Accepting Bergen's addition.

5317   *to*. Accepting Bergen's addition.

5324   *yeven*. MS: *gif*.

5332   *he*. MS: *him*.

5335   *Enbroudrid*. Bergen emends to *Enbroudid*.

5363   *No*. Bergen emends to *Nor*.

5364   *not to*. Bergen emends to *to*.

5372   Hector's fatal error in trying to despoil the dead Greek king recalls his earlier effort to despoil Patroclus, and so Achilles's vengeance on him reflects a special irony.

5383   *Allas*. MS: *Allas the while*. See 3.5396.

5402   *to*. Accepting Bergen's addition.

5422   *for*. Accepting Bergen's addition. See 3.4089 and the office of aiding lovers to lament their misfortune which Chaucer's narrator takes on at the beginning of *Troilus and Criseyde* (1.22–56).

5431   *ever*. MS: *alle*.

5445   *to*. MS: *for.*

5454   *A drery fere*. See Chaucer's *Troilus and Criseyde* 1.13.

5462   *boget*. Bergen emends to *boket.*

5487–88   *desolat . . . discounsolat*. Lydgate apostrophizes Troy in the same language
            that Chaucer employs in Troilus's lamentation before Criseyde's empty house
            after she has been delivered to the Greeks: "O paleys desolat, / O hous of
            houses whilom best ihight, / O paleys empty and disconsolat" (*Troilus and
            Criseyde* 5.540–42). Lydgate earlier describes Troilus and Criseyde as
            "Disconsolat" (3.4187) when they meet after the exchange for Antenor has
            been decided. He repeats the pairing of "desolat" and "disconsolat" in
            Achilles's speech urging the Greeks to abandon the war so that he can marry
            Polyxena (4.993–94). The phrasing in both *Troy Book* and *Troilus* and
            Criseyde echoes the opening of Jeremiah's Lamentations. The connection
            between the biblical lament and the loss of a worldly love object is made in
            Chaucer's translation of the *Roman de la Rose* when the dreamer is left "all
            sool, disconsolat" (*Romaunt*, line 3168) after Bel Acuel is driven off.
            Chaucer adds the phrasing from Lamentations; Guillaume de Lorris writes,
            "je remés tous esbahis, / Honteus et mas" (lines 2952–53).

5517   *mortal*. MS: *mortally.*

5526   *whom*. Accepting Bergen's addition.

5537   *token*. MS: *taken.*

5546   *boris*. Bergen emends to *bolis*, but I preserve the MS reading, which conveys
            the image of savage rage rather than sacrifice. "Wilde bore" is a fairly
            common image in Chaucer, notably in The Knight's Tale (I.1658), where it
            expresses the fury of Palamon and Arcite in their battle against each other.

5556   *make*. MS: *make make.*

5558   *Her pitous sobbynge*. MS: *The woful cries.*

5559   *The woful cries*. MS: *Her pitous sobbynge.*

5572   *Thei*. Bergen emends to *To*.

5595   *in sight it*. Bergen emends to *it in sight*.

5596   *lifly*. MS: *likly*. Accepting Bergen's emendation.

5603   *axeynge*. Bergen reads *axynge*.

5612   *the*. Bergen emends to *in*.

5613   *spake*. MS: *speke*.

5627   *al*. Accepting Bergen's addition.

5643   *Attenyng*. MS: *Attendyng*. MS reading is a confusion of the verb *extenden* (MED).

5653   *the*. Bergen emends to *this*.

5654   *good*. MS: *gret*.

5679   *many*. MS: *many a*.

5686   *a sowle that were vegetable*. The soul is traditionally divided into three parts — vegetative, sensitive, and rational — which correspond hierarchically to plants, animals, and men. The division goes back to Plato's analytic separation of the concupiscible, irascible, and rational souls. Scholastic philosophers insist on the unity of the soul. In their systems, the vegetative soul confers the power to live, the animal soul the power to feel, and the rational soul the power to think. Lydgate's reference conveys the idea that Hector's body is kept alive but the other faculties are dead.

5689   *semblably*. MS: *semblaly*.

5705   *were*. MS: *was*.

5714   *rejoysseden*. Bergen emends to *rejoyssed*.

5728   *on heighte*. MS: *o loft*.

5729	*Pluvius*. MS error for *Plinius*. The name in the corresponding passage in Benoît is *Plines* (line 16541). *Pluvius* is a surname for Jupiter, as the sender of rain. The source for the passage on ebony is Pliny's *Natural History* 12.8.17–12.9.20.
5733	*lond*. MS: *londes*.
5737	*is*. MS: *it is*.

Book 4

154	*it were no nede*. Bergen emends to *that it were no nede*.
159	*How I th'estat*. Grammatically parallel with *that I have governaunce* as direct objects of *muse* and *grucchen*.
163	*brocage*. MS: *procage*.
196	*dewly may*. Bergen emends to *may dewely*.
208	*shuld*. Bergen emends to *shulde*.
215	*obeied*. MS: *ben obeied*.
220	*compleyne*. Bergen emends to *pleyne*.
279	*highe*. Bergen emends to *your highe*.
287	*a*. Bergen emends to *the*.
301	In Lydgate as in Chaucer, *newe* usually carries a pejorative sense and represents a self-indulgent wish for novelty rather than stability and proven worth. In politics as much as in love, the poets censure *newfongilnes*. See note to 1.2090.
317	*in every cost*. Bergen emends to *aboute in every cost*, but the couplet remains a metrical problem. One alternative is to emend the next line to *The emperour*.

553   *sothly*. MS: *soth*.

556   *unto*. Bergen emends to *to*.

556–57   Achilles's attendance at the rites in Apollo's temple, where he falls in love
           with Polyxena, recalls Troilus's first sight of Criseyde in the temple at the
           feast of the Palladium (*Troilus and Criseyde* 1.161).

561   *wer*. Bergen emends to *was*.

564   *gadered*. Bergen reads *gadred*.

575   *lowe*. MS: *lawe*.

590   *to*. MS: *unto*.

592   *Of*. Accepting Bergen's addition.

603   *percyng stremys of hir eyen two*. Achilles falls in love with Polyxena in a way
           that recalls Troilus's falling in love with Criseyde as Love dwells "[w]ithinne
           the subtile stremes of hir yen" (*Troilus and Criseyde* 1.305; see also *Troilus
           and Criseyde* 3.129). Lydgate repeats the image at 4.673.

612   *lyke*. Bergen emends to *lykly*.

619   *lovis snare*. See Troilus's and Pandarus's descriptions of his predicament
           (*Troilus and Criseyde* 1.507 and 663), echoed later by Criseyde in the Greek
           camp (*Troilus and Criseyde* 5.748).

622   *best to do*. See *Troilus and Criseyde* 1.828 and 2.1485.

629   *This to seyn, the sonne wente doun*. Typical Chaucerian phrasing in the
           Canterbury Tales (I.181, I.1839, I.1857), perhaps best exploited for the effect
           of rhetorical deflation in The Franklin's Tale (V.1017–18).

640–43   See Troilus's taking to bed and making a mirror of his mind in which to see
           the image of Criseyde (*Troilus and Criseyde* 1.358–67). Lydgate injects a
           perhaps unconscious irony by using Troilus as a model for the figure who

will dispatch him without pity later in the poem and "Despitously" in Chaucer's poem (*Troilus and Criseyde* 5.1806).

645   *final cause.* In Aristotle's analysis of cause, the final cause is the reason for which an action is undertaken, as distinct from the formal, material, and instrumental causes. Lydgate conspicuously modifies Guido, who portrays Polyxena as the efficient cause of Achilles's love sickness.

673   *the stremys of hir eyen tweyne.* See above, 4.603.

674   *corve.* Bergen emends to *corven*; see 2.988.

686   *availlen.* Bergen emends to *availle. or.* Bergen emends to *nor.*

690   *outrage.* MS: *autrage.*

698–701   Once he falls in love with Polyxena, Achilles changes his assessment of Hector's worth.

712   *provyde.* MS: *pvyde.*

725   *fretyng.* The term used here to describe Achilles's lovesickness is applied elsewhere to anger; see Peleus's anger toward Jason (1.229) and Lamedon's fury in battle (1.4167).

730   *or.* Accepting Bergen's emendation for MS: *and.*

742   *mene.* See above, 3.4217. Lydgate's allusion to Chaucer's Pandarus plays off his straightforward use of the term earlier (4.709) to signify a course of action.

756   *And.* Accepting Bergen's addition.

756-84   Lydgate goes beyond Guido's spare account of the messenger's mission and describes his speech as a logical argument, proceeding through an ordered sequence of premises to a necessary conclusion. The messenger proposes that marrying Polyxena to Achilles will end a war caused in part by the loss of Hesione and Paris's abduction of Helen.

761   *Effectuously*. Bergen emends to *Effectuelly*.

773   *thorugh*. Bergen emends to *by* and avoids repetition with next line, which seems to be the rhetorical aim.

778   *performyd*. Bergen reads *parformyd*.

782   *him*. MS: *hem*. The emendation reflects the two conditions of the proposal: that the Greeks end the war and Priam (*him*) live in peace thereafter.

784   *knyt up in a cheyne*. The same image is used earlier to describe Achilles's relationship with Patroclus (3.611, 3.3835-39).

787   *or that*. MS: *that or*.

798   *To*. MS: *For*.

        for. Accepting Bergen's addition.

817   *to*. Bergen emends to *into*.

820   *for*. Accepting Bergen's addition.

835   *how*. Bergen emends to *that*.

881   *the treté*. Bergen emends to *this treté*.

907   *th'effect of this mater*. Chaucerian phrasing (Sir Thopas VII.958 and *Troilus and Criseyde* 4.890).

914   *alway*. MS: *away*.

918   *cast*. Bergen emends to *caste*.

920   *cruellé*. Bergen emends to *cruelly*.

933   *take*. MS: *toke*.

935 *a verray impossible*. See Aurelius's exclamation at the task Dorigen gives him in The Franklin's Tale: "this were an inpossible" (V.1009).

936 *ben so*. Bergen emends to *ben ay so*.

966 *flouring yit in fame*. Bergen emends to *floureth yit the fame* for grammar, but the MS phrasing is consistent with Lydgate's style.

974 *liften*. Bergen emends to *lifte*.

987 *Was*. MS: *As*.

993 *desolat*; see 3.5487–88.

1017 Bergen (4:223) notes that the phrase refers to Achilles rather than Hector.

1019 *yit*. Accepting Bergen's addition.

1035 *into*. MS: *to*.

1049 *gilt*. Bergen emends to *gilte*.

1051 *dyvos*. Bergen (4:223) notes that Guido does not mention divorce and that Lydgate here moves from canon to Roman law.

1052 *knowe*. Bergen emends to *iknowe*.

1089–90 The lines echo the beginning of Book 4 of *Troilus and Criseyde*, as Fortune withdraws her favor from Troilus: "From Troilus she gan hire brighte face / Awey to writhe, and tok of hym non heede, / But caste hym clene out of his lady grace" (4.8–10).

1095 *home that we*. Bergen emends to *that we home*.

1108 *to*. MS: *in*.

1109 *Whiche*. Bergen emends to *While*.

1111 *so*. Accepting Bergen's addition.

1119–29   Achilles ironically echoes the argument made earlier by Paris (2.2341–47) that a Greek woman should be taken as recompense for Telamon's seizing Hesione after the fall of Lamedon's Troy.

1134   Repeats the last line of Chaucer's The Franklin's Tale (V.1624).

1142   *perturbid.* Bergen reads *parturbid.*

1147   *nold.* Bergen emends to *nolde.*

1162   *the felde.* Bergen emends to *felde.*

1164   *yaf.* MS: *yaf in.*

1170   *the.* Bergen emends to *his.*

1197   *the request.* Bergen emends to *request.*

1213   *mendyn.* Bergen emends to *amendyn. repeire.* Bergen emends to *repare* to clarify rhyme with *spare*; see 4.857–58, where *contrarie* rhymes with *apaire.*

1221   *purpos.* Bergen emends to *purpose.*

2036   *That as the deth thei fledde fro his sight.* See Chaucer's description of Troilus's martial valor: "the Grekes as the deth him dredde" (*Troilus and Criseyde* 1.483).

2058   *tariyng.* Bergen emends to *lettyng.*

2059   *throwe.* MS: *threwe.*

2075   *myghty.* MS: *myghte.*

2085   *han.* Bergen emends to *had.*

2088   *the knyghthod.* MS: *his knyghthod. the highe.* MS: *his highe.*

2095   *ridyng.* Bergen emends to *hym ridyng,* to emphasize that the knights are riding around Agamemnon in an escort.

2103 *ther.* MS: *thei.*

2110 *hym.* Bergen emends to *hem.* In the MS reading, Agamemnon sees the distress Troilus has inflicted on him and how the Greeks are unable to resist Troilus.

2111 *the.* Bergen emends to *his.*

2139 Lydgate adds reminiscences of Criseyde's interviews with Troilus in Book 3 of *Troilus and Criseyde*; Guido says that Diomede is lying in bed, not that Briseida sits on the side of it.

2144 Lydgate, unlike Chaucer, identifies the point at which Criseyde shifts her love from Troilus to Diomede. The source is Guido, Book 26.

2148 *Loo, what pité is in wommanhede.* Pearsall (1990), p. 48, relates this passage to *Troilus and Criseyde* 5.1048–50. See 4.2172, where Criseyde would rather be thought changeable than lacking pity. Lydgate's references to Criseyde's pity offer an ironic comment on Chaucer's repeated assertion in the *Canterbury Tales*, "pitee renneth soone in gentil herte." See above, 1.4266.

2150 *olde.* MS: *newe.*

2151 *late slyppe asyde.* See Chaucer's description of Criseyde: "Ne nevere mo ne lakked hire pite; / Tendre-herted, slydynge of corage" (*Troilus and Crisyde* 5.824–25).

2155 *Lombard Strete.* Lombard merchants settled in London in the twelfth century. In 1318 Langbourn Street changed its name to Lombard Street. The name was in common use in the fourteenth century. From the early years of Edward I's reign onwards, Lombards served as bankers to the English crown. Their influence caused frequent resentment. In 1359, Lombards were attacked during riots. In 1376, the Mayor, Aldermen, and commons of London petitioned the King to forbid Lombards to live in the city or act as brokers in retail sales. Lombards were a target during the Rising of 1377.

2175 *to.* Accepting Bergen's addition.

2660 *And withinne.* Bergen emends to *Withinne.*

2679   *worthiest*. Bergen emends to *worthieste*.

2681   *I fele myn herte*. Bergen emends to *myn herte I fele*.

2697   *of highe*. Accepting Bergen's addition to MS: *highe*.

2726   *to lasse and to discres*. Bergen emends to *gan to lasse and discrese* without repairing the meter fully.

2732   *at*. Bergen emends to *under*.

2734   *worthy*. MS: *manly*.

2741   *grounde*. Bergen emends to *ygrounde*.

2748   *severed*. Bergen emends to *severe*.

2750   *man*. Bergen emends to *wight*.

2763   *cruel cursed*. Bergen emends to *cursed cruel*.

2764   *thought pleynly*. Bergen emends to *thoughte platly*.

2773–79   Achilles's mistreatment of Troilus's body is the same that he shows Hector's corpse in the *Iliad*.

2783   *that he*. Bergen emends to *he*.

2801   *unto*. MS: *to*.

2836   *arace*. MS: *race*.

2840   *so foule is*. MS: *is so foule*.

2849   *for*. Accepting Bergen's addition.

3105   *with hevy*. Bergen emends to *ful hevy*.

3113   *of Troylus*. Bergen emends to *Troylus*.

3121   *of right and equyté*. Hecuba's justification for plotting Achilles's death is the same that Priam uses earlier (2.1203, 2.1214, 2.1253) to urge retaliation for Hesione's abduction; Hector uses the phrasing in his interview with Achilles (3.3897), and Priam repeats it in arguing that King Thoas should be put to death after his capture (3.3139).

3155   *firé*. Bergen emends to *firy*; see Pro.11 and 2.3748

3161   *whan*. MS: *wan*.

3171   *temple*. Bergen emends to *the temple*.

3190   *the*. Bergen emends to *his*.

3191   *therwithal*. MS: *therwith*.

3204   *body was*. MS: *bodies wern*.

3210–11   See Chaucer's reproval of the pagan world at the end of *Troilus and Criseyde* (5.1849–55).

3213   *knot*. See Chaucer's The Squire's Tale: "The knotte why that every tale is toold" (V.401). The term is repeated at 5.2301.

3227   *thei*. MS: *the*.

3228   *hem*. Accepting Bergen's addition.

3766   *custom*. Bergen emends to *custome*.

3772   The Amazons' service to Mars is an ironic echo of the service to Venus conventionally offered by chivalric heroes; see, for example, Palamon's wish to die in Venus's service in The Knight's Tale (I.2243).

3835   *the*. MS: *hir*.

3843   *to*. Bergen emends to *hir*.

3864   *famous*. MS: *grete*.

3865   *kyng.* MS: *quene.*

3885   *Rounde.* MS: *Ronde.*

3888   *And.* Bergen emends to *But.*

3896   *myght.* Bergen emends to *myghte.*

3905   *that.* Accepting Bergen's addition.

3908   *the.* Bergen emends to *this.*

3941   *had.* Bergen emends to *hadde.*

3946   *as a sturdy wal.* The image used to describe Hector (3.4938) and Troilus as well as Nestor (1.4084) is applied to Diomede. Guido says only that Diomedes offered wondrous resistance to the Amazons (Book 28).

4307   *gan.* Bergen emends to *dide.*

4318   *maked.* MS: *maketh.*

4326   *the Grekis.* Accepting Bergen's emendation for MS: *Grekis.*

4340   The dismemberment of Penthesilea looks forward to Pyrrhus's dismemberment of Polyxena after the fall of Troy (4.6852–57).

4341   *so.* Bergen emends to *to.* See 4.4427

4398   *al.* Bergen reads *all.*

4414   *burie.* Bergen emends to *burie it,* but the syntax suggests that the Trojans want the body to bury and inter (*grave*).

4429   *that.* Bergen emends to *how.*

5121   *thei.* MS: *ye.*

5152   *ben.* Bergen emends to *were.*

5166   *that*. MS: *that ye*.

5193   *the*. Bergen emends to *this*.

5198   *foreyns*. MS: *forereyns*.

5220   Lydgate here tropes the repeated phrase *crop and rote*, meaning "the whole."

5221   *of*. MS: *of a*.

5236   *to holde champartie*. In OF *champart* is the Lord's share in the crop of a tenant's land (MED). "To hold champartie" means "to hold one's own" or "to contend successfully."

5245   *though*. MS: *yough*.

5256   *that*. Accepting Bergen's addition.

5259   *with*. Bergen emends to *by*.

5262   *also*. MS: *also of*.

5274   *Wherfore*. Bergen emends to *Therfore*.

5280   *in mewe*. Antenor's use of the term contrasts with earlier associations with love and desire; see 1.1901 and 2.3600.

5286   *al*. Bergen reads *all*.

5294   *pes*. Bergen emends to *a pes*. *with*. Bergen emends to *for*.

5553   *goddes*. MS: *goodes*.

5575   The clause requires the verb *was* to be understood.

5579   *it in*. Bergen emends to *in*.

5588   *ywrought*. MS: *wrought*.

5590   *in the Rose*. Lydgate refers anachronistically to the story of Pygmalion in the *Roman de la Rose*, lines 20817–21214.

5596   *sent*. MS: *it sent*.

5634   *immortal*. Bergen reads *inmortal*.

5636   *that*. Accepting Bergen's addition.

5638   *of*. MS: *in*.

5639   *and*. Bergen emends to *of* and glosses "from all assault and danger; dangerous attack."

5670   Bergen (4:224) suggests a colon after *dwelle* to indicate that the priest will be spoken to privately. Antenor seems, however, to be telling Ulysses to stay calm.

5671   *outher*. MS: *outhe*.

5695   *and*. Bergen emends to *to*.

5732   *as*. Bergen emends to *that*.

5742   *And*. MS: *And to*.

5752   *in*. MS: *and*.

5756   *pleinly*. Bergen emends to *platly*.

5767   *ensclaundrid*. Bergen emends to *esclaundrid*.

5768   *shal shape*. Bergen emends to *shape shal*.

5775   *with*. Bergen emends to *of*.

5783   *partener*. MS: *parcener*.

5788   *that*. Accepting Bergen's addition.

5791	*aweye.* Bergen reads *aweie.*
5795	*his.* MS: *to his.*
5818	*no.* Bergen emends to *in.* There is nothing in Isidore, Pliny, or Trevisa to suggest that gold can penetrate steel and marble; Lydgate seems to suggest that these substances resist gold but the priest does not. See 3.2063 and 4.1529.
5820	*shal his purpos.* MS: *his purpos shal.*
5829–30	The verb *were* must be understood with *dismaied* and *outtraied.*
6023	*Bysshop Calchas.* Lydgate's syntax is convoluted here, but the phrase stands in apposition to *hym* in the main clause at 4.6038: *Recorde of hym.*
6028	*To.* MS: *Te.*
6045	*How.* MS: *How the.*
6047	*shal yow.* Bergen emends to *shal.*
6102	*of the.* Bergen emends to *of.*
6135	*be.* Bergen emends to *was.*
6163	*Duringe.* MS: *Durige.*
6185	*the.* Bergen emends to *this.*
6202	*into.* MS: *unto.*
6212	*whiche.* MS: *the whiche.*
6277	*Tenedoun.* Tenedos is an island off the coast of Troy that the Greeks captured (see summary of Book 2.4896–6576) and used as a mustering point. In their ruse it remains a secure place from which to rally their troops in short order.

6285 *he*. Accepting Bergen's addition.

6290 *to*. Accepting Bergen's addition.

6294 *On*. MS: *An*.

    horsebak. MS: *horsbak*.

6295 *Troye*. Bergen reads *Troy*.

6314 *toke*. Bergen emends to *ne toke*.

6331 *Now*. MS: *And now*.

6338 *Wherof*. MS: *Wherfore*.

6345 *her*. MS: *the*.

6347 *bareyn and bare ymaked*. Bergen emends to *bare and bareyne maked*.

6356–60 The Greeks' despoiling of the Trojan temples recalls Paris's desecration of the temple at Cythera (2.3809–27).

6365 *in*. Bergen emends to *and*.

6366 *And*. MS: *And of*.

    the. Bergen emends to *that*.

6376 *Mi penne shuld of verray routhe rive*. See the narrator's phrase in *Troilus and Crisyde*: "Thise woful vers, that wepen as I write" (1.7).

6388 *on the*. Bergen emends to *the*.

6389 *fals*. Accepting Bergen's addition.

6400 *raught*. Bergen emends to *raught away*.

6402 *party*. MS: *part*.

6403   *nor*. Bergen emends to *or*.

6418   *aside*. Bergen emends to *beside*. In Guido (Book 30) Pyrrhus slays Priam in the sight of Aeneas and Antenor. MS reading gives the sense that the traitors both allow the murder to occur and witness it.

6425   *her*. Bergen emends to *the*.

6427   *with*. Accepting Bergen's addition.

6428   *with his*. Bergen emends to *his*.

6458   *traitour*. MS: *troitour*.

6460   *him*. MS: *hm*.

6488   *the*. Accepting Bergen's addition.

6500   *be so*. Bergen emends to *so be*.

6550   *how*. Accepting Bergen's addition.

6739   *conselit*. Bergen emends to *conseled*.

6747   *now that I*. MS: *that I now*.

6748   *this*. MS: *the*.

6772   The understood subject "I" must be supplied for this clause.

6779   *wrathe*. MS: *wroth*.

6794   *bewepe hir virginité*. Lydgate appears to echo Jephthah's daughter, another innocent destroyed by men's misguidance (Judges 11.37)

6795   *pitous*. Bergen emends to *this pitous*.

6805   *unto*. MS: *to*.

6818   *me*. Bergen emends to *here*.

6831   *the*. Accepting Bergen's addition.

6853   *Dismembrid*. Pyrrhus's vengeance recalls the death of Penthesilea (above, 4.4340–41). In Ovid (*Metamorphoses* 13.445–48), the ghost of Achilles demands that Polyxena be sacrificed on his tomb. *swerd*. Bergen reads *swerde*.

6866   *ful*. Accepting Bergen's addition. *ybe*. MS: *be*.

6880   *wisly*. Bergen emends to *wistly* but glosses the line under *wysly*.

6888   *the*. Bergen emends to *this*.

6899   *a*. Accepting Bergen's addition.

6914   *ther men*. Bergen emends to *men ther*.

6929   *take*. MS: *toke*.

6931   *to*. Accepting Bergen's addition.

6938   *forget*. Bergen emends to *forged*.

6940   *confusioun*. MS: *conclusioun*.

6944   *the*. MS: *to do*.

        unto. MS: *to*.

6948   Lydgate's repudiation of the pagan gods, like Chaucer's rejection of "payens corsed olde rites" (*Troilus and Criseyde* 5.1849), also implies a repudiation of the poetic narratives associated with the gods. See also Lydgate's remarks at 4.7029–31.

6951   *Mars, Pallas*. MS: *Pallas Mars*.

6956   *Nouther*. MS: *Nor*.

6969–70   Lines transposed in MS.

6975   *Genyus the prest*. Genius was originally a deity assigned to individuals, but his most important role is as a god connected with the process of birth and regeneration. In this capacity, he appears as a figure in the *Cosmographia* of Bernardus Silvestris and the *De planctu naturae* of Alan of Lille. Jean de Meun incorporates and amplifies Alan's portrayal in the *Roman de la Rose*. Genius is the Lover's confessor in John Gower's *Confessio Amantis*.

6984–85   See Chaucer's The Wife of Bath's Tale (III.873–75)

6986   *fawny*. MS: *fauner*. Bergen emends to *fauni*. The form *fawny* appears elsewhere in the MS (2.5652, 2.7702 — not in selections for this text) and in Chaucer (*Troilus and Criseyde* 4.1544).

6991   *the*. Accepting Bergen's addition.

7018   *exanple*. Bergen emends to *example*, but the MS form is attested elsewhere in Lydgate's works in the sense of instructive narrative (*exemplum*).

7027   *have*. Bergen reads *han*.

7033   *May now ought*. Bergen emends to *What may now*.

7035   *allas*. Accepting Bergen's addition.

7036   The lament for fallen cities is a common topic in classical, biblical, and Near Eastern literatures; one prominent example is the medieval poem *Pergama flere volo*.

7057   *gret*. Bergen emends to *grete*; see 4.2732.

7058   *Jeremye*. The Book of Lamentations, a sequence of five poems on the fall of Jerusalem to the Babylonians in 587 B.C., was commonly ascribed to the prophet Jeremiah.

7062   *transmygracioun*. MS: *transmutacioun*. Bergen's emendation fits the historical context. Chaucer uses *transmutacioun* in something close to Lydgate's sense in *The House of Fame* when he speaks of "dyvers transmutacions / Of estats, and eke of regions" (lines 1969–70). OED cites a rare late-sixteenth-century usage of the term that means the transmigration of souls from one body to another.

7066   *Babilon*. MS: *Bailon*.

7068   *he that was departed with a sawe*. According to apocryphal tradition, the prophet Isaiah was sawed in two during the reign of Manasseh. St. Paul makes reference in Hebrews 11.37, as does the ninth-century commentator Christianus Stabulensis in his *Expositio in Euangelium Matthaei* (chs. 4 and 35).

7095   *sympelnesse*. Bergen emends to *symplesse*; see Env.63.

7096   *blottid*. MS: *blottid be*.

7106   *that*. Accepting Bergen's addition.

7108   *fifthe*. MS: *fithe*.

Book 5

5   *lady of the eyr*. Juno is the wife and sister of Jupiter and queen of the pagan gods; she is traditionally associated with the moon. She is identified with the air by Augustine, *De civitate Dei* 7.16 and 10.21 (compare *Sermo* 197) and by Vatican Mythographer 2 (chs. 6 and 9).

11   *any*. Accepting Bergen's addition.

15   *And*. The conjunction is needed for rhythm and sense.

16   *Fortune*. Lydgate's description of Fortune, which he adds independently to the story, explains the downfall of the Greek victors as a Boethian tragedy.

26   *and*. MS: *and of*.

1788   *and smothe*. MS: *now smothe*.

1809 *pleinly*. Accepting Bergen's addition.

1826 *Kyng Ydumee*. King Idomeneus comes with King Merion from Crete, leading eighty ships. After Agamemnon's murder, he shelters and raises Orestes, and later arranges his marriage with Hermione.

1847 *Mirma*. In *Odyssey* 9, Odysseus comes to a land in Thrace; Guido (Book 33) calls it Mirna.

1862 *Clanstafages*. Lydgate's rendering of Guido's "Calastofagos." Griffin (p. 283) notes that Benoît and Guido have made Dictys's *Lotophagos* (Lotus eaters) into a port.

1875 *pensif*. Bergen emends to *so pensif*.

1882 In Guido the brother kings of Sicily are called Strigona and Ciclopa. Lydgate preserves the names of their sons but adds the detail that Polyphemus is a giant (5.1908), apparently to harmonize Guido's version with Ovid. In the *Metamorphoses*, Polyphemus uses a pine as a walking stick (13.782) and says that he is as large as Jupiter (13.842). Guido mentions Alphenor's love for Polyphemus's unnamed sister, but Lydgate embroiders the episode with the conventions of courtly love.

1895 *thei*. MS: *ther*.

1919 *narwe*. MS: *nawe*.

1920 *upon*. MS: *on*.

1921 *alwey*. Bergen emends to *ay* to avoid repetition.

1938 *myght*. Bergen emends to *myghte*.

1945 *my*. MS: *me*.

1958–75 *like as writ Ovide*. Telemus foretells the blinding of Polyphemus in *Metamorphoses* 13.770–75 and Achaemenides tells the story in *Metamorphoses* 14.167–222.

1987 *wondirfully*. Bergen emends to *wonderly*.

2000 *abood*. MS: *bood*.

2004–06 Mention of Telegonus here prepares for Ulysses's death at the end of the poem. Guido (Book 33) does not mention Telegonus's name.

2007 *reherse*. Bergen emends to *wel reherse*.

2009 *secré*. MS: *socre*.

2012 *myght*. Bergen emends to *myghte*, but the MS form gives an acceptable Lydgate line.

2048 *Goddes myght*. See the repeated phrase in Chaucer, "Goddes pryvytee."

2071 *he*. MS: *thei*.

2082 *man*. Bergen emends to *a man*.

2102 *by southe and nat by est*. In Guido (Book 33), Ulysses says only that he has circled the world and now come to this land.

2110 *it doth to me*. Bergen emends to *to me it doth*.

2120 *also*. MS: *as*.

2132 *meyné*. MS: *money*.

2140 *desirous*. The verb "was" is understood here.

2146 *as*. MS: *a. an*. Accepting Bergen's addition.

2152 *yit grene*. MS: *grene yit*.

2156 *example of wommanhede*. Penelope's wifely virtue is a conventional part of the defense of women that is included within the tradition of medieval misyogyny. See Dorigen's lament in Chaucer's The Franklin's Tale (V.1443) and the Balade in the *The Legend of Good Women* F 252 and G 206. Gower tells of Penelope's fidelity in *Confessio Amantis* 4.147–233, and makes several subsequent allusions to her steadfastness and wifely truth — 4.1822; 6.1461; 8.2621.

2160   *auctours*. The term encompasses both authors and the texts they write, the latter conceived as creations participating independently in a tradition.

2165   *ay*. Accepting Bergen's addition.

2174   *inportable*. Bergen reads *importable*.

2185   *dremes*. Bergen emends to *a dreme*.

2192   *be*. MS: *he be*.

2195   *se*. Bergen emends to *yse*.

2198   *ben*. MS: *bem*.

2232   *thei*. Accepting Bergen's addition.

2236   *on*. Bergen emends to *of*.

2240   *had*. Accepting Bergen's addition.

2250   *lond*. MS: *hond*.

2261   *on the*. Bergen emends to *the*.

2275–2314   Lydgate's extravagant sentence is organized as an extended consecutive thought: "Yif . . . Yif . . . It were to long tariyng for my boke . . . [and] Men wolde deme me. . . ."

2286   *ilyche*. Bergen reads *iliche*.

2295   *mediacioun*. MS: *meditacioun*.

2299–2300   The final narrative of *Troy Book* shows how the survivors of the Trojan War establish alliances in the generation that follows them. See below for the reconciliations of Achilleidos and Lamedonte and of Telemachus and Telegonus. In this passage, the wedding of Nausia and Telemonus foreshadows the wedding of Henry and Katherine (5.3420–23), which likewise joins two realms and ends strife.

2301 *knotte.* The term refers as well to the main point of a story or argument; see Chaucer's use in The Squire's Tale (V.401, 407) and *Romaunt*, line 4698, and Lydgate's earlier use at 4.3213.

2314 *untwyne.* Bergen emends to *to untwyne.*

2937 On the fate of Ulysses compare Gower's Tale of Ulysses and Telegonus (*Confessio Amantis* 6.1391–1778). Gower bases his tale on Benoît, lines 28571–28666 and 29629–30092. Benoît includes some details not found in Guido.

2939 *glad.* Bergen emends to *glade.*

2947 *Lyk.* Bergen reads *Lik.*

2964 *fairie.* MS: *faire.*

2977–78 These lines are misplaced with lines 2979–80 in MS.

   But. MS: *And.*

2978 *she.* Accepting Bergen's addition.

2979 *And.* MS: *But. the more he gan to purswe.* Bergen emends to *the more that he gan purswe.*

2985–3000 Lydgate's Ulysses uses an aureate, courtly diction that is not in Guido.

2994 *my.* Bergen reads *myn.*

3021 *of.* Accepting Bergen's addition.

3022 *Ful of fysshes betyn.* Gold or some other metal is hammered into images, and then they are sown onto the banner (Guido, Book 35). Benoît (lines

30021–24) seems to be the source for details in the passage. See 5.3208–09, where Telegonus glosses this image by describing his birth.

3026   *parte.* MS: *parten.*

3032   *he sodeynly.* MS: *sodeynly he.*

3033   *fantasie.* In scholastic psychology, fantasy refers to a faculty of imagination that allows apprehension or recollection of sense data and images. See 2.2817 and 3.4806.

3052   *on.* MS: *oon.*

3058–64 Lydgate describes the mechanism of Ulysses's downfall by means of Boethian tragedy. Ulysses misperceives the situation before him and acts in a seemingly rational way that ironically carries him further toward catastrophe.

3060   *But wenyng he.* "He" is the subject of the sentence, and "wenyng" takes "to have be prudent" as its complement.

3066   *the speris.* Accepting Bergen's addition to MS: *speris.*

3093   *noon.* Accepting Bergen's addition.

3102   *for.* Accepting Bergen's addition.

3140   *Monday.* Latin *dies lunae* ("day of the moon"), hence a symbol of mutability.

3142   The porter's abuse of Telegonus recalls the remote origin of the Trojan War, when Jason feels that Lamedon treats him discourteously.

3155   *roof.* Bergen emends to *brast.*

3158   *lepen into flood.* Bergen emends to *lepe into the flood.*

3175   *Hent.* MS: *Rent.* Emendation is consistent with Lydgate's usage immediately above at 5.3169.

3178   *That.* Accepting Bergen's addition.

3178   *he*. MS: *that he. nedis*. Accepting Bergen's addition.

3197   *it with*. Bergen emends to *with*.

          darte. Bergen reads *dart*.

3205   *Ulixes*. MS: *hym*.

3242   *aswowne*. MS: *aswone*.

3248   *I*. "Cursid" is understood.

3252   *begat*. MS: *gat*.

3257   *Circes*. MS: *Cures*.

3261   *inportable*. Bergen reads *importable*.

3267   *founde*. Bergen emends to *hath founde*, but *founde* is in the preterite, parallel with *saw*, *knewe*, and *hent*.

3306   *his*. Bergen records this as an emendation, but the reading occurs in the MS.

3319   *Thelagonyus*. Bergen emends to *this Thelagonyus*.

3323–25   Lydgate follows Guido (Book 35) in having Telemachus reign seventy years and Telegonus sixty; in Benoît (line 30268), Telemachus reigns eighty years. There is no reference in Guido or Benoît to Telemachus and Telegonus's going to Jupiter. Lydgate's addition recalls Castor and Pollux, the ideal figures of brothers united in death.

3360   *Latyn*. Bergen emends to *of latyn*.

3367   *just*. Bergen emends to *juste*.

3368–69   Bergen (4:2n) suggests that Lydgate's poem was completed late in 1420.

3370   *manhede*. MS: *maidenhede*.

3372	*maide*. Bergen emends to *a maide*.
3373	*The eyghte yere*. Henry V was crowned 9 April 1412.
3380	*passeth*. MS: *passed*.
3383	*to withseyn*. MS: *withseyn*.
3392	*he is made regent*. In July 1414, Henry sent an embassy to Paris to demand the cession of Normandy, Touraine, Maine, Anjou and Aquitaine. In 1415, he rejected efforts by a French embassy to stave off the English invasion. In these actions, he renewed the English claim to the French throne, initiated by Edward III who argued his claim by descent from his mother, Isabella of France. Henry's military campaign in Normandy began in August 1415 with the siege of Harfleur. Most of the Normandy campaign was carried out in 1417-19, and it led to the Treaty of Troyes in 1420, which made Henry regent of France and heir to the French throne after the death of Charles VI. These are the terms of the *convencioun* (5.3398). As part of the treaty, Henry married Charles's daughter Katherine of Valois on 2 June 1420. The father referred to at 5.3393 is Charles.
3400	*the olde worlde called aureat*. The literary commonplace of a Golden Age of original harmony originates with Hesiod's *Works and Days*, lines 109-20; for the Middle Ages, Ovid's *Metamorphoses* 1.89-112 and the *Roman de la Rose*, lines 8357-8458 are important expressions of the idea.
3411 ff.	See note to 5.3392. Lydgate writes in the future tense about the union of England and France, though he may be expressing a hope rather than referring to an impending event following Henry's marriage. Lydgate's call for peace is doubtless genuine, but it is also a commonplace in the literature of princely advice. How far he advocates a specific policy, as distinct from offering good advice, is not certain. But his role as a *de facto* royal propagandist limits the extent to which he can put forth personal views. Henry, as Pearsall (1994, p. 386) remarks in the case of Thomas Hoccleve, Lydgate's nearest competitor as a court poet, was more interested in being seen to take advice than in actually following it.

3424   *Kateryne*. In the *Legenda aurea*, Jacobus de Voragine etymologizes Saint Catherine's name as "total ruin," meaning her humility destroyed the edifice of pride, and as a "small chain," which signifies the good works by which she climbed to heaven.

3466   *boistous and rual*. See the Franklin's description of himself as "a burel man" (V.716).

3481   *her*. MS: *his*.

3482   *correcte*. The common literary pose of the medieval poet is to be "under correccioun"; see Chaucer's use of the convention at the end of *Troilus and Criseyde* 5.1858. See also note to Pro.63–75 where Lydgate first introduces the idea.

3490   *set behynde*. MED records two relevant senses of the term: "given up" and "downgraded, treated as unimportant."

3493   *that*. Accepting Bergen's addition.

3499   *lak*. Bergen emends to *a lak*.

3506   *Baiard*. See above, 2.4731.

3520   Chaucer's poem to his scribe, Adam, belies Lydgate's claim that Chaucer cheerfully ignored blemishes in the texts of his works.

3549–62   Lydgate's list recalls the roster of felonies that Arcite sees depicted on the walls of the temple of Mars in The Knight's Tale (I.1995–2040).

3551   *plounget*. Bergen emends to *plounged*.

3570   The metaphor of life's pilgrimage is a medieval commonplace. Guillaume de Deguilleville's *Le pelerinaige de vie humaine* is one of the most important late medieval allegories. Dante's *Divine Comedy* incorporates the metaphor as the basis of its narrative.

3579   *to Hym that starf uppon the Rode*. Lydgate's phrasing invokes the ending of *Troilus and Criseyde*: "that sothfast Crist, that starf on rode" (5.1860).

3586   *With a fewe ageyn gret multitude.* Henry's victory at Agincourt in 1415 was against a vastly larger French force.

3602   *after that.* Bergen emends to *afterward. nynthe spere.* See above, 3.4382. Here Lydgate simply means heaven.

3604   *God.* MS: *good.*

Envoy

Lydgate shifts from couplets into the English stanza, sometimes referred to as rhyme royal, used by Chaucer in *Troilus and Criseyde.*

1   *sours.* MS: *flour.*

4   *the worthi nyne.* The Nine Worthy are chivalric heroes representing gentiles (Hector, Julius Caesar, Alexander the Great), Jews (Joshua, David, Judas Maccabeus), and Christians (Arthur, Charlemagne, Godfrey of Bouillon).

12   *rekned.* This is the verb governing the sentence that extends over the first four stanzas of the Envoy. Bergen emends to *y-rekned.*

14   *the hous of fame.* From other echoes in *Fall of Princes* (8.2735–36 and 9.3468), it appears that Lydgate's reference is to the roster of historical writers and poets in Chaucer's *The House of Fame.*

18   *evermore.* MS: *overmore.* MS reading makes syntactic sense, but *evermore* accords better with *in memorie.*

21   The following stanza is not separated by a space in the MS.

36–49   Lydgate's list combines biblical and classical kings who are mentioned for their qualities of character. Joshua is the follower and successor of Moses, and he enjoys divine favor as a military leader (Isidore of Seville, *De ortu et obitu patrum*, ch. 26). Solomon is known for his wisdom and justice (Isidore, *De ortu*, ch. 34). David is a figure of patience and humility (Isidore, *De ortu*, ch. 33 and Augustine, *De civitate Dei* 17.20). Caesar symbolizes both ambition and greatness of spirit (Augustine, *De civitate Dei* 5.12 and Vincent of Beauvais, *De morali principis institutione*, ch. 16).

37   *conveied*. The verb "to be" is understood.

43   *meynt*. Probably to be construed with the verb "to be": "Your mercy is mingled with your magnificence."

             magnificence. As Aristotle explains in the *Nicomachean Ethics* (4.2), magnificence is a moral virtue akin to generosity but differing from generosity by being on a larger scale and directed toward public display.

52   *scepter*. MS: *swerde*.

63   *sympilnesse*. Bergen emends to *symplesse*.

64   *eke*. Accepting Bergen's addition.

67   *received*. MS: *recerved*.

68   *twey mynutes*. Mark 12:41–44 and Luke 21:1–4 record Jesus's example of the widow who contributes all she has to the temple's treasury.

73   *gift*. MS: *gilt*.

77   *al*. Accepting Bergen's addition.

92   *Go, litel bok*. See *Troilus and Criseyde* 5.1786–92, the stanza that marks the beginning of Chaucer's Envoy.

99   The following stanza is not separated by a space in the MS.

100–01   See earlier echoes of Chaucer's Franklin at 2.192–97 and 3.551–56.

Glossary

abo(o)de *delay*
abreide *speak*
advert *notice*
albe *although*
alder *of us all*
asterte *escape*
auter *altar*
availle *be of use*
aviseness *consideration*
await *ambush*
ay *always*

be *by, be*
brenne *burn*

cast *foresee*
ceriously *in due order, point by point*
char *chariot*
cher(e) *countenance, mood*
clene *clean, pure, purely*
condescende *agree*
confusioun *destruction*
contune *continue*
cors *corpse*

dede *deed; dead; did*
dool *sorrow*
durste *dared*

eke *also*
entere *entire, complete*
everychone *everyone*

fere *companion; fear*
feris *companions*
ferre *far*
foon *foes*
fre *generous, liberal*
fredam *generosity, liberality*
fyn *end, goal*

hem *them; themselves*
hent(e) *seized, took*
her *her, their; hair; hear*
hight(e) *was called*
hole, hoole *whole*
hye *hasten*

ifere *together*
issed *issued, went*

kerve *cut, carve*
kynde *nature*

list *lest; it pleases*
lorn *lost*
lyche *like*

Martis *Mars*
maugre *despite*
meynt(e) *mixed*
moo *more*
morwe *morning, morrow*

Glossary

of *of; off*
or *before*
outterly *utterly, completely*

pes *peace*
platis *plate armor*
platly *plainly, openly*
pres *mob, crowd, warriors*
prevely *secretly*

quike *alive*

rathe *quickly, readily*
rede, reed *advice; read*
renomed *renowned*
rood *rode; Cross*
rote *root*
routhe *pity*

sege *siege*
sikerness *certainty*
sithen *since*
slawen *slain*
sleighti *crafty, tricky*
smet *smote*
soth(e) *truth*
sotil *subtle*
spere *sphere*
stede *steed, horse*
stele *steel, armor*
sterve *die*
stoundemel *from time to time*
strond(e) *shore*
sue, swe *follow, pursue*
swevene *dream*
swich(e) *such*
sythes *times*

thilke *that, that same*
trew *truce*
tweyne *two*

un(n)ethe *scarcely, hardly*

wawe *wave*
wende *go*
wene *doubt*
wenyng *thinking, expecting*
wer(r)e *were; protect; war; doubt*
wher *whether; where*
wo(o)d *mad*
wist *knew*
woye *way*
wyght *person*

yeve *give*
yif(fe) *if*
yove *given*